Naval Ceremonies, Customs, and Traditions

D0961158

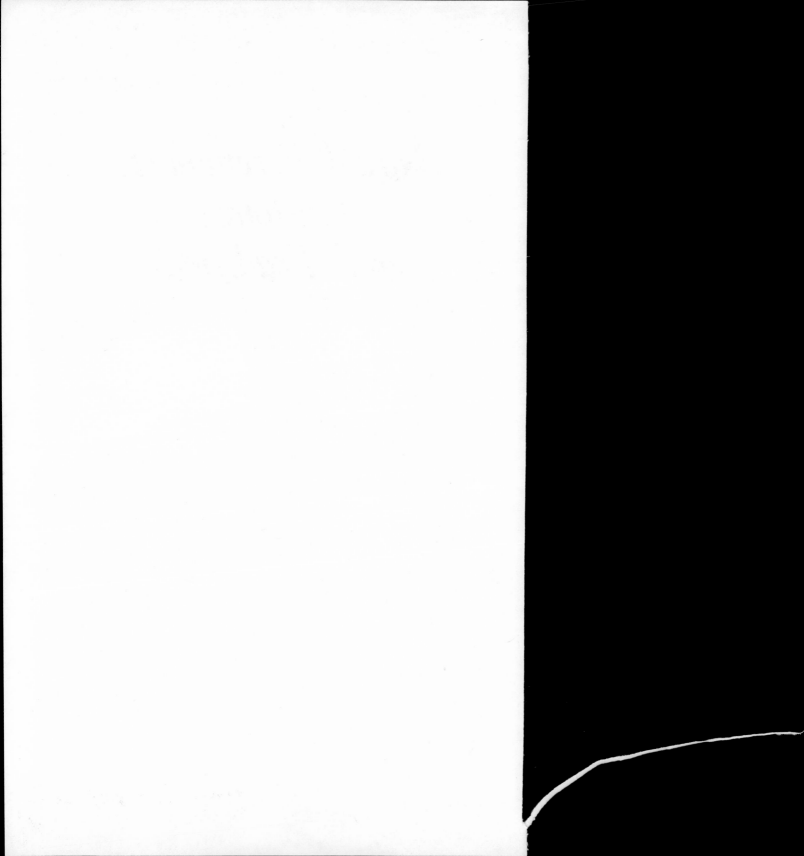

FIFTH EDITION

Naval Ceremonies, Customs, and Traditions

By Vice Admiral William P. Mack,
U.S. Navy (Retired)
and
Lieutenant Commander Royal W. Connell,
U.S. Navy

NAVAL INSTITUTE PRESS
Annapolis, Maryland

Library of Congress Cataloging in Publication Data
Lovette, Leland Pearson, 1897–
    Naval ceremonies, customs, and traditions.
    Previous editions published under title: Naval
customs, traditions & usage.
    Bibliography: p.
    Includes index.
    1. Naval ceremonies, honors, and salutes—United
States.   2. Naval art and science—Terminology.
I. Connell, Royal W., 1948– II. Mack, William P.,
1915– III. Title.
V310.L6 1980   359.1'336'0973   79-92236
ISBN 0-87021-412-8

Printed in the United States of America on acid-free paper ∞

12 11 10 9

I wish to dedicate my work to my father, Royal W. Connell, Colonel, U.S. Air Force, whose life and death have taught me the importance of both the continuity of tradition and of the love of my country.

Royal W. Connell
Lieutenant Commander, U.S. Navy

I dedicate my work to my father, Commander Albert R. Mack, U.S. Navy, and to my father-in-law, Rear Admiral George J. McMillin, U.S. Navy, whose examples and advice were invaluable to me throughout my career.

William P. Mack
Vice Admiral, U.S. Navy (Retired)

Contents

Preface to the Fifth Edition

The first four editions were written by Vice Admiral Leland P. Lovette, U.S. Navy (Retired).

This edition has drawn extensively on the thorough and painstaking research and composition of Admiral Lovette. A general reorganization has been accomplished, and a more up-to-date approach has been taken in certain subjects. World War II and subsequent wars and years brought many changes in ceremonies, customs, and usages, and these have been incorporated. At the same time, every effort has been made to describe the preservation through these changing times of those time-honored traditions that remain relatively constant.

In the period following the fourth edition, the position of women in the Navy has changed radically. The number of women serving has increased almost tenfold. Women attend the U.S. Naval Academy. Women fly all types of aircraft and are trained to serve in all types of ships. Only the law, which proscribes their serving in combatant billets, prevents their complete participation in every facet of the Navy. In due time, they will contribute increasingly to the Navy's traditions. The authors have attempted to recognize these facts in this edition, but this recognition does not take the form of changes in nomenclature. The first dictionary definition of "man" is "a member of the human race," and the second definition is "a male of the human race." A seaman is therefore a member of the human race who goes to sea, and the word has no male connotation. A woman entitled to the richly traditional title of midshipman deserves that title without qualification or differentiation.

The authors of the fifth edition would like to acknowledge the spirit with which Admiral Lovette approached his work by quoting verbatim the following paragraph from the fourth edition.

> We may expect many changes in customs and usage; however, there are some eternal verities, "things that perish never": one of which, and perhaps the most important, is man's indomitable spirit that continues dauntlessly to meet formidable challenges inherent in the profession of arms and in the careers of those who battle the elements. It is for these that often the remembrance of things past, merely the memory of splendid heroism of other days, effects an unshakable resolution in the face of adversity. And of them who so react, it may be said that a great tradition has begun or continued, if action and deed clearly went beyond the call of duty.

Annapolis, Maryland
January 1980

William P. Mack
Vice Admiral, U.S. Navy (Retired)

Royal W. Connell
Lieutenant Commander, U.S. Navy

Acknowledgments

In connection with a work of this kind it is difficult to give proper credit to all sources of information and material and to acknowledge all those who assisted in its preparation.

Admiral Lovette's original work remains as the basis for this edition, and his outstanding work is gratefully acknowledged, as are the individuals and institutions named by him in the previous edition.

Naval Ceremonies, Customs, and Traditions

PART I

Customs, Ceremonies, Traditions, and Usage

CHAPTER 1

The Interrelationship of Customs, Ceremonies, Traditions, and Usage

What men will fight for seems to be worth looking into.
                                        H. L. Mencken

May we not who are of their brotherhood claim that in a small way at least we are partakers of their glory? Certainly it is our duty to keep these traditions alive and in our memory, and to pass them on untarnished to those who come after us.
                                        Rear Admiral Albert Gleaves, USN

Among the Americans who served on Iwo Island, uncommon valor was a common virtue.
                                        Admiral Chester W. Nimitz, USN

The Regular Officer has the tradition of forty generations of serving soldiers behind him, and to him the old weapons are the most honored.
                                        T. E. Lawrence

THROUGHOUT LIFE, traditions, ceremonies, customs, and usage exert a profound influence upon human behavior. The effect is particularly marked in such professions as the military organizations which—because of imposed discipline—lend themselves to passing on and perpetuating the more venerated customs, heroic traditions, and dignified ceremonies. Such stimuli when appreciated and properly applied engender ideals and service *esprit de corps* of incalculable value.

This high incentive, this pride in great tradition inculcated in the regular establishment, serves well when in time of war professional leaders are required to train millions in the profession of arms on the land, the sea, and in the air. Pride in the "outfit," and knowledge of the exploits of heroic soldiers, sailors, and airmen who have gone before, comprise the warp and woof of tradition; these are the things which impel American manhood to go forth and do likewise. As Disraeli said: "Nurture your minds with great thoughts. To believe in the heroic makes heroes." In time of war, however, much that should be done in the matter of imbuing trainees with military history and tradition must necessarily be lightly touched or omitted because of the need to speed up specialized training for early combat. As one instructor during the war against Hitler phrased it at a navigational school for patrol boat captains: "This course will take only two weeks, and if any of you stay out too long in the men's room, you will miss your whole sophomore year." The rapid assimilation of professional knowledge by young Americans in time of war has become traditional.

The naval officer of the nuclear power, guided-missile, jet-plane age is required to devote more and more of his time keeping abreast of a profession that becomes increasingly complex with the advance of science; there is time for little else. The personal factor remains, however; it is still men who drop bombs and fire atomic missiles, men who still must sail the seas and fly jet planes.

In recent times officers and men of the armed forces have been individually and collectively tested in the crucible of a prisoner-of-war atmosphere. In World War II the Japanese treated severely, but rarely tortured, our prisoners, but in the Korean War the North Koreans reached a new high in harsh, illegal treatment of prisoners. The majority of prisoners in this war were young, ill-prepared Army infantrymen. It was to be expected that they would offer little resistance to torture. After this war the Defense Department was unable to document a single case of successful resistance to torture.

In the war with Vietnam many prisoners were Navy and Air Force pilots of middle rank. Most had college educations, and many were products of the service academies. In spite of the severity and bestiality of North Vietnamese torture for periods as long as seven years, many officers were able to resist successfully. Commanders Stockdale, Denton, and Lawrence took the worst the enemy could offer and at the same time offered outstanding leadership to their more junior camp mates. At the end of long confinement they came home to heroes' welcomes and continued their career to flag rank. Vice

Naval personnel who become prisoners of war must be prepared to resist their captors in the traditional ways established by those who were captives of the North Vietnamese.

Admiral Stockdale publicly credited his ability to resist and to perform far beyond the call of duty to his Naval Academy training. For him, tradition provided strong moral guidance in an atmosphere of uncertainty.

Others reported similar reactions. Prior to the Korean war, POWs were told to acknowledge only name, rank, and serial number. After the failure of this policy in the Korean war, it was modified to permit expanded exchange with the enemy under duress, and in the war with Vietnam this change was successful. On occasion POWs appeared to be cooperating with the enemy by making movie and television appearances, but it was readily evident that these occurrences were *in ex-*

tremis and in some cases provided valuable intelligence information. In general, a new tradition was born—that of resisting captors to the utmost, maintaining the chain of command whenever possible, and communicating with and helping fellow POWs.

The personal factor is still preponderant. Because of this, and because men are actuated by the same motives and drives, the same loyalties and devotions as from time immemorial, those training and conditioning routines that make better Americans and more efficient members of the armed forces should not be overlooked. There was a let-down after World War II and the war in Vietnam, a decided trend to do away with some of the time-honored customs conducive to smartness and discipline. *It did not work.* As the pendulum of official opinion swings back, eternal credit should be given those senior officers of the naval service who never for a moment underestimated the value of naval traditions, customs, and ceremonies—professional leaders who knew the immeasurable value of spiritual cement in a military organization.

The Navy saga from John Paul Jones to Nimitz, Spruance, and Burke tells the whole story. A distinctive feature of our naval history is its continuum of success; and one of the reasons for this success is that from the days of the American Revolution when John Paul Jones reported officially, "If midnight study and the instructions of the greatest and most learned sea officers can have given me advantages, I am not without them," down the years to the most modern courses in nuclear fission set up by the Navy Department, the Navy has had a tradition of preparedness by education. Probably nothing contributed more to the success of the naval service in war.

The Navy emphasizes its customs and traditions in times of peace, because the memory of them inspires men in times of stress and in battle. The effect that old customs had in the formulation of naval regulations is a marked example of the influence of tested usage. The courtesy of the sea and the worth of ceremony rest mainly on the fact that they bind us to the past and at the same time lend an air of dignity and respect in official relations, whether at home or abroad. There are no greater "goodwill ambassadors" than the visits of our ships to foreign ports. Here is where dignified and time-honored nautical ceremonies play their part, because ceremony is to a marked degree the cement of discipline, and upon discipline the service rests. Tradition, when coupled with courage and pride, gives to the officer corps its highest incentive to carry on both in peace and in war. It is good that one should ask oneself: "Am I living up to the best traditions of those who have gone before?"

Privations and a "hard school" produced our outstanding sailors of other years. This does not mean that high naval authorities have not kept pace with modern American trends in providing better living conditions. The modern "hard school" is a continuation of the old tradition of keeping the sea—of daily drills, frequent target practices and maneuvers, without which our customary high standards of readiness could never have been realized. The sea captains of the American Revolution and the War of 1812 long ago set the pace.

Sailors must have the sea habit. World-wide commitments make it necessary to deploy fleet elements beyond the ideal one-third at sea and two-thirds at home ratio, and this makes it "tough on the ships and on the people," according to Admiral Robert B. Carney, who also told over 1,200 officers of the Washington area that he wanted a toughening up of command throughout the Navy. He warned that if a military service is to be successful in war there can be no abridging of authority, and added:

> War is highly competitive; we are trying to train people to endure
> the hardships and strain of war, and we would be doing ourselves
> and our country a disservice to adopt measures which would
> soften the fibre of the men in uniform.

It is for this training and the carrying out of the Navy's high mission that the finer traditions of other years provide support and inspiration. An examination, however cursory, of the loyalty and devotion, both individually and *en masse*, to the brotherhood that has passed on, gives striking evidence of the tremendous worth of the traditional ethics of the naval code. Theodore Roosevelt while President said: "Every officer in the Navy should feel in each fibre of his being an eager desire to emulate the energy, the professional capacity, the indomitable determination, and dauntless scorn of death which marked John Paul Jones above all his fellows." Those who wear the Navy blue will find much that puts iron in character and enhances professional value if they take time to look closely at the brilliant tapestry of naval tradition.

In fact, tradition is even more important in this age when awesome responsibility can be placed on very young officers. In the case of the initiation of strategic bombing attacks, Navy pilots of junior rank will be launched in aircraft loaded with nuclear weapons, and they will be charged with making accurate delivery on military targets. Significant error on their part may kill thousands of civilians. Only strong tradition based on a firm base of ethics and morals can bring such a young man through safely.

Junior officers in modern times are given extremely important responsibilities when they must be prepared to be launched with nuclear bombs. An error in judgment could kill thousands of civilians.

Because this work treats of custom, ceremonies, tradition, and usage, both in a general sense and in particular detail, it may be helpful to define the terms.

First, let us examine the word *custom*. Custom is defined as "repetition of the same act or procedure, established manner or way." Woolsey, in his introduction to a treatise on international law, wrote, "Custom within each country existed before statutes. . . ." Emerson once remarked, "We all live according to custom," while Bacon, commenting on customs in the Elizabethan Age, wrote, "Since custom is the principal magistrate of men's lives, let men by all means obtain good customs."

Customs are to a major degree authoritative and often stand in the place of law and regulations for the conduct of groups of men, though it must be remembered that some customs may die or be abolished. G. E. Moore in *Principia Ethica* said: "There is a strong probability in favor of adhering to an existing custom, even if it be a bad one." Customs may change, however, as do fashions and manners, either for better or for worse. Custom has an important role in all systems of jurisprudence. A favorite phrase of English law is: "a custom whereof the memory of man runneth not back to the contrary." And in this century this important word was used in a repetition of an ancient legal maxim: "Custom is the best interpreter of the law."[1] Nevertheless, those who chafe under the restraint of customs may remember the old Latin proverb: "Custom is a tyrant." (*Usus est tyrannus.*)

Usage is best defined by comparing it with the meaning of *custom*. In its simplest sense, *usage* means an accepted way of acting, hence the "ancient usages of Parliament." Here it is applicable to procedures or ceremonies. The Century Dictionary explains that technically, in English law, *usage* has a different signification from *custom*, in not implying immemorial existence or general prevalence. Some American writers use the term as practically equivalent, except in regarding *usage* as the fact by which the existence of *custom* is proved. Others treat *usage* as the habits of individuals or classes—such as those engaged in a particular trade or business—and *custom* as to the habit of communities or localities. One could say, "The naval *usage* of playing the national anthem at the end of receptions became a *custom* in the community." However, the Navy would say, "It has always been our *custom*."

Usage can become crystallized, but changes much more frequently than custom. Shakespeare implies the power of usage in the line: "How use doth breed a habit in a man!"[2]

When *usage* is referred to in the Navy, it is usually in reference to matters of general etiquette, social procedures, correctness in matters of correspondence, and generally with the intent of determining the *best accepted practice*. For example: What is the accepted time for making formal calls on Army families at posts? Is it generally accepted usage to send flowers when attending birthday functions in Latin American countries? When not specified, what has been the usage as to the number of copies to make for certain reports? Should civilian clothes or uniform be worn? Some will say: "Matters of small moment." Yet a little foresight, thought, and tactful inquiry will, particularly when abroad, often spare official representatives of the United States varying degrees of personal embarrassment.

"Try to do it right." Madame Celnart, an expert on manners, said, "The grand secret of never-failing propriety of deportment is to have an intention of always doing right." This implies a sincere effort to conform to the best usage at home and abroad, and that requires observation and application.

Tradition from the Latin *tradere* to hand down, is a word of vexatious connotations. The Century Dictionary defines it as: "The handing

---

[1] *The Code of Canon Law*, II, May 19, 1918.
[2] Shakespeare, *The Two Gentlemen of Verona*, Act V, Scene 4.

down of opinions, practices, rites, customs, from one generation to another by oral communications, without written memorials." *Traditional* is sometimes confused with *legendary*, and even *mythical*. A standard authority of correct expression cites three words that are sometimes interchanged with tradition by the unwary. Crabb wrote, "The *traditional* splendor of a noble family, for instance, means splendor enduring from generation to generation both in memory and reality; *legendary* splendor means splendor described in old stories, existent long ago, but not now; *mythical* splendor means that which is said to be but is not; *fabulous* splendor, splendor now existent but so great as to seem impossible."

Therefore, we are correct in assuming for the purpose of this work that naval traditions are accumulated experiences and deeds passed on from sailor to sailor "both in memory and reality."

A secondary definition of tradition as set forth in the Century Dictionary and applicable to "members of professions" and others is: "The accumulated experience, advance, or achievement of the past." This accumulated experience, some of which will be shown to date back to man's earliest adventures on the sea, comprises a huge reservoir of fact and fancy from which has flowed the stream of deeds, ceremonies, and sea language that is our heritage. A not altogether regrettable conservatism, typical of all navies, has enabled ours to pass on to future generations our established customs and definite traditions. For

Foreign navies still lay great stress on the custom of exchanging official calls. Here the commander Seventh Fleet returns such a call on a fleet commander of the Japanese Maritime Self Defense Force aboard his flagship.

the Navy, they constitute in the main the essence of heroic enterprise, moral fibre, pride in the service, and correct deportment.

Apart from the spiritual value of this legacy, there is one of every-day practicality. Customs of the service have the full effect of law when they fulfill the naval legal definition. It has been held that they can be "taken as precedents to follow when intrinsically proper in themselves and supplementary of the written law and regulations on points on which the latter are silent."[3] Moreover, customs of the service are again legally acknowledged in that "specifications of naval courts-martial must on their face allege facts which constitute a violation of some law, regulation, or custom of the service. . . ."[4]

Customs antedate most of the laws as we know them today. As a rule, customs of the service, when established by long-continued usage, have led to definitive regulations. This fact is noted in the *Naval Digest*: "Customs and usages of the service, whether originating in traditions or in specific orders or rulings, are now, as such, not numerous in the Army (or Navy), a large proportion, in obedience to a natural law, having changed their form by becoming merged in written regulations." It is apparent that regulations are merely customs that have crystallized because of long usage.

Customs have a legal definition. The *Naval Digest*, 1921, states:

> Elements necessary to establish the principal conditions to be fulfilled in order to constitute a valid military custom are: (a) it must be long continued; (b) it must be certain and uniform; (c) it must be compulsory; (d) it must be consistent; (e) it must be general; (f) it must be known; (g) it must not be in opposition to the terms and provisions of a statute or lawful regulation or order.[5]

In general, any research that concerns the development of regulations and law clearly indicates that usage has led to custom, and custom to laws, regulations, and established ceremony.

It is of interest that, to a large degree, the function of ceremonies in military and naval organizations is analogous to the place of ritual in religious worship. "The chief task of routine in religion is to organize the activities necessary to its stability and continuity as a social institution, in order that all available spontaneity and initiative may be directed into spiritual channels."[6] In loose paraphrase of the above, it could be said that the chief task of ceremonies in military and naval

---

[3] *Court-Martial Orders*, 43 (1906), 3.
[4] *Court-Martial Orders*, 33 (1914), 6.
[5] *Naval Courts and Boards*, 1917.
[6] *Encyclopaedia Britannica*, 14th ed.

Inspection of the Honor Guard on the occasion of an official call ashore.

services is to organize their activities in such a way that by the stability and continuity thus engendered, they will be ensured as military organizations, and that all available initiative and energy will be directed into those channels that prepare those organizations to defend the Republic. Ceremonies, like rituals, tend to make the body one.

One of the most interesting phases of sociology is the history of ceremonies and forms. Whether the research be confined to ecclesiastical, legal, military, or naval ceremonies, the student will find a wealth of source material, and throughout such an investigation he will be impressed with the continuity of tradition and custom. We are, here, concerned particularly with ceremony, usage, and customs from the point of view of the naval service. Although it is beyond the scope of this study to treat ceremony and form from a sociological point of view, it is fitting that this historical aspect be mentioned.

A coronation in the Abbey Church at Westminster, both in setting and magnificence, presents the most lustrous pageantry and moving ceremony that remain on earth with the exception of the coronation of a Pope; the latter is, of course, strictly religious. The enthronement of a British monarch combines the rhythmic and stately grace of royalty and nobility in high ceremonial with venerable, symbolic rites that derive partly from paganism as well as from Christianity—all to conse-crate and dedicate a sovereign. And to the informed, there are ever-present reminders of the beginnings of British history.

In essence, a coronation reanimates the tale of continuous national life staged in a historic church that is an eloquent memorial to all that was greatest and most famous in British history. Here near the sepul-chers of monarchs, close by the dust of Chaucer, Spenser, Sam John-son, Tennyson and Browning, solemn oaths are taken by the sovereign to the people, and by liege lords to the Crown.

There, near the tomb of Edward the Confessor, is performed the mystic sacrament of Holy Communion, some lines of which date from Edgar, crowned in 973. The ceremony of sitting on fabled stones, such as the Stone of Scone, goes back to the five Saxon monarchs of the ancient Kingdom of Wessex. The order for the procession in the Abbey dates from 1189. One thinks of civilizations long dead, when reminded that the anointment with holy oil is done in conformance with the ceremony of the Bible that records that the early kings of Israel, Saul and David, were anointed by the prophet Samuel. Regal robes that in style and rich material derive from those worn by Byzan-tine emperors, and a crown that imitates the golden circlets of the rulers of imperial Rome, add to the dramatic splendor of the historic rites. As the Archbishop of Canterbury wrote, it is "a noble drama of religious and national emotions. But at heart is a deep simplicity." It is a lofty example of "customs, traditions and usage." With all the drastic changes in modern history, the ceremony still symbolizes the ancient and unbroken tradition of the Anglo-Saxon and Norman races, and at the same time gives our English-speaking ally, the old mother-country, inspiration for the future by evoking memories of her past glories.

Because of the evolution of the above ceremony from the days of absolute monarchy and the divine right of kings, it may be of interest to the read the conclusions of an expert.

Thorstein Veblen, in *The Theory of the Leisure Class*, discusses ceremonial institutions from their inception, with comment on their ethnological bearing. Since most ceremony has a different connotation today from that understood in its early practice, it is interesting to read Veblen's comments on the slow change in the significance of cere-monial rule:

> We have seen how ceremony originates from fear: on the one side supremacy of a victor or master, on the other side dread of death or punishment felt by the vanquished or the slave. And under the regime of compulsory co-operation thus initiated, fear

develops and maintains in strength all forms of propitiation. But with the rise of a social type based on voluntary cooperation, fear decreases. The subordinate ruler or officer is no longer wholly at the mercy of his superior; the trader, not liable to be robbed or tortured by the noble, has a remedy against him for non-payment; the laborer in receipt of wages cannot be beaten like the slave. In proportion as the system of exchanging services under contract spreads and the rendering of services under compulsion diminishes, men dread one another less; and, consequently, become less scrupulous in fulfilling propitiatory forms.

Ceremonies that evolved from servility, that originated in fear and awe, are accepted today in military organizations as dignified gestures of respect to the symbols of the state and the state's officials. Ceremonies are a function of discipline. Definitive regulations exist for important ceremonial occasions and are tributes to worthy tradition. It follows that if the respect for lawful authority and the symbolism of the flag are worthy of preservation, they must be revered by their defenders: half measures will not do.

A worthy member of the armed forces has pride in uniform, pride in service, and pride in his respect for the flag. Of Admiral Lord Jervis, the Earl of St. Vincent, master seaman and classic disciplinarian, Mahan writes:

> He wisely believed in the value of forms, and was careful to employ them, in this crisis of the mutinies, to enforce the habit of reverence for the insignia of the state and the emblems of military authority. The discipline of the cabin and wardroom officer is the discipline of the fleet, said the admiral [St. Vincent]; and savage almost were the punishments that fell upon officers who disgraced their cloth. The hoisting of the colors, the symbol of power of the nation, from which depended his own and that of all the naval hierarchy, was made an august and imposing ceremony. . . . Lord St. Vincent made a point of attending always, and in full uniform; a detail he did not require of other officers . . . the very atmosphere the seamen breathed was saturated with reverence.

Mahan again relates how Jervis adhered strictly to custom and ceremony:

> . . . to pay outward reverence to the national flag, to salute the quarterdeck as the seat of authority, were no vain show under him. "Discipline," he was fond of quoting, "is summed up in the one word obedience," and these customs were charged with the obser-

vance which is obedience in spirit. They conduce to discipline as conventional good manners, by rendering the due of each to each, knit together the social fabric and maintain the regularity and efficiency of common life; removing friction, suppressing jars, and ministering constantly to the smooth and even working of the social machinery.

It was thus that Jervis, by inculcation of spirit, regular drill, and observance of ceremony, welded the weapon that won for him the decisive victory of Cape St. Vincent and passed on to Nelson the great British fleet that the hero of Trafalgar commanded with incomparable genius.

In every phase of human behavior we encounter tradition, whether good or bad. John Selden, in *Table Talk*, reminds us, "Say what you will against tradition; we know the Signification of Words by nothing but Tradition." Or again in the realm of manners and of law, Herbert Spencer observes, "While in the course of civilization written law tends to replace *traditional* usages, the replacement never becomes complete."

Years add glamor to the courageous or heroic acts of those who have gone. Mankind tends generally to weave some embroidery on the fabric of the actual event. Often romantic and sentimental traditions may hold little truth, yet often they may have commendable inspirational value as folklore.

There is also a practical justification for the fostering of traditional customs. Think of the difficulty should the officer of the deck be left to decide on each occasion whether the starboard or port side would be the ceremonial side, or whether it may or may not be well to "sound taps" at a funeral, or what side of the quarterdeck should be cleared for the captain. Early customs became established traditions and exact regulations.

When should we change custom and usage? Whenever necessary. A reactionary spirit is only to be commended when it clings to an old tradition, custom, or usage, in certainty that a change will effect neither enlightenment nor improvement.

Mahan in his essay, *Military Rule of Obedience*, wrote:

> The value of tradition to the social body is immense. The veneration for practices, or for authority, consecrated by long acceptance, has a reserve of strength which cannot be obtained by any novel device. Respect for the old customs is planted deep in the hearts, as well as in the intelligence, of all inheritors of English-speaking polity.

The "reserve of strength" pointed out by Mahan should be pondered by the commissioned personnel of each generation. The outstanding officers of the service have never failed from the days of the

The Navy and Flogging. Captain Uriah P. Levy exhibits the cat-o'-nine-tails and describes its use to a group of statesmen in Washington. The abolition of corporal punishment in the U.S. Navy was largely due to his efforts. On March 28, 1939, the British government disclosed that the Admiralty had asked it to abolish the centuries-old punishment of flogging. Until 1881, the cat-o'-nine-tails was used frequently for various breaches of discipline. *Puck's Pictorial History*

infant Navy to recognize the power of tradition. In a desire to emulate the progenitors of tradition, one becomes imbued with some of the spirit that prompted the original words and deeds: of an imponderable but vital factor that so influences morale that men often die without complaint when in full knowledge that they have done their duty for country and organization, as did those who went before. "Don't give up the ship"; "Fight her till she sinks"; "Damn the torpedoes, full speed ahead"; "Surrender? I have not yet begun to fight!" and "We are ready now"; "Take her down"; "Attack! Attack!" are not mere words of sound and fury but rather carry lofty connotations—majestic overtones —of valor, of self-sacrifice, of proud glory. They are the essence of priceless tradition.

Worthy traditions also cause the voice of conscience to whisper to the patriot: "Can you go and do likewise?" Fate, or call it luck, may decide for the man on active service whether the ordeal of decision comes early or late. There may be no fame or glory, for the decision may result only in deeds and actions that will bring others fame and glory. There may be painful personal decisions that involve friends, loved ones, and shipmates; yet whether taken in the face of death or a peaceful locale, the remembrance of the traditions of honor and duty that have ever characterized the service will bring to mind the principle that should prevail: *Is what I am about to do in keeping with the highest traditions of the United States naval service?*

The highest praise that could be paid an officer or an enlisted man at his retirement or death is that he lived and worked according to the best traditions of the service. And this of course means both in peace and in war. Those who would live squarely up to this superlative code should early in their careers know something of its most distinguished exemplars—particularly, their contributions to the defense of the Republic, and the heritage they have bequeathed to the successive generations who will wear the uniform. If this you do, you will be proud to say: *The lines are fallen unto me in pleasant places; yea, I have a goodly heritage.*[7]

[7] Psalms XVI, 6.

CHAPTER 2

An Account of the Development of the Laws of the Service

Herein are the good ordinances of the sea, which wise men, who voyaged round the world, gave to our ancestors, and which constitute the books of the science of good customs.

The Consulate of the Sea

Uncharted the rocks that surround thee,
Take heed that the channels thou learn
Lest thy name serve to buoy for another
That shoal, the Courts-Martial Return.
Though armour the belt that protects her,
The ship bears the scar on her side;
It is well if the court will acquit thee;
It were best hadst thou never been tried.

Captain Hopwood, RN, "The Laws of the Navy"

Time is the best interpreter of every doubtful law.

Dionysius of Halicarnassus, *Roman Antiquities*

Let the law never be contradictory to custom: for if the custom is good the law is worthless.

Voltaire, *Philosophical Dictionary*

Ever since the beginning of navies, there have been laws peculiarly applicable to the sea and seafaring people.

Rear Admiral Albert E. Jarrell, USN

ALL THE DISCIPLINE and justice of the Navy until 31 May 1951 derived from the *Articles for the Government of the Navy*, laws called "Rocks and Shoals" by generations of sailors. On the aforementioned date the *Uniform Code of Military Justice* went into full effect and at the same time the *Articles of War* of the Army, the *Articles for the Government of the Navy*, and the *Disciplinary Laws of the Coast Guard* became null and void. The *Uniform Code of Military Justice* superseded them all. It is with an understandable regret that the Navy said farewell to these old Articles under which the Navy had, with good discipline, high morale, and superb leadership, fought wars successfully. Also, many of the new naval regulations and instructions conformed, in spirit if not in letter, to the venerable "constitution" of the Navy.

Why the change? A factual answer with statements of the pros and cons would require much more space than appropriate to this book. Nevertheless, it may be said that when the National Military Establishment was created, strong pressure was brought to bear that all differences in the systems of justice of the armed forces and the Coast Guard be erased. Mr. Forrestal, Secretary of Defense, deemed it a necessary measure to effect a unification of the armed forces, and in 1948 set up an interdepartmental committee to draft a uniform code. The mission was:

> To unify, consolidate, revise and codify, the Articles of War, the Articles for the Government of the Navy, and the disciplinary laws of the Coast Guard, and to enact and establish a Uniform Code of Military Justice.

The Code, the work of the committee, was sent to Congress, and after many hearings and numerous changes, Congress passed the bill, and it was signed by President Truman on 5 May 1950. One year was allowed to make the sweeping change.

"The Uniform Code of Military Justice," writes Hanson W. Baldwin, "was a by-product of some of the military 'reforms' that followed World War II." Most of these so-called reforms were designed to have the overall effect of protecting to a greater degree the rights of the innocent, increasing morale, and making life in the service more pleasant. The traditional salute off posts and places of duty was waived, and other measures were taken to break down customary social distinctions of officers and men. It was thought at the time that this would result in increased enlistments and reenlistments. That this was not achieved is a matter of statistical fact supported by the testimony in congressional hearings of the senior officers of the armed forces. The salute was restored to its rightful place in military etiquette; dress uniforms for evening affairs are now in order; and in the Navy the sword has again been decreed a part of uniform when appropriate. All of these details give tone and cohesion to the service, continue worthwhile custom, and help to maintain traditions passed on by generations of dedicated officers. And may we never forget that the morale of the services depends primarily upon the morale of the officers corps.

The first American naval articles were adopted by the Continental Congress, 28 November 1775. This first "Blue Book" was called *Rules for the Regulation of the Navy of the United Colonies.* The old English custom prevailed to the extent that it was decreed that the *Rules* were to be posted in "public places of the Ship." The infant Navy of the New World was administered by a Committee of Congress, called the Marine Committee, and to John Adams of this committee the task was given of drafting the first rules of the Navy. As will be later shown, they were modeled after existing British regulations. John Paul Jones considered them inadequate; nevertheless, they served for the period of the War for Independence. On 2 March 1779, a code of fifty articles was made effective.

Eleven of the original thirteen states fitted out one or more armed vessels. New Jersey and Delaware were the two exceptions. Various state laws were promulgated relative to discipline, prizes, and general administration. The largest forces were maintained by Massachusetts, Connecticut, Pennsylvania, Maryland, Virginia, and South Carolina. New Hampshire had only one ship, and Georgia commissioned four galleys. No state navy was as large as that of the Navy authorized by Congress, but their work was in most cases effective, and their deeds belong to the common naval tradition.

Despite the excellent performance of the American Navy in the War of the Revolution, public interest and congressional sympathy grew cold to the needs of a naval service, and by 1785 the last ship of the fleet had been disposed of. In fact, it was in 1798 that our Navy was truly "born again."

In the establishment of the new federal government, no provisions in the way of laws or regulations were made for the Navy. It was in 1798 that a Naval Department was formed, and we may consider that this year marks the beginning of the permanent service that has been maintained ever since. Moreover, it marked the drafting of the original "Articles for the Government of the Navy." The articles grew from the 1775 *Rules and Regulations*, just as the articles until 1951 grew from those of 1798.

In order to secure a historic background for our naval law, it is necessary to examine the development of ancient customs and laws of the sea that had merged with the British naval regulations, such as those in force at the time of the American Revolution.

Although no definite organization that could properly be called an English Navy existed until the latter part of the Middle Ages, an organization did exist known as the "King's Ships." The quaint title "Keeper of the King's Ships" appears upon an appointment made by King John of England. In time, Lords of the Admiralty were created to carry on the duties of the Keeper. The titles "Keeper and Governor of the King's Ships" and "Clerk of the King's Ships" survived until past the middle of the sixteenth century. Early English sea power was in reality a fleet of private donations. The King owned a few ships, but the towns of the Cinque Ports (Hythe, Romney, Hastings, Dover, and Sandwich) were obliged to return for royal favors to furnish the King with fifty-seven vessels upon request.

This maritime power of England was governed for many years by the general tenets of the Code of Oléron. The Laws of Oléron were based upon the sea law of the Republic of Rhodes, derived from old Roman law and codified previously by other Mediterranean cities and states. Although this code was one of the five or six existing codes of the time, it is recorded that Richard Coeur de Lion used it at Marseilles

Flogging a Seaman. The seaman to be flogged is lashed to a grating while the petty officer with the cat-o'-nine-tails stands ready to administer the punishment. *George Cruikshank, 1825.* Old Ship Prints *by E. Keble Chatterton.*

in 1190 while awaiting transport for his Crusade to the Holy Land. William de Forz of Oléron, who was one of the five commanders of Richard I on this expedition and afterwards became one of the justiciaries of the English Navy, was probably instrumental in urging its adoption. Alphonso X introduced and adopted the same code in Castile in the thirteenth century. It was Richard I after his return from the Crusades, who with additions introduced the Code of Oléron to England. It is of interest to note that the Code of Oléron was originally compiled and promulgated by Eleanor, Duchess of Guinne, mother of Richard I of England. Parts of the Code were embraced in manuscripts of the fifteenth century, collectively called the *Black Book of the Admiralty*.

The original *Black Book*, a most valuable legal codification, was lost at the end of the eighteenth century but fortunately was found in 1874 in an old chest. Inasmuch as it was the basis of British sea law, a brief description of this rare book may be of interest. It was written in Norman-French, which at that time was the language of Court as well as the language of judicial and legal proceedings. The book is 9½ inches high, 6¼ inches wide, and 2 inches thick. The first part of the

Keelhauling. In this most cruel punishment, a gun was fired to add to the culprit's misery before he was hauled beneath the ship and brought aboard on the port side. *Heck's Iconographic Encyclopedia*

book dates from Edward III, the latter belongs to the reigns of Henry IV, Henry V, and Henry VI. E. Keble Chatterton in his book, *Sailing the Seas*, writes in regard to the *Black Book*, "What immediately interests us is that we see order emerging out of chaos."

A few of the laws of the Code of Oléron are set forth to illustrate the inhumane punishments of that day:

> Anyone that should kill another on board ship should be tied to the dead body and thrown into the sea.
>
> Anyone that should kill another on land should be tied to the dead body and buried with it in the earth.
>
> Anyone lawfully convicted of drawing a knife or other weapon with intent to strike another, or of striking another so as to draw blood, should lose his hand.
>
> Anyone lawfully convicted of theft should have his head shaved and boiling pitch poured upon it and feathers or down should then be strewn upon it for the distinguishing of the offender; and upon the first occasion he should be put ashore.

The duties of an admiral in the fifteenth century were manifold and he exercised autocratic authority. The very power of creating a navy was delegated to him, as well as to appoint lieutenants, to impress ships and men of the kingdom, and to administer justice "according to the law and ancient customs of the sea."

These beginnings of definitive rules and punishments led to "orders for war." They in time were merged with maritime law such as was embraced in the Code of Oléron and Laws of Wisby.[1]

Although British authorities trace the descent of English men-o'-war and men-o'-war's men from the "buscarles" or sea police of nine centuries ago, it was not until the time of Henry VIII and his daughter Queen Elizabeth that the Royal Navy was shaped as an administrative entity with a book of *Orders for War*. It is recorded that Sir Thomas Dudley, an aide to Henry VIII, framed the first book of *Orders of War* to be used on land and sea. One of the instructions was:

> First, the laws which be written what every man ought to do in the ship towards his Captain to be set in the main mast in parchment to be read as occasion shall serve.

On the fourth offense of a man sleeping on watch the following "mild" punishment was ordered:

---

[1] The sea law of the northern maritime countries of Europe as adopted in the island of Gotland in the Baltic. Some writers claim these laws antedate the Code of Oléron.

A court-martial on deck. *Heck's Iconographic Encyclopedia*

The Brig. The two men are secured to the iron rod by leg irons. *Heck's Iconographic Encyclopedia*

Being taken asleep he shall be hanged to the bowsprit end of the ship in a basket, with a can of beer, a loaf of bread, and a sharp knife, and choose to hang there until he starve or cut himself into the sea.

There are to be found during this period certain special instructions such as those issued by the Earl of Essex and by Lord Howard of Effingham during the Cadiz Expedition. These instructions consisted of twenty-nine articles. They were to be "openly read" twice each week. The first article ordered that religious exercises take place twice each day. Another quaint article is that the watch was "to be set every night by eight of the clock, either by trumpets or drum and singing the Lord's Prayer, some of the Psalms of David, or clearing the glass."[2]

Punishments have in no measure been uniform throughout the years. Although cruel and drastic were the punishments of the early years, as late as 1750 more death sentence offenses were added, while the inhuman practice of flogging was exercised on the slightest pretext. For example, for blasphemy, by the Code of Oléron, the offender was fined in silver. In the early seventeenth century, the offender was gagged and his tongue scraped; in 1644, there was an order to the effect that blasphemy was to be punished by burning the tongue of the offender with a red-hot iron. The strong religious instinct may be clearly followed through the Elizabethan and post-Elizabethan age in the reverence shown in the Psalms and Holy Writ, and in the severe sentences for impiety and blasphemy. But in the seventeenth and eighteenth centuries the religious fever of former days was disappearing.

The Elizabethan period of maritime history gives the first inkling of some system of standardized discipline. The court-martial is the present-day heir of the *Curia Militaris*, or Court of Chivalry, called also the Marshal's Court. This was originally the only military court that was established by the laws of England.[3]

Originally this court was held before the Lord High Constable and the Earl Marshal jointly. In the reign of Henry VIII, the office of Lord High Constable was made extinct, and all cases regarding civil matters of the military were held before the Earl Marshal.

The court by statute (13 Richard II, c. 2) had jurisdiction over "contracts and other matters touching deeds of arms and war" both in

---

[2] *Clearing the glass:* Reversing the sand in the hour or half-hour glass.

[3] There is no etymological connection between *martial* and *marshal*. The one is derived from the Latin adjective *martialis* meaning sacred to Mars or pertaining to him. The other from the Old English *mearh scalc*, which meant literally horse boy, but was the title of a high officer at the Saxon court.

the kingdom and without. Originally it was purely a military court, or court of honor, when held before the Earl Marshal, and a criminal court when held before the Lord High Constable. Because of their weak jurisdiction and lack of power to enjoin their judgments, and because they were not courts of record, both courts fell into disuse.

The constitution of military courts as we know them was adopted by ordinance in the reign of Charles I, and was in a great measure borrowed from the *Articles of War* of Gustavus Adolphus. Their adoption was expedited by the mutiny of a number of English and Scottish dragoons that had been ordered to Holland to replace certain Dutch troops ordered to England.

The first statutes setting forth the courts-martial (as distinct from the Court of Chivalry) are found in the original Mutiny Act, 1689 (1 William and Mary, c. 5). This act was annually renewed "for the regulation of the Army."[4] By this act the sovereign was authorized to grant, when he desired, "commission, under his royal sign manual," giving to any officer not under the rank of a field-officer authorization for holding a general court-martial. It further provided that he could by warrant give the lord lieutenant of Ireland, the governor of Gibraltar, or governors of "any of the dominions beyond the sea" necessary authority to appoint courts-martial.

Although it has been nearly two hundred and fifty years since the above was enacted, it is still the source of military law of the English-speaking peoples. It exists in modified form in the United States, and many striking similarities will be found in a comparison of these statutes of 1689 and our own courts-martial system of precepts and jurisdiction.

Naval law and military law in England originally had many wide divergences. In the early days, the Lord High Admiral issued the instructions and regulations of both the Royal and the Merchant Navy. Commanders administered at their discretion naval law under the general instructions of the Lord High Admiral. Sentences at times were excessive: death sentences were even given in peacetime at the discretion of the commanders.[5]

---

[4] The reason for the annual passing of the Army Act or Mutiny Act is that the existence of a standing army in Britain is prohibited by the Bill of Rights. The existence of the army is authorized by the act. If the king fails to call parliament one year, the act lapses and the army discipline is void, so that the army cannot be used for oppressing the people in the absence of parliament.

[5] Blackstone says, "If anyone that hath commission of martial authority doth, in time of peace, hang, or otherwise execute any man by colour of martial law, this is murder; for it is against Magna Charta."

The first regular naval tribunal was instituted by the leaders of the Long Parliament in 1645. They passed a measure called "An Ordinance and Article of Martial Law for the Government of the Navy." It was this act that for the first time authorized "general and ships' courts-martial with written records," the former for captains and commanders, and the latter for subordinate officers and men. It was in a later law (Art. 13, Charles II, c. 9) that the Lord High Admiral was given the power to issue commissions (precepts) to officers to hold courts-martial. The first *Articles of War* for the Royal Navy were promulgated in the rule of Cromwell; these were gathered from a collation of pertinent instructions issued by admirals in command, and approved about 1661 during the reign of Charles II. In 1749 Parliament enacted new *Articles of War*, mainly through the efforts of Lord Anson. It was in these articles that so many death penalties were incorporated, and without doubt this accounts for the numerous death penalties in our old *Articles for the Government of the Navy*.

The Cromwellian *Articles for War* were not sufficient for naval administration. Commanders of the fleet and their immediate subordinates found it necessary from time to time to issue instructions and "details of service and discipline." With these instructions as a foundation, and guided by the best usage and customs of the sea, there appeared in 1731 the first issue of the *King's Regulations and Admiralty Instructions*.

British naval law, maritime history, and general sea traditions were common knowledge to the educated and well informed of our seaboard colonies. In fact, British maritime law as well as common law was the existing law of the Colonies; furthermore, there had been colonials, both officers and men, in the British Navy. John Adams used the British Admiralty regulations as his guide for the first *Rules* of our service. In some places the regulations were quoted verbatim, while in other cases slight modifications were necessary. The *King's Regulations* were comparatively new as a compilation (1731).

One of the staunchest supporters of the new-born Navy in the Continental Congress was John Adams who compiled the *Rules for the Regulation of the Navy of the United Colonies* adopted by the Continental Congress on November 28, 1775. These *Rules* formed the basic articles of the government of the Navy. Inadequate as they were, they served during the period of the Revolution. John Adams ever evinced a keen interest in matters maritime, and although he had no experience as a sea officer, as a lawyer he had considerable knowledge of the legal aspects of military and naval discipline and knew something of the Admiralty Law of England.

To augment the new *Rules and Regulations*, individual letters of instruction were issued to commanding officers, with directions such as "Use your people well, but preserve strict discipline; treat prisoners if any you make with humanity; and in all things be duly attentive to the honor and interest of America." The above is an extract of a letter of August 23, 1776, now preserved in the Library of Congress, and written to Lieutenant John Baldwin, commander of the schooner *Wasp*.

In a letter of November 1, 1776, it was urged upon Captain Elisha Warren of the Continental sloop *Fly* that

> Although we recommend your taking good care of your vessel
> and people, yet we should deem it more praiseworthy in an officer
> to lose his vessel in a bold enterprise than to lose a good prize by
> too timid a conduct.

The 1775 articles, or *Rules* as they were called, comprised about forty paragraphs. They sketchily defined the rights and the duties of officers, the reports required, and certain punishments for infractions of the rules. Flogging was sanctioned, and the issue of rum was authorized: one half-pint of rum a day for each man.

There were some quaint regulations in the Colonial *Naval Rules* of 1775. The third article reads:

> If any shall be heard to swear, curse, or blaspheme the name of
> God, the Commander is strictly enjoined to punish them for every
> offense by causing them to wear a wooden collar or some shame-
> ful badge, for so long a time as he shall judge proper.

In the fourth article regarding punishments, it is stated:

> No commander shall inflict any punishments upon a seaman be-
> yond twelve lashes upon his bare back with a cat-o'nine-tails; if the
> fault shall deserve a greater punishment, he is to apply to the Com-
> mander-in-Chief of the Navy in order to the trying of him by a
> Court-Martial, and in the meantime, he may put him under
> confinement.

The 1775 articles had a general declaration that covered extraordinary offenses as well as those not otherwise covered. This regulation reads:

> All other faults, disorders, and misdemeanors which shall be com-
> mitted on any ship belonging to the thirteen United Colonies,
> and which are not herein mentioned shall be punished according
> to the laws and customs in such cases at sea.

The lawmakers of the United States were fervently occupied at this time with the codification of law. Penalties and offenses became definitive. British customs and usage served as a general precedent in the lawmaking of the legislative assemblies, except that in the old *Articles for the Government of the Navy* we find no reference to custom or the "ancient common law of the sea." In this connection, it is notable that in keeping with the British legal system and the fact that British common law is unwritten law, the present *Queen's Regulations and Admiralty Instructions*, as well as the *Naval Discipline Acts* (corresponding to United States *Articles for the Government of the Navy*) refer to "customs of the sea." Section 44 of *Naval Discipline Acts* states that persons shall be proceeded against and punished "according to the laws and customs used at sea." Again, in Part III of *Naval Discipline Acts* there is found the phrase, "according to the custom of the Navy." One finds a general cover-all in the *Naval Discipline Acts*, known as the "Captain's Cloak":

> Every person subject to the act who shall be guilty of any act, disorder, or neglect to the prejudice of good order and naval discipline not hereinbefore specified, shall be dismissed from His Majesty's Service with disgrace, or suffer such other punishment as is hereinafter mentioned.

The old form of the first one of the original *Articles for the Government of the Navy* was as follows:

> The commanders of all ships and vessels belonging to the thirteen United Colonies are strictly required to shew in themselves a good example of honor and virtue to their officers and men, and to be very vigilant in inspecting the behavior of all such as are under them, and to discountenance and suppress all dissolute, immoral, and disorderly practice, and also such as are contrary to the rules of discipline and obedience, and to correct those who are guilty of the same, according to the usage of the sea.

With little change to the above, Article 1102 of naval regulations reads:

> All commanding officers and others in authority in the naval service are required to show in themselves a good example of virtue, honor, patriotism, and subordination; to be vigilant in inspecting the conduct of all persons who are placed under their command; to guard against and suppress all dissolute and immoral practices, and to correct, according to the laws and regulations of the Navy, all persons who are guilty of them; and to take all

necessary and proper measures, under the laws, regulations, and customs of the naval service, to promote and safeguard the morale, the physical well-being, and the general welfare of the officers and enlisted persons under their command or charge. (10 USC 5947)

Various other British regulations were embodied in the 1798 *Naval Regulations*. The following quotations show striking similarity:

REGULATIONS AND INSTRUCTIONS
RELATING TO HIS MAJESTY'S SERVICE AT SEA

Printed in the Year 1790

The Cook[6]

Article I

The Cook is to have the charge of the Steep-Tub and to be answerable for the meat put therein, if any part thereof shall be lost through his want of care.

II

He is to see the meat duly watered and the provisions carefully and cleanly boiled, and issued to the men according to the practice of the Navy.

*   *   *   *

NAVAL REGULATIONS
ISSUED BY COMMAND OF THE PRESIDENT OF THE
UNITED STATES OF AMERICA

January 25, 1802
Of the Duties of a Cook[7]

1. He is to have charge of the steep tub, and is answerable for the meat put therein.
2. He is to see the meat duly watered, and the provisions carefully boiled, and delivered to the men according to the practice of the Navy.

On reflection, it is obvious why a small, new-born navy of identical race and language should copy and adhere to many of the regulations and customs of what was then called the "English Fleet" or the British Navy. Britain claimed the mastery of the seas and was the

---

[6] The cook was an important warrant officer at that time. For many years after the above dates, the duties of the midshipmen were listed in the *Naval Regulations* after those of the cook. The "watering," soaking, of meat was an attempt to remove the salt.

[7] The following is quoted from the personal copy of Thomas Truxtun.

undisputed master after crushing the French and Spanish navies at Trafalgar (1805). In 1812, the London *Times* reported that the British Navy outnumbered the United States Navy seven to one in armament. Although at the time, "There was little to choose between a Yankee and a Briton. Both were cold and hardy, cool and intelligent, quick with their hands, and showing at their best in an emergency. They looked alike and spoke alike; when they took the trouble to think, they thought alike; and when they got drunk, which was not an infrequent occurrence, they quarreled alike."[8]

The old Articles are no more. All that pertained to punishments, execution of sentences, and the administration of justice have been modified and adjusted in the new Code. That which dealt with the duties and general responsibilities of commanders' duties have been made a part of the U. S. Navy Regulations.[9]

Thus have tradition, custom, usage, and experience given form to the basic laws of the Navy. It is a source of pride that

> The rules of the greatest and most glorious game in the world are not a thing of yesterday or the day before. They were born of the travail and the trial of ages; they are the result of centuries of experience and experiment; heated at the forge of battle, hammered into shape on the anvil of practical knowledge; tested and approved by great heroes of the sea. Any man in the navy that has a heart to understand and appreciate the spiritual in life must breathe freer and walk with a firmer step when he recalls that he is obeying the same laws that Rodney and Nelson and Napier obeyed; that he is under the same discipline that Decatur, Macdonough, and Perry, Dahlgren and Porter, Farragut and Dewey, and a host of other patriots have honored and made illustrious.[10]

[8] Theodore Roosevelt, *The Naval War of 1812.*

[9] As should be expected of a new republic based upon democratic principles, the U. S. Navy was the first of the navies of the world to abolish flogging and other inhuman punishments. It is of particular interest that in 1962 the Secretary of the Navy sent a letter praising Uriah P. Levy, naval officer and founder of the Washington Hebrew Congregation, upon the 100th anniversary of the death of the commodore, to Rabbi Norman Gerstenfeld of the Congregation. The letter, praising the commodore for his philanthropic and patriotic contributions, was read by Rear Admiral Robert D. Powers, Jr., deputy judge advocate general of the Navy. In particular, the letter referred to Levy's "fervent belief in the dignity of man that spurred him to fashion his most lasting memorial," which was the abolition of corporal punishment, brought about mainly by the commodore and Senator Stockton of New Jersey. In short, Congress in 1852 abolished flogging forever in the American Navy.

[10] Charles R. Williams, "History of Discipline in the Navy," U. S. Naval Institute *Proceedings*, March 1919, p. 376.

Few Americans ever appreciated more than Theodore Roosevelt the significance and power of great tradition, and particularly its effect upon the morale of armed forces. In an address called "Washington's Forgotten Maxim," delivered at the Naval War College, June 1897, Roosevelt, then Assistant Secretary of the Navy, said: "We but keep to the traditions of Washington, to the traditions of all great Americans who struggled for the real greatness of America, when we strive to build up those fighting qualities for the lack of which in a nation, as in an individual, no refinement, no culture, no wealth, no material prosperity, can atone."

PART II

Sea Manners and Shore Manners

.

CHAPTER 3

Honors, Salutes, and Ceremonies

Salutes and salutations were, in their origin, marks of submission. We take off our hats because of old the conquered took off their helmets; we bow, because the vanquished were used to bend their necks to the conqueror; and salutes were fired, shot and all, that the place or ship might be thereby without the means of present defense. Thus from the bloody forms of turbulent ages are derived the ceremonies of polished life.

The Lady's Magazine, 1821.

Because so many honors and ceremonies are international in character, it is important that they be rendered and conducted in a manner that reflects credit on both the U.S. Navy and the United States.

Watch Officer's Guide, 1979.[1]

[1] Eleventh edition revised by Commander K. C. Jacobsen, USN. This manual, published by the Naval Institute Press, is a valuable training aid and important professional book. Recommended for the sea library of all junior officers.

The officer of the deck shall see that all regulations concerning salutes, honors, and ceremonies, except as modified by orders of competent authority, are carefully observed.

U. S. Navy Regulations, 1948.

THIS CHAPTER, by the very nature of its content, is directed more to the naval officer than to the general reader. It is, of course, the naval officer, particularly when serving as officer of the deck, who must understand and execute the various traditional honors, salutes, and ceremonies that must be performed aboard his ship. Nevertheless, the general reader has undoubtedly witnessed or heard of these observances; therefore, this chapter should help him to become better informed regarding these time-honored procedures, closely associated with the Navy and its history.

The effect of these usages, both to the executing officer and the observing layman, derives first of all from the smartness of their execution. With this in mind, the officer of the deck should always observe the following principles:

(1) Keep informed and insist on a "sharp lookout" by signalmen and the quartermaster of the watch.

(2) Correctness, promptness, and smartness should be the aim in rendering honors.

(3) Check and recheck honors by regulations or existing instructions where there is doubt.

(4) The promptness of a man-of-war in returning the dip of merchant ships is usually a gauge of her smartness regarding honors in general. Remember that this is an honor that is paid your flag, so be prompt to return the courtesy.

(5) Ensure that ensign, flags, and pennants fly free and are hoisted to the very top of the hoist. Learn, as in the days of sail, to cast your eyes aloft.

(6) When a senior ship passes, order "attention" sounded before she does, and ensure that "carry on" is given after she gives it.

(7) Exercise great care that honors are never rendered of a less degree than due. In the matter of side boys for foreign officers—if unsure, err on the high side.

(8) In addition to the correctness and smartness that one must show in the attention to honors, remember to make sure that all persons coming alongside or visiting the ship are courteously treated. That means thoughtful, dignified military courtesy.

(9) Insist that the signalmen in charge of the signal watches maintain bright lookouts for boats approaching or passing with pennants and flags of senior officers flying. Inform the signal bridge when calls are expected, in order that timely information may be given the quarterdeck. Never let a V.I.P. (very important person) get alongside or aboard without your knowledge.

(10) When officer of the deck of flagships, maintain a close liaison with flag lieutenants, and keep the admiral thoroughly informed, but remember always to make prompt reports to your commanding and executive officer.

Morning quarters—the Lord's Prayer. "*All Hands*" by R.F. Zogbaum. *Courtesy Harper and Bros.*

(11) Give attention to your personal appearance on watch, with particular regard to gold braid, cap, and accoutrement.

THE QUARTERDECK

Few modern ships have quarterdeck space comparable to that of the larger types in the "Old Navy." In 1932, because of the installation of "new fangled" catapults on the quarterdeck and the necessary upkeep incident thereto, the commander, Battleship Divisions, in an official letter to the commanding officers of twelve battleships called attention to the Navy Regulations regarding the limits and use of the quarterdeck. He observed a tendency of some men in the area to loaf, to smoke, and to engage in loud conversation. This, he pointed out, was not "conducive to smartness," and added, "the Navy's traditions and customs with respect to the 'sanctity' of the quarterdeck are gradually being ignored." In many ships today the "quarterdeck" is where the commanding officer says it is, because additional deck structures, anti-aircraft guns, and special equipment required in modern warfare have usurped the old quarterdeck space.

> The commanding officer of a ship shall establish the limits of the quarterdeck and the restrictions as to its use. The quarterdeck shall embrace so much of the main or other appropriate deck as may be necessary for the proper conduct of official and ceremonial functions.[2]

It is normally on the main deck near the gangways. It is marked off by appropriate lines, deck markings, cartridge cases decoratively arranged, or fancy work. It is always kept particularly clean and ship-shape. Men not on duty should not be allowed on or near the quarterdeck. The dignity and appearance of the quarterdeck are symbols of the professional and seamanlike attitude of a ship and her crew.

A CEREMONY OF CHANGE IN COMMAND
ABOARD SHIP

Such ceremonies as this should be formal and impressive, with close attention to detail designed to strengthen that respect for authority which is vital to a military organization. In older, more genteel times such ceremonies were announced by official invitation to the participants. Since World War II, however, the tendency has been to pro-

[2] *U. S. Navy Regulations*, 1948.

mulgate the plans by naval message, with formal invitations being sent to those whom the principals desire to attend.

In general, the order of the ceremony is as it has been for decades. The uniform for participants is normally Full Dress in keeping with the dignity of the occasion. The officers, chief petty officers, and crew are formed in ranks such that they are not excluded from the ceremony and that they might observe the event which so affects their lives. Additionally, side boys, honor guard, color guard, and bands are paraded as available and appropriate. When all preparations are complete and the guests are present, the official party will arrive amid the required ceremonies and salutes. After the invocation, the remarks of the guest speaker (usually the next senior officer in the chain of command) shall follow and then the remarks of the officer being relieved. Upon completion of his remarks he and then his relief will read their orders. The ceremony then reaches its simplest and most impressive part, with the words used traditionally at the changing of the watch: "I relieve you, sir" and "I stand relieved." The two then report to their superior and, after the traditionally brief remarks of the new CO and a benediction, the ceremony is over.

Change of command aboard the USS *Antietam*.

The following details of the ceremony are noteworthy:

(1) In the days when the quarterdeck was aft, the officer to be relieved and his staff paraded on the honor side, the starboard side of the quarterdeck. If the ceremony should take place on the forecastle or other parts of the ship, then the officer to be relieved should be to the right, the honor side of the officer relieving.

(2) At such ceremonies the officers of the ship stand together. A variation in this arrangement was to have visiting officers forward and amidships and ships officers and chief petty officers just abaft the visiting officers and amidships. Guests first.

(3) Fifty years ago, after such occasions officers repaired to the suitable mess to "splice the main brace," but today soft drinks, coffee, and tea are offered instead.

(4) The change of command was never, formerly, a mixed social affair; however, since World War II, there has been a trend towards inviting the families of the officers and crew as well as friends of the two officers involved. The rule concerning "guests first" applies in this instance, and such guests should be seated in such a position as to allow them the best possible view of the event. The increase in morale which this action provides can, however, backfire if the crew is relegated to a secondary role or placed in a position where they cannot observe the ceremony.

(5) Ensure that all publicity media that may be interested are given sufficient advance information as to the ceremony and what facilities may be offered them.

(6) *Prepare and promulgate a detailed plan*, and include a sketch if thought necessary.

THE CEREMONY OF COMMISSIONING A NAVAL SHIP

The following procedure conforms to the general practice of the Navy as determined by custom in commissioning a large ship such as a carrier and is easily adapted to all types because the principles are the same.

Two main principles govern in commissioning a naval ship: The ship has usually been turned over by the builders to the commandant of a naval district and is his responsibility until commissioned. Therefore, no ensign, jack, or commission pennant flies before commissioning. This means that when the commandant or his delegated representative comes aboard to turn over the ship, no honors other than the

Change of Command at Sea. Although most changes of command take place in port, this ceremony can also occur at sea. On this occasion the Seventh Fleet changed commanders just out of range of gunfire during the height of the war with North Vietnam. Within an hour, the flagship was firing again.

courtesy of meeting him at the side are rendered. Honors are given him at departure.

It is the best established practice in commissioning to have the basic and official ceremony first, and after that has terminated and the ship is in commission, to continue the program with the personal remarks, official speeches, presentations, etc. This ensures that at all times responsibility is clearly placed; and even though very inspiring and eloquent speeches may continue for another hour, officers and men are on duty at their assigned stations for port watches and should be able to cope effectively with any emergency that might arise. Furthermore, such a procedure adheres to the letter of the only naval regulations on the subject:

(1) The formal transfer shall be effected by the district commandant or his representative.

(2) As many of the officers and crew of the ship as circumstances permit, and a guard and music, shall be assembled and properly distributed on the quarterdeck or other suitable part of the ship.

(3) The officer effecting the transfer shall cause the national ensign and the proper insignia of command to be hoisted with the

appropriate ceremonies, and shall turn the ship over to the prospective commanding officer.

(4) The prospective commanding officer shall read his orders, assume command, and cause the watch to be set.

STEPS IN THE COMMISSIONING CEREMONY

(Destroyers and smaller craft)

(1) A dais or platform should be constructed a few feet above the deck and decorated with signal flags. A lectern and public address system should be provided and a plan drawn for seating distinguished guests and the principals on the platform. Printed invitations and programs lend tone to the occasion and provide appropriate souvenirs for officers, men, and invited guests. The executive officer (small ships) should cover all details in the plan of the day. Check arrangements and

A naval vessel is commissioned. The first watch has been ordered to man their stations.

allocation for guests who may be invited for refreshments in the respective messes. A rehearsal of getting men expeditiously to and away from dress parade stations will make for smoothness on commissioning day.

(2) Officers fall in aft at dress parade stations on the quarterdeck or fantail, and the crew is marched by divisions aft to assigned stations. It is customary for officers to fall in amidships and face aft. The guard and band fall in aft at stations for colors but face the ceremony until the ensign is hoisted. Visitors should be assigned chairs or seats with an unobstructed view.

(3) Because of restricted space on destroyers and smaller ships, it has been customary to have the band and a marine guard of the district take stations on the pier abreast of the place of ceremony. When this is done, it is usual to give the commandant honors when he gets out of his car on the dock. He is obviously making an official visit. Often the commandant or his representative will come aboard a few minutes early and spend a short time with the prospective commanding officer in the cabin.

(4) The executive officer should report to the prospective commanding officer that "Officers and crew are up and aft and all is ready for the commissioning ceremony." The admiral or delegated representative and the prospective commanding officer should proceed to the place of ceremony. All come to attention and "carry on" when the principals reach the platform.

(5) The ceremony commences with the invocation by a chaplain.[3]

(6) The officer effecting the transfer reads the orders for the delivery of the ship, and orders the prospective commanding officer to "Commission the USS ————." The captain, through the executive officer to the navigator (officer of the deck), relays the order. Attention is sounded on the bugle, the national anthem is played, the ensign, the commission pennant, and jack are hoisted simultaneously. If an admiral effects the transfer, then his flag is hoisted and remains until he departs.

(7) The prospective commanding officer reads his orders from the Navy Department, salutes the officer effecting the transfer and says, "I assume command of the USS ————." Immediately he orders the executive officer to "set the watch." This is most effective when all the boatswain's mates commence piping at one time to pass the word

---

[3] In the commissioning ceremony program of the attack carrier *Forrestal*, the invocation came immediately after the Commandant of the District accepted the ship from the builders. This is good practice when taking over new ships directly from builders.

fore and aft. The officer of the deck takes his station and makes the first entry in the log. *The ship is now officially commissioned.*

(8) The commanding officer then formally introduces the commandant or his representative, who customarily makes a short talk to the officers and men of the newly commissioned ship.

(9) The address of the commanding officer.

(10) Should there be a presentation of silver service or other gifts to the ship by a city, state, or organization, it is fitting that the ceremony come at this point. In this event it is expected that the command-

An Official Visit. At that time, the salute consisted of holding the bill of the cap or raising it. *"All Hands"* by R.F. Zogbaum. *Courtesy Harper and Bros.*

ing officer will reply to the speech of presentation by expressing the thanks of the Navy Department and his officers and men for the gift and the motives that prompted its presentation.

(11) The benediction concludes the ceremony.

(12) Departure of official party.

(13) Reception and refreshments in appropriate quarters and messes.

GUN SALUTES

First Regulations on Gun Salutes[4]

When a public character, high in rank, shall embark on board of any of the United States' ships of war, he may be saluted with 13 guns.

When a commanding officer anchors in any foreign port, he is to inform himself what salutes have been usually given or received by officers of his rank of other nations, and he is to insist on receiving the same mark of respect. Captains may salute foreign ports with such number of guns as may have been customary, on receiving an assurance that an equal number shall be returned—but without such assurance, they are never to salute.

Foreigners of distinction, on visiting the United States' ships of war, are to be saluted with such a number of guns as may suit their rank and quality.

[4] *Rules, Regulations, and Instructions for the Naval Service of the United States, 1818.*

CHAPTER 4

Naval Social Customs

Look about you today! See the confusion and chaos that reign over all questions of doctrine, diet, hygiene, behaviour; the relations of man to man, and above all of sex to sex; and ask yourself whether everything does not already bear the indelible stamp of having been left too long without the discriminating guidance of taste. Where traditional usages are breaking down, what is rising to take their place? Where old institutions are losing their power, where are the substitutes offered by the present age?
Anthony M. Ludovici, *A Defence of Aristocracy*

Let public apathy starve our material into inaction or degenerate us into an epidemic of scraping and painting, of bright-work and holy stones, if so be it that we remain a personnel determined that the niceties of plain good manners, manners learned at home and polished up with military terms into military courtesy, shall not perish from the sea; if so be it that these manners of Paul Jones, of Lawrence, of Farragut, of Dewey; if these sea manners passed down to us by these sea-gentlemen be preserved through us of today to sea-gentlemen yet unborn; if so be it we remain determined that the heart and soul of the Navy shall not go to hell!
Admiral F. B. Upham, USN

Life is not so short, but that there is always time for courtesy.
Emerson, *Letters and Social Aims*

IN AN AVERAGE CAREER, the naval officer will have relations with the representative citizens and subjects of many countries. Because of the large number of ships in our far flung fleets, such relations are far more frequent than ever before; because of international tensions our foreign relations were never more important. It is generally recognized that all information acquired that pertains to the history, customs, and accepted usage of foreign states will prove useful: specifically because the acquisition of such knowledge furthers the conduct of official business, and leads to ease in official and social intercourse. But as a starter, it is essential that the naval officer be familiar with and appreciative of his own sea manners, customs, and best usage, ashore and afloat.

The traditional unwritten law of naval etiquette, sea manners, and shore manners is best learned in an officer's youth. That is why young officers are constantly reminded that they should set good examples for their men. By the same token, it is logical to assert that as the older officers observe sound and time-honored usages so will the younger officers conform to example and precept. If seniors give but scant attention to sea manners, why should juniors consider them worthy of adoption?

The comments upon some of the important "small things" that are set forth in this chapter were in the main prompted by observations and opinions of experienced officers of the Navy, both on the active and retired lists. The subjects range from the ordinary manners and courtesy always expected of the officer aboard ship and ashore to the amenities that constitute everywhere the *savoir faire* of men of the world.

In the reminders that follow, details and manner of execution require the judgment and initiative of the individual officer: the custom, the principle, and in some cases the sincere gesture are the points to which attention is here invited. It is comparatively easy to know what to do; often the real difficulty is to know what to avoid.

OLD CUSTOMS ON DECK

At one time it was always customary to send a side boy or messenger to the foot of the accommodation ladder when guests of flag rank came aboard. This ensured that the boat would be held snugly alongside, and that parcels or luggage would be expeditiously handled. In short, it was a courtesy that had a practical value and was a distinctive attention that was not often overlooked. In like manner, ladies should be assisted getting in or out of boats.

It was once a custom that the junior officer of the deck, a junior officer, or even the officer of the deck go to the foot of the accommodation ladder and inform a visiting commanding officer when it was not convenient for the commanding officer to receive the visitor in person. The captain is often precluded from attending the side because of conferences, inspections, etc. This fine old custom was a courtesy that saved the visiting captain a useless trip up the ladder when he was only making a friendly and informal visit. There was a time when this custom was never neglected.

To give side boys to foreign senior officers after dark or sunset when making calls or attending official dinners and receptions, was once a gracious courtesy often rendered. This is done by some foreign navies today.

To hold in mind the "sanctity" of the quarterdeck and observe its traditional etiquette—this should be ever foremost in the minds of those who respect their profession and the smartness of their ship.

In the days of the large quarterdecks, it had long been the custom that the starboard side aft be reserved exclusively for the admiral or captain when on deck. A captain, if on deck, would shift to the port side if the admiral came topside, particularly if he accompanied another flag officer or senior visitor; this gave the senior officer more privacy. The port side abaft the quarterdeck was for the use of the commissioned officers, and the starboard side forward was reserved on many ships for the warrant officers. The large "foc'suls" of those days gave the crew ample space for fresh air and recreation.

In the days of sail, admirals and captains customarily walked the weather side of the quarterdeck. This was an extension of a major tradition and custom of the sea.

This point is made by C. S. Forester: ". . . and he began to stride up and down the weather side of the quarterdeck, hands behind him, head bowed forward, in the old comfortable attitude. Enthusiasts had talked or written of pleasures innumerable, of gardens and women, wine or fishing; it was strange that no one had ever told of the pleasure of walking a quarterdeck."[1]

EXTRAORDINARY NAVAL COURTESIES

An interesting custom and extraordinary courtesy is that of delaying the "official sunset" in order that regulation day-time honors may be

[1] C. S. Forester, *Commodore Hornblower* (Boston: Little, Brown & Co., 1946), p. 53.

rendered. This was done aboard the USS *Arizona* at Callao, Peru, in August 1921, in order that honors and a salute could be rendered the President of Peru, who did not leave the ship until after dark.

When the Prince of Wales passed through the Panama Canal on his cruise to Australia, a ship of the Special Service Squadron rendered full honors after dark.

On 4 July 1923 all ships of the Royal Navy present in Hong Kong, by direction of the commander in chief of the British Asiatic Fleet, rendered a 21-gun salute, although the only American ship present was the gunboat *Pampanga*, too small to be rated as a saluting ship. It is such sincere and timely gestures that aid in maintaining the cordial relations that should exist between public officers and the inhabitants of friendly states.

One recalls also the aerial salute that was given by Rear Admiral T. P. Magruder, U. S. Navy, to the populace of Wellington, New Zealand, in 1925. Planes were launched in heavy winds and taken aboard in a choppy sea: the gesture was exceptional and timely. Admiral Magruder also executed, as a mark of respect to the Governor of Tasmania, a very difficult naval evolution at high speed, both upon entering and leaving Hobart, Tasmania. It might have been called "cutting a dido," but the smart effect of the division of light cruisers in rendering this exceptional honor was taken as a compliment to the governor and much appreciated by the inhabitants. Such things are long remembered.

A most interesting custom, still remembered by older officers of the retired list, was that of using lanterns after dark to light the way from the gangway to the hatchway leading to the officers' quarters. The anchor watch lined up and held six lanterns for the admiral, four for the captain, and two for a wardroom officer. After the introduction of electric lights, this custom fell into disuse. It is reported, however, that when Admiral W. H. Brownson commanded the armored cruiser squadron before World War I, he instituted the practice of using a portable electric lead which carried eight lamps. The picture on the front cover of *All Hands* Magazine, May 1955, shows a revival of this quaint old honor as rendered to Vice Admiral T. G. W. Settle, USN, by eight night side boys, when he, as the Commander Amphibious Force Pacific, visited the USS *Mount McKinley*.

 There is another memory that will always live in the minds of the officers and men who witnessed it; and that is the cheering led by Admiral Beatty, RN, on 7 December 1917 when Admiral Rodman's division of United States battleships joined the Grand Fleet as the Sixth Battle Squadron. Admiral Beatty's waving his cap with the cheering

British bluejackets was a sincere gesture on a momentous occasion. It was the first time since the days of John Paul Jones that the United States had joined a foreign Navy as a unit. Certainly the "Farewell" on 1 December 1918, rendered by the British Fleet commanded by Admiral Beatty, involved extraordinary honors. An officer who was an eye-witness aboard the flagship *New York*, reported as follows:

> The Sixth Battle Squadron weighed anchor, broke from its maintops long streaming "homeward bound" pennants, and proceeded out of harbor (Rosyth, Scotland). Our band burst forth with "Homeward Bound" and followed it with "Good Bye-e-e." Cheers were exchanged with every vessel we passed between the columns, while their bands played our airs, and messages of comradeship and good luck floated in a score of different versions from as many yardarms. Nor was that the end. The *New York* followed by the *Texas, Nevada, Arkansas, Wyoming,* and *Florida* in column was escorted to May Island, twenty miles outside, by the ships of the Fifth Battle Squadron (British), our sister division, and the Eleventh Destroyer Flotilla. . . . There was music and cheering nearly all the way, culminating as we reached May Island. The British units turned gracefully outward swinging through 180 degrees. There was a sustained roar of cheers as the great ships parted from us. . . . From the masthead of Admiral Levenson's *Barham* was displayed at last the plain English hoist: "G-O-O-D B-Y-E-E-E-E." Simultaneously a message was received from Lord Beatty, the Commander-in-Chief, Grand Fleet: "Your comrades in the Grand Fleet regret your departure. We trust it is only temporary and that the interchange of squadrons from the two great fleets of the Anglo-Saxon race may be repeated. We wish you good-bye, good luck, a good time; and come back soon."[2]

An earlier example of mass cheering took place in 1895 aboard the USS *New York* then in the harbor of Kiel, Germany. Captain Robley D. Evans, "Fighting Bob," in command welcomed the emperor of Germany, his brother Admiral Prince Henry, and ten other admirals to dine. When the emperor came aboard Captain Evans informed him that the *New York* had the champion twelve-oared cutter in the American Navy, and requested, on the part of his crew, the honor of naming her after the emperor's daughter—Victoria Louisa. The Emperor graciously granted the request and "was really touched by the compliment." Captain Evans wrote: "I turned to the crew and called for

[2] Francis T. Hunter, *Beatty, Jellicoe, Sims, and Rodman* (New York: Doubleday, Page & Co., 1919), pp. 186–187.

three cheers for the *Victoria Louisa*, and then three cheers and a tiger for the emperor. I don't think he ever heard such cheers before."

The Kaiser expressed a desire to inspect the engine rooms at 1:00 A.M. He then asked Captain Evans how long it took to close all watertight doors, and was told about two minutes at night. Unfortunately, there was not enough steam on the siren to give the alarm, but Evans, ever resourceful throughout his distinguished career, touched the general alarm, which called "all hands" to quarters. Captain Evans reported:

> The emperor took the time himself, and in one minute and a half the entire ship was ready for action with all watertight doors closed. It was 2 A.M., the royal [imperial] standard at our main and the searchlight of the USS *Columbia* turned on it, the ship ready for action and the emperor complimenting the captain on the forecastle. I find myself in some funny positions.[3]

Captain Evans also gave what he called a "dancing reception" for the German officers and their ladies and the officers of the other foreign ships at the gala celebration of the opening of the Kiel Canal. The old sea dog knew how to give a party. In speaking of this affair for nine hundred guests, he wrote in his journal: "The flowers were beautiful, the women more so, and the food excellent—they drank nineteen kegs of beer and thirty gallons of punch."[4]

One of the most dramatic occasions of cheering witnessed in the States in World War II took place on a bleak November day in 1942 when the war-scarred USS *Boise* moored at the pier in the Philadelphia Navy Yard. The commandant, Rear Admiral M. F. Draemel, USN, and senior officers of the District and yard assembled with a band on the assigned pier to welcome the gallant ship and those in her who had so bravely fought the heroic night action against the Japanese off Cape Esperance on October 11–12, 1942.

HMS *Royal Sovereign* was moored on the other side of the pier assigned the rusty *Boise*. Everyone in the yard knocked off work to witness the moving ceremony. An officer observer, Lt. Wilcox, wrote:

---

[3] Robley D. Evans, *A Sailor's Log* (New York: Appleton, 1931), pp. 382–387.

[4] A Spanish general, on his king's birthday, during the stay of the British Fleet in Cadiz, "intended to entertain all the English, Dutch, and Spanish officers with a bowl of punch [bowl of large fountain] to celebrate the Birth of his Master and to keep that amity that was between themselves" had made a punch that contained: "English Barrels of Water, amounting to 432 gallons; of Brandy there was 188 Gallons; of sugar 400 weight, of Lemmons, which the garden itself afforded, about six thousand; a pound of nutmegs, and there was ordered 180 weight of Biskets but there was none put in."

As the cruiser drew within hailing distance, the band sounded off and the music was like a tropical sunrise the way it burst out. Orders were passed and the crew of the *Royal Sovereign* manned rails. All hands on the *Boise* not required for ship's work also manned rails and there was not an inch of her [rails] topside unoccupied.

Heaving lines curved ashore. Mooring hawsers were passed and as the first one was secured . . . three cheers were proposed aboard the *Royal Sovereign*. They were given lustily from more than a thousand throats, and thus did a ship of our British ally pay homage to a gallant ship.

Done in a time-honored way, it was a modern enactment of the ancient evolution. . . .[5]

The leave-taking of Captain E. J. "Mike" Moran took place a few weeks later. He had the noonday meal with the wardroom officers. Afterwards the officers and ship's company mustered on the dock abreast the brow from which he was to depart. The captain made a forceful "fight talk" and touching farewell, at the conclusion of which the executive officer proposed three cheers which were enthusiastically given; then Captain Moran was piped over the side, a chief boatswain's mate piping with four other chief petty officers serving as sideboys. The captain passed down the line on the pier. He shook hands with each officer as he passed—juniors to seniors in inverse order of rank. And there was no more to say or do—Moran and the saga of the *Boise* became history and tradition. Continues Wilcox:

The faces of the crew were interesting to watch as they returned aboard. There were many a wet eye and sniffling nose. Among the most moved were veterans with two or three hash marks, and the Marine detail was sad-eyed as the rest.

Things such as this do not bulk large in the over-all considerations of a grim global war, but certainly have some permanent niche in the history which is being created these days. Both ceremonies deeply impressed and moved me.

THE OFFICERS' MESS

An officers' mess should be comparable to a gentleman's club in its efficient service, its standard of behavior, and tone of conversation.

---

[5] Lt. (j.g.) E. E. Wilcox, USNR, in a personal letter to the Director of Naval Public Relations, February 14, 1943.

The laxity that has been observed in some ships is attributed to many causes. Some assert that the heavy work incident to present-day fleet training and competitions leaves little time for the "fancy stuff." Others state that the "slackening off" is the result of an influx of officers during World War II who did not have proper junior officer training. Another group considers the regulation prohibiting wine in the mess has limited formal entertainment to the extent that the large parties of the "good old days" are never given, and with them have gone the attendant amenities of the formal dinner. Whatever may be the cause or causes, some of the sea manners and usages that were once observed and are now in many particulars disregarded deserve a word of attention.

WARDROOM CUSTOMS AND ETIQUETTE

Wardroom country is each officer's seagoing home, a home in which he should be proud to entertain his relatives and friends. It is also his club where he may gather with his fellow officers for moments of relaxation, such as a discussion of the daily problems; a movie; radio; musical or TV program; or just a game of acey deucey over a cup of coffee. Whatever the event, it is a place where members should conduct themselves within the ordinary rules of propriety, common sense, and good manners, in addition to observing the rules of etiquette founded on customs and traditions.

(1) The presiding officer should be punctual for the commencement of meals. If delayed, he should inform the next senior whether or not to proceed with the meal.

(2) Members should be prompt in order that all the mess may be seated when the presiding officer takes his seat. The old custom of arriving from three to five minutes ahead of mealtime is recommended. If late, make apologies to the senior member, and if required to leave before the termination of the meal, ask the presiding officer, as well as those near you, to be excused. Never under ordinary circumstances leave the table precipitately.

(3) Refrain from a discussion of ladies and religion in the mess, and show restraint in discussions of politics and matters dealing with racial characteristics. This taboo once included the Civil War. A friendly, cheerful atmosphere should prevail; it is a time for pleasantries and good conversation. Rare old Ben Jonson put it well: "Delectable and pleasant conversation, whose property is to move a kindly delight, and sometimes not without laughter."

A good rule that has official sanction is: " 'Shop talk' anytime, 'ship talk' only after coffee."

(4) Good usage and custom have never sanctioned smoking throughout a meal. At a formal meal, and this is strictly complied with abroad, never "light up" until your host or seniors have. This will generally be after coffee is served. All of this has to do with manners, and as Thomas Gray said: "Manners speak the idiom of their soil." It is recommended that "the president should privately counsel those whose deportment brings down the tone of the mess."

(5) Well-regulated messes have a written policy regarding guests, with a clear-cut differentiation made between guests of the mess and those of the individual, as well as a scale of charges for the respective meals.

Officers should be encouraged to bring their guests aboard ship for dinner. Every guest that enters the mess should be treated as the guest of the entire mess, and it is the duty and privilege of each member to carry out his social obligation as co-host to the best of his ability. Introduce all members present to your guests. Each member should come forward to meet them.

(6) It was once customary in the larger ships, particularly when anchored near populous centers or abroad, to designate a night each week as "guest night"; the officers dressed, flowers and place cards were in order, and the Number One dinner was served. This assured that invited guests received the most favorable impression of the mess, the ship, and the service.

(7) The criterion of a mess is that it shall be one in which officers are proud to bring a distinguished guest at any time, and know that he will be tendered the same dignified hospitality that he would expect to receive in a gentlemen's club or at a dinner given by gentlemen. This type of mess is not obtained except by the sincere cooperation of *all members*.

(8) It is the duty of the commanding officer to ensure that the wardroom mess which he commands, generally exercising his command through the president of the mess, maintains high standards in tone and behavior and reflects credit on the naval service both at home and when abroad.

A WELL-REGULATED WARDROOM

One of the best-conducted wardrooms in the old Battle Fleet (1932–1935) attributed its fine reputation to the following customs and regulations:

(1) The executive officer never failed to be in the mess a few minutes before the scheduled time for meals, and decreed that with the exception of breakfast all officers not on watch were expected to be seated with the executive officer.

(2) If officers were called away from the table before finishing the meal, they were expected to ask the executive officer to be excused.

(3) Officers were encouraged to bring guests aboard for dinner. Special arrangements could always be made for boats if they were needed. Officers were enjoined to have guests on board sufficiently in advance of dinner in order that all could be presented and learn their places before being seated. The matter of promptness greatly helped the steward to serve hot and appetizing food. The steward once said: "I know to the minute when I serve the courses on the ship."

(4) It was expected that all games played in the mess such as cards, chess, and checkers would terminate one-half hour before meal times.

(5) The mess was made exceedingly attractive by interior decoration and lighting. The mess boys of the watch were required to tidy up the mess every two hours. Officers cooperated in returning magazines to their proper racks and stowing any gear such as gameboards, etc., in the place from which they were taken. The mess was always neat and presentable. A mess, as a rule, is a composite reflection of its members.

(6) The mess caterer gave special instruction to stewardsmen in serving correctly, and arranged for the cooks to get some special instruction in first class restaurants and hotels, and paid meticulous attention to the menus. Care in the preparation and prompt serving of food was stressed. Discriminating taste was the aim of those charged with the conduct of mess affairs.

(7) At frequent intervals special dinner parties were given when all officers and guests were required to wear formal evening dress. At sea on special occasions, officers were given the opportunity to make short prepared dinner speeches and to learn the etiquette of toasts. To such affairs the captain was often invited.

(8) Personal guests were made to feel that they were guests of the mess. Senior officers took special pains to pay attention to the guests of junior officers. Senior officers made it a point to present their guests to junior officers.

(9) Officers never loitered in the wardroom in working hours and never appeared in the wardroom out of uniform.

The hour of dinner has been pronounced by Dr. Johnson to be, in civilized society, the most important hour of the twenty-four. In the wardroom described above, the etiquette of the dinner table had an emphasis commensurate with the importance of the event.

In connection with a mess, it is of great interest to read Colonel Stewart's description of Admiral Lord Nelson's routine on the *St. George*:

> His hour of rising was 4 or 5 o'clock, and of going to rest about 10; breakfast was never later than 6, and generally nearer to 5 o'clock. A midshipman or two were always of the party, and I have known him to send, during the middle watch, to invite the little fellows to breakfast with him, when relieved. At table with them, he would enter into their boyish jokes and be the most youthful of the party. At dinner he invariably had every officer of the ship in their turn, and was both a polite and hospitable host.

In commenting upon Nelson's courtesy to subordinates, and his desire to teach young officers the amenities of polite society, Admiral Mark Keer, RN, in *The Sailor's Nelson* writes:

> It is impossible to overestimate the value of this [in those days] unusual procedure in forming the discipline, good feeling, and mutual confidence of the generations who have followed him in the naval service; it has been and still is one of the principal priceless legacies that Nelson has bequeathed to the service, which looks up to him as a model for all time.

CALLS REQUIRED OF AN OFFICER AFTER HE REPORTS ON BOARD SHIP

The young officer should give thought at the outset of his naval career to the fact that there are visits and calls that are required by regulations, by customs, and by courtesy. A personal choice or selection in the matter of visits is not the prerogative of those in official life. Good usage decrees that certain calls be as scrupulously returned as they are expected to be made.

In delivering verbal communications from senior to junior, it is customary for officers of the Navy to use the form, "Rear Admiral Smith presents his compliments to Captain Brown and says, . . ." A junior never presents his compliments to a senior. Upon making a social or official call upon a senior, it is perfectly correct and customary to say, "Admiral Smith, I came to pay my respects," or to the orderly before entering the cabin, "Tell the captain (or admiral) that Lieutenant Jones would like to pay his respects."

Navy Regulations require that

an officer joining a ship or naval station shall, in addition to reporting for duty, make a visit of courtesy to his commanding officer or commandant within 48 hours after joining.

The courtesy call is made on the commanding officer in his cabin on board ship, and to the commandant or other senior officer at his office on shore. This courtesy visit is made even though the officer has reported to the commanding officer or commandant for duty in person, although such will seldom be the case. Officers report first to executive officers if afloat, and to chiefs of staff or other staff officers of the senior commands ashore, and at the same time inquire when it will be convenient to call upon the captain or the admiral. When reporting for duty in person, always carry the orders that effected your transfer of duty. This is not required for courtesy calls.

A courtesy visit made on board or to an office ashore should last not longer than ten minutes. Naturalness in demeanor and restraint in conversation are to be recommended for the junior. Although not necessary, it is courteous to leave a card. If for any reason it is not possible to see the captain when making the call, then a card should be left. Obviously, in military and naval service this type of call is not returned.

UNIFORM REGULATIONS

The Navy Uniform Regulations prescribe the correct manner of wearing the uniform, but the purpose of its wearing goes far deeper. It is primarily designed to identify the wearer as a member of the naval service; moreover, it identifies his rank and therefore the authority and responsibility assigned to him by law. The evolution of the present-day uniform has entailed many changes, thus it embodies many of the traditions of the service.

Obviously, the manner of wearing the uniform creates a lasting impression upon the observer and reflects the pride the member has in his profession. It is incumbent upon all members of the service to demand excellence in uniform appearance, for no one wishes to be associated with an organization typified by slovenly dress.

SOCIAL CLUB ETIQUETTE

Naval officers are often given cards to private membership social clubs for the short stays of the ship or the fleet in ports both at home and abroad. It is a privilege that the Navy has always enjoyed, and under no condition should it be abused. For the benefit of young officers who have never been honorary members of the larger or more exclusive clubs, a few "navigational aids" are not amiss.

The visitor has no special rights in the club, but is expected to conform to the club rules, the same as any member. In fact, dignified courtesy should be rendered to all members, remembering always that the uniform and rank of the officer permit him to enjoy the facilities of clubs, while often others wait many years to become members. Club members gauge the social and intellectual caliber of the Navy by the officers they meet in the club. Although there are all kinds of clubs, the better clubs are not "back-slapping, political-rally" organizations, and are therefore not fit places for large class reunions and the gayer parties that should be held elsewhere. There is an air of dignity about the best clubs, both at home and abroad, such as is found in the best homes. Men of affairs, men of letters, and "those who spin not" use a club for meeting other members, both in a business and social sense, as well as to take advantage of facilities such as the library, the reading and writing rooms, and the dining room. To many it is their home. Often men of wealth and affluence, after a family has been dispersed, prefer permanent residence at clubs and, of course, expect the same atmosphere to prevail that once obtained in their homes. In no sense is a club a hotel, and the better ones are not fraternal organizations. A prominent club man once remarked:

> In a very smart London club, you keep your hat on and glare about. In Paris you take your hat off and behave with such courtesy and politeness as seems to you an affectation. In New York you take your hat off and behave as though the rooms were empty, but as though you were being observed through loopholes in the walls.

Possibly these remarks are ultrasophisticated but they adequately express the "tone" of the smart and more exclusive clubs.

Officers who have been given cards as guests of a club for a stated period of time and wish to accept the courtesy should sign the club register. This formality has a practical reason. The servants know who you are, and members are able to know what officers have visited the club. Leaving cards or signing the register permits club members to look for old friends, as well as know the names of those for whom special courtesies may be extended. One should also observe whether or not there is a card board and, if so, leave a visiting card on the board. This is always customary in British clubs. Leaving a card signifies that you have appreciated the invitation and have paid your respects to the members. Senior officers leave their cards when convenient in person or send them by a member of the staff.

An officer should be prompt in meeting all financial obligations incurred at a club where he is tendered the privilege of signing checks. It is embarrassing for a senior officer to receive an official letter after sailing, to the effect that an officer under his command sailed without paying his club debts. There is a certain stigma attached to the non-payment of club debts. "Tailors sometimes have to wait for a short time, but club bills are paid promptly," so saith the old clubman.

It is customary for the senior officer of a division or squadron and commanding officers of ships acting singly to address a letter to the club before sailing, in which they express thanks for the kindnesses and courtesies that have been tendered the officers of their commands during the stay of the ship or ships in port. This letter is usually addressed to the secretary of the club; in some cases, the letters are addressed to the president of the club.

It would be difficult to improve on Emily Post's remarks on good manners in clubs:

> A perfect clubman is another word for the perfect gentleman. . . .
> Good manners in clubs are the same as good manners elsewhere—
> only a little more so. A club is for the pleasure and convenience
> of many; it is never intended as a stage setting for a "star" or
> "clown" or "monologist." There is no place where a person has
> greater need of constraint and consideration for the reserves of
> others than in a club. In every club there is a reading-room or
> library where conversation is not allowed; there are books and easy
> chairs and good light for reading both by day and night; and it is
> one of the unbreakable rules not to speak to anybody who is read-
> ing or writing.
>
> When two people are sitting by themselves and talking, an-
> other should on no account join them unless he is an intimate
> friend of both. To be a mere acquaintance, or, still less, to have
> been introduced to one of them, gives no privilege whatever.[6]

It is also well to remember that the more exclusive clubs have customs which one calls in the Navy "special rates"—R.H.I.P. That is, the oldest members have certain corners or small rooms in which they lounge, certain tables they habitually use in the dining rooms, certain desirable chairs that for years they have occupied near the windows

---

[6] Emily Post, *Etiquette*. (By permission Funk & Wagnalls Co.)

on the street. Observation on the part of the young officer will usually disclose this distinct deference that is paid to age and rank.

In conclusion, an excellent rule for a young man to obey in a meeting of gentlemen, whether in clubs or out, is George Washington's 66th "Rule of Civility," "Be not forward but friendly and courteous; the first to salute, hear, and answer, and be not pensive when it's a time to converse."

GENERAL COURTESY

It is an unwritten law that warrant officers and junior officers remove their caps when in wardroom country; also that all officers uncover when passing through the captain's or admiral's country. This is not done when in full dress or wearing sword.

Those versed in the niceties of old custom *always* remove their caps when passing through the crew's quarters at meal times.

When officers enter the sick bay on inspection trips and otherwise, it has been customary for them to remove their caps. This custom is probably derived from the old mark of respect paid the sick and suffering. Men were about ready for "slipping the cable" when they were admitted to sick bays in the days of sail.

Strictly speaking, officers are not supposed to uncover in the open except for divine worship, funerals, and other religious ceremonies. Since standing at attention and rendering the hand salute is the highest respect that one pays the colors or the commander in chief of the Navy afloat or ashore, it should suffice for the meeting with gentlemen or ladies in the open. The doffing of the headdress passed when it was decreed that the salute to flag and superiors would be the hand salute. This, of course, does not apply to receptions and social occasions on deck.

The very old courtesy of passing a senior going in the same direction with a "By your leave, sir," is not supposed to be forgotten when the midshipman leaves the Naval Academy.

In walking with a senior ashore, or acting as an aide, the position of honor is to the right. An aide should be to the left and one or two paces in the rear when approaching presentations or meetings between seniors, whether it be military, naval, or civil officers. If the aide is to make the introductions, he should step to the side, facing both officers who are presented. The custom of the "right hand rule" is very old. It is quaintly expressed in Washington's 30th "Rule of Civility":

In walking, the highest place in most countries seems to be on the right hand, therefore place yourself on the left of him whom you desire to honor; but if three walk together the middle place is the most honorable. The wall is usually given to the most worthy if two walk together.

The above rule applies to riding in carriages or automobiles with seniors. A proper "gangway" for seniors should be scrupulously observed. Again, one reads in Washington's 29th "Rule of Civility":

When you meet with one of greater quality than yourself, stop and retire, especially if it be at a door or any straight place to give way for him to pass.

TOASTS AFLOAT AND ASHORE[7]

The custom of welcoming guests at a repast by special libations in honor of the head of the state of the visitor, or the country from which the guest hails, or the organization to which he belongs, is very ancient. In old days it was also customary for the host to take a sip of the cup first to show that the beverage was not poisoned. A survival of the custom lingers in the usage that is observed when a sip of wine is poured in the glass of the host so that he may determine its quality before filling the glasses of the guests.

Although "official drinking" antedates the Caesars, it is of interest that the term *toast* is of Anglo-Saxon derivation. A piece of toast was at one time placed in the glass with certain wines and beverages in the belief that this would improve the flavor of the wine. The following quotations indicate the custom of the day:

It happened that on a publick day a celebrated beauty of those times [of Charles II] was in the Cross Bath [at Bath] when one of the crowd of her admirers took a glass of water in which the fair one stood, and drank her health to the company. There was in the place a gay fellow, half-fuddled, who offered to jump in, and swore, tho' he liked not the liquor, he would have the *toast*. Tho' he was opposed in his resolution, this whim gave foundation to the present honour which is done to the lady we mention in our liquors, who has ever since been called a *toast.—Tatler*, No. 24 (June 4, 1709).

[7] See Appendix C, "Ward Room Etiquette and Toasts in H.M. Canadian Navy."

Let the toast pass
Drink to the lass
I'll warrant she'll prove excuse for the glass.
                              —Sheridan, *School for Scandal.*

Go fetch me a quart of sack; put a toast in 't.
                              —Shakespeare, *Merry Wives of Windsor.*

It is universally acknowledged that at official dinners given in honor of visiting foreign officials, toasts are to be drunk first to the head of the state, or to the country, or to the organization of the guests. For example, at a dinner given by an Italian admiral to an American admiral, the Italian would propose a toast to the President of the United States, and shortly afterwards the senior honored guest, the American admiral, would propose a toast to the President of Italy. There are occasions where some confusion might arise in those messes where a toast is always drunk at dinner to the sovereign. For example, it was once observed in a British mess at a dinner that was not official, that the president of the mess toasted the King, then shortly afterwards proposed a toast to the United States Navy. The proper reply by the American officer should have been a toast to the British Navy. At an official dinner the Britisher would toast "the President of the United States" and the senior American reply "The Queen."

Because of General Order No. 99 and the Eighteenth Amendment, toasts nearly died in the service afloat. They may be revived in the future and they may not, but it is part of the social education of a naval officer to know how they are given in all foreign navies, and to know what to do if the occasion arises.

Ceremonies differ somewhat as to the time when the first and ceremonial toasts are drunk. At an official dinner given, for example, by a British admiral for an American admiral, the routine may be as follows: the British admiral at a point before completion of the dinner, usually at or after dessert, rises and toasts the President of the United States, the orchestra playing "The Star Spangled Banner," upon the completion of the toast. After the officers are seated and a minute or so afterwards, the American admiral should rise and toast "the Queen"; immediately thereupon the orchestra will play "God Save the Queen." After these toasts, short speeches are sometimes made, followed with a toast to the respective services. It is understood that there are British military messes wherein no one but the reigning monarch may be toasted. This was especially waived at one time for Admiral Farragut—an extraordinary courtesy.

Officers of the Royal Navy have the privilege of remaining seated when they toast the sovereign. Some authorities write that this honor was accorded the Royal Navy by William IV, while the popular service opinion is that it was Charles II who established the custom. The story goes that Charles II, when returning to England in 1660 in the *Royal Charles*, bumped his head because of the low overhead of the wardroom when replying to a toast that had been drunk to him. He made the statement forthwith that royal naval officers would never again rise to toast the British sovereign. The late Marquis of Milford Haven, then Admiral of the Fleet and at that time the Prince of Battenberg, established the custom of rising in the British Navy only when the toast to the King was followed by "God Save the King." Officers in the royal yacht rise to toast the sovereign. This is in all probability a custom that arose from the desire of the officers of the royal yacht to be distinctive in this respect. In 1964, in honor of the 300th birthday of the Royal Marines, Queen Elizabeth II ruled that the marines would make their toast to the Queen sitting down.

In the British service at the present time the youngest member of the mess is called upon to reply on Saturday night to the toast on behalf of "The Ladies."

Although the manner of toasting in military and naval messes is not in all respects uniform, some general principles may be outlined:

(1) Do not drink a toast that is proposed to you or your service. All drink to the President, King, Queen, or a dignitary.

(2) The highest officials as a rule propose toasts to the heads of the state. The host honors the guest first.

(3) At smaller dinners and semiformal ones, the toast may be drunk to the navy of the visiting country, the country of the visitors, and in some cases to the senior officer and officers of the squadron or ship. These toasts may also follow the toasts to the heads of the respective states.

(4) Replies to toasts should be of similar nature and of corresponding subjects.

(5) Toasts to sovereigns and heads of state should be short and not prefaced by irrelevant remarks.

(6) Some British officers are superstitious as to drinking toasts with water—even grape juice is preferable.

The French, with the politeness characteristic of their race, usually say "I have the honor, etc." At a dinner for a French admiral or senior French officer, the American officer would say, "I have the honor to propose a toast to the President of the French Republic." The French officer would reply, "It is my great honor to propose a toast to the President of the United States" or simply "To the President of the United States." At regular mess dinners in the British Navy, the senior member of the mess proposes the toast "The Queen," and all members in a low tone repeat "The Queen" and drink a sip of the toast.

The German Admiralty published a book called *Handbook for Relations with Foreign Navies* wherein various toasts are set forth for all occasions. Among these toasts were:

Messieurs,
    C'est un grand honneur et un vif plaisir pour nous autres Allemands d'avoir l'occasion aujourd'hui (ces jours-ci) de voir parmi nous des représentants de la Marine Française. C'est pourquoi je prends la liberté de prier mes compatriotes (camarades, collègues) de s'associer avec moi pour souhaiter à ces Messieurs bien cordialement la bienvenue en Allemagne (à bord), et je vous demande de vous joindre à moi pour porter un toast à la santé des Officiers Français ici présents.

Messieurs,
    J'ai l'honneur de proposer un toast pour (à la santé de) le Président de la République Française.

Messieurs,
    J'ai l'honneur de vous proposer de lever vos verres et de boire (de les vider) à la santé des Officiers de Marine ... (à la santé et à la prospérité de Marine ...).

It also contained such cordial expressions as,

    I request my fellow countrymen to raise their glasses and join me in the toast of ...
    I ask the officers of the ... to rise and to drink the health of ... wishing them success always and everywhere.
    And in now drinking the health of ... we testify our keen appreciation of what they have done for us and wish them happy days and good luck.

The old Royal Italian Naval Academy, in its textbook on *Most Prevalent Usage in Social and International Relations*, taught in regard to toasts:

    As a rule toasts should be few and short.
    At dinners aboard that are not strictly private, it is advisable to adopt the English usage of a single toast to the King (the simple

words, long live the King). If there are foreign guests, however, it will be well to drink a toast of the occasion, by saying a few cordial words of welcome and concluding with homage to the nation of the guest. It is best to speak in one's own tongue, if the others are not known well. It is to be remembered in such case that utmost brevity is indispensable.

Much care should be taken in the choice of the subject, all political allusions being avoided, unless specially authorized or directed. Good subjects may be drawn from naval history by recalling glorious feats of arms, possibly common to the two navies, and finding in them reasons for predicting glory and prosperity for the future.

To a toast of this nature reply is made by the ranking member of the visiting body, who follows a similar course. If the first toast is made in honor of the Navy and its representatives, reply is made in the name of the whole Navy, expressing the deepest appreciation for the complimentary words, etc., etc., and giving assurance of ineffaceable memory of the days past in such pleasant company, everlasting gratitude for the cordial hospitality received, etc. etc.

At official dinners attended by high authorities it is necessary that all toasts be previously agreed upon at least as to the spirit and subject to be treated.

This is particularly necessary at dinners attended by sovereigns or princes of royal blood, in which case, if there has been no means of previous understanding with someone in the suite, it is preferable to abstain from any manifestation whatever.

In some foreign countries (northern) it is customary not to make any toasts, but to drink successively to the health of each individual guest, expressing one's own wishes with a look or gesture. It is proper to reply by at least one sip and a nod of the head, and then to return the compliment a few minutes later.

In those countries, it may happen that while at table in a public place, a polite acquaintance may send a waiter to inform you that he wishes to drink to your health. In such case it is proper for everyone to remain seated, make a gesture of thanks and, turning to the gracious person, take at least one sip, and then return the courtesy.

In countries of non-European civilization, other customs prevail, all of which it would be impossible to recall. In every case and wherever it may be it will be well to show the greatest cordiality without, however, considering oneself obliged to drink or eat the food and drink to which one is not accustomed.

Short, dignified exchanges of toasts are far more agreeable than the interminable speeches that have become a part of so many banquets and official dinners. At any rate, it is safe to be prepared. A well-told joke or anecdote; short, sincere remarks addressed to the host or hosts, all in the spirit of the occasion—that is the real secret of effective after-dinner speaking.

A successful toastmaster once stated that he always learned all that he could about those who were to respond to toasts, with particular emphasis upon any exceptional services or duties that they had performed or outstanding honors they had received. He used this information in making short, pleasing introductions. Moreover, he never failed to make a brief comment on the toasts proposed, and tried to temper the spirit of his commentaries to the mood of the toasts. He always interspersed his introductions with short anecdotes and timely jokes. The great secret, he said, was to relate short "yarns," if possible, in which various guests present had participated, but under no circumstances to indulge in stories that were unpleasant or sarcastic, or make a diner uncomfortable or embarrassed.

Even if grape juice is used, the time-honored custom of toasting at a formal dinner in honor of foreign officers is in good taste. At informal dinners, a short word of welcome is also correct, and may or may not be followed by a toast to guests. Give thought to and plan as much as possible in advance.

OFFICER AND GENTLEMAN

Attention is drawn to the two words that are supposed to be synonymous—"officer and gentleman." The officer corps attains its highest distinction when the two nouns have, in a general sense, the same connotation. To the customs and usages of civilized countries, the gentlemen will conform, for, as Cardinal Newman said in his classic definition of a gentleman: "He even supports institutions as venerable, beautiful, or useful, to which he does not assent." And an officer could also ponder what a celebrated French author had to say: "A gentleman is one who has reflected deeply upon all the obligations which belong to his station, and who has applied himself ardently to fulfill them with grace."

Thoughtful adherence to those standards of military conduct that were of importance during the many years before the present active list entered the Navy would be a worthy goal. The service has certain fine old usages that are worthy of respect, and no matter how pressing duties might become, there is always time for their observance. It is not tradition and custom alone that compel these observances; instinct also lends its voice. Some say that times have changed. Yes, they have changed in many ways, but good manners, personal dignity, punctilious courtesy without sycophancy, attention to those niceties not in the regulation book, all based on loyalty and consideration for others, still remain the hallmark of the officer and the gentleman.

CHAPTER 5

Social Usage–Prescribed and Proscribed

As you from this day start the world as a man, I trust that your future conduct in life will prove you both an officer and a gentleman. Recollect that you must be a seaman to be an officer; and also that you cannot be a good officer without being a gentleman.
Advice from Admiral Lord Nelson
to a young man just appointed a midshipman

He became an officer and a gentleman, which is an enviable thing.
"Only a Subaltern." Rudyard Kipling

It is almost a definition of a gentleman to say he is one who never inflicts pain.
Idea of a University. The Man of the World.
Cardinal John Henry Newman

To be a gentleman is to be one the world over, and in every relation and grade of society.
The Amateur Immigrant (1896).

We all did our duty, which, in the patriot's, soldier's, and gentleman's language, is a very comprehensive word, of great honour, meaning, and import.
Travels of Baron Munchausen. Rudolf Erich Raspe

Montaigne, whose essays have been best sellers for ten generations, and whose work has gone into seventy-five European editions with translations in all civilized tongues, wrote:

I have often seene men proove unmanerely by too much maners, and importunate by over-much curtesie. The knowledge of entertainment is otherwise a profitable knowledge.[1]

By all means, it is the "profitable knowledge" that should be gained. Sincerity and common sense should always govern, and nothing that makes for ease and decorum in polite society should be neglected by those in the service. The thorough gentleman moves and talks with the ease that everywhere marks the well-bred people, the "cultes of the imperturbable,"[2] people who in reality are unconscious of "manners."

The heritage of the Navy, with no appreciable qualification, is certainly one of superior behavior and unquestioned honesty. Superior behavior comprises self-restraint, consideration for others, and a gracious conformance with the best social usage of the time. The high standards of honor and integrity in the Navy have become traditional —a fashioner of character throughout one's career.

High birth and aristocratic background are privileges of the few; but the habits and manners of a gentleman may be acquired by all. In the humblest of homes, children can be taught the basic social virtues— to pay proper respect to age and office; to treat ladies with chivalrous regard; to aid the unfortunate and helpless; and above all to meet life with a sense of decency and fair play. Such training leaves an indelible stamp: its breakdown in American life has caused much of our juvenile delinquency—the most lamentable defect and greatest blot on American civilization.

Far too little attention is paid today to that indispensable discipline called home training. It has shaped the careers of our greatest men and women: the illustrious as well as the solid citizenry that made America. It was the dying mother of Abraham Lincoln who touched with loving fingers the tear-stained face of her boy and whispered, "Be somebody, Abe." Likewise, "The basic precept of David's and Ida's [parents of President Eisenhower] religion was the fatherhood of God and the sonship of man; the dignity of man, the independence and equality of man. Their job, as they saw it, was to establish firmly in their sons that same conscience that guided their own lives. With that established, all problems could be resolved."[3]

[1] John Florio, *Translations of the Essayes of Michael Lord of Montaigne* (New York: AMS Press, 1967), p. 360.

[2] A term that has become classic since Austin Dobson in the *New Chesterfield* explained Chesterfield's scheme of conduct for his son in *Eighteenth Century Vignettes*.

[3] Bela Kornitzer, *The Great American Heritage, the Story of the Five Eisenhower Brothers* (New York: Farrar, Straus and Cudahy, Inc., 1955), p. 19.

Hopefully the fundamentals can be gained in childhood and early youth, but those not so fortunate can learn by careful observation of good manners in others, a searching self-criticism and vigilant attention to deportment and bearing to feel at ease in any company, no matter how formal, official, or dignified the assembly. An officer should strive for the possession of the intellect and manners that make him worth meeting, at home and abroad.

It is difficult to define "gentleman," one of the most abused terms in the English language, but we all have a conception of the ideal, well knowing that it is neither the "gent" of vulgar circles nor the conceited, arrogant cad found in some of the upper reaches of society. *Gentlemen* fits neither those who are afraid they will not be taken as gentlemen nor those who tell the world they are gentlemen.

A proper appreciation of social values and the exercise of superior manners require no justification: "It is a wise thing to be polite; consequently, it is a stupid thing to be rude." Neither are good manners incompatible with the role of seamen, notwithstanding the extreme "he-man" and "hairy-chested-sailor" school of thought. Suffren, Jervis, Howe, Nelson, Perry, Lawrence, Decatur, Porter, Farragut, Dewey, Sims, Yarnell, Halsey, Nimitz and King were gentlemen, even though some were bluff or gruff. They knew the value of tradition and dignified ceremony: and, above all, they were men of character.

Again, the naval service sometimes forgets that foreign officials' impressions of the culture of the United States are formed to a large extent by their contact with the officers of our foreign service and the armed forces. Do we not as a rule judge the people of a country by their official representatives? By *Navy Regulations*, it is the duty of the naval officer to respect the customs of foreign lands. To learn some of the history, outstanding customs, modes of living, and social amenities of foreign countries is an important phase of a liberal education. Naval officers do not roam the world as fact-finding politicians, freelance writers, professors and sociologists; rather it is their duty to keep in mind that they are usually official guests or allies, and as such to criticize publicly their hosts is to commit a grave breach of etiquette. We as Americans have no monopoly on customs or manners. Our basic code of manners and etiquette first saw light in the Old World. Would it not be more profitable if we spent more time in mending our own fences and correcting our own shortcomings, and had a little less criticism of the established customs of other people?

Religion plays a major role in the daily life of many foreigners. It is important that the naval officer have some basic knowledge of the

A naval officer and his wife must know and observe the customs and traditions of the people of foreign lands. This is a rice-pounding ceremony in Japan.

world's great religions in order that he not say or do something offensive to people of other countries who may be of other religions.

In their international application good manners require a reasonable conformance to the best usage of foreign states, as well as self-restraint and consideration for others. Of course, the American abroad sometimes finds an amount of antiquated ceremonial, as well as dreary forms of stilted etiquette, bordering closely on servility. Some of it may seem mummery, but it should be politely accepted. While in Rome do as the Romans do—that is, if one wishes to learn something, have a good time, and be invited back.

This brings us to an important rule in official social relations, and that is to ascertain in advance what will be expected—the ceremonies and customs that obtain on certain occasions. This policy if pursued has two practical advantages. First, all ceremonies, such as formal presentations, levees, and audiences, go more smoothly when all know the "drill." Second, although senior officers are at times required by virtue of rank to attend official ceremonials, some may by advance information forego the "pleasure," if not in sympathy with the ceremonial or the principals.

Upon inquiry, all details may generally be ascertained in advance of official functions. Where the occasion is that of luncheon or dinner, the senior officer will often be called upon to say a "few words," whether he knows or does not know the significance of the memorial, celebration, anniversary, or feast day. As usual, preparedness should be the rule. Know what is expected of you. Formal or informal inquiry through the United States consular or diplomatic channels will generally secure the desired advance information. This is part of the business of the foreign service.

TITLES

George Washington, in his 39th "Rule of Civility," wrote: "In writing or speaking, give to every person his due title according to his degree and custom of the place." This excellent rule is universal in its application. In the thousands of extant letters written by Washington, few mistakes are found in titles and points of address. Again, it is well to be forehanded enough to find out who will be at the ceremonial, celebration, or dinner. How are they addressed? What are their official titles? How are their names pronounced? What is the correct etiquette of the occasion? A young American naval officer in England once addressed the wife of an Earl as "Mrs." For a second her embarrassment was apparent, for it was probably the first time in her life that she had been so addressed, but as a great lady she paid no further attention to it. It should be remembered that she had the same legal right to her title that the naval officer had to his rank—it was fixed by law. Her title was not even a custom, upon which many United States titles (excepting the military and naval) depend. The individual should be given the benefit of the doubt, but where titles are established by law, be they civilian, military or naval, one should be precise in giving "every person his due."[4]

Attention to official amenities is a factor that is conducive to good morale. Particularly on foreign duty how many times one has heard, in substance, "Our admiral (or captain) knows what to do at the right time and the right place." It goes without saying that this engenders pride in ship and service, and it imbues junior officers with the desire

---

[4] Official lists, rosters, registers, *Who's Who* (American and British) and for high British titles, Debrett's *Peerage*, Burke's *Peerage*, and *British Landed Gentry* will generally give all that is needed.

to emulate the actions of the superior, and to learn from example, what to do and when to do it, when their time comes. In fact, the true spirit of the gentleman aids considerably in the competent exercise of the art of command.

Captain Basil Hall, RN, who wrote a most detailed and descriptive journal of his career on the sea, said in this connection over a hundred years ago:

> And certainly as far as my own observation and inquiries have gone, I have found reason to believe that those officers who are the best informed and the best bred, and who possess most of the true spirit of gentlemen, are not only the safest to trust in command of others, but are always the readiest to yield that prompt and cheerful obedience to their superiors, which is the mainspring of good order. Such men respect themselves so justly and value their own true dignity of character so much and are at all times so sensitively alive to the humiliation of incurring reproach, that they are extremely cautious how they expose themselves to merited censure. From the early and constant exercise of genuine politeness, they become habitually considerate of the feelings of others; and thus, by the combined action of these great principles of manners, officers of this stamp contrive to get through far more work, and generally do it much better, than persons of less refinement. Moreover, they consider nothing beneath their closest attention which falls within the limits of their duty; and, as a leading part of this principle, they are the most patient as well as vigilant superintendents of the labours of those placed under their authority, of any men I have ever seen.

The truth and value of these observations has not altered through the years.

RULES OF CIVILITY

So-called grand manners—the haughtiness of the *grand seigneur*, for example—do not in all cases indicate basic good manners. Rules of civility are vested with the authority of good usage. Experience has proved their worth. Our generation did not make them, nor did our fathers, but they will exist when our last cruise is over. There is a marked universality in some of them. The Chinese sage Confucius "saw the courtesies as coming from the heart," and wrote that "when they are practiced with all the heart, a moral elevation issues."

After the fall of Rome, "a revolution," writes Gibbon, "which will ever be remembered, and is still felt by the nations of the earth," manners and social codes of the various classes became vague and in some instances nonexistent. The Norman, William the Conqueror, introduced the beginnings of the medieval institution of chivalry with the conquest of England. This was a civilizing force that instituted certain rules for peace and war in contrast to the savage fight-to-the-death, and influenced those who bore arms to observe codes of courtesy and civilization. The organization of the Church by William in England also did much to ameliorate the general condition of savagery.

It was much later that we find the first collection of rules for the deportment and manners of gentlemen, although an unwritten code existed for gentlemen-at-arms. From this first book of etiquette came the *Rules of Civility* that George Washington conformed to throughout his career.

The original rules styled *Bienséance de la Conversation entre les Hommes* were composed and collated by the *pensionnaires* of the French Jesuit College of La Flèche in 1595. They were sent to their brothers at Pont à Mousson where Father Perin translated them into Latin, adding a chapter of his own on behavior at the table. Father Perin's edition appeared in 1617. Editions were published in Spanish, German, and Bohemian. A French edition appeared in 1640, and at the same time Francis Hawkins published an English edition in London. This little book in its various translations was used as a text book in many of the best institutions of learning responsible for the education of the young gentlemen of the day. A copy of the date 1698, stating that it was "Newly revised and much enlarged," is to be found in the British Museum. Obadiah Walker, Master of University College, Oxford, compiled a version called *Youth Behaviour*, a form of which seems to have been transcribed by George Washington in his youth.

Washington's *Rules of Civility and Decent Behaviour in Company and Conversation* was most probably derived from his brothers, Augustine and Lawrence, and not from the Reverend James Mayre, as explained by Maurice Conway. Research fails to establish the fact that Washington ever attended a regular school. These rules, though old-fashioned and quaint, carry in essence that fundamental precept of any social code—*polite deference* and *respect* to others.

It would be preposterous, however, to state that the memorization of a set of rules will create a gentleman. In the last analysis, gentility is a reflection of the inner man. The rules only give guidance to the spirit; for as James I said to his old nurse: "I'll mak' your son a baronet

gin ye like, Luckie, but the de'il himself couldna mak' him a gentleman."

SOME NAVAL SOCIAL CUSTOMS

Official Calls

In civilian life formal visits are seldom made, though in some areas of
our country informal calls (visits) are made by neighbors on new
arrivals. In the services, families moving into government housing areas
will usually be called upon informally by nearby service families and
should return these visits within two weeks. Calling cards are seldom
used, but if used, cards should be left on the return visit. Prior to
World War II the calling system in the armed services was quite formal. After World War II, for many reasons calling became very informal and much less uniform. Lack of domestic help, the difficulty of
obtaining sitters for children, the uncertainty of ship schedules, and
the lack of free time all contributed to the change. Each ship, shore
station, and area has a different custom, and it is wise to inquire after
arrival of the flag lieutenant, executive officer's assistant, or other
source as to the local custom and the desires of senior officers. In many
areas, "at homes" or ship or station parties are used as substitutes for
calls made and returned.

Some commanding officers still expect more formal calling to be
carried out, however, and it is better to know what to do in such a
case. For this reason an explanation follows. Past usage decreed in the
Navy that juniors and seniors should meet in each other's homes, with
emphasis that the first call should be made by the junior in the customary first official calls ashore, or "duty calls" as they are termed.
This includes calls on the commanding officer and his wife, the executive officer and his wife, and as soon thereafter as practicable the heads
of department (your own, first), and then the next senior in your
department. This is the old, established ship custom. However, shore
stations that usually have a large number of officers conform in general
to the following usage unless there are instructions to the contrary:

> Upon joining a unit, the naval officer makes an *official call* upon
> his commanding officer as soon as possible, subject to the senior's
> convenience. In many commands the new officer and his wife also
> pay an *official social call* upon the commanding officer and his
> wife in their home, also as soon as possible, subject to the con-
> venience of the senior couple.

The whole purpose of this call is for the senior couple to become acquainted with you in a relaxed and informal atmosphere, and to welcome you in a social way to the unit. It should be the beginning of a continuing agreeable relationship.[5]

All first calls should be returned within two weeks because they are formal calls; cards are always left whether the host is home or not; fifteen to thirty minutes (and never more) comprise the duration of a formal call—after this such meetings are termed visits. These informal neighborly visits may be arranged by telephone and are informal. Visits are paid to neighbors and friends. One does not telephone a senior and say, "We are coming over to visit if convenient," when proposing to make a first call. It is made without telephoning or prior arrangements unless the commanding officer or other senior officer has requested otherwise.

Always inquire when first on ship or station if the commanding officer or senior officer present entertains with an at-home or reception at which "all calls are made and returned." Such affairs are formal and cards are left, as in making a call. Only the senior officer has the *prerogative* of holding receptions with the general understanding that for those who attended, "all calls are made and returned."

First calls serve the purpose of ensuring that the officers of ships or stations and their wives meet and become acquainted in a dignified, orderly manner. This permits juniors and seniors to meet at other times than in the official discharge of duties.

For young officers and their ladies there is an educational aspect. There will always be a certain amount of formality incident to the career of an officer: only by means of calls and social visits to seniors will the young officer and his wife develop a smoothness and *savoir-faire* in these matters of his own service that will serve him in good stead when he has his first official social relations and calls in foreign lands, where he will usually find a more formal atmosphere than at home. The young officer and his wife are also given the opportunity to act as host and hostess in receiving formal visits in their own home when the calls of all ranks of the Navy are returned. Dignified cordiality, graciousness, and pleasant conversation mark those who excel as hosts and hostesses.

---

[5] Jean Ebbert, *Welcome Aboard, An Informal Guide for the Naval Officer's Wife*, (Annapolis: Naval Institute Press, 1974), p. 229. A valuable contribution that covers a broad field with much that is necessary, useful, and important for the wives of younger naval officers.

Occasionally, a relatively senior officer and wife have not had the opportunity to make the first call or the return call, whichever it may be, but are having a dinner party or social affair to which they should like the couple to attend, although they have not called upon them. A note or telephone call is all that is required to explain the delay in calling, at which time the couple is invited to the affair or afterwards sent an invitation. One of the principles of first calls and their return is that it establishes social relations between the callers—as an old timer once said: "It breaks the ice."

Unless a bachelor is very senior and has quarters of his own, it is not established usage that married couples return his call. However, if done, only the husband leaves a card. This conforms with the inviolable rule of polite society that ladies do not call on gentlemen. It has become a custom that if the two officers are about the same age and rank, instead of returning the call of a bachelor, the husband invites him home for a drink, or dinner, or some other social courtesy at which the lady of the house is present. It is perfectly correct for a husband to leave a card at an Officer's Club or Bachelor Officer's Quarters as recognition of a first call made upon him and his wife. This is done abroad. However, if it is someone that the couple should desire to know better, or a bachelor of another country, then it is proper to invite him informally to the couple's quarters or abode as one does at home. That should suffice for the return call. Again it is reiterated that one should always inquire as to the local customs of those of the particular service. Europeans in particular conform to a much more rigid etiquette than Americans, and for this reason it is important that naval officers make every effort to learn and do what is expected when abroad.

In the Navy one is prompt in paying calls on newlyweds. This is particularly so when the couple is married while the officer is attached to the ship or station. If an officer reports for duty with a bride, the obligation still remains of making a first call on the commanding officer and wife. However, the right is waived by the commanding officer to receive the first call; instead, he and his lady endeavor to call promptly on the young couple and welcome the bride to the Navy. "There is," writes Florence Johnson, "an obligation on both sides in this instance; it is just a question of who gets there first." A junior can never go wrong by erring on the safe side in borderline cases.

On leaving a ship or station it is obligatory that one call and leave cards on the commanding officer and the executive officer and their wives at their quarters about twenty-four hours before departure. If the officers are not at home, you may leave cards with "p.p.c." written in the lower left hand corner with either pen or pencil which indicates the callers came "pour prendre congé" or to take leave. In fact, this generally recognized custom of polite society throughout Europe and South America sanctions the mailing of p.p.c. cards to acquaintances and friends if one is leaving and unable to call to say good-bye. This, under no circumstances, relieves one of the courtesy of saying good-bye to one's best friends, colleagues, and immediate seniors, or thanking in person or by note all who have been most kind. Old but true— *it's the little things that count.*

CARD ETIQUETTE

It is curious how important small matters may, on occasions, become, as for instance who should leave his visiting card on whom. On the continent of Europe, and in the diplomatic corps the world over, in general terms the lastcomer makes the first call. This is also agreed to in all navies, and followed in all armies. While Great Britain and the United States officially subscribe to this, in everyday life and among wives the opposite custom obtains, and everyone is expected to call upon the newcomer. In the Navy, officially, among officers, a commanding officer of a ship, division, or squadron makes the first call on his superior in command of a ship, division, squadron, or naval station. Among those not in command and among the wives, where no real rule is respected, it should be remembered that an unmade call may lead to uncertainties, misunderstandings, and hurt feelings. In all cases, the first call should be made and returned in person, and the expectation is that it will be. In the diplomatic corps it is, in fact, often bluffed through, and careless diplomats have been known to rely on the office boy or the stationer from whom visiting cards are ordered, to make the first round of card-leaving visits. In all navies, calls of officers are made in person and returned in person within twenty-four hours.

> Aside from any mere formality or formalism, the exchange of
> visits and of visiting cards implies a "recognition" which forms the
> entire basis of social or official relations, and any one who belittles
> it is a nonentity.[6]

It is expected that all officers of the Navy have properly engraved calling cards. The good engravers cost little more and know the best

---

[6] Captain A. P. Niblack, "Letters of a Retired Rear Admiral to his Son," U. S. Naval Institute *Proceedings*, March-April, 1915.

usage in size, engraving, and taste. The wife of an officer is also expected to have cards; good taste decrees that the engraving be the same as that of the officer's. Married couples frequently use the double or joint card, for example:

Commander and Mrs. John Racine Smith

The officer's branch of the service should not be indicated on the joint card but *always* on his single card.[7]

Carry sufficient cards at all times so that when needed they are readily accessible. One is expected to leave cards at some formal receptions and of course at all formal calls, therefore the old rule: "Always carry your cards. Have them convenient. Look out for the card tray." In calls on foreign officers ashore at their offices, an aide, attendant, or orderly will often take the card to the officer called upon before one is shown in. If this is not done, leave the card unobtrusively on a convenient table or stand.

It is discourteous to call when one knows the people are not at home unless time or some other important consideration compels it. However, the call is made if one calls and leaves cards.

In England and some British possessions, one usually "signs the book" when making official calls at the homes of the very senior civil, military, and naval officials. Someone directs the visitor to the register at the doorway of the house; one signs and departs. Visiting officers who have signed are usually invited at a later date to tea or an At-Home.

If there is any doubt as to who should make the first call, do not stand on the doubt *but make the call.* In large cities such as Washington, however, it is impossible for seniors to return many calls. Check with the officer you relieve as to local procedure.

FORMAL INVITATIONS AT HOME AND ABROAD

Formal invitations must always be replied to "by hand" in the formal third person style and in the prescribed form. The writing must be spaced with the proper indentations conforming to the formal invitation.

Dinner invitations must be declined or accepted as soon as possible after receipt and always within twenty-four hours. Informal dinner

---

[7] Specific rules for the design and usage of calling cards are included in the book *Service Etiquette*, and this work is recommended to those who require further information on the subject. Oretha D. Swartz, *Service Etiquette*, 3rd ed rev. (Annapolis: Naval Institute Press, 1977), pp. 79–96.

invitations should receive the same prompt attention as formal invitations.

The hour and date of the dinner must be placed in the note of acceptance, although it is not required in notes of regret. This holds for all replies to invitations of a formal nature.

"R.s.v.p." (*répondez s'il vous plaît*) invitations of all descriptions must be replied to. The custom is growing in the United States of indicating "Please reply to ————," or "Telephone reply to ————," instead of "r.s.v.p."

English has become the business and scientific language of the world, but because French was for generations the diplomatic language, the tongue of *politesse*, it is well to reply to a French invitation in French. In all other cases, irrespective of the language, reply to the invitation in English.

When a number of officers of a ship make replies to the same shore social affair abroad, it is good practice to send all individual replies together by officer messenger to our embassy, legation or consulate, where, if requested, they will be despatched by messenger to the proper address. The Navy has always found the officers of our foreign service valuable advisors in all matters of local customs and things social.

When invitations are issued for ships' receptions, dances on board, and formal dinner parties, it is good form and a great convenience to place the name of the pier from which the boats leave in the lower corner of the invitation. For large affairs of any description cards should be issued to those invited that will give admittance to boats at the pier or landing designated thereon. This is most useful to civilians who know little about the piers and waterfronts of their own cities.

In our own and foreign services, replies to formal invitations are made to flag lieutenants and in the armies to aides-de-camp. Replies to invitations of royalty are made to the Lord Chamberlain, or to equerries. To whom the reply is to be sent is usually found in the lower left corner of the invitation. Our flag lieutenants should ensure that on all formal invitations sent to civilians an exact and clear address should be given on the invitation, one that will provide the quickest and surest way of receiving replies.

FORMAL DINNERS

Flag Lieutenants' and Staff Officers' Duties

The flag lieutenant or staff officer charged with the details, after checking the guest list given him by the admiral, should make a neat seating diagram and submit it to the admiral or his senior officer for approval. Precedence must be correct; therefore, if there is any doubt when abroad, consult with the senior United States official ashore or a member of his staff.

Use place cards. Check the menu with the steward with a view to having good food, served promptly and properly. The menu should do justice to the rank of the guests. Arrange for buying flowers, and check their arrangement before the dinner.

Give the officer of the deck a written memorandum as to the time when it is desired to send barge and/or gig for guests. It is good practice to ascertain personally that the boat officer has a list of the guests expected. Boat officers must be provided on all formal occasions. For informal occasions when a boat officer is not sent, give the coxswain a list of the guests with instruction to wait a certain time in the event a guest is late.

Inform the admiral or senior officer when his guests are approaching the ship. An officer should go to the lower ladder to aid the ladies of the party as well as the elderly gentlemen. Escort the ladies to the area reserved as a cloakroom for them.

Ensure that as many introductions as possible are made before dinner. See that the steward announces dinner promptly. Show the guests the seating diagram. If it is a large dinner, small cards given the gentlemen indicating names of dinner partners will aid in prompt seating. Observe carefully all table service. If there is any irregularity speak to the steward, but in a low tone.

The flag lieutenant assists the admiral at all times to see that guests are comfortable and their wishes gratified. The musical program for dinner is usually left to the flag lieutenant. He should check the bandmaster's program in advance, and if toasts are required and the national airs of foreign states are to be rendered, make a written memorandum as to details for the information of the bandmaster and for the senior officer. Finally, check and ascertain that the bandmaster thoroughly understands the signals of execution for national airs after the respective toasts.

If the captain is invited, or if not aboard, then his cabin—usually near or by that of the admiral's—is an ideal location for guests to meet and chat before the luncheon or dinner is announced; also it is a convenient place for the ladies to retire after dinner until joined by the gentlemen. See that the admiral's (or senior officer's) guest book is signed. Shore-going people often appreciate souvenirs of ships.

If the showing of motion pictures is decided upon as entertainment, be sure to get the latest and best picture that is suitable for the guests.

The flag lieutenant, an officer of the staff, or a boat officer should accompany the guests on the boat trip ashore. He should remain until all guests have departed from the pier or landing.

At both formal and informal lunches and dinners with civilians and foreign officers, conversation should be kept on a high plane. This does not bar the amusing or pointed anecdote nor the inevitable discussion of the differences in language and the humorous mistakes that each country makes when employing the idiom of the other. One should refrain from a discussion of women, death, religion, local politics, and embarrassing points of difference in our respective foreign policies, and particularly naval shop talk, unless guests ask questions. Endeavor to make all guests comfortable and at ease with special attention to dividing the time in conversation with the guests on either side.

Two good thoughts merit the attention of those who have the opportunity to dine with notables and senior officials of our own country and those abroad. One is the old saying: "I ain't never learned nothing when I was talking." The other from the *Autobiography of Benjamin Franklin*: "I made it a rule to forebear all direct contradiction to the sentiments of others, and all positive assertion of my own . . . I even forbid myself . . . the use of every word or expression in the language that imported a fix'd opinion, such as *certainly, undoubtedly*, etc., and I adopted instead of them, *I conceive, I apprehend*, or *I imagine* a thing to be so and so; or *it appears to me at present*. . . . I soon found the advantage of this change in my manner; the conversations I engag'd in went more pleasantly."

PRESENTATIONS AND AUDIENCES

Wear the prescribed uniform and arrive at the designated time, or better, a few minutes ahead of time.

On replying to a monarch, one says, "Yes" or "No, Your Majesty"; nevertheless, also remember that the old word "Sir" is always correct in replying to royalty, nobility, or those of high officialdom. To a Queen "Ma'am" is perfectly correct; "Sire" is also used in formal address to kings.

At any presentation learn the ceremonial in advance, if possible. Maintain a military bearing but endeavor to feel at ease.

In either formal or informal conversation, it is considered bad form to question royalty. It is never correct to turn directly away after formal presentation to commoner or king, but rather to back away a step or so and if necessary, to the side.

Some of the ancient ceremonies observed by European courts, the church and foreign naval and military organizations are most interesting, and should afford lasting memories for years.

At some official receptions on the Continent, guests of honor are announced individually and are expected to step forward and bow to the assembly. Consequently, it is well to be prepared to be announced and presented *tout seul*. This requires all the poise and dignity that the average person is able to muster, but as an experienced foreign-service official said, "The best rule is to take it easy with a trace of smile."

One kneels, as customary of nineteen centuries, during a papal audience; and should touch lips to the papal ring when personally blessed by His Holiness.

LETTERS OF APPRECIATION AND THANKS

All naval officers, and particularly commanding officers, before or just after leaving port, must never neglect the amenity of writing notes of thanks, of appreciation, and of farewell to those clubs, societies, officials, and individuals who rendered courtesies and favors to him and his command. In fact, it is all the thanks that some receive for their many courtesies and their kindness to officers of the fleet.

Some of the expressions of thanks in this day of fast communications may take the form of dispatches or telegrams.

In these days of air travel, naval officers often visit military installations in the course of their official duties and are frequently entertained by local officers, particularly those residing in public quarters. Social usage requires that a note of appreciation be addressed promptly to the host and hostess when one has been an overnight guest. It is also a mark of good manners to send a note of thanks when one has been a guest at a meal or other social event.

THE FIGHTING MAN IN GENTLE COMPANY

Brusqueness, the "hard-boiled" exterior, the accentuated "he-man" pose indicating indifference and disdain for the refined and cultured is the antithesis of poise and good manners. Rude and unpleasant strains in social intercourse are conspicuously absent in a Nelson, a Wellington, a Washington, a Farragut, and a Lee. Thackeray's social climber who "licks the boots of those above him and kicks the faces of those below him on the social ladder," is a shining example of what a gentleman *is not*.

Chivalric demeanor is the hallmark of the officer corps. This means a consideration of the feelings of others rather than the aggressiveness and chip-on-the-shoulder attitude of certain classes and individuals. Strength of character may be displayed without bombast; dignity, without frigidity; friendliness, without garrulousness; while an appreciation of art, music, and *belles-lettres* does not lessen the essentially professional character of the officer.

It is important that the officer corps acquire the tastes of refined society and enlightened men, and that serious thought be given to civilian points of view. Discussions pertaining to "shop" and war should not monopolize conversation with those not of the profession of arms. Your gauge as a warrior and qualifications as an officer are not exemplified by whetting swords in society, nor by displaying indifference to the manners and tastes that mark the finer types of the social order. Castiglione wrote in 1528 in his *Book of the Courtier*:

> Because to such men as this, one might justly say that which a
> brave lady jestingly said in gentle company to one whom I will
> not name at present (supposed to have been a brave soldier of for-
> tune, one Captain Fracassa) who, being invited by her out of com-
> pliment to dance, refused not only that but to listen to the music,
> and many other entertainments proposed to him, saying always
> that such silly trifles were not his business; so at last the lady said,
> "What is your business then?" He replied with a sour look, "to
> fight." Then the lady at once said, "Now, that you are in no war
> and out of fighting time, I should think it were a good thing to
> have yourself well oiled, and to stow yourself with all your battle
> harness in a closet until you be needed, lest you grow more rusty
> than you are." And so, amid much laughter from the bystanders,
> she left the discomfited fellow to his silly presumption.

The code of a gentleman may not be encompassed within a few written rules, or even in a volume. To some extent, it is a progressive education throughout life. There are many commendable, terse private codes of conduct. And from many examined, one has been selected: the code of a once active naval officer, a gentleman who loved the sea and who became the beloved sovereign of a vast empire—a friend of the United States, George V.

The code, which was said to have been framed and hung in his bed chamber, is:

> Teach me to be obedient to the rules of the game.
> Teach me to distinguish between sentiment and sentimentality,
> admiring the one and despising the other.
> Teach me neither to proffer nor to receive cheap praise.
> If I am called upon to suffer, let me be like a wellbred beast
> that goes away to suffer in silence.

Teach me to win if I may; if I may not, teach me to be a good loser.

Teach me neither to cry for the moon nor to cry over spilt milk.

One might end these notes with the "Code of a King"; but for purposes of contrast, a final point is presented—an observation that not only marks the catholicity of good manners, but also exemplifies the impressions created by the possessor of good manners.

Mr. R. D. Blumenfeld, a onetime American newspaper reporter, who became the doyen of Fleet Street editors and an outstanding personage in the British newspaper world, once recalling the high spots of his successful career, spoke of the celebrities he knew intimately— of the rulers and political leaders who had trusted him with many confidences. When asked who was the greatest, he dismissed them all and named Jimmy Aylett, a plain, smiling, cheerful, silent, poor man of Essex, "a natural poet, a philosopher, a true gentleman." Blumenfeld said:

> Jimmy Aylett was my week-end cottage gardener thirty years ago. He was eighty. He was born next door, as his father and grand- father and great-grandfather before him. He knew the earth which gave to his spade and his hoe, and what it could stand and could produce. He knew all about clouds and rain and sun.
>
> Jimmy Aylett lived his simple, honest, beautiful life without violence, without temper, without malice. He went to church o' Sundays with a little bunch of flowers in his cleanly brushed Sunday coat. He had the courtesy and the gallantry of the courtier. He knew naught of London or the world. His philosophy lay in Mother Earth and what she would provide. He was kind to dogs and hated traps for rabbits. Always in his pocket there was an apple or a pear or a few dusty sweets for children.

Blumenfeld considered Jimmy Aylett the greatest man he ever knew,

> for he taught me above all things that the important things in life are not to be achieved in the making of money or in the chasing of social rainbows.

The noble character of a Jimmy Aylett should not be dismissed as irrelevant in any study of social relations. After all, associations with human beings "are the stuff that outward existence is made of"—and manners constitute one fine, one beautiful art that may be cultivated by all.

PART III

Symbols of
Great Tradition

CHAPTER 6

The Flag of the United States

A thoughtful mind when it sees a nation's flag, sees not the flag only, but the nation itself; and whatever may be its symbols, its insignia, he reads chiefly in the flag, the government, the principles, the truths, the history which belong to the nation that sets it forth.

Henry Ward Beecher
The American Flag

In the American flag are happily blended the symbols of the old and the new, of history and prophecy, of conservatism and progress, of the stability of the unchanging past with the promise and potency of the future.

William Elliot Griffis
Matthew Calbraith Perry: A Typical American Naval Officer

Life on a man-of-war is well calculated to inspire love for our national flag . . . the ceremony with which the colors are hoisted in the morning and lowered at night when the sunset gun is fired . . . the salutes in its honor at home and abroad, the never ceasing watch for its appearance at sea or in foreign ports, the constant reference to it in nautical conversation, the carrying of it in all small boats, are only a few of the ways in which it deepens its hold upon heart and memory.

Elizabeth Douglas Van Denburg
My Voyage in the U.S. Frigate Congress

> *The things that the flag stands for were created by the ex-*
> *periences of a great people. Everything that it stands for was*
> *written by their lives. The flag is the embodiment, not of senti-*
> *ment, but of history. It represents the experiences made by men*
> *and women, the experiences of those who do and live under*
> *that flag.*
>
> Woodrow Wilson

FROM TIME IMMEMORIAL, flags, standards, and banners have been employed by kings, noblemen, knights, military and civil organizations,
and religious bodies and faiths to denote by visual symbol the distinctive character of those who claimed the colors or insignia. By similar
devices the presence of the supreme commander was made known, the
camps of military units and tribes were differentiated, and enemies
distinguished. Banners as distinctive tribal devices were used by the
Tribes of Israel. David in the Psalms wrote, "We will rejoice in thy
salvation, and in the name of our God we will set up our banners."
The wise Solomon used the simile: "Terrible as an army with banners."
The units of the army of ancient Egypt had distinctive standards; the
chariot of Darius, the Persian, carried its regal badge; and after it the
eagle standards of the Caesars were recognized by barbaric tribes at
the outposts of the known world.

Flags and symbols have played a conspicuous part in the history of
religion. The fanatical fervor of the Crusades, in its intensity unsurpassed in history, was inspired by the cross as well as the crescent. It
is recorded that in the sixth century Saint Augustine and his followers
carried to Canterbury banners of the Cross of Christianity. Richard
the Lion-Hearted bore the "Cross of Saint George" to the Crusades.
In fact, the history of the Crusades, and the bitter feelings and cruel
wars of Moor and Christian in Western Europe, were symbolized by
constant allusion to the conflict of the banners of the "Cross and of
the Crescent."

In the Middle Ages when chivalry was at its height, the nobleman,
knight, and squire each had his distinctive device. Many of these banners were carried to the Crusades and were accorded a devotion by
their followers that was close to worship. The banners brought home
were sacredly preserved, and counterparts of the insignia were in time
placed on the seals, symbols, and flags of the respective countries. It
was in this romantic and religious age that heraldry came into being,
and it is from this point that the expert is able to trace the evolution
and changes, as well as the fixed symbols, that comprise the history of

of flags and standards. Even in the formulation of the Flag Code of the United States, certain ancient but established principles of heraldry govern.

The effect of the Crusades upon European art, architecture, and letters is incalculable. The cross previously surmounted many crowns, but after the "Holy Wars," the motif of the cross was predominant; it became the symbol of countries, kings, and leaders. The triple-cross flag of Great Britain, and the flags of Norway, Sweden, Denmark, Iceland, and Finland carry to this day the cross, indicative of the devotion that the early Christian symbolism inspired. Robert Phillips, in his work on the American flag, wrote:

> Out of the chaos and romance of this golden epoch there emerged
> a universal addiction to the display of personal and family coats
> of arms, and of the colors of knightly and religious orders. The
> records of the time teem with allusions to standards, banners,
> banderols, guidons, gonfalons, pennons, pennoncels.

In this connection and for those interested in the earliest arms and banners arising from the spirit of the Crusades, one is referred to a quaint, unique, and interesting book, *Knowledge of All the Kingdoms, Lands, and Lordships That Are in the World*, written by a Spanish Franciscan in the middle of the fourteenth century, and setting forth a detailed and faithful description of the arms and devices of each land as well as those of the ruling kings and lords.

Only in the last few hundred years have the flags in a number of countries really symbolized the land and the people. Early in the twentieth century, arms and devices on most European flags carried imperial and royal arms. Their removal usually resulted from revolutionary changes in the respective governments.

For example, before the establishment of various democratic national flags, we have record of the *fleur-de-lis* of the Bourbons, the black eagle of the Hohenzollerns, the double-headed eagles of the Hapsburgs and Romanoffs. It is of interest that long ago both the Hohenzollerns and the Hapsburgs discarded their family arms and adopted the arms of their territories. In a vague, traditional way, the double-headed eagles of both imperial Austria and Russia symbolized their claim to the rule of both the former Eastern and Western Roman Empires. Napoleon revived a proud Roman tradition by adopting the eagles of the Caesars. Hitler brought back the ancient symbol of the swastika that for a hectic time stood for about everything free men abhor; Mussolini, in trying to echo the grandeur of imperial Rome, revived some of the ancient ceremonies and the Roman salute. As did Napoleon, *Il Duce* again used the eagle as a symbol for his Italian legions.

It is asserted that the flag, called the *Dannebrog*, of Denmark, is the oldest national flag of a present-day state. Tradition tells us that the flag was adopted in 1219 after the Danish King Waldemar beheld, at a critical point in battle, a shining cross in the sky. The red swallow-tailed flag with the white cross was then adopted and has remained the flag of the country until the present. The second oldest flag is that of Switzerland, a white Greek cross on a red field, adopted in the seventeenth century. It is interesting to note that the flag of the Red Cross is that of Switzerland with the colors reversed. The X-like cross that has been placed on many flags, both public and private, is the Cross of Saint Andrew, the patron saint of imperial Russia and symbolical of the Scots of the United Kingdom.

The first Russian ensign before adoption of the Saint Andrew's Cross was hoisted on the *Santa Profitie* on July 21, 1694, and by a strange quirk it was the Dutch flag upside down.[1]

The flag of Saint Andrew, the ensign of the Russian Imperial Navy until the Bolshevik Revolution in 1917, was hoisted near Bornholm for the first time on August 5, 1716, in the presence of ships from England, Holland, and Denmark which appropriately saluted the new flag of a great power. Peter the Great in 1698 established the Order of Saint Andrew, and the distinctive cross was shown on medals, insignia, and some flags before its use by the Navy. Research discloses, however, that England and Scotland had a prior claim to Saint Andrew; it was part of the original national flag of England in 1606 before the Union with Scotland in 1706–07.

Considering their ages as a political entity, the national flags of some European countries in their present form are not old. The royal standard of Spain was adopted in 1785. The first well-known sea flag was that flown by the ships of Prince Henry the Navigator in the

---

[1] A. W. Meyerson, one time lieutenant commander in the Imperial Russian Navy, writes: "When the Dutchman by name Botman completed the first Russian naval warship as such in July, 1694, he asked the Tsar Alexey Michailovich what flag he should hoist at launching. The Tsar then asked what Hollanders did. Apparently until full commission the custom was to hoist the flag of Holland upside down. This was done, and when it was explained to the Tsar that it was in practice a distress signal, he ordered the double-eagle of the Romanoffs to be placed on the middle white stripe. Description of such a flag can be found in English literature." "This," said Meyerson, "is undoubtedly the starting point of naval tradition in the Russian Navy."

fifteenth century. The tricolor of France was born of the French Revolution and is a combination of the white of the Bourbons with blue and red, the colors of the city of Paris. The Union Flag (or Banner) of Great Britain and now Northern Ireland was adopted in 1801 on union with Ireland.[2] The British or Union Flag perpetuates the union of England, Scotland, and now Northern Ireland, and is an ingenious overlay of the crosses of Saint George and Saint Patrick on the Cross of Saint Andrew. This should not be confused with the Union Jack. " 'Jack' is the name given to the colours worn on a staff at the stem or on the bowsprit by ships or vessels at anchor or alongside. It is a smaller flag than the corresponding ensign and can be square or rectangular in shape."[3]

The traditional origin of oriental flags, banners, and devices is an absorbing story. As far back as A.D. 1169, the Emperor of Japan used the red disc of the sun as the royal emblem. In 1859, after contact with the Occident, Japan adopted the red sun with diverging rays on a white field. In 1826, Imperial China officially promulgated the design of its flag: triangular and of deep yellow color, with an "imperial dragon thereon." When the republican form of government supplanted the empire, the ancient dragon flag gave way to a national ensign consisting of five equal horizontal stripes of colors that represent the races of China in order of their importance. At the top, red for the Chinese race; then yellow for the Manchurian; blue for the Mohammedan; and at the bottom, black for the Tibetan. Then came the "Sun Yat-sen flag" of Nationalist China, that remains the flag of the Chinese Nationalists on Taiwan. On the mainland, Communist China has a flag with five gold stars on a red field. China is an interesting example of how political history is symbolized by the changes in flag design.

Because of the numerous changes in the flags of many countries, the flag of the United States of America is considered among the oldest of the national standards of the world. This remark should be qualified with mention that the forty-ninth and fiftieth stars were added to the original design in 1959 and 1960 when Alaska and Hawaii were admitted to the Union.

---

[2] Lieutenant Philip Chaplin (SB) RCN (R) writes: "The flag you refer to is properly called the Union Banner of Great Britain and Northern Ireland, but the word banner has acquired a special meaning outside heraldic usage, and so it is usually called the Union Flag (technically) or Union Jack (colloquially). And it is understood in the British Navy, that any flag of the same design should be called a Union Flag. This distinction is observed in British Navies, and by heraldic authorities, but it is not generally observed in colloquial usage."

[3] *Manual of Seamanship*, Vol. I, Lords Commissioners of the Admiralty, 1964.

The American flag with its fifty stars is the symbol of the nation's progress and growth, a reminder of the ideals and aspirations of the heroic founders of the Republic, and an emblem of the bond that unites every American to every other regardless of racial blood or religious creed. And significantly, from the days of our first commander in chief, George Washington, until the present day, it stands for the sacrifices in war that men and women have made for its sake—the essence of military, naval, and air tradition.

Although there is a variance of opinion as to where the flag was first flown in battle, and some question as to minor details in the first design and place of fashioning remains, the following chronological account gives its general history.

First we must go back to colonial days. For a century before the Revolutionary War, the American colonists flew the Red Ensign of Great Britain with distinctive devices for the various colonies, much as the Blue and Red Ensigns of Great Britain are used today by the British Commonwealth.[4]

This banner or flag of St. George flown in the Colonies had been used for centuries in England; it was later combined with the crosses of St. Andrew and St. Patrick, but it had always been a national and not a royal flag.[5]

We know that the primitive British flag, that of St. George, a white field with a red upright cross on it, was in use in Massachusetts in 1635, because at that time a complaint was entered "that the ensign at Salem was defaced"; viz., one part of the red cross was taken out. This was not done in disrespect to England, but "upon the opinion that the red cross was given to the King of England by the Pope, as an ensign of victory, so a superstitious thing, and a relic of anti-Christ." The court gave no verdict, and after referring the matter to the next higher court, a new flag was proposed, and the matter referred to the

---

[4] Royal Governors in those colonial days flew the flag of the colony governed. We find "Order of the King in Council on petition of Thos. Lord Culpepper Governor of Virginia to have the same honor and privilege of all his Maj. Governors of plantations in America of wearing a flag in the main top as soon as he has sailed out of the limit of the Narrow Seas; directing the Lords of the Admiralty to allow the same if any of his Maj. Governors under the same character have actually enjoyed the privilege. Whitehall, November 28, 1679."

[5] Lt. Philip Chaplin, RCN (R) writes: "In the film *Henry V*, the king wore his personal armorial bearings on his shield and on his coat; his squire rode with him carrying his spear which bore the banner of England, the Cross of St. George. This was his command flag, and to this day the flag of a General Officer Commander in Chief overseas is the Union Flag, and an admiral's flag is still the Cross of St. George." In short the Union Flag is the military flag of the British.

crown for the purpose of obtaining "the judgment of the most wise and godly there." As early as the fourteenth century the badge of St. George was universally worn by the soldiers of England as an emblazonment on the "jack" or leather surcoat.[6]

The Union Flag became distinctive of the Royal Navy in 1634. The land forces and the merchant ships flew either the Cross of St. George or that of St. Andrew. After the execution of Charles I in 1649, the English ships reverted to the old flag of St. George. From all accounts the American colonists preferred the Union flag during this period. It was in 1707 that Queen Anne decreed that a flag of a red field with a "Union Jack" (here is where the confusion first came) in the canton, should now be flown by all who had previously carried the flags of either St. George or St. Andrew. This flag today is the well-known Red Ensign of the British Merchant Service. The Blue Ensign is the distinctive ensign of the Royal Naval Reserve, and of merchant ships commanded by officers on the retired list of the Royal Navy, and officers of the Royal Naval Reserve. And it is ordered that all Her Majesty's ships of war in commission shall wear a white ensign with the red St. George's Cross and the Union in the upper canton.

It is reasonable to assume that the Crosses of St. George and St. Andrew, banners flown in the New World by the earliest colonists from the British Isles, were carried by the Jamestown colonists when they landed in Virginia in 1607, and by the Mayflower colonists at Plymouth Rock in 1620. However, the British colonists in America at an early date secured permission to place a distinctive colonial design on the Union Flag. Up to 1776 four main changes had been made in the basic design. In 1737, the United Colonies of New England were authorized to use a blue flag, with the red cross of Saint George in a white canton, and in the upper corner of the canton next to the staff, a globe representing the world. One of the popular designs of pre-Revolutionary days was that of a red field with a tree instead of a globe in the canton.

---

[6] This may have been the derivation of the name "jack" for a flag. The more probable is from James I, who signed his name "Jacques" and under whose direction the original National Flag of England was formed by the banners of St. George and St. Andrew conjoined. John Cabot and the early English explorers flew St. George as the national flag of England. It is interesting that the realms of England and Scotland were not united in 1606 when James I ordered both crosses united on the same flag. He thought a common flag would effect a closer union; most Scots, of course, thought differently. However, the union became legal in 1707.

SOME EARLY FLAGS BORNE BY UNITS OF THE
CONTINENTAL ARMY

Date	Description	Remarks
1775 Bedford Flag	Designed originally in England for Three County Troop in King Phillip's War. A maroon ground with mailed arm holding a short sword, on a scroll the motto *Vince aut morire* (conquer or die).	Carried by Cornet Nathaniel Page at Concord.
1775	No illustration has been preserved. A red ground with the Connecticut motto *qui transtulit sustinet* (He who transplanted still sustains); on the reverse side a pine tree with the early motto of Massachusetts, "an appeal to heaven." It is almost identical with the Connecticut state flag of today.	Said to have been a present from John Hancock to General Putnam for the gallant fight of his troops at Bunker Hill. First unfurled at Prospect Hill, Boston.
1775 Philadelphia Light Horse Troop Flag	Of yellow silk 40″ by 30″ with a shield and elaborate rosette design of blue and silver. L.H. was also intertwined on the flag, and underneath the motto, "For these we strive." In the upper left-hand corner were thirteen blue and silver stripes, the first flag that symbolized the thirteen colonies by stripes.	This flag was first carried by the Philadelphia Troop of Light Horse when it escorted Washington from Philadelphia to New York to take command of the Continental Army at Cambridge. Probably carried at battle of Trenton; the Light Horse Troop was there.
Jan. 1, 1776	Had seven red and six white stripes with the cross of Saint Andrew and St. George on the blue field of the canton.	This flag was hoisted over the troops of George Washington about January 1 or 2, 1776, on Prospect Hill; at Charlestown on 3d; at Cambridge on 4th. It was designed for naval use. Washington wrote August 4, 1776, "We hoisted the Union flag in compliment to the United Colonies and sa-

SOME EARLY FLAGS OF THE CONTINENTAL ARMY (*Cont.*)

Remarks

luted it with thirteen guns." Tradition relates that Commodore Esek Hopkins sailed in February 1776 from Philadelphia "amidst the acclamation of thousands assembled on the joyful occasion, with the display of a Union Flag with thirteen stripes emblematical of the thirteen Colonies."

In 1649 a new Union Flag was designed for the British Navy, and in design symbolized the union of England and Ireland. In 1658, the old Union Flag, called by some "Union Jack," was reintroduced with the "harpe" imposed thereon for Ireland. It is of record that in 1660 the harpe was removed, "it being offensive to the King." One may safely say that it was also perfectly agreeable to the Irish that the harpe be removed from an English flag. In 1801 the British flag became the flag the world knows today, and in its strictly technical symbolism the Cross of St. Patrick now represents Northern Ireland.

Although the "Union" of Washington's "Grand Union Flag" of 1776 was supposed to stand for the union of the United Colonies, the traditional ties to the mother country were not overlooked, for in the canton one sees the crosses of Saint Andrew and Saint George.

One may observe from the above outline that Revolutionary flags of all descriptions were carried. Some of them were designed as stirring, inflammatory Revolutionary banners, while others more dignified expressed the fervor and seriousness of the patriotic colonists. The Grand Union or Cambridge flag was never authorized by Congress and was in reality "half British." It was on July 4, 1776, that the Declaration of Independence terminated forever the "King's Colors" and the Grand Union flag in the United Colonies of America.

EARLY FLAGS FLOWN AT SEA

The Grand Union flag was designed primarily for use at sea, but various other flags were worn by Continental ships, state ships, and privateers.

"Don't Tread on Me" Flag

Thirteen stripes without a union, with a rattlesnake undulating across the flag, and underneath the motto, "Don't tread on me." It is reported that it was hoisted by Hopkins, December 5, 1775, at the mainmast of the *Alfred* at the time Lieutenant John Paul Jones raised the Grand Union flag. A portrait of Commodore Hopkins was printed in London in August, 1776, and it clearly shows on his right the "Don't Tread on Me" flag, while on his left may be observed the "Liberty Tree" flag (Pine tree on white field with inscription "Liberty Tree" at top and "Appeal to God" underneath).

Washington's Navy Ensign or Pine Tree Flag

Green pine tree on white field bearing inscription, "An Appeal to Heaven." It was adopted in 1775 and carried by some of the first naval vessels of the United States. It is noted that the pine tree was used on various New England flags, because previous to the Revolution it had been a symbol on banners and flags of some of the New England colonies.

Merchant and Privateer Ensign

A plain flag of seven red stripes and six white ones without a union, used at sea from 1775 until 1795.

OTHER FLAGS OF THE WAR FOR AMERICAN INDEPENDENCE

Gadsden's Standard, February, 1776

A bright yellow flag with a coiled rattlesnake in the center and underneath the motto, "Don't Tread on Me." This flag has a peculiar interest in that Gadsden, a member of the Naval Committee, presented it to Congress with the request that it be designated as the personal command flag of Commodore Hopkins, the commander in chief of the Navy. So far as can be learned, nothing was ever done about it, and the flag hung for some time in Congress. Nevertheless, a chart of early flags published in 1974 by the Washington Bi-Centennial Congressional Committee states underneath a cut of this flag that it was hoisted by Hopkins on the *Alfred*. It is regretted that no proof is to be found to this effect.

Pine Tree Flag, 1775–1776–1777

The outstanding device on the majority of these flags was a pine tree with the motto, "An Appeal to Heaven," underneath. This type of flag was used by the floating batteries of the Delaware. It was borne by the Massachusetts and New Hampshire regiments. John Fiske writes that this flag was carried by many naval vessels until the adoption of the new flag in 1776.

There were many unique flags carried by troops in the War of the Revolution. The Culpepper Minute Men, commanded by Patrick Henry, had the snake with the two mottos: "Liberty or Death" and "Don't Tread on Me." Morgan's Rifles had "1776" on their flag, with the words "XI Virginia Regiment" and "Morgan's Rifle Corps" devised thereon. Count Pulaski, who so gallantly cast his lot with the American colonists and lost his life for the cause, carried into his last battle at Savannah, Georgia, a crimson silk banner covered with many devices.

There is still preserved the flag used by the Washington Light Infantry. The fiancée of Colonel William Washington hastily made this flag out of a red curtain. This flag saw victory at Cowpens on January 17, 1781, and was carried at the battle of Eutaw Springs which was conceded a British victory.

JOHN PAUL JONES'S CONNECTION WITH THE EARLY AMERICAN FLAG

John Paul Jones was so closely connected with the first American flags afloat that it is relevant to flag history to mention his association with the tradition of the first "breaking" of the flag, and the first salute to the Stars and Stripes.

Paul Jones's commission as a first lieutenant in the first organization of the American Navy was dated December 22, 1775, and was presented to him in Independence Hall by John Hancock in person. It is recorded that immediately upon receipt of his commission, in the company of John Hancock, Thomas Jefferson, and others, he repaired on board the *Alfred*, the flagship of Commodore Hopkins. Captain Saltonstall, the flag captain, was not aboard, and for that reason it has been related that Hancock directed that Lieutenant Jones take charge. He immediately hoisted to the masthead a new ensign, probably the first "flag of America" ever displayed at the mast of an American man-of-war. Admiral Preble in his exhaustive and authoritative study of flags was of the opinion that the flag hoisted by Jones was in all probability the "Grand Union Flag" which was hoisted two weeks later over Washington's Army at Boston. But later writers seem to agree that it was a combination of the "rattlesnake" flag and the "pine tree" flag. This flag had the rattlesnake coiled around the pine tree and the motto, "Don't Tread on Me" underneath. We are certain that the snake was on the flag, for Jones wrote later in his journal:

> For my own part, I could never see how or why a venomous serpent could be the combatant emblem of a brave and honest folk, fighting to be free. Of course I had no choice but to break the pennant as it was given to me. But I always abhorred the device and was glad when it was discarded for one much more symmetrical as well as appropriate a year or so later.

The Union flag was flown when this little force that marked the beginning of the American Navy sailed from Philadelphia. The order of the day that prescribed the sailing of the fleet down the Delaware on February 17, 1776, specifically said that all vessels should fly "Saint George's ensign with stripes at the mizzen-peak." In all probability this was the Grand Union flag at the hoist of honor, with "the standard at the main top." The standard referred to must have been the "rattlesnake" flag (i.e., seven red stripes, six white stripes, a rattlesnake placed diagonally on the flag, with the motto, "Don't Tread on Me" underneath).

The first operation of the infant navy was against New Providence in the Bahamas. A writer for the London *Ladies Magazine* wrote at the time that the American ships there had colors "striped under the Union with thirteen stripes and their standard a rattlesnake." This checks closely with the order of the day.

THE FIRST STAR-SPANGLED BANNER

It is to be regretted that we shall never know who stood up in the Continental Congress on Saturday, June 14, 1777, and motioned for the adoption of the resolution which read that:

> the Flag of the united states be 13 stripes, alternate red and white, that the union be 13 stars white in a blue field representing a new constellation.[7]

---

[7] The handwriting of the original resolution is that of Charles Thompson, Secretary of the Continental Congress. It is of interest that "Flag" is spelled with a capital "F" but "United States" is spelled with a small "u" and small "s." Note— it is the "Flag of the United States," not "the United States Flag."

This marks the birth of the flag in design about as we know it today. Colonel Nicholas Smith in his book on the flag wrote:

A flag was wanted to harmonize with the growing spirit of Americanism, one that would beautifully symbolize the aspirations of the thirteen states.

One of the most curious coincidences in American naval history is the fact that at the same hour that the new flag was adopted, the dauntless Jones was ordered to command the *Ranger*. His orders and the flag adoption were not in the same bill, but passed in the same hour. Jones was surely cognizant of this event, for afterwards he wrote:

That flag and I were twins; born in the same hour from the same womb of destiny. We cannot be parted in life or death. So long as we can float, we shall float together. If we must sink, we shall go down as one.

All that is mortal of John Paul Jones rests at the United States Naval Academy under the flag he so heroically fought for.

THE OFFICIAL UNITED STATES FLAG'S BAPTISM OF FIRE

It has long been a point of discussion and dispute as to where the first official United States flag went into battle. There are several claimants for the honor. Fort Stanwix (Schuyler), now Rome, New York, is the oldest contender for the honor. Colonel Peter Gansevoort then in command defended the fort on August 3, 1777, against a force composed of British and Indians. Massachusetts reinforcements brought news of the adoption by Congress of an official flag. It is recorded that the soldiers cut up their shirts to make the white stripes; scarlet material to form the red, so tradition states, was secured from red flannel petticoats of officers' wives, while material for the blue union was secured from Captain Abraham Swartwout's blue cloth coat. A voucher is extant that the captain was paid by Congress for the loss of his coat. But whether this flag was the Grand Union or the Stars and Stripes is still questioned by historians. Of all claims to being the first flag in battle, the claims of this flag are the most widely accepted.

After the engagement at Fort Schuyler came the battle of Bennington. The two American flags carried in that battle are still in existence. They are curious flags in design. A good part of one of them is well preserved. The flag has a blue canton with thirteen stars painted thereon. A part of the green field is still attached to the canton.

The other flag is now in the possession of the Bennington Battle Monument and Historical Association. It is certainly a "Stars and Stripes" of a peculiar size and design. The flag is 10 feet long and 5.5 feet wide, with seven white stripes and six red stripes. The striping makes both the bottom and top stripe white. In this connection, it is of interest that when the original certificate of the Society of the Cincinnati was designed in Paris, the engraver used this arrangement of stripes, because it was in accordance with the rules of heraldry. The canton of the flag spanned nine stripes instead of the present seven; it was blue with thirteen white stars. Eleven stars were arranged in an arch, with one in each upper corner. All the stars are seven pointed, with the point directed upwards. Large Arabic numerals "76" are under the arch. It is the oldest Stars and Stripes in existence.

Although there are no records to the effect, it is quite possible that General Gates in command of American troops flew some description of "Stars and Stripes" at the surrender of General Burgoyne in the decisive battle of Saratoga.

There is a third claim that the new official flag was first flown in action at Cooch's Bridge, near Newark, Delaware, on September 3, 1777. Here Maxwell's advanced corps met the British under Howe, and Washington wrote "pretty smart skirmishing" occurred. No reference can be found in official records that the flag was flown there. This corps had been through Philadelphia on its southern march to check the advance of the British, and there is every reason to believe that an official flag was secured in Philadelphia, inasmuch as it had been adopted by Congress on June 14, but was not officially promulgated until September 3.

In a letter to the *New York Times* dated September 12, 1932, Mr. C. W. Heathcote of West Chester, Pennsylvania, brings additional evidence as to the presence of the first official flag being flown at the Battle of Brandywine. He writes:

> However, for the first critical battle of the Revolution, the battle of the Brandywine, the official flag floated. In carrying on research for a considerable period of time, I found a copy of a sermon preached by the Rev. Joab Trout, a chaplain near Washington's headquarters, on the eve of the battle, September 10, 1777. He said, "It is a solemn moment, Brethren, does not the solemn voice of nature seem to echo the sympathies of the hour? The flag of our country droops heavily from yonder staff; the breeze has died away along the green plains of Chadd's Ford, the plain that lies before us, glittering in the sunlight, the heights of the Brandywine

arising gloomy and grand beyond the waters of yonder stream. All Nature holds a pause of solemn silence on the eve of the up-roar, of the bloodshed and strife of tomorrow.

We believe we are correct in assuming that the flag the chaplain refers to is the official flag. It is not likely that Washington would fly any other from his headquarters, and that inasmuch as he was ever correct in matters of military regulations, he would not fly the Stars and Stripes until he received its official promulgation. We therefore believe that the new United States flag received its baptism in the Battle of the Brandywine. The above information is presented as an interesting side light of flag history, although the question of "first flying in battle" has not been definitely settled by historians.

THE FIRST UNITED STATES FLAG IN EUROPEAN WATERS

Tradition records that Captain John Paul Jones was presented a flag for the *Ranger* that had been made from the best silk gowns of the ladies of Portsmouth, New Hampshire. Jones furnished the specifications, and as the story goes the work was done at a quilting party, and the white stars were cut from the bridal dress of one Helen Seary. It is most probable that this is the flag that was first saluted at Quiberon Bay, France. Jones describes this most important salute in American history as follows:

> I also demanded and obtained a salute from the Flag of France both at Quiberon and at Brest, before the treaty of alliance was announced.

This official report was made to the American Board of Admiralty in March 1781, as a reply to certain questions that were propounded. History records the fact that Jones saluted the French Admiral La Motte Picquet with thirteen guns, while the return salute to Jones was nine guns. In the thirteen-gun salute, it was intended that there should be one gun for each state. It is also a matter of record that Jones ascertained in advance that his salute to the white flag of the Bourbons would be returned, although he was disappointed that it would not be returned gun for gun. A kingdom at that time gave a republic (Holland, for example) only nine guns. This is the first record of a salute of honor to the Stars and Stripes at sea.

That Jones's flag received the first salute on February 14, 1778, is generally accepted, but in this connection it is of historic importance to know that John Adams wrote in a letter to Josiah Quincy that the first American vessel to receive a salute from a foreign power was the *Andrea Doria* in November 1776, at St. Eustatius in the Dutch West Indies. The flag carried by the Doria was probably the Grand Union flag. It was certainly not the Stars and Stripes. Cooper wrote: "For this indiscretion the Dutch governor was subsequently displaced."

It is of great interest that the salute to the flag in France was rendered before the Treaty of Alliance with France, the first and only treaty of alliance that the United States government made until World War II. Had it not been for French aid, it is very doubtful whether the United States would have won the War of Independence.

The first five vessels commissioned by the Congress in December 1775 flew the first flag of the infant navy. John Adams, a member of the Marine Committee, wrote:

> The first was named *Alfred*, in honor of the greatest Navy that ever existed; the second, *Columbus*, after the discoverer of this quarter of the globe; the third, *Cortez*, after the discoverer of the northern part of the continent; the fourth, *Andrea Doria*, in honor of the great Genoese admiral; and the fifth, *Providence*, the name of the town where she was purchased and the residence of Governor Hopkins and his brother Esek, whom we appointed the first captain.

It is true that a salute to the American flag was rendered by the Dutch on November 16, 1776, after the *Doria* had saluted the Dutch flag, as set forth in John Adams' letter. Nevertheless, it was not a salute to the authorized Stars and Stripes. It is highly probable that the *Andrea Doria*, commanded by Isaiah Robinson, wore the "Union Flag" that Washington hoisted over his army at Cambridge, a flag that was never legalized. The St. Eustatius salute was given by the Dutch about eight months before the legal birth of the Stars and Stripes.

THE FLAG IN EUROPEAN WATERS

Jones had the supreme honor of carrying this first flag into action on the seas. As Buell in exuberance writes:

> This was the first edition of the Stars and Stripes that Europe ever saw; the first to be saluted by the guns of a European naval power, but far beyond, and beyond anything, it was the first and last flag that ever went down or ever will go down flying on the ship that conquered and captured the ship that sunk her.

It is a glorious tradition for a sea service to start with. Jones in his report eloquently describes the sinking of his vessel, the *Bon Homme Richard*, after those of his crew that were alive had been transferred to the ship of his foe, HMS *Serapis*. Jones writes,

> The ensign-gaff shot away in action had been fished and put in place soon after firing ceased, and ours torn and tattered was left flying when we abandoned her. As she plunged down by the head at last her taffrail momentarily rose in the air so the very last vestige mortal eye ever saw of the *Bon Homme Richard* was the defiant waving of her unconquered and unstrucken flag as she went down. And as I had given them the good old ship as their sepulcher, I now bequeathed to my immortal dead the flag they had so desperately defended, for their winding sheet.

The Stars and Stripes that Jones flew on the *Serapis* after taking her as prize is preserved. It has twelve stars in the canton. It is a tradition that one star was cut off and given to President Lincoln as a gift.

THE NEW FLAG 1795

After Vermont and Kentucky had been admitted to the Union, they strongly requested to be included in the symbolism of the United States flag. After considerable involved debate in the House of Representatives, a bill was passed that provided that from the first day of May 1795, the flag of the United States be fifteen stripes of alternate red and white, and that the union be fifteen white stars in a blue field. This bill was approved by President Washington January 13, 1794. It was passed by a vote of fifty yeas to forty-two nays.

THE LAST ALTERATION TO THE FLAG

For twenty-two years the flag of 1795 was hoisted ashore and afloat, over civilian, military, and naval activities. It was the conquering flag in thirteen out of eighteen naval battles of the War of 1812. It was truly the flag of our golden age on the sea. In 1814 at Fort McHenry, it had inspired the words of the stirring song "The Star Spangled Banner," that in 1931 became our official and legal national anthem. The epic of America was taking shape, and from the frontiers five new states were admitted to the Union. There was again considerable de-debate on the change in the flag. Representative Wendover in a speech on the floor said:

And even on those who predicted that in nine months the striped bunting would be swept from the seas, it possessed the wonderful charm, that before the nine months had elapsed, "fir buildt frigates" and "Yankee Cock Boats" were magnified in ships of the line; and his Majesty's faithful officers, careful for the preservation of British oak, sought protection for their frigates under the convoy of 74-gun ships.

It is interesting to note that in that time there was no uniformity in the number of stripes of the flag. Wendover said:

> That, on the hall of Congress, whence laws emanate, has but thirteen, and those of the navy yard and marine barracks have each eighteen. Nor can I omit to mention the flag under which the last Congress sat during its first session, which from some cause or other unknown had but nine stripes.

In reality it was a hit or miss period of flag manufacture; there was little uniformity.

A bill was finally passed that provided from the Fourth day of July, 1818:

> The flag of the United States be thirteen horizontal stripes of alternate red and white; that the union have twenty white stars in a blue field; that one star be added on the admission of every new state in the Union; and that the addition shall take place on the 4th of July next succeeding such admission.

The bill passed on March 31, 1818, and was signed by President Monroe on April 4, 1818.

The signing of this bill marked the settlement of the troublesome national flag question. By the admission of states in the years that followed, the flag of forty-eight stars became fixed in appearance and design. An Act of Congress on October 26, 1912, decreed that there should be forty-eight stars arranged in six horizontal rows of eight each, with five-pointed stars, one point on each star pointed upwards. When Alaska became a state in 1959, the forty-ninth star was added; on July 4, 1960, the fiftieth star was added for the new state of Hawaii. The stars are arranged in nine staggered rows, with six in the top row, five in the next, and so on.

"THE STAR SPANGLED BANNER"

After years of inactivity, bickering, and attempts by cliques and individuals to secure recognition of other words and music, on April 21,

1930, the House adopted the words and music of "The Star Spangled Banner" as the national anthem. It became a law after being adopted by the Senate on March 3, 1931. Although Congress three times rejected the bill of Congressman Linthicum of Maryland, he finally presented a petition which was reported to bear 5,000,000 signatures that were obtained through the cooperation of various patriotic societies. Without commenting on the musical merits of "The Star Spangled Banner," it is interesting to note that when the argument was advanced that the song was pitched too high for popular singing, Mr. Linthicum was instrumental in bringing about a hearing before the House Judiciary Committee at which two sopranos sang and the Navy Band played the strains. The passage of the bill indicates approval.

In brief, the history of "The Star Spangled Banner" is here given. Francis Scott Key was inspired to write the words of "The Star Spangled Banner" during the bombardment of Fort McHenry by a British fleet in 1812. Dr. William Beanes, an old and prominent resident of Upper Marlborough, Maryland, was made prisoner by General Ross of the British Army and confined on Vice-Admiral Sir George Cockrane's flagship, HMS *Surprise*. Francis Scott Key, a very close friend of Dr. Beanes, determined to request the doctor's release and for that reason repaired on the flagship. Admiral Cockrane received Key most cordially; he consented to release Dr. Beanes but informed him that, in view of important operations, it would be necessary for them to remain aboard for a few days.

On the night of September 13, 1814, the heavy shelling took place. Key, with Beanes and John Skinner of Baltimore, who had accompanied Key, were transferred to the British tender *Minden* just before the attack. After a night of bombardment, Francis Scott Key looked out at dawn towards the fort of his homeland for signs of life. His vision was greeted by "The Star Spangled Banner"; although torn and shell-rent, it still floated over the gallant defenders of the old fort. It was then that he wrote the first draft of the song, inscribing the words on the back of an old envelope.[8] His reference to the "foe's haughty host" alluded to the British soldiers of General Ross at North Point.

The motives that gave birth to our national anthem need no commentary.[9] The tradition for our reflection is that noble sentiment and

[8] The original draft of "The Star Spangled Banner" was purchased by the city of Baltimore in 1934 and is now owned by the Maryland Historical Society in that city.

[9] To secure the petitions in support of the measure that ultimately made the "Star Spangled Banner" the legal national anthem, great credit must go to a Spanish-American War veteran, "Daddy" Joyce, who worked zealously for nine

pride in country and flag inspired the legal national anthem of our country. Maryland now observes September 14 as Defenders' Day. The flag that flew through the night may now be seen in the Smithsonian Institution, in Washington. It is pierced with eleven shot holes.

The fourteenth of June is now observed in practically all states as Flag Day. Its observance is based on custom and conventionality, which are often of greater authority than are decrees and statutes.

FEDERAL LAW AGAINST DESECRATION

Surprisingly, until 1968 there existed only one federal statute which protected the flag throughout the country from desecration. This law provided that a trademark cannot be registered which consists of or comprises among other things, "The flag, coat of arms, or other insignia of the United States or any simulation thereof." On July 5th, 1968, President Johnson signed the law which made it a crime, punishable by a fine of $1,000 or one year in jail, or both, for "knowingly" casting "contempt" on the flag by "publicly mutilating, defacing, defiling, burning, or trampling upon it."

SYMBOLISM OF THE FLAG

The National Flag Conference of 1924, in an appeal to the honor and loyalty that should be accorded our colors and to the significance of its history, concluded:

> It embodies the essence of patriotism. Its spirit is the spirit of the
> American nation. Its history is the history of the American people.
> Emblazoned upon its folds in letters of living light are the names
> and fame of our heroic dead, the Fathers of the Republic, who
> devoted upon its altars their lives, their fortunes, and their sacred
> honor. Twice-told tales of national honor and glory cluster thickly
> about it. Ever victorious, it has emerged triumphant from eight
> great national conflicts. It flew at Saratoga, at Yorktown, at Palo
> Alto, at Gettysburg, at Manila Bay, at Chateau-Thierry. It bears
> witness to the immense expansion of our national boundaries, the
> development of our national resources, and the splendid structure
> of our civilization. It prophesies the triumph of popular govern-
> ment, of civic and religious liberty, and of national righteousness
> throughout the world.

---

years on this measure. Mrs. Harvey L. Miller, Chairman of the National Legislation Committee of the Veterans of Foreign Wars Ladies' Auxiliaries, gained mainly by her own efforts the final legislative support required to pass the Linthicum Bill.

For the professional man-at-arms, the flag means many things; all of which, in varying degrees, he feels; much of which, he finds difficult fully to explain. Herein lies a paradox: the fact that one sworn to defend the flag and country against all enemies, living figuratively under its folds day and night, may have no standard and pat answer of its meaning to him, other than that it is a visible, external, national symbol that serves as an embodiment of his patriotic faith. And some, because of strong personal feelings for its meaning that could be over-simplified as love for a mute symbol that stands for all we are and all we ever hope to be, as in the instances of people with deep, personal religious convictions, do not care to discuss or reveal to others its meaning to them. There are others who will immediately say that it means many things, but that uppermost, it stands for "the land of the free and the home of the brave," and more specifically, that it is the reminder of our precious freedoms—the human and property rights embodied in the Constitution.

For the true American, the flag is an ever-thrilling inspiration. Its historic associations with wars and victories throughout the world provide immeasurable incentive for its defenders of the present to do as well as its defenders in the past. That means an esprit de corps, a loyalty, and a devotion to cause that compels men—against all odds, if necessary—to defend it as the colorful symbol of the country they love.

THE SALUTE AT "COLORS" ON BOARD SHIP

The venerable system of saluting the quarterdeck has been recounted, but strangely only at a comparatively recent date were naval personnel ordered to give appropriate recognition, by salute, or attention if uncovered, to the national ensign at the ceremony of colors.

The first order found on the subject is that of Rear Admiral James E. Jouett, U.S. Navy, in a squadron order dated November 22, 1884:

> The attention of the squadron is called to the fact that at colors no custom has hitherto prevailed of giving appropriate recognition, by salute or otherwise, to the flag, the emblem not only of the national authority at home, but of liberty and progress throughout the world. Under the conviction that such a recognition is fitting and desirable, and that the custom, if adopted by all, should be the spontaneous expression of a general sentiment, the commander in chief deems it only necessary to express the wish that on board the ships of the North Atlantic Squadron all officers and men who may be on deck at colors will uncover, as far as practicable without serious interruption to the occupation of the moment.

Traditionally, all naval ships and stations make colors at 0800.

In 1884, all salutes were rendered by removing the headdress. And although there was a ceremony for the Guard and others who were on duty at colors, the above order clearly indicates that previously those in the vicinity paid no attention to the ceremony. The custom of standing at attention and saluting became in time a naval regulation. Thus the "wish" of an admiral became a general custom, and afterwards the order of our day.

THE FLAG CODE[10]

In order that the officers of the service may have the most authoritative opinions and collected usage pertaining to flag etiquette, there is set forth the Flag Code adopted at the National Flag Conference, Washington, D.C., June 14–15, 1923, as revised and endorsed at the Second National Flag Conference, Washington, May 15, 1924. The original Flag Conference was convened at the request of the American Legion in cooperation with sixty-eight other organizations in Memorial Continental Hall of the National Society of the Daughters of the American Revolution.

SALUTE TO THE NATIONAL ANTHEM

When the national anthem is played and no flag is displayed, all present should stand and face toward the music. Those in uniform should salute at the first note of the anthem, retaining this position until the last note of the anthem. All others should stand at attention, men removing their headdress. When the flag is displayed, the regular "Salute to the Flag" should be given.

NOTES ON THE FLAG[11]

When displayed either horizontally or vertically against a wall, in a show window, or elsewhere:
    The blue field is uppermost and to the flag's own right, that is, to the observer's left.
    The reason for displaying the flag with the blue field uppermost and to the flag's own *right* (the observer's *left*) is this: the blue field, according to the rules of heraldry, is the honor point and should, therefore, occupy the position of danger. But the position of danger is the position of the arm which holds the sword, that is, the right arm. Therefore, the blue field of the flag, which faces the observer, should be to its right.
    A simple "rule-of-thumb" that tells how to display the flag correctly in either a horizontal or vertical position is this: We always speak of the flag as the Stars and Stripes, never as the stripes and stars.

---

[10] On June 22, 1942, Congress did give special recognition to the Code by emphasizing its importance under Joint Resolution 623. Subsequently, the Resolution was amended and became Public Law 829 on December 22, 1942. Uniformity was the aim of the law. All states have flag laws with varying penalties of fines and imprisonments for flag abuse.

[11] *Reserve Officers' Manual, U. S. Navy* (1932).

Therefore, when we look at the flag it should read "stars and stripes," that is, the stars (in the blue field) should come first.

When carried in a horizontal position by a number of people, as it sometimes done in parades:

The blue field is at the right (flag's own right) and front. However, it is a violation of the Flag Code to carry the flag in this manner and it is to be regretted that it is ever done. Everything possible should be done to discourage the practice, which, however good the intentions of those concerned may be, is considered by most people as an unnatural, unusual, and undignified display of the flag. When carried this way, the flag is often allowed to sag in an ungainly manner, frequently touching the ground, which sometimes leads to the abuse of using the sagging flag as a receptacle for hats and other articles. Hence, it is most desirable that the practice be discontinued.

When used to cover a casket:

The flag should be placed so that the union is at the head of the casket and over the left shoulder of the deceased. The casket should be carried foot first.[12]

The flag must not be lowered into the grave, nor allowed to touch the ground.

The position of the blue field is reversed on a casket to indicate mourning. With the blue field on the right as the flag faces the coffin it may be said that the flag is embracing the deceased who in life had served the flag.

To indicate mourning when the flag is not on a staff but is displayed flat:

A black crêpe bowknot, either with or without streamers, is placed at the fastening points. Since the flag symbolizes the nation, it should be half-masted or dressed with crêpe only in cases where it is appropriate to indicate that the nation mourns. If it is desired to show that a state, a city, a club, or a society mourns, then the state, city, club, or society flag should be half-masted or dressed in crêpe. The flag should not be both half-masted and dressed with crêpe, nor should it ever be tied in the middle with crêpe to indicate mourning.

---

[12] "In accordance with an old custom based on the belief that a chaplain, even in death, should always face his flock, the body of a chaplain is carried head first into and out of the chapel and from the caisson or hearse to the graveside. Committal services for a chaplain are conducted at the foot of the grave." *Naval Funerals*, NavPers 10068, Art. 147.

INTERESTING FLAG HISTORY AND
EXTRAORDINARY SALUTES

The Turkish Flag Flies over Bainbridge in
Command of a United States Frigate

In September 1800, the twenty-six-year-old Captain William Bainbridge in the United States ship *George Washington*, first American man-of-war to enter the Mediterranean, delivered tribute from the United States government to the Dey of Algiers. The Dey, after much protest on Bainbridge's part, commandeered the *George Washington* for use in sending a special ambassador to the Sultan of Turkey with money and rich gifts.

The American Consul, General Richard O'Brien, went on board; the Turkish flag was hoisted at the main of the United States ship, and saluted with seven guns. Captain Bainbridge wrote at the time to a friend:

> The Dey of Algiers, soon after my arrival, made a demand that the United States' ship, *George Washington*, should carry an ambassador to Constantinople with presents to the amount of five or six hundred thousand dollars, and upwards of two hundred Turkish passengers. Every effort was made by me to evade this demand but it availed nothing. The light in which the chief of this regency looks upon the people of the United States may be inferred from his style of expression. He remarked to me, "You pay me tribute, by which you become my slaves; I have therefore a right to order you as I may think proper." The unpleasant situation in which I am placed must convince you that I have no alternative left but compliance, or a renewal of hostilities against our commerce. The loss of the frigate and the fear of slavery for myself and crew were the least circumstances to be apprehended, but I knew our valuable commerce in these seas would fall a sacrifice to the corsairs of this power, as we have here no cruisers to protect it. . . . I hope I may never again be sent to Algiers with tribute unless I am authorized to deliver it from the mouth of our cannon. . . .[13]

Tunis Salutes First

The first national salute by the Regency of Tunis to the U. S. flag was fired to the flagship *North Carolina*, Commodore John Rodgers, in

---

[13] Thomas Harris, *The Life and Services of Commodore William Bainbridge* (Boston: Gray & Bowen, 1832), p. 163.

February 1827. This salute was fired at the request of Dr. S. D. Heap, U. S. Consul General to Tunis. The salute was immediately returned by the *North Carolina.*

First Stars and Stripes in an English Port

Captain Bedford of Massachusetts brought the *Bedford* to London on February 6, 1783, and reported a heavy cargo of whale oil to the London Custom House. British and American peace envoys were still negotiating in London as to the terms of the peace treaty. The daring Yankee skipper was moored in sight of the Tower of London where Henry Laurens and a large number of officers and men were still prisoners of war. The ship was described as "American built, manned wholly by American seamen, wearing the Rebel colors, and belonging to Massachusetts." The *London Chronicle* of February 7, 1783, said:

> There is a vessel in the harbor with a very strange flag. Thirteen is a number peculiar to rebels. A party of prisoners, lately returned from Jersey, says the rations among the rebels are thirteen dried clams a day. Sachem Schuyler has a topknot of thirteen stiff hairs which erect themselves on the crown of his head when he gets mad. It takes thirteen paper dollars to make one shilling. Every well-organized household has thirteen children, all of whom expect to be Major Generals or members of the high and mightly Congress of the thirteen United States when they attain the age of thirteen years. Mrs. Washington has a tomcat with thirteen yellow rings around its tail. His flaunting tail suggested to Congress the same number of stripes for the Rebel Flag.

Stars and Stripes Fly over British Parliament

The flag of the United States flew over the highest spire of the British Parliament Building on April 20, 1917, in celebration of the entry of the United States in World War I. It was the first foreign flag ever to fly there.

Joint Operations—Americans and British

"When the two British cutters broke the boom at Oran (November 1942) with American Rangers on board, they went into action for the first time in our history wearing both the United States and White Ensigns."[14]

---

[14] Of this daring exploit, Churchill wrote: "They encountered murderous fire at point blank range, and both ships were destroyed with most of those on board." Their mission was accomplished; they broke the boom.

Flag Carried Around the World

Captain Robert Gray, sailing from Boston on September 30, 1787, in command of the sloop *Washington*, took command of the *Columbia* in the northwest country. Gray sailed with a cargo of guns to China and returned to Boston on August 10, 1790, "having carried the thirteen stars and thirteen stripes for the first time around the world."

Flag Hoisted over the Louisiana Purchase

The Stars and Stripes were first hoisted in Louisiana, December 20, 1803. It was not until March 10, 1804, that the formal transfer of upper Louisiana took place. St. Louis, Missouri, has the unique distinction of having been under three flags in twenty-four hours. On March 9, 1804, the Spanish flag was hauled down and that of France was hoisted. On March 10, 1804, the flag of the United States was raised for the first time over the vast territory of upper Louisiana.

First Flown from an Old World Fort

By the grace of God, a few Marines, one midshipman, and thirty-odd Greeks and some Arabs, Lieutenant Presley N. O'Bannon, U. S. Marine Corps, a Kentuckian, captured the battery that defended the city of Derna, Tripoli. O'Bannon routed the enemy, turned the guns on the fleeing Tripolitans, and planted the flag on the fort, April 1805.[15]

The Origin of the Term "Old Glory"

The story found in various books and papers states that Captain William Driver of Salem, Massachusetts, gave the name "Old Glory" to a flag that was presented to him by a committee of ladies in 1831. The original "Old Glory" was hoisted on his brig, the *Charles Daggett*, and afterward carried by the captain twice around the world.

At the time of the occupation of Nashville, Tennessee, by the federal troops, on February 25, 1862, a United States flag was first hoisted by the Sixth Ohio Volunteers, but was hauled down a few minutes later and Driver's original "Old Glory" hoisted in its place.

In an article titled "Adventures of Old Glory," William E. Beard, relates that:[16]

---

[15] Hemet, claimant for Pasha of Tripoli, is said to have presented O'Bannon a sword Hemet carried with the Mamelukes in Egypt. The sword was of a pattern later called "the Mameluke sword." This sword, reports Col. Clyde H. Metcalf, U. S. Marine Corps historian, has been with slight interruption (1859–1875), "that carried by Marine officers since a few years after the Tripolitan War."

[16] William E. Beard, "Adventures of Old Glory," U. S. Naval Institute *Proceedings.*

Perry transfers his flag at Lake Erie. "If a victory is to be gained, I'll gain it." *W.H. Powell. Now in the Capitol in Washington, D.C.*

> Captain Driver, at the time of the occupation of Nashville, retired from the sea and residing in the Tennessee city, had sacredly preserved his flag during the exciting times of secession and had the distinction of raising it with his own hands over the state house. Nashville thus became the only city over which the original "Old Glory" ever floated as an emblem of war.

Hoisted over the Castle of Chapultepec, Mexico

After Mexican General Santa Anna had been forced out of Mexico City by Pillow's and Quitman's Divisions, Captain Benjamin S. Roberts of Vermont, on orders, on September 1847 planted a stand of colors on the ancient palace of the Montezumas.

Lowering and Raising the Flag at Fort Sumter

On Sunday, April 14, 1861, the United States flag of Fort Sumter was lowered and saluted with fifty guns during the lowering, by order of Major Robert Anderson, U. S. Army, in command. A premature discharge of a gun during the salute resulted in the death of a United States soldier, the first fatality of the Civil War. The fort had made a game defense but could not withstand the heavy Confederate bombardment. The lowering of this flag marks the beginning of the bloody, long-drawn-out Civil War.

The Confederates were not forced from Fort Sumter until February 17, 1865. To celebrate and mark the restoration, it was ordered that five days later on Washington's birthday, 1865, West Point and all forts, arsenals, and garrisons in the United States fire a national salute.

"General Order No. 50," Adjutant General's Office, Washington, dated March 27, 1865, ordered:

> That at the hour of noon on the fourteenth day of April, 1865, Brevet Major General Anderson will raise and plant upon the ruins of Fort Sumter, in Charleston Harbor, the same U.S. flag which floated over the battlements of that fort during the rebel assault, and which was lowered and saluted by him and the small force of his command when the works were evacuated on the fourteenth day of April, 1861.
>
> That the flag, when raised, be saluted by 100 guns from Fort Sumter, and by a national salute from every fort and rebel battery that fired upon Fort Sumter.

The American Flag Replaces That of Spain at Santiago

Admiral Sampson and Commander Schley defeated the Spanish fleet of the gallant Spanish Admiral Pascual Cervera after it emerged on July 3, 1898, from the harbor of Santiago, Cuba. The naval action and the success of the United States Army in the battle of San Juan Hill and El Caney forced the surrender of Santiago on July 17, 1898. General Castellanos formally surrendered the government to General John Brooke, U. S. Army, on January 1, 1899, and the Spanish flag with the arms of Ferdinand and Isabella, the sovereigns for whom Columbus discovered the new world, was lowered at Morro Castle, Havana. By this act the last vestige of Spanish sovereignty was lost in this hemisphere.

The Spanish Lieutenant Müller y Tejerio wrote on July 17, 1898, in regard to the surrender of Santiago:

> In conformity with the terms of the capitulation, the surrender of the city to the American Army took place today. At 9 P.M., the Spanish flag was hoisted on Punta Blanca Fort and saluted by twenty-one guns; shortly after, it was lowered. At 9:30 Generals Toral and Shafter, commander in chief of the Spanish and American forces, respectively, the latter accompanied by his staff and many of the commanders and officers of the American fleet, witnessed the marching by, under arms, of a company of the former, representing all the Spanish forces, as it was difficult to assemble them. The American forces presented arms and beat a march.
>
> The heights of Conosa were the theater of this sad scene. . . .

The troops having evacuated the city, 1,000 men of the United States Army entered it, hoisting the flag of that nation at the Palace and the Morro.[17]

Flag Flies over Manila in the Philippines

Commodore Dewey and the American Asiatic Fleet destroyed and captured the Spanish fleet of Admiral Montojo at Manila on May 1, 1898. It was not until August 12, 1898, that the protocol of agreement was signed between Spain and the United States. On August 13, Dewey sent the following dispatch to Washington:

> Manila, August 13. Secretary Navy, Washington: Manila surrendered today to the American land and naval forces, after a combined attack. A division of the squadron shelled the forts and entrenchments at Malate on the south side of the city, driving back the enemy, our Army advancing from that side at the same time. City surrendered about five o'clock, the American flag being hoisted by Lieutenant Thomas M. Brumby. About 7,000 prisoners were taken. The squadron had no casualties; none of the vessels were injured.
>
> On August 7, General Wesley Merritt and I demanded the surrender of the city, which the Spanish general refused.

The Discovery of the North Pole by a Naval Officer

The world was excited on receipt of the following message: "Indian Head Harbor, via Cape Roy, N. F., September 6, 1909. To Associated Press, New York: 'Stars and Stripes' nailed to North Pole. Peary."

It was after twenty years of arctic exploration that Robert E. Peary, civil engineer officer, United States Navy, on April 6, 1909, became the first person to reach the top of the earth. The fragment of the flag he deposited there in a glass bottle was a part of the silken flag presented to him by his wife fifteen years before. Small fragments had been left by Peary at all his "farthest norths" in the years that preceded his success.

Byrd Makes First Flight in Airplane over North and South Poles

On May 9, 1926, Lieutenant Commander Richard Evelyn Byrd, U.S. Navy, made the first airplane flight over the North Pole. A

---

[17] The American ensign hoisted over the Morro at the harbor entrance was a yacht ensign. This flag was sent by Captain E. T. Pollock, USN (Retired), in 1933, to the Naval Academy.

weighted American flag was dropped by him on the calculated "top of the earth." On November 29, 1929, Commander Byrd flew over the South Pole in an airplane, and from a trap door in the plane dropped an American flag weighted with a stone brought from the grave of his comrade, dear friend, and pilot on the North Pole flight, Floyd Bennett, former Chief Aviation Pilot, U.S. Navy. At a later date, Byrd made another flight over the Pole and in memory of Scott and Amundsen dropped the flags of their respective countries on the "bottom of the earth."

An Army Flag that Was Never Surrendered

After the American forces reoccupied Luzon in World War II, Major General Oscar W. Griswold accepted with tear-dimmed eyes the regimental flag of the 26th Cavalry that had been preserved and treasured by American survivors of Bataan and "The Death March." Lt. Henry Clay Connor, Jr., who commanded this small group of Americans, said: "Take an ordinary man back in the States. . . . He doesn't know how much faith means. Those of us out here who didn't have faith these last three years in America, who didn't have something to hold like this flag, just went to pieces."

A Flag Raising that Will Never Be Forgotten—Iwo Jima

One of the most savage battles in World War II took place at Iwo Jima. In this bloody siege of five weeks by U. S. Marines, 6,000 Americans were killed and 20,000 wounded. On February 23, 1945, four days after the landing five Marines and a sailor raised the American flag on Mount Suribachi.[18] This heroic and historic event is immortalized in the photograph by Joe Rosenthal, and the giant statue of the Marine Corps Memorial at Washington, D.C., as adapted by the sculptor, Felix de Welden.

An Historic Flag of the Army and Air Force

General Carl Spaatz, U. S. Air Force, ordered the now-faded, bomb-torn flag that flew over Hickam Field when it was attacked by the

---

[18] This honored flag was presented to General MacArthur in Manila after American occupation. It was taken on to Tokyo where the general, less than a dozen officers, and a small color guard, all visibly moved, saw it hoisted over the American Embassy there. "It was," wrote General Bonner Fellers, U. S. Army, (Ret.), "the end of a long and frustrating and heartbreaking and bloody trail. And as our beautiful flag unfurled in the blue over Tokyo, emotion shook every one of us to the marrow of his bones."

Japanese December 7, 1941, to be hoisted again at the same flag pole at 7:55 Hawaiian time, five years later. The order read: "Troops of the Seventh Air Force, with Headquarters at Hickam Field, will pass in review while an honor guard attends the raising." It is of historic interest that this same flag was first raised after the Pearl Harbor attack over the headquarters of General George C. Kenney, Commanding General of the Far Eastern Forces, when he arrived in Tokyo with General MacArthur's staff and the first occupational troops.

First Official Flag of the Navy

On April 24, 1959, President Eisenhower approved a new "blue and gold emblem" that gave the Navy an official flag for the first time in its 184 years. All the other armed forces had official flags, but the banner flown by the Navy during ceremonial and parade occasions was the United States Navy infantry flag. This is the familiar blue rectangle with a blue anchor (fouled) set on a white diamond. Nothing can be found in standard Navy reference books or papers that give the origin of this flag.

The executive order describes the new flag as of dark blue material with a two and one-half inch yellow fringe. In the center, in colors, is part of the seal of the Navy Department, enclosed in a circle of yellow rope. A yellow scroll below this circular emblem is inscribed "United States Navy" in dark blue letters.

Flag Procedure in Washington, D.C.

Since World War I, the flag of the United States has flown night and day on both the east front and west front of the Capitol of the United States. The flags are only lowered to be replaced with new ones.

A Presidential Proclamation of March 1, 1954, placed under the General Services Administration the task of seeing that flags are properly handled over most official federal buildings, but exempted from its jurisdiction are the Treasury Department and its subdivisions, the Smithsonian Institution, the Government Printing Office, and all buildings on Capitol Hill.

Until this change the White House had to make a proclamation at the death of each high official. Most flags on Capitol Hill are half-masted without orders on the death of a senator or representative, but special orders are given by the vice president or Speaker of the House for half-masting colors at the deaths of other officials.

On the death of a president of the United States, flags are half-masted for thirty days at all legations and military establishments abroad; also on all government buildings, grounds, and naval vessels in

the District of Columbia, the United States, its territories and possessions.

First Airplane to Land at South Pole

Rear Admiral George J. Dufek, who commanded the U. S. Navy's
Operation Deep Freeze, 1956–59, for construction and maintenance of
the South Pole Station as part of the U. S. contribution to the International Geophysical Year, in preliminary operations landed on October 31, 1956, in an airplane at the South Pole. Many planes had flown
across, but this was the first landing. Seven Navy men accompanied
him. A hole was hacked in the ice, a certificate of landing was deposited, on top of which an American flag was placed. It was 58° below
zero. Admiral Dufek and men were the first persons to set foot at the
Pole since the British Expedition commanded by Robert Falcon Scott,
in January 1912.

U. S. Flag at South Pole

On March 22, 1957, Dr. Paul A. Siple, Scientific Leader of Amundsen-
Scott South Pole Station (IGY project of National Academy of Science, maintained by Navy Operation Deep Freeze), stood with some
colleagues and for the first time in the life of man saw the sun disap-
pear below the horizon at the Pole. It was coincidental but fitting that
the torn, wind-whipped, American flag at the Pole be lowered at that
time from half-mast where it was flown for ten days following the
death of Admiral Richard E. Byrd.

First Ship to Reach North Pole

On August 3, 1958, the United States Navy's atomic submarine *Nautilus*, skippered by Commander William R. Anderson, reached the
North Pole, cruising 1,839 nautical miles in four days, while passing
from the Pacific to the Atlantic under the great ice mass of the Arctic
Ocean. A few days after the cruise of the *Nautilus*, the *Skate*, the
Navy's third nuclear submarine, spent ten days beneath the pack-ice
making studies, frequently surfacing, and reached the Pole twice. At
some of the festive homecoming celebrations for officers and crew of
the *Nautilus*, Rear Admiral, now Admiral, Hyman G. Rickover, father
of the nuclear submarine, shared some of the glory.

   The crossing of the 2,000-mile-wide, frozen continent of Antarc-
tica about six months before by the British Commonwealth Expedition,
led by Dr. (later Sir) Vivian Fuchs, and the brilliant achievement of
the *Nautilus* are considered by the *National Geographic*'s editor as
"two of the greatest achievements in the annals of exploration."

First Men on the Moon

At 10:56:20 EDT on 20 July 1969, Astronaut Neil A. Armstrong was the first man to set foot on the moon, and as the world watched the event, he and Astronaut Edwin E. Aldrin planted the Stars and Stripes

Color Guard. The Color Guard of the United States Naval Academy includes the National Ensign, the Marine Corps Flag, the Navy Flag, and the Naval Academy Flag.

on the Lunar plains. They returned to earth after their historic walk, leaving behind them their footprints and a plaque honoring the five men who gave their lives for the conquest of space.

A NAVAL OFFICER'S ALLEGIANCE TO THE FLAG

The allegiance of a naval officer to the flag of his country is more absolute than that of a soldier or civilian. In the very nature of the case that symbol of nationality, borne aloft upon the high seas and receiving tributes of respect wherever displayed in distant ports, comes to be regarded as the ever-present proof of a people's entity, as the blazon of that people's honor and power. To bear it nobly, and—away from government and officials—under sudden and trying circumstances, to maintain its dignity unsullied, is the pride of the true sailor. To extend its protection and relief in lonely places, is his frequent duty. To uphold it manfully in the face of opposition is his special trust. Bound up in that flag are his highest and holiest hopes. It gladdens his eye in the sunshine of peace, and covers his head in the day of battle. He rejoices in the deep-toned thunders which salute its presence, and glories in the grand defiance which leaps from under its folds. His world lies within its shadow. Its service is his reward, and by this token are his companionships confirmed.[19]

A TRIBUTE BY A SOLDIER

The importance of the true meaning of the flag of our nation, its significance in the past, what it symbolizes now, and what it stands for in the future cannot be too strongly stressed.

General Dwight D. Eisenhower

[19] Charles C. Jones, distinguished Southern historian of the nineteenth century and biographer of Commodore Josiah Tattnall.

CHAPTER 7

The Golden Age—
The Naval War
of 1812-1815

*This war should be studied with increasing diligence; the
pride of two peoples to whom naval affairs are so generally familiar
has cleared all the details and laid bare all the episodes, and at
every step can be seen that great truth, that there is only success
for those who know how to prepare for it.*

Admiral Jurien de la Gravière, *Guerres Maritimes*

*The material results were not very good, at least in their effect
on Great Britain, whose enormous Navy did not feel in the slightest degree the loss of a few frigates and sloops. But morally the
result was of inestimable benefit to the United States. The victories
kept up the spirits of the people, cast down by the defeats on
land; practically decided in favor of the Americans the chief question in dispute—Great Britain's right of search and imprisonment
—and gave the Navy, and thereby the country, a worldwide
reputation.*

Theodore Roosevelt, *The Naval War of 1812*

*Not once or twice in our rough island story
The path of duty was the way to glory.*

Tennyson[1]

*What you from your fathers have inherited,
Earn it, in order to possess it.*

Goethe

[1] After Admiral Lord Fraser's ships sank the German battleship *Scharnhorst*,
Winston Churchill reminded him of the lines from Tennyson's "Ode on the
Death of the Duke of Wellington."

"THE GOLDEN AGE" is a general term applied to the brilliant portion of a phase of history, or department of activity. Such ages in a particular field of human endeavor tower above other periods, as mankind looks back along the bridge that links the present with the past. To students of these divisions of history, generally accepted as epochal, they become a source of inspiration and give a better understanding of some of the forces that determine mankind's advance.

In the profession of arms both ashore and afloat, there have been golden ages, when leaders of unquestioned superiority had followers so inspired by ardent loyalty to them and devotion to cause that for long periods victory was certain. One recalls the campaigns of Caesar, Gustavus Adolphus, Frederick the Great, and Napoleon, the success of the mariners of Elizabethan England as well as the superb genius that was exemplified in all that Lord Nelson did. Considering the limited number of ships employed, it is doubtful that any naval campaign of similar duration exceeded the brilliant exploits, the inspired leadership, the high morale of crews, and the superb seamanship of the U. S. Navy during the War of 1812. It is not merely a heroic saga for lovers of high adventure; there is practical value. The impetus that the Navy of 1812 gave to a new service is incalculable; the wealth of tradition that was bequeathed as a heritage is priceless. We should be proud that King, Nimitz, Halsey, Spruance, Kincaid, Mitscher, Burke, and many others passed on this legacy embellished and untarnished.

When routine duties become irksome, when years of attention to minute details dull the imagination, when even an appreciation of great tradition with its inspirational value waxes cool within us, it is wise to turn to the thrilling exploits of the officers and men of other days without whom we might not have a Navy today. These people, who fought against great odds, who won the respect of a powerful foe and the praise of all civilized nations, deserve our homage. "Heroism," wrote Amiel, "is the brilliant triumph of the soul over the flesh"; in some of the 1812 actions, our Yankee sailors proved it.

There comes a time in every leader's career when he experiences the need of precedent, inspiration, and the memories of how others followed the hard path of duty. Much inspiration may be ours if we will give some study, time, and reflection to great men and their deeds.

Let us, for a few minutes, examine some heroic actions of the United States War of 1812–1815 on the sea, and see what support there is for the thesis that it was a heroic, golden age for a new navy in a new world: a navy that in time, would surpass in size that of the old mother country from which our language and many of our customs derive.

The War of 1812 was fought primarily over opposite views of the United States and Great Britain as to the rights of belligerents and neutrals on the high seas. It was the result of the long conflict between the British doctrine, "once a subject always a subject," and the American law which conferred citizenship on British subjects after five years of American residence and the execution of certain forms. Moreover, there was the British system of impressing crews for warships which had been a customary practice in the British Navy, and which had caused national bitterness when the British extended the policy to the search of American ships for British seamen. Also, Great Britain held that she had the right to search any neutral ship for property and the nationals of her enemies. Because of impressment in the British Navy, many British seamen deserted and sailed under the American flag. Nevertheless, Theodore Roosevelt, in his *Naval War of 1812* noted: "Equally probable is it that the American blockade runners were guilty of a great deal of fraud or less thinly veiled perjury."

In fact, many incidents over a period of years led up to this "second war of the Revolution." The Navy had never forgotten the *Chesapeake-Leopard* affair when, without declaration of war, HMS *Leopard* (54 guns) made a surprise attack on the USS *Chesapeake* (38 guns), killed or wounded twenty-two of the crew, and took off four alleged deserters. One alleged deserter was hanged by the British. Captain James Barron was suspended from duty for five years on charges that his ship was not ready for action. The British captain, however, received a letter of commendation from his admiral which stated:

> You have conducted yourself most properly. I hope you mind the published accounts as little as I do. We must make allowances for the state of the populace in a country where law and every tie, both civil and religious, is treated so lightly.

The small, weak service foresaw war on the horizon. Weak materially, how was it in personnel? What was the caliber and character of the officers and men of the Navy? What type of training and discipline had this "substantially similar" branch of the English race afloat? The officers and men had had for the most part very active service. Traditions had been made. Some of the older officers and men had served in the War of the Revolution and recounted tales of Barney, Jones, and the roving privateers of the preceding century. It had been a hard, rough school, but it had developed skilled seamen.

The officers were all practical seamen. In the small United States Navy their promotion had been won mainly by their skill in ship handling and their attention to the drill of their crews, both in seamanship and gunnery. Their mettle had been tried against the French, and at Tripoli their prowess against the Moors had become history. Theodore Roosevelt refers particularly to the officers' devotion to duty and flag.

> Beyond almost any of his countrymen, he [the American naval officer] worshipped the Gridiron Flag and, having been brought up in the Navy, regarded its honor as his own. It was, perhaps, the Navy alone that thought itself a match, ship against ship, for Great Britain. The remainder of the nation pinned its faith to the Army, or rather to that weakest of weak reeds, the Militia. The officers of the Navy, with their strong *esprit de corps*, their jealousy of their own name and record, and the knowledge, by actual experience, that the British ships sailed no faster and were no better handled than their own, had no desire to shirk a conflict with any foe, and having tried their bravery in actual service, they made it doubly formidable by cool, wary skill.

General apathy on the part of the legislative branch of the government caused the little service to band together more closely, to maintain the highest discipline and morale. For in 1808 the Navy had in full commission only one frigate and two smaller vessels. Jefferson did not desire to build a Navy but considered that 257 small defense gunboats could protect the coasts. He wrote to a friend:

> Believing that gunboats are the only water defense which can be useful to us and protect us from the ruinous folly of a Navy, I am pleased with everything which promises to improve them.

The administration of the Navy Department was grossly inefficient for a period of years prior to 1812. When it was proposed to lay up the small Navy in port during the war, it was extremely fortunate for the Navy and the country that Charles Stewart and William Bainbridge were in Washington. Their ardent protests helped to prevent the execution of this policy.

The seamen of this period were as efficient and competent in their spheres as the officers. They were shrewd, bold, and daring. For the most part, their training had been acquired in the Merchant Service, with the exception of a scattering of the man-of-war's men who were in the War of the Revolution, in the two victories of the *Constellation*, and possibly some who were with Decatur when he cut out the *Philadelphia* at Tripoli with a handful of men. These seamen of 1812 already had traditions to live up to. Training and the "sea habit" were theirs. Before entering the service, they had followed their calling in the East India trade, or run the blockade to France with the Baltimore clippers, or sailed in the whalers of New Bedford to the border of the Antarctic. Most of the New Englanders had in their youth been to the Grand Banks after cod and halibut. Sailormen all.

This sturdy stock of the New World may have overemphasized the abstract word "liberty," but they knew it did not lie in impressment on British ships. They detested the British Navy, the British flag, in other words, the system, though they had no particular grudge against those of their own blood, the English seamen.

In general, there was very little difference between the Yankee and British sailor. At that time, they looked much alike and had the same speech. Both English and American seamen were then the boldest, coolest, and most intelligent seamen in the world. Roosevelt comments:

> What choice there was, was in favor of the American. In point of courage there was no difference whatever. The *Essex* and the *Lawrence*, as well as the *Frolic* and the *Reindeer*, were defended with the same stubborn, desperate, cool bravery that marks the English race on both sides of the Atlantic. But the American was a free citizen, anyone's equal, a voter with a personal interest in his country's welfare, and, above all, without the degrading fear of the press gang perpetually before his eyes.

So much for the seamen—what kind of ships did they fight?

Action between the *Constitution* and the *Guerrière*. War of 1812. *Courtesy Naval Historical Foundation.*

The frigates of 1812 did credit to their builders. They were for the most part fast sailers, and in the hands of trained seamen, they were handled with consummate skill. It is true that the American 44-gun frigate was a more formidable ship than the British 38s, but the statement has often been made by British historians, particularly by James, that they were "disguised line of battle ships." This is a misstatement of fact. The smallest line of battle ships of that day, the 74, threw a broadside of 1,032 pounds, while the broadside of the United States frigate *United States* threw a nominal 846 pounds and a real 786 pounds. In fact, the British ship of the line compared to the United States frigate in broadside threw three to two, or two to one. Credit must be given where due, and although it is to the credit of the service and the builders of its ships that the American frigates surpassed the British frigates in armament, it was in the use of the guns that the superiority was marked. Roosevelt goes into detail to compare the weight of broadside, and in their well-known actions he itemizes the guns and carronades and gives the following totals:

Constitution			*Guerrière*	
Broadside, Nominal	736 lb.		Broadside	556 lb.
Real	684 lb.			
United States			*Macedonian*	
Broadside, Nominal	846 lb.		Broadside	547 lb.
Real	786 lb.			
Constitution			*Java*	
Broadside, Nominal	704 lb.		Broadside	576 lb.
Real	654 lb.			

The *Constitution* found the 42-pound carronades too heavy, and in the *Java* action carried carried ten less than in the *Guerrière* action. Long 18s were the largest British guns employed in the above actions against the *United States*'s long 24s. The defeat, however, was actually accomplished by superior seamanship and gunnery on the part of the Americans. This gunnery superiority has been conceded by various British writers. In a comprehensive study and authoritative text on the customs and history of the British seamen, *The British Tar in Fact and Fiction*, by Commander Robinson, RN, and John Leyland, one marks a British opinion:

> After Trafalgar, the Navy stood at the height of its splendour, and its officers felt the fullest confidence in their prowess. They had despised their foes, and when they encountered the young American Navy they despised their new foes also. They had begun to

pay less attention to gunnery, and the failure in this matter, resting partly upon too much pride and self-confidence, prepared the way for many discomfitures. . . . The lesson of the war is so clear that it should be unnecessary to point it out. Two races had met in conflict, each of them high in intelligence, and each of them possessing the true fighting edge, and the victory often went in the single-ship actions to that side which had earned it by thoroughness of preparation. Here we notice also that when equality of fighting power is reached, and ships and squadrons are handled equally well by their officers generally, it is the quality of the gunnery officers and seamen gunners that tells most in the deadly effect of the gunfire, and thus it was that the seamen of the United States, in the War of 1812–15, often with some advantage in the weight of their broadsides, exercised in many of these minor actions the deciding influence for success.

When war had been declared, what went by the name of a Navy Department had done little to meet the approaching crisis. It is unthinkable that a weak Navy such as ours, with war imminent, should have been so widely scattered. With the exception of Commodore John Rodgers's squadron, it would be difficult to conceive of greater naval unpreparedness. The *Constellation, Chesapeake, Adams,* and *John Adams* were out of commission. The *Constitution* was at Annapolis shipping a new crew. But by the twenty-first of June, all of Commodore John Rodgers's squadron was ready with the exception of the *Essex.* The doughty, competent old Commodore's broad command pennant flew on the 44-gun frigate *President.* With him were the *United States* (44), *Congress* (38), *Hornet* (18), and *Argus* (16). We must not forget that Captain Stephen Decatur commanded the *United States* and Lieutenant James Lawrence, the *Hornet.* Rodgers started the cruise and the war by calling all hands to quarters, and in sailor style said:

> Now lads, we have got something to do that will shake the rust from our jackets. War is declared! We shall have another dash at our old enemies. It is the very thing you have long wanted. The rascals have been bullying over us these ten years, and I am glad the time has come when we can have satisfaction.

Rodgers had been watching the situation; he knew that a British convoy from Jamaica had sailed on May 20 and should be off our coast and decided that a bold, powerful stroke should be made at once. By prompt sailing, after concentration on June 21, he missed the orders from the Navy Department to the effect that he establish a patrol on the coast. Some time after this move he wrote:

My calculations were even if I did not succeed in destroying the convoy, that leaving the coast as we did would distract the enemy, oblige him to concentrate a considerable portion of his active navy, and at the same time prevent his single cruisers lying before any of our principal ports, from their not knowing to which and at what moment, we might return.

Frost, in *We Build a Navy*, says: "This idea was an inspiration of genius and stamps Rodgers as the leading strategist of our early Navy."

After the *Constitution* sailed from Annapolis with new gun crews, she fell in with Broke's squadron off the coast. Here the brilliant seamanship of Hull and his first lieutenant, Morris, was displayed in escaping by kedge hauling. When it looked as if escape was impossible, Captain Hull calmly told Lieutenant Morris: "Let's lay broadside to them, Mr. Morris, and fight the whole. If they sink us, we'll go down like men!" However, they cleverly eluded Broke's five ships.

The *Essex* was not ready for sea, and so Captain David Porter did not sail with Rodgers. But Porter's later ventures and long, thrilling cruise in the Pacific fill pages of naval history.

The *Essex* was not properly armed, for instead of the usual 18- or 24-pound long guns, she was given but six long 12s and the rest of the broadside were carronades, a very useful short-range, point-blank gun, but of no use for long-range work. Porter protested, but the Navy Department of the day refused to change the armament.

But here we gain a useful lesson, a fine tradition. After protest and recommendation to improve the commands, the sea officers of that day redoubled their efforts to make the most of what they had. This Porter did. He knew that with his carronades he would have to fight close action and attempt whenever possible to carry the day by boarding. Farragut, a midshipman on board, wrote:

> Every day the crew was exercised at the great guns, small arms, and single stick. And I may mention here the fact that I have never been on board a ship where the crew of the old *Essex* was represented but that I found them to be the best swordsmen on board. They had been so thoroughly trained as boarders that every man was prepared for such an emergency, with his cutlass as sharp as a razor, a dirk made by the ship's armourer out of a file, and a pistol.

Porter's officers and crew always reflected splendid training and constant drill. This is the David Porter who, after the shortcomings of Jeffersonian naval policy were apparent, said:

The vital error, if not criminal neglect of the government, is in not introducing the naval element into the Navy Department. Experienced officers would have avoided the terrible mistakes which have been committed within my recollection, and we would have had now such a respectable force of frigates that Great Britain would not have dared to go to war with us, for fear of having her commerce destroyed. Thirty frigates on our side would make her respect us.

What is the result of ponderous moral pretensions without power? Upon whom will the blame rest when a navy has to fight that has been made purposely inadequate? To reflect upon such questions, to counsel and to recommend, is certainly the duty of the service, today as it was in 1815.

One of the most decisive and intense frigate duels in our history occurred during the twenty-five minutes that it took Hull in the *Constitution* to dismast and defeat the *Guerrière*, commanded by the gallant Dacres. This victory was the sea-Saratoga of the War of 1812; it bolstered the administration, raised the morale of the people, and gave the Navy a high mark at which to shoot.

Much inspiration for the officer of today may be derived from an examination of the action of Captain Hull. Smith, a gun sponger, who wrote the most vivid narrative extant of the action, said:

> Hull was now all animation. He saw the decisive moment had come. With great energy, yet calmness of manner, he passed around among the officers and men, addressing to them words of confidence and encouragement. "Men," said he, "now do your duty. Your officers cannot have entire command over you now. Each man must do all in his power for his country." The Stars and Stripes never floated more proudly than they did at that moment. All was silent beneath them, save the occasional order from an officer, or the low sound of the movement of our implements of war! *Every man stood firm, to his post.*

News was widespread of the *Constitution-Guerrière* action. The London *Times* wrote: "Never before in the history of the world did an English frigate strike to an American." John Paul Jones's victory should not have been forgotten so soon, for not only did the *Serapis* strike but Jones sailed away in her after seeing his command, the *Bon Homme Richard*, sink with colors flying.

For high adventure of the Captain Hornblower school, one should read of that grand old sailor Barney, of Baltimore, who started a pri-

vateering cruise in the Baltimore schooner *Rossie*. Barney's capture of
the *General Monk* in the War of the Revolution and a review of his
sea career of forty years compel one to conclude that he was a master
seaman and an officer who feared nothing. Barney had the distinction
of serving in two wars, as well as in the navy of France. He was perhaps at his best as a privateersman, for once in eleven days he captured
twelve ships.

Barney left a comfortable farm to seek adventure. At the age of
sixteen he commanded a merchantman in the Mediterranean, at which
time a Spanish admiral forced him to join in an attack on Algiers. He
served in the state navies of Maryland and Pennsylvania, and the Federal Navy. Not only did he command many private ships, but at the
time of the French Revolution accepted a commission in the French
Navy as *chef de division des armées navales*, and for this received severe censure in the United States.

Benjamin Franklin was extremely fond of him and presented him
at the court of Versailles where he kissed the cheek of Marie Antoi-
nette and dined with Louis XVI. At another time he had a private
audience with Napoleon and "saluted the hand of the Empress Jose-
phine." Barney was a faithful friend of Robert Morris in his days of
adversity. Always a close friend of John Paul Jones, the intrepid Barney once accompanied him across the Atlantic for a landing in Plymouth, England. As a commodore in the French Navy in 1798, he
became the friend and adviser of Toussaint L'Ouverture, the celebrated
black dictator of Haiti. After visiting the Washingtons at Mount
Vernon, he accompanied General and Mrs. Washington to the in-
augural ceremonies in New York City, a duty that gives him the honor
of being the first naval aide of a president of the United States.

The remarkable Barney fought in seventeen battles in the Revolution, and in nine in the War of 1812, with a score of twenty-five victories. He was successful in all but the last battle—the so-called battle
of Bladensburg, Maryland—a fight to defend Washington. There, with
a small detachment of bluejackets and marines, the doughty commodore "held his ground against a rush of British troops which scattered
General Winder and his militia like chaff before the wind."[2]

As much at ease on a horse as on the quarterdeck, he had a mount
shot under him at Bladensburg and there received British lead in the
thigh that he carried to the grave. Always seeking new adventures, he

[2] Albert Gleaves, U. S. Naval Institute *Proceedings*, January 1925, p. 174.

started with his family to take possession of extensive lands he owned on the wild Kentucky frontier but died en route and was buried at Pittsburgh. As a skillful, courageous sea fighter and maker of naval tradition few have been his equal.

Next came Decatur in the *United States* and the capture of the *Macedonian*. It was a long-range gunnery duel in contrast to Hull's close action in the *Guerrière* fight. The *United States* and the *Macedonian* compared in size and armament with the *Constitution* and *Guerrière*. By the system of British tonnage measurements, the *Constitution* was 1,426 tons to 1,338 for the *Guerrière*. The Yankees carried 24 pounders while the British considered 18 pounders more effective. The United States frigates were about one inch thicker. The British considered that the increased weight would make clumsy sailors. But a seaman's heart must have thrilled at Decatur's seamanship and maneuvers in the *Macedonian* duel. British gunnery was very poor and in ninety minutes Decatur had inflicted 104 casualties. With eleven casualties in the *United States*, Decatur achieved a decisive victory.

Bainbridge commanding the *Constitution* fought the *Java* in probably the fiercest action of the "second war for American Independence." Bainbridge was badly wounded but kept his station on deck. Lieutenant Aylwin fell with wounds that caused his death—Aylwin who saw also the battle ensign of the *Guerrière* lowered. Another Yankee victory! Bainbridge was feted in Boston. "Old Ironsides" was laid up for overhaul and the British Admiralty issued orders that British frigates were not to engage American 44s in single action.

Then came the occasion for James Lawrence's immortal slogan that became the battle cry of the Golden Age: "Don't give up the ship!" The criticism of Lawrence's judgment in fighting the *Shannon* under the able Broke will not be discussed. There is a variance of opinion. Suffice it to say that Lawrence was a chivalrous soul, as ambitious as a Nelson, as brave as John Paul Jones. He landed with Porter in Tripoli; he made that hazardous climb over the *Philadelphia*'s side with Stephen Decatur; he thirsted for fame and the superiority of American arms. Broke was a brilliant and competent captain. After devastating and superior gunfire, Broke boarded the *Chesapeake*. His men were seasoned and experienced; Lawrence had taken over a new ship, and there had been little drill together. He did not have a team.

Lawrence fell mortally wounded. After being carried below to the cockpit, he cried out: "Go on deck, and order them to fire faster and to fight the ship till she sinks; never strike, let the colors wave while I live." When he knew that the defeat was decisive, he said over and over again: "Don't give up the ship, blow her up."

The fighting had been fierce, and 146 Yankees had been killed or wounded; Lawrence lived four days after the action and, in intense suffering of mind and body, kept saying "Don't give up the ship." Nevertheless, the *Chesapeake* was captured, and he died aboard.

What indomitable courage, what devotion to duty! Nelsonian in every attribute. Before his death he talked to his officers of why he failed. Washington Irving wrote:

> It was thus he devoted the last of his moments to usefulness and instruction, teaching his friends how to improve upon his precedent, showing the survivors the way out of the wreck to rise.

Lawrence left us a double tradition, the willingness to fight against superior odds and the realization that an officer's greatness often lies in his willingness to admit mistakes, so that others may profit by the lessons of experience.

Next, we lost the *Argus* to the British *Pelican*. Allen, the American captain, had poor gunners; he had not devoted enough time to drills. In the first few minutes, a shot tore off Allen's leg. He fell, but by raising up from the deck, he continued to give orders. He fainted, his life blood ebbing, and he died at his post. His ship was taken by boarding; the crew left their posts, one of the few times recorded in all our naval history. It is a blot on their record, this leaving their posts by the crew. The captain died at his.

The American *Enterprise* met the *Boxer*. Both ships were evenly matched. Captain Blyth of the *Boxer* was killed in the first few minutes of action. Burrows was mortally wounded, and he too lay on the quarterdeck voicing the tradition of Lawrence, repeating that the colors must not be struck. Just before his death, Burrows received the sword of the enemy and said, "I am satisfied, I die contented."

Each captain did his duty, and each died as a promising naval career seemed to loom ahead. Burrows, the American, and Blyth, the Englishman, were buried side by side at Portland, Maine.

Finally, there was brave Macdonough on Lake Champlain. After this action, Sir George Prevost hastily returned to Canada, and the northern frontier was never again seriously menaced. There is little doubt that Macdonough's decisive victory strongly affected the peace negotiations.

After a detailed and comprehensive study of Macdonough in the *Naval War of 1812*, Theodore Roosevelt said:

> But Macdonough in this battle won a higher fame than any other commander of the war, British or American. He had a decidedly superior force to contend against, the officers and men of the two

sides being about on a par in every respect; and it was solely owing to his foresight and resource that he won the victory. He forced the British to engage at a disadvantage by his excellent choice of position; and he prepared beforehand for every possible contingency. His personal prowess had already been shown at the cost of the rovers of Tripoli. . . . His skill, seamanship, quick eye, readiness of resource, and indomitable pluck are beyond all praise. Down to the time of the Civil War, his is the greatest figure in our naval history. A thoroughly religious man, he was as generous and humane as he was skillful and brave; one of the greatest of our sea captains, he has left a stainless name behind him.

We had defeats, losing the *Chesapeake*, the *Essex*, and the *President*. But Chauncey made history on Lake Ontario, while the twenty-seven-year-old Perry prepared his squadron on Lake Erie. We know of no better conclusion to this sketch of a golden age than Perry's victory after the conference with his captains in the *Lawrence*. He brought back a flag that hangs today in a conspicuous place of honor at the U. S. Naval Academy. It is of blue, with rough white muslin letters, the words thereon being those of the chivalrous Lawrence, "DON'T GIVE UP THE SHIP"—it was the battle signal and hoisted at the beginning of the engagement in the lake. Perry won, but only after losing four-fifths of the crew of his flagship, the *Lawrence*, and after transferring in an openboat to the *Niagara* with this now historic battle flag. The Canadians, English, and some of French extraction "fought as well but no better than the Americans," wrote Theodore Roosevelt. Frost appropriately says in his detailed study of the War of 1812: "Ah! what a battle flag to fight under! Every vessel of our Navy should today carry an exact copy of this famous flag to be hoisted before going into action."

Some of the outstanding actions of this heroic age of the Navy have been presented. Mistakes were certainly made, some of them glaring ones, but we are concerned here with the motives that inspired the service and their total effect on the outcome of the war. The greater tradition is not the advisability of action on Lawrence's part, but rather how he fought and how he died.

The spirit of the offensive, a cardinal principle of war, was not new to the officers of 1812. It was in a great measure a heritage from the War of the Revolution. For example, when Captain Pearson testified at his court-martial for losing the *Serapis* to John Paul Jones, he stated:

Long before the close of the action, it became clearly apparent that the American ship dominated by a command will of the most unalterable resolution, and there could be no doubt that the intention of her commander was, if he could not conquer to sink alongside. And this desperate resolve of the American captain was fully shared and fiercely seconded by every one of his ship's company.

> *Why even death stands still,*
> *And waits an hour sometimes*
> *for such a will.*

Such a gallant service tradition lived on. More than three decades after Jones, Stephen Decatur in his report to the Secretary of the Navy relative to the capture of the *Macedonian* declared:

> The enthusiasm of every officer, seaman, and marine on board this ship on discovering the enemy—their steady conduct in battle, the precision of their fire could not be surpassed. Where all met my fullest expectations, it would be unjust in me to discriminate.[3]

Could a sea captain demand or expect more?

In summary, the United States Navy in 1812–13 won at sea because it demonstrated that a well-drilled navy, although small, can win single-ship actions against the detached units of superior sea power; and that American frigates were as well constructed and fitted out as any in the world. This war accentuated and conclusively proved that accuracy in gunnery is largely dependent upon drill and practice at sea. A majority of the sailors in the frigates, brigs, schooners, and flotillas on the Great Lakes were trained in the hard school of the merchant ship.[4]

Keeping the Yankee flag flying at sea when pitted against a vastly superior navy was a *tour de force* unsurpassed. Fenimore Cooper speaks of "that aptitude of the American character for the sea" in his account

---

[3] Report of Stephen Decatur to the Hon. Paul Hamilton, written at sea, October 30, 1812.

[4] James's *Naval History of Great Britain* speaks of Commodore Perry picking his crews in the vessels on the lakes. Roosevelt refutes this and states that Perry had once sent in his resignation on account of the poor quality of his crews and had with difficulty been induced to withdraw it. It seems that Perry's men were not up to the standard of the blue-water American sailor. Many of the officers learned their seamanship and gunnery in privateers. A number of the officers and men were engaged in the short war at sea with France; others had fought the corsairs of the Barbary Coast. Sailors learn their duties on oceans, and there is no known substitute for "the sea habit."

of the War of 1812. This is true, but one must not forget that we were fighting a nation which practiced impressment, and American sailors would fight to the end to resist the exercise of that practice. Moreover, freedom was more precious than security! And never would they relinquish their recently hard-won liberties.

Things that men fight for must never be underestimated. It is characteristic of golden ages to be marked by definite ideals, and the great military-naval periods by a fervent belief in cause. This was true of the War of 1812. In short, it was a willingness to resist all in defense of the political principles upon which the new republic was founded that engendered the high moral and physical courage which spurred a small navy fearlessly to combat the world's largest and most seasoned sea power. The victories at sea greatly enhanced the prestige of the United States in the world.

Cooper further observes that "A stern discipline, a high moral tone, rare models in seamanship, active warfare, the means of comparison, and a spirit of emulation that is sure to carry the national character to the highest level, whenever the national energies can be permitted to exhibit themselves, had conspired to produce this end."

PART IV

The Sea

CHAPTER 8

The United States
Marine Corps

Semper Fidelis
First to Fight
When they aren't fighting they're working.
General Ben H. Fuller, USMC

There was one thing that won this battle . . . and that was the
superior courage of the Marines.
General Julian Smith, USMC

Come on you crazy s-o-bs. Do you want to live forever?[1]

RIGOROUS METHODS OF SELECTION, tough realistic training, and a pride in corps that stems from traditions of past glory have given to the United States Marine Corps its enviable and well-justified reputation as an elite corps. There has been a continuity and consistency of performance from the days of John Paul Jones in the *Bon Homme Richard* with his marines under Lieutenant Stack in 1779, to the heroic fight out of the grim trap of the Changjin Reservoir by marines under "Chesty" Puller, "Big Foot" Brown, and O. P. Smith of the First Division in Korea in the dreadful winter of 1952.

The glorious heritage of the Marine Corps is not only a part of the nation's tradition of military valor and victory but also reflects the

---

[1] Gunnery Sergeant Dan Daly, USMC, to his platoon, Belleau Wood, June, 1918. Gunnery Sergeant Daly as an enlisted man won two Medals of Honor, the Navy Cross, the Distinguished Service Cross, and three French decorations. He is said to have told the press afterwards in Paris, "Why, you know a non-com would never use bad language. I said: 'For goodness' sake, you chaps, let us advance against the foe!'"

141

spirit of the people and the history of America. As General Lemuel C. Shepherd, Jr., Marine Corps Commandant, said when he presented the Marine Corps memorial to the American people on November 10, 1954: "The five marines and the sailor depicted are, themselves, only a symbol. The men do not represent just the Marine Corps—nor is this a monument to war.

"To all who shall ever review this memorial—it will speak of the courage, the spirit, and the greatness of the American people—the people from whom these men and their ageless comrades came."

The Flag of Victory. On February 23, 1945, five U.S. Marines and a U.S. Navy hospital corpsman raised their battle flag on Mount Suribachi, Iwo Jima.

Tarawa was a typical Marine Corps amphibious action. Marine Major General Julian T. Smith (lower right) escorts Admiral Nimitz (behind him) and Army General Richardson (to his left) across a portion of the battle field.

Marines have a venerable history that in duties and general mission shows little variation throughout the centuries. There have been changes in weapons and extent of operations, but marines have been landing as sea soldiers from ships of war on foreign shores since the dawn of recorded history. It is written that the marines of Phoenicia, Egypt, Greece, Carthage, and Rome had duties similar to those of the marines of today; that because they were the soldiers on board fighting ships, they were usually the spearhead in all landing operations. Although the Royal British Marines were not organized until 1664, some of their ancestors may have been forced by Roman marines to serve under the eagles of Julius Caesar before the Christian Era. British-American colonial marines (Lawrence Washington, brother of George Washington, was one) served under Admiral "Grog" Vernon, RN, at Cartagena and in Cuba in 1741. A marine was closely associated with the first battle of the Revolution; for when Major Pitcairn, RBM, cried out at Concord, "Disperse, you rebels," there followed immediately the "shot heard around the world."[2]

It was on October 5, 1775, that the Continental Congress first referred to "marines." Because of the thousands of marines then serving in armed vessels of the states as well as in privateers, Congress created an *organization* or corps of marines. After the war of the Revolution, the Army, Navy, and the Corps of Marines were, for reasons of national economy, completely disbanded and discharged from all duties. Afterwards Congress authorized a number of marines as part of the complement of every vessel ordered to be constructed during the period of 1794–98. It was on July 11, 1798, that John Adams and Congress officially created the modern organization known as the United States Marine Corps. The headquarters was moved in 1800 from Philadelphia to Washington.

The Marine Corps has always been a military organization which, with the exception of services rendered by the Navy such as medical and dental assistance, and the Judge Advocate General's Department, has administered itself completely.

General Ben H. Fuller wrote:

> The Marine Corps is an element or unit of the naval service and normally subject to the laws and regulations established for the government of the Navy, but Marine Corps Headquarters is not an intimate part of the Navy Department in the same sense as the Bureau of Navigation, or bureaus of the Navy Department. The Marine Corps is a military organization (composed of soldiers trained to the ways of the sea) adapted to naval conditions. The Corps is always available for immediate use at the direction of the Secretary of the Navy acting for the President.

In 1954, Secretary of the Navy Robert Anderson termed the Marine Corps a "unique but not separate service." The Chief of Naval Operations as the senior military officer of the naval establishment has been delegated by the Secretary with responsibility for certain Marine Corps matters, but in the new policy the Marine Corps Commandant

---

[2] Each year on March 1, the U. S. Marine Corps sends anniversary greetings to the British Regiment, the Royal Welsh Fusiliers, commemorating the friendship established when that regiment and the first Marine Regiment served together in China, in 1900, in the Boxer Rebellion. When General John J. Pershing, on June 10, 1917, as the Commander of American Forces, stepped on British soil from the gangplank of the steamer *Baltic*, the guard of honor was the 23rd Foot, the Royal Welsh Fusiliers; a regiment that under Lord Cornwallis had fought with "uncommon gallantry" against the Continental Army at Yorktown, Virginia, before the surrender in 1781.

will be directly responsible to the Secretary of the Navy. The only marine units placed under Navy command are those on duty aboard ships or attached to Navy shore stations. The Commandant of the Marine Corps sits with the Joint Chiefs of Staff in consideration of all matters.

The marines have participated in all the wars of their country—the Revolution (1775–83), French Naval War (1798–1801), war with Algiers (1805), War of 1812, war with West Indian pirates (1818–30), war with Florida Indians (1835–42), Mexican War (1846–48), Civil War (1861–65), war with Spain (1898), Chinese Boxer War (1900), Philippine Insurrection (1899–1904), World War I (1917–18), World War II (1941–45), Korean War (1950–53), and most recently in Vietnam.

The Marine Corps has also served directly under the Army. This authority is set forth in the Revised Statutes wherein it provides that

> the Marine Corps shall at all times be subject to the laws and regulations established for the government of the Navy, except when detached for service with the Army by orders of the President; and when so detached they shall be subject to the rules and articles of war prescribed for the government of the Army.

By this or similar provision, the Marine Corps had units at the Battle of Princeton in the Revolution; the Battle of Bladensburg and Battle of New Orleans in the Second War with Great Britain; in the Florida Indian Wars of 1836–37, when the Commandant of Marines commanded the "Fighting Brigade" of the Army of the South; at the capture of the forts of Vera Cruz, the heights of Chapultepec, and Mexico City in the Mexican War; in the Army of Cuban Pacification, 1906–09; in Mexico in 1914; with the American Expeditionary Forces in France, Belgium, Luxemburg, and Germany; and in World War II and the Korean War. The terrible fight of 7,500 leathernecks at Belleau Wood in France will be remembered together with Guadalcanal, Tarawa, Iwo Jima, and Okinawa as long as there is a United States Marine Corps.

The story of the minor wars and landings of the marines throughout their history is already the subject of many books. The international police duties, such as the twenty years in Haiti; the rendering of aid at earthquakes, fires, and other catastrophes; the supervision of elections in Central America; the administration of foreign states; and the guarding of United States mail has demonstrated the versatility, competency, and efficiency of this alert combatant organization. In addition, the United States Marine Corps is probably the most completely prepared of any similar organization in the world, in respect to plans and state of readiness for landing operations. Just a week after the North Koreans crossed the 38th parallel, General of the Army MacArthur requested the immediate dispatch of marines. They are specialists in amphibious warfare, initial seizures, assaults, and defense of advanced bases—and they are *ready*.[3]

It is difficult for one not a member of the Marine Corps to understand all the subtle factors that make for its high *esprit de corps*. Some of these imponderables were tersely expressed by one of the bravest warriors of their thrilling history, General John A. Lejeune:

> The willing, thorough-going, and practical devotion of the marine to the cause of his Navy, and of his country, is perpetuated in his motto *Semper Fidelis*, and represents his most sacred tradition. We have always appreciated the superior importance of personnel over material. That famed *esprit de corps* attributed to the marines is but an evidence of the constantly increasing recognition
>
> of the importance of personnel over the material, more especially that quality of personnel animated by a general spirit of faith in, and loyalty to, the organization and its purposes. No improvement in its material can outdistance in importance such a quality.

It was this superb quality of marine personnel that gave the marines their clear-cut victories. They had luck also; for example, in World War I they were placed as a great fighting outfit on the front at critical times and in critical places. Military historians say that when the American 18th Division, the American 2d Division, and the Moroccan 18th Division attacked south of Soissons on July 18, 1918, the war was lost on that day to the Central Empires.

One dreads to think what might have happened if Vandegrift had lost Guadalcanal. The marines get the tough assignments, and their success is attained by discipline, expert rifle, machine gun, and bayonet tactics, and the iron will to win; in short, select personnel, high standards of training and unsurpassed morale. The marines are justly proud that their name is written on the battle flags of the American 2d Divi-

---

[3] When Secretary of the Navy Frank Knox awarded the Distinguished Service Medal to General Holland Smith, USMC, the citation read: "He laid the groundwork for amphibious training of practically all American units, including at various times the First and Third Marine Divisions, the First, Seventh, and Ninth Infantry Divisions of the Army and numerous other Marine Corps and Army personnel. His proficient leadership and tireless energy in the development of high combat efficiency among the forces under his supervision were in keeping with the highest traditions of the United States Naval Service."

sion, and words fail to express their deep sentiment and pride in the thirty-four battle streamers carried on the Marine Corps flag.

Great traditions exact a heavy toll of self-sacrifice. For example, the casualties of the Marine Brigade in France were over 55 percent.

> Such things carry little meaning except to men who can remember the dreadful wheat field to the west of Belleau Wood, and shrapnel-flailed slopes between Blanc Mont and St. Etienne, and the line of dead engineers on the path between the heights of the Meuse near Pouilly and the place where the bridge was the last night of the war.
>
> For the rest there is transmitted a certain old blood-stained glory, peculiarly of the marines and of the United States naval service. That was the Marine Brigade.[4]

It takes self-sacrifice to win wars. At Guadalcanal, the bitter jungle fight to hold Henderson Field was won after six months of battle at a cost ashore of 6,111 American casualties, army and marine, including 1,752 killed or missing in action. The United States Navy won Guadalcanal in a costly struggle.

In November 1943 at Tarawa 685 marines were killed, 77 died of wounds, 169 were missing, and about 2,100 were wounded.

And at Iwo Jima, one of the most viciously fought battles in history, ending March 26, 1945, 6,821 Americans died, of whom 5,931 were marines, and another 19,217 were wounded, to win that seven-and-a-half square miles of volcanic ash and rocks.

At Okinawa, in an eighty-two day operation that broke Japan's back, there were 49,000 total American battle casualties of which about 12,500 were killed or missing. Thirty-six American ships were sunk and 368 were damaged. In this costly, hard-fought battle, the Japanese suffered severely: 110,000 killed and about 7,400 taken prisoner. About 7,800 planes were knocked down by American fighters and antiaircraft fire. The splendid cooperation of the Army and Marine Corps in this decisive battle is a matter of special comment by military historians. In this epic operation the Navy took higher casualties than at any comparable period in its history, with 4,907 killed and 4,824 wounded.

In World War II combat, 727 officers and 12,565 men of the U.S. Marine Corps were killed, and a total of 63,611 wounded in action. Marines do not talk about it much, but one may be assured that they never forget the sacrifices that win the battles, and give the Corps "that certain old blood-stained glory."

---

[4] Major John W. Thomason, Jr., USMC, "The Marine Brigade," U.S. Naval Institute *Proceedings*, November 1928, pp. 963–68.

How are men trained, if necessary, to die and to maintain such high standards of discipline? In all training, marine instructors, usually veterans who have fought their "country's battles on the land as on the sea" stress initiative of the individual along with intelligent team work. Officers and men learn the job of the next higher billet, how immediately to fill the shoes of certain seniors, if the occasion arises in action. Certainly, this doctrine has led to standards of training that have educated the junior and the noncommissioned officers of the Marine Corps to a degree of military *savoir faire* probably unequalled, definitely unsurpassed, by those of any comparable organization in the world. This can also be said of the enlisted men after they have received the standard training.

While many of its leaders had much to do with directing its destiny, its outstanding *esprit de corps* has grown up and been maintained largely through the efforts of its rank and file. While the noncommissioned of the organization are not as frequently mentioned as the commissioned officers, they maintain its efficiency and fighting spirit, especially in times of great stress.

In no service have splendid traditions of heroic exploits and old tales of victory been more jealously cherished, and in none is the common heritage more widely shared. It also is a part of the naval tradition, and with the Navy lies the Corps' most promising future, firmly built upon an affiliation and association that has lasted for nearly two hundred years.

One may still hear the old saw, "Tell it to the marines." But when it comes time *to do*, one may be assured that the job will be done with the determination and efficiency implicit in the message scrawled for higher authority by Marine Captain Myers in the Boxer War at the siege of Peking. He wrote: "*We will do our best.*" And the world has come to know that there is no better *best*.

SOME FIRSTS AND OTHER INCIDENTS IN
MARINE CORPS HISTORY

> Their greatest accomplishment has been to transmit "their temper and character and viewpoint and tradition" to successive generations. This is the most difficult of all military training missions—to make the glories and durable disciplines of the past part of the living principles of a changing present.[5]

[5] Hanson Baldwin, "Homage to the Marines," *New York Times,* November 11, 1954.

November 1775

Upon the establishment of the marines by congressional resolution on November 10, 1775, Captain Samuel Nicholas was ordered to recruit two battalions of marines with the specification that personnel selected be "good seamen or so acquainted with maritime affairs as to be able to serve to advantage at sea."[6]

A Corps of Marines was authorized by the Act of July 11, 1798, which provided for an organization of: "one major, four captains, sixteen first lieutenants, twelve second lieutenants, forty-eight sergeants, forty-eight corporals, thirty-two drums and fifes, and seven hundred and twenty privates, including marines who had been enlisted." The first headquarters were opened August 23, 1798, at a camp near Philadelphia with William Ward Burrows, appointed by President John Adams, as the Major Commandant.

December 1775

The first U. S. Marine Corps unit was the detachment on board the *Cabot*, December 1775, as part of the naval squadron under Commodore Esek Hopkins, first Commander in Chief at sea.

October 1776

First American marines in European waters during the Revolution were those aboard the *Reprisal*, which took Benjamin Franklin to France in 1776 and later captured several British prizes. A unit fought under John Paul Jones in 1779, in the *Serapis-Bonhomme Richard* fight when on demand for surrender, Jones gave the immortal reply: "I have not yet begun to fight."

March 1776

In their 181 years of service, the marines have made more than 200 landings on foreign shores. As Continental Marines they made their first amphibious landing and thereby captured Fort Montague on the island of New Providence, in the Bahamas.

January 1777

A marine battalion accompanied George Washington when he crossed the Delaware near Trenton, New Jersey, and afterward it fought in the Second Battle of Trenton and the Battle of Princeton.

---

[6] The original two-story Tun Tavern building where the two battalions were recruited was on Water Street between Market and Chestnut. The Marine Corps War Memorial Foundation has laid the foundation for a reconstruction of this famous building, just a couple of blocks south of the original site, on S.E. Spruce and Mattis Streets, Philadelphia, Pa.

Sharpshooting Marine riflemen dominate the action between the USS *Wasp* and the HMS *Reindeer*, 1814.

April 1805

Lieutenant Presley N. O'Bannon commanded the marines who hoisted the American flag over the Barbary fortress at Derna, Tripoli. This was the first and only time (prior to World War I) that the American flag was flown over an "Old World" fort, or on the continent of Africa.

September 1814

After the national Capitol was burned and partially destroyed by the British, Congress moved into Blodgett's Hotel, Washington, D.C., and the legislators were guarded by the marines.

January 1815

A detachment of marines commanded by Major Daniel Carmick, USMC, fought under General Andrew Jackson at the battle of New Orleans.

July 1846

Marines raised the American flag over the custom house at Monterey, California, and took possession from the Mexican commandant.

September 1847

Under the supreme command of General Winfield Scott, marines participated in the capture and storming of the Castle of Chapultepec. A part of a company of marines under Captain George H. Terrett, which operated as a unit with a detachment of soldiers under Lieutenant U.S. Grant, captured the San Cosme gate of the city of Mexico and technically were the first troops to enter the stronghold. The detachment was ordered to retire from the exposed position, but after a reorganization of troops, marines took part in the major successful assault of the gates and the formal entry.

Next day the "mud-spattered and blood-stained" troops moved on to the Plaza where a line was formed to render honors to General Scott and the American flag hoisted over the National Palace—"The Halls of Montezuma."

"It was during the battle of Chapultepec," wrote Colonel Clyde H. Metcalf, USMC, "that the fighting spirit of the American Army probably reached the highest pitch of determination and willingness to do or die that it has ever attained."

1853 and 1854

Marines accompanied Commodore Matthew C. Perry's two Far East expeditions that resulted in the "opening of Japan."

October 1859

A detachment of marines under Colonel Robert E. Lee, USA, captured John Brown at Harpers Ferry.

March 1861

A Confederate Marine Corps was organized in Richmond, Virginia.

July 1861

Marines participated in the first battle of Bull Run.

May 1898

The American Flag was first raised over the Philippines by a detachment of marines that took possession of Cavite.

June 1898

During the Spanish-American War, the first landing in Cuba was made by Huntington's Battalion of Marines at Guantánamo Bay.

May 1900

Marines first assigned to guard the American Legation in Peking, China.

1904–05

Marines assigned as Legation Guard at Seoul, Korea.

A brigade of marines occupied for more than eight years the Dominican Republic, and provided the force for military intervention in Haiti for approximately twenty years, 1914–1934.[7] As a result of interventions in Nicaragua and at the request of the Nicaraguan government, a Nicaraguan constabulary "on a non-partisan basis, to be commanded by American officers" was organized. The old Guardia was reorganized by the marines and became the Guardia Nacional de Nicaragua, a military organization under officers of the Marine Corps that in eleven years had approximately 510 encounters with bands of outlaws. It has been estimated that the Guardia killed well over a thousand bandits, capturing and driving out of the country a large number, with a loss to the Guardia of about 200 killed or wounded.

The tune of *The Marine's Hymn*, first sung after the Mexican War of 1847, is that of an old Spanish folk song. It is also a melody in Jacques Offenbach's French comic opera *Geneviève de Brabant*. The U. S. Marine Band, known as "The President's Own" and which has played for all important social occasions at the White House and for every president since Thomas Jefferson, is credited with having, in 1908, the custom of always standing at attention throughout the playing of *The Star Spangled Banner*. Audiences soon followed suit. John Philip Sousa when he was leader of the U. S. Marine Band played his *Washington Post March* for the first time on June 15, 1889.

World War I

In recognition of the gallant action of the marines at Belleau Wood, June 1918, the French changed the name of the sector to the Bois de la Brigade de Marines. In the last bitter days of the war that included the crossing of the Meuse river, the Marine Brigade from November 1 until the Armistice Day on the 11th suffered losses of 323 killed and

---

[7] In 1959, a small marine military mission returned to Haiti at the request of the Haitian government.

1,109 wounded. Two Marine Corps regiments, the 5th Marines and 6th Marines, received the French Fourragère for valorous service.

In World War I, the Marine Corps reached a maximum strength of 75,101, which included approximately 250 "Marinettes" or Women Marines. In World War II, the peak strength of 485,113 was reached on August 31, 1945, of which over 22,000 were Women Reserves.

World War II

In World War II, marines were stationed on board over 500 ships of the U. S. Navy. Also, there are some little-known but impressive percentages that officially show that over 96 percent of the male officer personnel and 89 percent of the male enlisted personnel served overseas during World War II.

The above facts about the U. S. Marine Corps bespeak a colorful, historic past through which runs an unbroken golden thread of heroism, devotion to duty, and a "blood-stained glory" that should inspire generations of men yet unborn.

CHAPTER 9

Some Traditions, Ceremonies, Customs, and Usages of the Service

The worth of a sentiment lies in the sacrifices men will make for its sake. All ideals are built on the ground of solid achievement, which in a given profession creates in the course of time a certain tradition, or in other words a standard of conduct.

Joseph Conrad

I should like to emphasize the confidence that our citizens have in their first line of defense. It is a faith of free men in the defenders of the democratic tradition; it is a trust that our citizens repose in a Navy that has never failed its country.[1]

Franklin D. Roosevelt

Hold the traditions which ye have been taught.

II Thessalonians

IN CHAPTER I the relationships of traditions, customs, ceremonies, and usages were set forth. Some of our best-known, established naval customs and ceremonies originated in antiquity; others grew from practices in the Middle Ages; and the great Age of Discovery passed on ceremonies and customs that have become naval regulations.

The following are the more commonly known traditions, customs, ceremonies, and usages of our naval service. These customs are a part of the naval profession; to overemphasize them is a mistake; to underestimate them displays a lack of perspective. For, as Bacon said in regard to ceremonies:

[1] In Navy Day letter to the Acting Secretary of the Navy, October 26, 1939.

Not to use ceremonies at all is to teach others not to use them
again, and so diminish the respect to himself; especially, they ought
not to be omitted to strangers and formal natures; but the dwell-
ing upon them, and exalting them above the moon, is not only
tedious, but doth diminish the faith and credit of him that speaks.

It is by the proper employment of dignified ceremony that discipline
and order are buttressed to a degree that is not to be underestimated.

A NEW NAVY IN A NEW WORLD

From the British Navy came the greater share of the American Navy's
first usages and written regulations. This was true particularly in the
early regulations, *Articles for the Government of the Navy*, and ship's
organization. John Adams, in drafting the first regulations, was influenced by the logic of modeling his draft on the instructions and tried
regulations of the largest, most powerful Navy in the world at the
time. In a study of American traditions and customs of the sea, one
must ever turn to the archives of maritime Britain for valuable source
material; in fact, "The Father of the U. S. Navy" was born a British
subject.

THE FATHER OF THE NAVY
JOHN PAUL JONES 1747–1792 UNITED STATES NAVY
HE GAVE OUR NAVY ITS EARLIEST TRADITIONS OF HEROISM AND VICTORY
ERECTED BY CONGRESS
A.D. 1912.[2]

As might be expected of him who wrote after the Revolutionary
War that "In time of peace it is necessary to prepare, and be always
prepared for war by sea," Jones gave profound thought to matters
affecting the defense of the country and proffered much constructive
criticism when the U. S. Navy was founded. In 1776, Jones wrote:

I propose not our enemies as an example for our general imitation,
yet, as their Navy [British] is the best regulated of any in the
world, we must in some degree imitate them, and aim at such further improvement as may one day make ours vie with, and exceed
theirs.

Again, in 1782, Jones wrote to the United States Minister of Marine: "We are a young people, and need not be ashamed to ask advice
from nations older and more experienced in marine matters than our-

---

[2] Inlaid in letters of bronze near his marble sarcophagus in the Crypt of the
Naval Academy Chapel at Annapolis, Maryland.

selves." The letter was prompted by Jones's plea that the *Navy Regulations* of 1775 be modified. He strongly urged that all captains of the line should be tacticians, with emphasis on what could be learned at the time from the Navy of France.

SALUTING THE QUARTERDECK AND THE COLORS

It is generally believed that the salute to the quarterdeck is derived from the very early seagoing custom of the respect and obeisance that all paid to the pagan altar on board ship—and later to the crucifix and shrine. There are a few competent authorities on customs and traditions who do not fully support this belief, but trace the custom to the early days of the British Navy when all officers who were present on the quarterdeck returned the first salute of the individual by uncovering. (The original personal salute consisted of uncovering.) Nevertheless, the majority opinion is that it was a salute to the seat of authority, the quarterdeck, the place nearest the colors. At any rate, it is definitely established that genuflections and obeisances were made to pagan shrines aboard the ship in the days of Greek, Roman, and Carthaginian sea power—the gods of the sea were frequently propitiated. With the advent of Christianity, the same respect was paid the shrine of the Virgin. The flags of the suzerain or sovereign became in time symbolical of the religion of the state and emblematical of the royal or imperial house of the ruler. Subsequently, the colors had a twofold significance—religion and state. The custom of obeisance or mark of respect survived after the shrines were moved from on deck. Or to put it another way, kings for a long time ruled by the now outmoded theory of "divine right," and as eventually the "king's colors" were symbols of church and state combined, the colors became the dominant symbol to respect. In this connection, it is interesting to note that today many Catholics raise their hats on passing in front of a Catholic church or shrine. Europeans uncover or salute when passing the tombs of their respective Unknown Soldiers: all are forms of honors rendered to something greater than the institution or the individual.

The quarterdeck has been a "sacred" area from the earliest days. Captain Basil Hall, RN, writing in 1831 of his midshipman days, said:

> Every person, not excepting the captain, when he puts his foot on this sacred spot, touches his hat; and as this salutation is supposed to be paid to the privileged region itself, all those who at the moment have the honor to be upon it are bound to acknowledge the compliment. Thus even when a midshipman comes up and

takes off his hat, all the officers on deck (the admiral included, if he happens to be of the number) return the salute.

So completely does this form grow into a habit, that in the darkest night, and when there may not be a single person near the hatch-way, it is invariably attended to with the same precision.

When reaching the top of the ladder, civilian dignitaries on official visits and all those in civilian dress should uncover when paying respect to the flag. This is the equivalent of the military salute by those in uniform. When uncovered, one should stand at attention for a moment and bow toward the colors.

It is sufficient to say that it is an old and impressive tradition—a short, dignified, personal recognition of the colors, the symbol of the state, the seat of authority.

THE HAND SALUTE

The hand salute in the American Navy came to us by way of the British Navy. The gesture of the hand salute was borrowed by the British Navy from the British Army. The tradition of its origin is of interest, but, as in the derivation of saluting the quarterdeck, it has various explanations. That it is the first part of the movement of uncovering is generally agreed; that there was nothing in the hand is a possible explanation of the British and French Army salute with the palm turned out.

From the earliest days of organized military units, the junior has uncovered in addressing or meeting the senior. A survival of this custom is noted in the Guard Regiments today in that they remove their caps when salutes are rendered in fatigue dress. Admiral the Earl of St. Vincent, in 1796, promulgated an order to the effect that all officers were to take off their hats when receiving orders from superiors, "and not to touch them with an air of negligence." One finds in Jones's *Sketches of Naval Life*, written on board the USS *Constitution* in 1826, an account of Sunday inspection on board and a description of the salute of the day:

> The Captain and First Lieutenant, Mr. Vallette, are now on deck; they pass around and examine every part of it, each man lifting his hat as they pass or, in default of one, catching hold of a lock of hair.

There is a certain plausibility in placing the origin of the salute in the days of chivalry. It was customary for the knights in mail to raise their visors, in order that those of the same order, as well as friendly orders, could see the face. In time, the gesture denoted membership in the same order of knighthood, or another friendly organization. Because of the strict gradations of social class and rank in the days of chivalry, it is believed that the junior was required to make the first gesture, and therefore distinction in class and grade entered at the very beginning of the custom.

Today, the personal salute is a significant military gesture. It is the act of military and naval men looking into the eyes of another companion in arms, and by a proper gesture of the hand, paying due respect to the uniform of another defender of the Republic. On through the scale, from the "jack of the dust" to the commander in chief, the junior salutes first. But humble and high meet on common ground when the circle is completed by the respect that all pay the flag, the highest symbol of the state.

Salutes are always rendered with the right hand by Army and Air Force personnel. Naval personnel may use the left hand if the right hand is encumbered. A soldier or airman may salute while sitting down or while uncovered. Naval personnel do not salute when sitting down or uncovered. They may do so when failure to return a salute from a member of another service would be embarrassing.

The salute is rendered when the person to be saluted is near enough to recognize that he is to be saluted and still has time enough to return the salute. Six to ten paces is considered normal.

Although the U. S. Army salute is the same as that of the U. S. Navy, such is not the case in the other armies of the world. A good explanation of this is made by Lieutenant Commander Lowry, RN. He sets forth the training ship regulations of 1882, in which the salute is defined as follows:

> The naval salute is made by touching the hat or cap or by taking it off, always looking the person saluted in the face. By touching the hat is meant holding the edge with the forefinger and thumb.

We see that the naval salute evolved from the palm "inboard." In 1888 this British order was amended to read:

> The naval salute is made by touching the hat or cap, or taking it off and looking the officer saluted in the face. Admirals, captains, officers of the same relative rank and the officers commanding the saluter's ship of whatever rank, are on all occasions saluted by the hat being taken off.

In practice, however, there was a great lack of conformity. Therefore, in January 1890 the hand salute *only* was decreed by Queen Victoria because of her displeasure at seeing officers and men uncovered when they appeared for royal commendation.

In the United States Navy, officers in the open uncover only for divine services. Men uncover when at "mast" for reports and requests, at certain division inspections, and in officers' country when the men are not under arms.

Both officers and men uncover when passing through compartments where naval personnel are at meals. Nothing gives a better indication of the state of discipline of a ship or organization than prompt execution of the salute—the most common form of military courtesy.

THE SWORD—SYMBOL OF AUTHORITY—BADGE OF OFFICE

You should have seen him as he stood,
  Fighting for his good land,
With all the iron of soul and blood
  Turned to a sword in hand.

  There is no refutation in God's truth and man's duty for the
flash of a clean sword.[3]

The ancient Hebrew prophets dreamed of a golden era when swords would be beaten into plowshares, but, alas, that vision is far from being realized. Nevertheless, the sword, though its practical value was probably last demonstrated by cavalrymen, remains even in the nuclear age as a badge of office when it is worn officially by officers of the armed services of all nations and by the diplomatic officers of most foreign powers when wearing full dress uniform.

From the days of the Roman *gladius*, and even before, the sword was a highly personal weapon and of symbolic importance. The surrendering of officers' swords has always been a token of submission. Officers of the United States possess today some swords of Japanese officers who turned them over after the surrender of Japan; many of these had been passed on in the warrior clans for hundreds of years. Nothing could denote Japanese family honor more than possession of a sword carried in defense of the Emperor and the homeland. Many Americans are justly proud to possess the swords and sabers carried by their forebears through the wars of the United States. It was sometimes the custom in olden days to take an officer's sword and break the blade if he was dismissed in disgrace. Before World War II any officer of the

---

[3] Dr. Frederick Brown Harris, "A Clean Sword," Washington *Sunday Star*, December 26, 1955.

Navy, who was placed under arrest pending court-martial, was required by regulation to deliver his sword to his commanding officer until after the verdict of the court.

To leave behind a"clean sword" whether death be in peace or war remains the high goal of officers of the armed forces. In other days, swords, hats, and caps remained on the caskets until time of burial. Today a sword may be leaned against a casket at funeral services. From his first commissioned days, a naval officer's sword may be carried to inspections and ceremonials, worn at his wedding, and also at his retirement ceremony; worn at all assumptions and reliefs of command; and finally may rest by his casket—all of which may explain why so much sentiment has always been attached to the sword and its symbolism.

One of the supreme honors that can be conferred upon an officer is the award by Congress or by state legislatures of a sword in recognition of services to the country. The magnificent gold sword, with the inscription "Louis XVI, the rewarder of the valiant avenger of the sea avenged," presented to John Paul Jones by the King of France may be seen in the Crypt near Jones's sarcophagus at Annapolis. The City of London, England, knew of no higher symbol of respect and gratitude to present to General Dwight D. Eisenhower at the close of World War II than a reproduction of the great two-handed sword of the Crusades.[4]

In 1954, the sword was officially returned as traditional accouterment for commissioned and warrant officers of the Navy. This occasioned a few jibes by the press. There was not much that could be said in reply by the service, but over the years the sword has gained wide acceptance as a symbol of the uniqueness of the seagoing service.

---

[4] This sword, along with eighty of the most historic swords of America, was shown at "The Sword in America" exhibition at the Corcoran Gallery of Art, Washington, D.C., December 1955. This fascinating exhibit commenced with a Viking sword and included those of Captain Miles Standish, young Lt. Colonel George Washington, O'Bannon, first hero of the Marine Corps when he planted the first American flag on foreign soil, Stephen Decatur, and Commodore Matthew Perry, who opened Japan to foreign trade. The two hits of the show were the swords of General U. S. Grant and General Robert E. Lee. Of interest was the last model of cavalry saber used before the advent of the armored tank; this model, designed by General George Smith Patton, Jr., was placed by his old cavalry saber.

In 1964, the Japanese Artistic Sword Preservation Society through the Department of Defense made an effort to effect the return of forty-two Japanese swords of "historic and cultural value" and designated as "National Treasures." All were reportedly turned over to personnel of the Allied Occupation Forces, 1945-46.

SWORD SALUTE

Again authorities differ when it comes to the derivation of the sword salute. The Royal Military Training College (British) taught for some years that it was derived from the oriental custom of the junior raising the sword and shading his eyes from the magnificence of the superior. The first etiquette or "school of the sword" was most probably of oriental origin. But all that can be found tends to indicate that the salute as we know it is probably of crusader origin.

The crucifix, symbolical of the cross, was in the days of chivalry symbolized on the sword by the handle and the guard. It was customary, in that tumultuous time of religious crusades, to kiss the sword hilt before entering battle and, of course, for vows and oaths. The cross on the sword survives: on British midshipmen's dirks; on the swords of the Scottish archers; on the undress swords of the Highland regiments, and the dress swords of diplomatic officers of several foreign countries. After Christianization, Norsemen had the Norse equivalent of the word *Jesus* etched on the sword hilt.

Most of the ancient history of the sword salute is displayed in the present-day salute. The sword held at arm's length was originally the hail or initial salute to the superior. The act of permitting the point to descend to the ground is the ancient act of submission or juniority. The start of both these movements—bringing the sword hilt to the mouth or chin—is a survival of the custom of kissing the cross on the sword.

The British Navy has an interesting sword custom. When an officer is tried by court-martial, he unhooks his sword and places it on the table just before the proceeding starts. If he is found guilty, his sword is then placed on the table with the point towards the accused; if he is found not guilty the hilt is placed towards him.

The sword salute on the march is a survival of the fancy turns and flourishes that were made by military officers in the reviews of the seventeenth century. Halberds and short swords were used in those days, and apparently the fancier the flourishes the better the show on parade and the more effective the salute. The fancy flourish of the drum major is a survival of this. Detailed instructions for the ceremonial use of the sword exist today. For example: When making a sword salute, be at least two sword lengths away from the one saluted; conceivably, you could prick a senior officer or wound a dignitary.

The most serious breach of unwritten sword etiquette would be to drop a sword when making a sword salute. Keep a firm grasp on the hilt. Those who have had no experience with swords should practice unsheathing, then the salute, and sheathing. You never know when you will be ordered to march in a parade, and remember *all* eyes are on you when passing the reviewing stand. We recall one officer in a parade who kept his sword at salute for a city block. When questioned. he called it a "Governor General's salute."

A sword should never be unsheathed in a church or sanctuary. At weddings of naval and military officers it is customary for the ushers in uniform to draw and arch swords outside the church door. After the nuptial ceremony, the bride and groom walk under the arch. This fine old English and American custom is a symbolic pledge of loyalty to the young married couple. In short, all for two. It also makes a good picture. Remember, no one but the newly married pair passes under the arch.

At the wedding reception, the officer should unsheath his sword, the Army officer his saber, and in a dignified manner the groom presents it to his bride. She should then cut a slice of the wedding cake, with the groom's right hand resting over hers on the hilt and with his left arm free to place around his bride.

Never draw a sword in a wardroom! Long ago this strict taboo may have been instituted to prevent some serious sword play when the flowing bowl stimulated argument. The fine for so doing in the old Navy was a bottle of champagne to be paid for by him who drew.

Swords were once worn at all Saturday personnel inspections and at all ceremonies. Gloves are always worn or carried when the uniform is "Swords." Check the uniform regulations to ensure that the sword knot is properly dressed and the sword properly hooked on the sword belt.[5]

GUN SALUTES

In theory, all sword or gun salutes were originally the friendly gesture by the one who first saluted of rendering himself or his ship powerless for the time of the rendition of the honors. The point of the sword on the ground at the finish of the sword salute rendered the saluter powerless for a moment. Guns in old days were kept shotted, and after firing a salute, an appreciable time was required before the guns could be fired again. In Henry VII's reign, to fire a gun three times or so in an hour was a good average.

---

[5] Possession of the sword, sword knot, and belt is required of all commissioned officers, lieutenant commander and above (except chaplains), for wear with full dress uniforms worn for ceremonial occasions.

The salutes to vessels flying the English flag started when the waters from the coast of Norway to Cape Finisterre were claimed as "English seas." It is known that before Norman days, sails of foreign vessels were lowered in those waters as a mark of respect to English sovereignty—a "mark of respect" that rendered the vessel powerless for a time. Of course, the ship had no appreciable way on after sails were lowered, and with decks cluttered with rigging and sail, the one saluted feared no attack. From this old custom grew the present regulations of "tossing oars," "lying on oars," "stopping engines," and in sail boats "letting fly the sheets" in order to render honors to superiors.

It is a very ancient superstition that gun salutes should be of odd number. In Boteler's *Dialogues* of 1685, published by the British Naval Records Society, the captain, referring to a very distinguished visitor aboard, says, "Have his farewell given him with so many guns as the ship is able to give; provided that they always be of an odd number."

"Admiral: 'And why odd?'"

"Captain: 'The odd number in ways of salute and ceremony is so observable at sea that, whensoever guns be given otherwise, it is taken for an expression that either the captain, or master, or master gunner is dead in the voyage.'[6]

"And this ceremony of giving of guns is also in use whensoever any prime passenger, or the captain of the ship, is to leave the ship and go to the shore."

Sir William Monson, in his *Naval Tracts* written prior to 1600, remarks:

> The saluting of ships by another at sea is both ancient and decent,
> though in this latter time much abused, for whereas three, five,
> or seven pieces may have been the ordinary use for an admiral, and
> never to exceed that proportion, and an admiral not to answer
> with above one or three, now they strive to exceed the number,
> thinking that many pieces add honor to the salutation; but the
> owners of merchant ships would be gladden it might be done with
> less cost and more courtesy in another kind. But tho the admiral
> cannot restrain this compliment in the ship that salutes, yet he may
> command his gunner not to return above one or three pieces
> according to the old manner.

[6] In the Coronation Program of George VI, a royal salute of forty-one guns, one for each completed year of his Majesty's age, was fired at St. James Park. At the actual moment of coronation a sixty-two-gun royal salute with twenty-one guns added, was fired at the Tower of London. A British army officer in a letter to the London *Times* recalled the ancient custom of odd and even guns, and continued: "It may be a foolish superstition to regard the firing of an even number of rounds in a salute to a live person as ominous, but it is a pity that old custom should be neglected in such an important ceremony."

For years the British compelled weaker nations to render the first salute, but in time international practice compelled "gun for gun" on the principle of equality of nations. In the earliest days, seven guns was the recognized British national salute. Here again we see that the number seven had a mystical significance, for in the Eastern civilization, seven was a sacred number. Those early regulations stated that although a ship would fire only seven guns, the forts ashore could fire three shots to each one shot afloat. In that day, powder of sodium nitrate was easier to keep on shore than at sea. In time, when the quality of gunpowder improved by the use of potassium nitrate, the sea salute was made equal to the shore salute—twenty-one guns as the highest national honor. Although for a period of time monarchies received more guns than republics, eventually republics gained equality. There was much confusion because of the varying customs of maritime states, but finally the British government proposed to the United States a regulation that provided for "salutes to be returned gun for gun." At that time the British officially considered the international salute (to sovereign states) to be twenty-one guns, and the United States adopted the twenty-one guns and "gun for gun" return, August 18, 1875.[7]

Previous to this time our national salute had been variable—one gun for each state of the Union. This practice was partly a result of usage, for John Paul Jones saluted France with thirteen guns at Quiberon Bay in 1778, when the Stars and Stripes received its first salute. This practice was not officially authorized until 1810. By the admission of states to the Union, the salute reached twenty-one guns in 1818. In 1841, the national salute was reduced to twenty-one guns. In fact, the 1875 adoption of the British suggestion was a formal announcement that the United States recognized twenty-one guns as an international salute.

The *National Geographic* says:

> This country has also an extra-special ceremony known as the "salute to the nation," which consists of one gun for each of the forty-eight [now fifty] states. This mimic war is staged only at noon on July 4 at American military posts, although it has been given on a few other occasions, such as the death of a President.

---

[7] When India was part of the British Empire, the King-Emperor would receive there an Imperial salute of 101 guns. Unless rendered to a president or the flag of a republic, twenty-one guns is called a royal salute in the British Isles, and even then it is called (colloquially) "royal" in the British Commonwealth. In short, it would be said of the president of the United States, if saluted in Canada, that he received a "royal salute."

The Navy full-dresses ship and fires twenty-one guns at noon on the Fourth of July and the 22nd of February. On Memorial Day, all ships and naval stations fire a salute of 21 guns, one every minute, and display the ensign at half-mast from 0800 until completion of the salute.

It seems that it was customary at dinners on board to fire a salute when toasts were drunk to high ranking officers, for Monson continues:

> The excessive banqueting on board is a great consuming of powder, for as men's brains are heated with wine, so they heat their ordnance with ostentation and professed kindness at that instant, and many times not without danger. . . . [It must be remembered that regular shot was fired.]

We are reminded of this custom in Shakespeare's Hamlet:

> No jocund health that Denmark drinks today,
> But the great cannon to the clouds shall tell. . . .

Monson was a very practical man, for in his command it was ordered that musketry be fired for toasts and leave taking. He used these honors as drills and directed that the muskets always be fired at a mark in the shape of a man. The Turkish Navy fired shotted salutes until 1910.[8]

The custom of returning gun for gun is very old. In 1688 Sir Cloudesly Shovel, writing on board the *James Galley* to Sir Martin Wescomb, said:

> I shall ever be careful in keeping especially my Royal orders,
> which positively command me to salute neither garrison nor flagg
> of any forrainer except I am certaine to receave gunne for gunne.

Today, for a revolutionary or *de facto* government to receive a salute from a foreign state is tantamount to recognition. At one time, when England maintained by force her proud title of "mistress of the seas," it was customary for kings of foreign states to salute the British flag on the seas. This, of course, held particularly in the Narrow Seas, for it was asserted for a long period after Edward I that England had claim to both sides of the Channel. In fact, one of King John's titles

---

[8] George Washington on September 17, 1781, made the second and last sea trip of his life, excepting two fishing trips in the presidential years, when, accompanied by Rochambeau, he visited Admiral Comte de Grasse off Cape Henry in his flag ship *La Ville de Paris*, then the largest ship in the world. At dinner aboard, gun salutes were rendered after each toast.

was Duke of Normandy. The Kings of England down to George II bore the title of King of France. The title and quartering of French arms was only dropped in 1801. Some of the sovereigns who were compelled to salute by cannon the English flag were King Philip of Spain on his visit to Queen Mary in 1554, and the King of Denmark on his return from an official visit to King James I at London. Also, foreign ambassadors and foreign captains were on occasions held accountable before a Court of Admiralty for failure to salute.

The most important salute in U. S. naval history is the first one to the Stars and Stripes by a sea power in recognition of our status as a sovereign state. This salute was received by John Paul Jones in the *Ranger* on the thirteenth of February 1778 at Quiberon Bay, France.

CHEERING

> In manning the rigging for cheering, the people should be chosen for their size, to stand together or on the same ratlines, observing the space of two or three ratlines between each. The men should be drest alike, the marines at the time drawn up on the gangway without their arms. After the three cheers have been given, if the Commodore returns the same number, it must be answered by one; if he returns but one no further notice to be taken, and the people called down.[9]

Cheering was also appropriate in the nineteenth century when distinguished passengers left the ship, and for shifts of commands. Research shows that it has long been a maritime custom of respect. In *Sketches of Naval Life* by Jones, a description of the cheering is given on Lafayette's departure from the USS *Brandywine*, as he went ashore in France after his last visit to the United States. A description is also given of the turning over of naval command in 1826. Jones writes in his log:

> Tuesday, 21 [January 1826]. The Commodore visited and inspected her, on the 19th; and today Captain Read went on board to take the command. He was received by Captain Patterson; the men had been ordered to clean themselves, and all hands were piped; the officers were summoned to the quarterdeck, where the orders of the Secretary for the exchange were read by one of the lieutenants, and the two captains then saluted each other, and bowed to the officers. The shrouds were next manned, and three cheers given. The cheers were repeated when Captain Patterson

[9] *U. S. Naval Instruction*, 1824.

left the ship; and in this manner he was also received by the *Constitution*.

The evolution was called "Manning the Yards and Cheering."

When sufficient advance notice could be had of the visit of a distinguished personage who would pass close aboard, all hands were ordered "to clean themselves." Then shortly afterwards, at the words "lay aloft," all hands would spring upon the rigging and cluster on to the tops around the topmost crosstrees and the top-gallant masthead. The second command was "Lay out upon the yards." The men spread each way and supported themselves by means of light life lines that were fastened to the lifts and masts. Next, when the order to cheer came from deck, the men took off their hats and waved them during the three cheers.

Manning the rail and cheering ship is a very old custom. A manuscript of Dr. Roger Marbecke in 1596, at the time of the English Cadiz Exposition, states:

> These hailings then are in this order. When after a day's absence or more, as occasion serveth, they come near to the Lord Admiral, and yet not too near, but of such seasonable distance as they may not endanger themselves of going foul of one another; they presently man the ship and place every one of their companies both upon the upper and middle deck and also upon the waist and shrouds and elsewhere to the most advantage they can to make the bravest show and appear the greater number. Then the masters and mates of the ships immediately join upon the sounding of their whistles in a pretty loud tunable manner, all the company shaking their hands, hats and caps, give a marvelous shout, with as much mirth and rejoicing as they can, which consisting of so many loud, strong, and variable voices maketh such a sounding echo and pleasant report in the air, as delighteth very much, and this ceremony is done three times by them and three times interchangeably answered by the Lord Admiral.

Herman Melville in *White Jacket* gives a description of how Dom Pedro II, Emperor of Brazil, was cheered on his official visit to the USS *United States* about 1849:

> But there they stood! Commodore and emperor, lieutenants and marquises, middies and pages! The brazen band on the poop struck up; the marine guard presented arms; and high aloft looking down on the scene, all the people vigorously hurrahed. A top-man next me on the main-royal removed his hat, and diligently manipulated his head in honor of the event; but he was so far out of sight in the clouds that the ceremony went for nothing.

DIPPING THE COLORS

The present custom of exchanging greetings between ships at sea by dipping the colors is an outgrowth of the old indication of submission of one warship to another or of a merchantman to a warship by the act of lowering topsails.

Before international standardization, salutes were often matters of controversy. National salutes are today based upon the equality of all sovereign states. But in olden days the weak saluted the strong, and the stranger usually saluted the country that claimed jurisdiction over the waters he entered. In 1594 one of the Fugger correspondents from Rome wrote:

> The disputes, which have so long prevailed among Christian powers about procedure at sea, have now been settled. Only the Pope and the King of Spain can sail their galleys with colors flying. If they meet, they must salute each other. All other nations must yield precedence to these two.

The old English Navy insisted on respect by all foreigners and English merchantmen. It is recorded that Richard Bullen, captain of HMS *Nicodemus*, was given a severe punishment in 1638 for not having forced a French ship of war to salute him.

An English merchant ship was fined £500 for not lowering topsails to Charles's fleet. In 1643 instructions to the Royal Navy read:

> If you chance to meet in his Majesties see any ships or fleet belonging to any foreign power or State and if they do not strike flaggs or take in topsail you are to force them thereunto.

Neither a U. S. man-of-war nor that of any other sovereign state ever dips her ensign except in return for such compliment. In fact it is not customary today for warships of any nation to dip their colors first. All ships of our Navy, however, should be alert when passing private vessels, and if this traditional salute (usually from merchant vessels, small craft, or yachts at sea) is rendered, it must be answered, dip for dip.

TENDING THE SIDE

The boatswain's pipe (whistle) is one of the oldest and most distinctive articles of personal nautical equipment. A pipe or flute was used in the days of antiquity, by which the galley slaves of Greece and Rome kept stroke. There is a record that the pipe was used in the Crusade of 1248 when the English crossbowmen were called on deck to attack by its

Admiral Kimmel is piped aboard the USS *San Francisco.*

signal. The pipe is mentioned by Shakespeare in the *Tempest*: "Tend to the master's whistle"; and Pepys refers to its use in his *Naval Notes.*

In time, the pipe came to be used as a badge of office, and in some cases a badge of honor. The Lord High Admiral carried a gold pipe on a chain around his neck; a silver one was used by high commanders as a badge of office, or "whistle of command," in addition to the gold whistle of honor. The whistle was used for salutes to distinguished personages, as well as to pass orders, and the old instructions read that on most occasions it was to be blown "three several times." In the action off Brest on April 25, 1513, between Sir Edward Howard, Lord High Admiral and son of the Earl of Surrey, and the Chevalier Pregant de Bidoux, it is related that when the Lord High Admiral was certain that he would be captured, he threw his gold whistle into the sea. The silver whistle of command was afterwards found on his body. The weight of a standard whistle of honor and names for its part were designated by Henry VIII. The monarch decreed that it should weigh 12 "oons" of gold, an oon being the original ounce, as derived from the Latin *uncia*. The chain was also to be of gold and to have an equivalent in gold ducats.

Aside from the use of the pipe as a badge of office and its use by officers for piping evolutions, it was used at the reception of high personages.[10] Boteler, in his *Dialogues* of 1645, describes the correct procedure: "In receiving, the Prince himself or his Admiral. . . . They were to be received publicly with ceremonies." He adds:

> The ship's barge to be sent to fetch the visitor having the cockson with his silver whistle in the stern. . . . Upon the near approach of the barge the noise of the trumpets are to sound and so to hold on until the barge comes within less than musket shot, and that time the trumpets are to cease and all such as carry whistles are to whistle a welcome three several times.

Tending the side with side boys, as we know it in modern practice, originated a long, long time ago. It was customary in the days of sail to hold conferences on the flagships both when at sea and in open roadstead; also, officers were invited to dinner on other ships while at sea, weather permitting. Sometimes the sea was such that visitors were hoisted aboard in boatswain's chairs. The pipe was, of course, used for "hoist away" and " 'vast heaving." Members of the crew did the hoisting, and it is from the aid they rendered in tending the side that the custom originated of having a certain number of men always in attendance. Some have reported the higher the rank, the heavier the individual. Tending the side is not to be confused with a guard of honor.

The piping of the side is a distinct nautical courtesy and so considered by the Royal Navy; however, the United States Navy has extended it to military, diplomatic, and consular officers, as well as to others of the legislative and executive departments of the government. In the British Navy, Commander Beckett writes that, by Admiralty regulations:

> No Military Officer, Consular Officer, or other civilian is entitled to this form of salute. By the Custom of the Service a corpse of any Naval Officer or man is piped over the side, if sent ashore for burial.

It is of interest that at the funerals of British monarchs since Queen Victoria the venerable custom of piping is part of the ceremony. In

[10] Also at their funerals: "The bells of Westminster Abbey began to toll, a bo'sun's whistle shrilled 'Admiral aboard' as the King's body was laid upon the gun carriage outside the door to Westminster Hall." *New York Times*, February 6, 1952.

this manner the Royal Navy, the "Senior Service," pays a seaman's tribute to the sovereigns of an empire built by sea power.

There is a tradition that the present form of the pipe (whistle) of the boatswain was adopted in commemoration of the defeat and capture of the body of the notorious Scottish pirate, Andrew Barton. Lord Edward Howard, in command of the British ships *Lion* and *Pirwin*, captured him after a severe battle. It is related that Howard took the whistle from the body of Barton. When Howard in time became Lord High Admiral, he caused its adoption. Whistles of other kinds had been in use prior to this date, but it is believed that the design and probably the idea of a more elaborate and costly model as a badge of office sprang from this capture.

In the seventeenth century, it is recorded that the master, the boatswain, and the coxswain, all three, rated the whistle. The coxswain had charge of the barge and the shallop, and was at all times to be in readiness to take the captain or admiral ashore. The orders were that the coxswain:

> "is to see her [the barge] trimmed with her carpets and cushions, and to be the person himself in her stern with his silver whistle to cheer up his gang. . . . And this is the lowest officer on the ship that wears a whistle."

LAUNCHING SHIP CEREMONIES[11]

> *And see! She stirs!*
> *She starts—she moves—she seems to feel*
> *The thrill of life along her keel,*
> *And, spurning with her foot the ground,*
> *With one exulting, joyous bound,*
> *She leaps into the ocean's arms.*–Longfellow

From the earliest days of seaborne craft, launching ceremonies have had a religious significance. There is a record of a launching ceremony in 2100 B.C. The custom originated as a propitiation to the gods of the elements. In Tahiti it was once the custom to shed human blood at the launching ceremonies. The Chinese have not changed in centuries their elaborate launching ceremonies, and today all the large junks carry a shrine in respect and propitiation to the Mother of the Dragon.

---

11 Acknowledgment to Robert G. Skerrett for use of material from his comprehensive treatment of the subject: "The Baptism of Ships," U.S. Naval Institute *Proceedings*, June 1909.

Wine was used in the rituals of the early days; however, the Greeks introduced water in the ceremony of lustration. Later, the Romans used water as a token of purification in the solemn priestly blessing. Christian ceremonials as in pagan ceremonials used wine as the sacrament, and water as the token of purification.

The religious zeal of the Middle Ages extended to things maritime. Ships were named after saints; shrines were placed aboard, and religious effigies found their way on figureheads and in the elaborate niches in the gilded stern galleries. The altars or shrines were placed aft in the same location as the image altars of the Greeks and Romans. The name "poop deck" survives the custom. This nautical word is derived from the Latin word *puppis*, a name the ancients gave to that ceremonial, sacred, honored deck where was kept the *pupi* or doll images of the deities. Here sacrifice was offered. One is impressed with the thought that the quarterdeck in reality has *always* been an area of honor.

In Catholic France throughout the eighteenth century and well into the nineteenth there was a launching ceremony that in most respects was analogous to the baptismal ceremony. This was performed by priests at the launching of merchant vessels and fishing craft in Brittany and Normandy. No wine was used in the ceremony of launching, but *vin d'honneur* was always served to those present.

It was only in the early part of the nineteenth century that women and those other than the clergy and high officials took any part in the ceremony of launching British ships. It is reported that Victoria inaugurated the religious portion of the ceremony that is now used in the launching of British warships. The civil ceremony usually consists in the naming of the vessel by a sponsor, a few words from the sponsor, and breaking a bottle of wine on the bow or stem of the ship as she slips down the ways. Because of the "noble experiment" of prohibition in the United States, this bottle-breaking custom was for a time held in abeyance.

Champagne has again taken its place as the customary liquid for launching ceremonies. The first time wine was used after the repeal of the Eighteenth Amendment was on November 21, 1933, at the launching of the USS *Cuttlefish*, built by the Electric Boat Company. Mrs. B. Saunders Bullard, wife of Commander C.C. Bullard, USN, cracked a bottle of champagne against the ship's bow as she left the ways. The USS *Guam* launched November 21, 1943, with the breaking of a bottle of champagne by Mrs. George J. McMillin whose husband, Captain McMillin, was the last prewar Governor of Guam and a Japanese prisoner of war on Formosa at the time Mrs. McMillin christened the ship.[12]

The first record found of a woman sponsor in the American Navy is that of a "Miss Watson of Philadelphia," who used a mixture of water and wine when she christened the *Germantown*, a ship of war, on October 22, 1846. The Philadelphia *North American* in describing the ceremony said, "Miss Watson was attired in pure white and wore in her girdle a neat bouquet of freshly culled flowers."

When the *Chicago* was sponsored in 1885, Mrs. Henry W. B. Glover released three doves from red, white, and blue ribbons. Mrs. Herbert Hoover released a flock of white pigeons when the ill-fated airship *Akron* was christened. The Japanese were the first to use birds in connection with launchings.

So many prominent women of the United States have launched ships that in order to preserve the records, Edith Wallace Benham and Anne Martin Hall wrote a book called, *Ships of the United States Navy and Their Sponsors.*[13] The Society of Sponsors of the United States Navy has preserved the interesting record of the christenings of all U. S. Navy ships since 1797.

Tradition has it that water was used in the first attempt to launch the *Constitution*, and "Old Ironsides" would not move; it apparently took wine to launch the ship. Admiral George Preble notes that the interesting story of her launching, after two attempts, may be found in the history of the Boston Navy Yard. The record states:

> Commodore James Sever stood at the heel of the bowsprit and according to time-honored usage baptised the ship with a bottle of choice old Madeira, from the cellar of the Honorable Thomas Russell, a leading Boston merchant.

In 1858, the USS *Hartford* was launched with three sponsors. Commodore Downes's daughter smashed a bottle of Hartford Springs water across the bows; Commodore Stringham's daughter broke a bottle of Connecticut River water across the ship's figurehead; Lieutenant Preble emptied a bottle of sea water on the bow. This was a "triple-barreled"

[12] When the USS *Guam* was commissioned September 15, 1944, the island of Guam had only been recaptured from the Japanese a short time. A committee of natives speaking for the people wrote a touching letter to the commanding officer of the *Guam* and said: "We of Guam, USA, request the pride and honor of serving in the USS *Guam.*" At the time over 1,000 men from the little island were serving in the U. S. Navy.

[13] Published by the U. S. Naval Institute.

water ceremony.[14] Once a U. S. Army Air Corps balloon was christened with liquid air.

COINS AT STEP OF MAST

The ancient custom of placing coins under the step of a mast at the time the vessel is built dates from antiquity.[15]

One explanation, given by Commander Beckett, RN, is that possibly it is a survival of the old Roman custom of placing coins in the mouths of the dead to pay their way to Charon for transportation across the River Styx; and if a ship met with mishap at sea, this ensured that the fare of all hands was paid.

This custom tends to show that some seafaring men still subscribe to outmoded superstition, and that sea services support many ancient traditions that have no particular bearing on modern sea life.

FUNERAL CEREMONIES

Much of the ceremony at military and naval funerals is traditional. The reversal of rank at funerals is an acknowledgment that at death all men are equal. Seniors take their proper precedence in the procession after burial.[16] This form of "the last shall be first and the first shall be last" is carried out in the recessional and processional of churches. There was a Roman custom of reversing all rank and position when celebrating the feast of Saturn.

The superstitions and significance of military funeral customs were set forth by one Stephen Graham, a private in the British Guards. This soldier wrote before the American Revolution:

[14] Mrs. Franklin D. Roosevelt christened the huge flying boat *Yankee Clipper* on March 3, 1939, at the U. S. Naval Air Station, Anacostia, D.C., with a bottle of water mixed from the Seven Seas.

In World War II days a group of ladies made strong petition to President Roosevelt and Secretary of Navy Knox that we "cease launching and christening of our boats with liquor," and recommended that they be launched by chaplains with "clear water only."

[15] An old Spanish wreck found in the Orkney Islands had under the mast and on the keel a coin dated 1618.

The officers of the USS *New Orleans* (commissioned 1934) during construction placed ten pennies beneath the foremast and two dimes, three nickels, and twenty-eight pennies at the heel of the mainmast. All coins were placed "heads up."

[16] For an unknown reason, this was not done at the funeral of Admiral George Dewey.

When a soldier dies, the Union Jack is laid upon his body in token that he died in the Service of the State, and that the State takes the responsibility of what it ordered him to do as a soldier.

The reversed arms are an acknowledgment of the shame of killing. Death puts the rifle to shame, and the reversal of the barrel is a fitting sign of reverence.

The three volleys fired into the air are fired at imaginary devils which might get into men's hearts at such a moment as the burial of a comrade-in-arms. An old superstition has it that the doors of men's hearts stand ajar at such times and devils might easily get in.

The last post is the *Nunc Dimittis* of the dead soldier. It is the last bugle call . . . but it gives promise of reveille . . . of the greatest reveille which ultimately the Archangel Gabriel will blow.

At the funeral of George Washington on December 18, 1799, the troops came first, then the clergy, and next the General's horse with two grooms. After the body, borne by Free Masons and officers, came the mourners, with Lord Fairfax as the last mourner.

BURIAL AT SEA

Death is at all times solemn, but never so much as at sea.
—Charles A. Dana

The most awesome ceremony of the sea is that which consigns mortal remains to the deep. It antedates all other ceremonies. Pagan burial rites were conducted at sea in the days of Greece and Rome; gods were then propitiated; coins were placed then in the mouths of the deceased for payment of fare to Charon for transportation over the River Styx.

According to a very old custom in preparing a body for burial at sea, the sailmaker, when sewing the canvas shroud, takes the last stitch through the nose of the deceased. Research has disclosed several instances of this custom. In *White Jacket*, Herman Melville speaks of this custom in recounting the conversation of an old American sailmaker with a seaman as to whether or not the stitch through the nose should be made. It was a time-honored custom in the British Navy that a guinea be paid from the public funds for each corpse sewn in a canvas shroud. Commander Beckett, in his *Customs and Superstitions*, reports that twenty-three guineas from government funds were paid to the rating who sewed up twenty-three bodies on a British man-of-war after the battle of Jutland. This duty is usually performed by a sailmaker, or by one of his mates.

Except in time of war, it is seldom necessary nowadays to bury at sea. Occasionally, officers and men who die ashore request that their ashes be spread on the deep; such requests must be submitted to the Navy Department.

In the event of a death aboard ship, it is customary for the ship's medical officer or whoever is in charge of "sick bay" to report the

"All hands bury the dead." *"All Hands"* by *R.F. Zogbaum. Courtesy Harper and Bros.*

death immediately to the officer of the watch, who in turn logs it, and reports it promptly to the captain and the executive officer.

If the deceased is buried at sea, the body is sewn in a canvas shroud or placed in a coffin that has been weighted to ensure sinking. The body is always carried feet first; over the coffin is draped the national flag whose union is placed at the head and over the left shoulder. The reading of Scripture, prayers, the committal, and the benediction constitute the religious rites, and may be performed by the clergy, but all else are usually performed by the military.

It has been customary for all officers and men not on duty to attend services when word is passed, "All hands bury the dead." The chaplain, or in his absence the captain or an officer detailed by the captain, reads the burial service at sea. The regulation is: "Any parts of the service may be omitted as necessary except that the committal should be said if possible." The Protestant, Catholic, and Jewish committals differ slightly. The Protestant committal reads:

> Unto Almighty God we commend the soul of our brother departed, and we commit his body to the deep; in sure and certain hope of the resurrection unto eternal life, through our Lord, Jesus Christ, Amen. (Tilt board and release body into the sea.)[17]

In order to illustrate an old superstition and at the same time show how funerals were conducted under circumstances at sea that will never occur again, there follows a description written by Captain Basil Hall, RN, in 1831. The funeral was that of one of his dearest friends, a young and much beloved midshipman of his mess who was buried off the shores of the United States during the War of 1812. As Hall records it:

> The peculiar circumstances connected with the funeral, which I am about to describe, have combined to fix the whole scene in my memory. Something occurred during the day to prevent the funeral taking place at the usual hour, and the ceremony was deferred until long after sunset. The evening was extremely dark, and it was blowing a treble-reefed topsail breeze. We had just sent down the top-gallant yards, and made all safe for a boisterous winter's night. As it became necessary to have lights to see what was done, several signal lanterns were placed on the break of the quarterdeck and others along the hammock railings on the lee gangway. The whole ship's company and officers were assembled,

---

[17] *The Ceremony of Burial of the Dead at Sea*, prescribed to be followed by all ships of the U.S. Navy where burial at sea is authorized, sets forth in detail both military procedure and the religious services of the three major faiths.

some on the booms, others in the boats, while the main rigging was crowded halfway up to the cat harpings. Overhead, the mainsail, illuminated as high as the yard by the lamps, was bulging forwards under the gale, which was rising every minute and straining so violently at the main sheet, that there was some doubt whether it might not be necessary to interrupt the funeral in order to take sail off the ship. The lower deck ports lay completely under water, and several times the muzzles of the main deck guns were plunged into the sea; so that the end of the grating on which the remains of poor Dolly were laid once or twice nearly touched the tops of the waves as they foamed and hissed past. The rain fell fast on the bare heads of the crew, dropping also on the officers, during all the ceremony, from the foot of the mainsail, and wetting the leaves of the prayer-book. The wind sighed over us amongst the wet shrouds, with a note so mournful that there could not have been a more appropriate dirge.

The ship, pitching violently, strained and cracked from end to end; so that what with the noise of the sea, the rattling of the ropes, and the whistling of the wind, hardly one word of the service could be distinguished. The men, however, understood, by a motion of the captain's hand, when the time came, and the body of our dear little brother was committed to the deep.

So violent a squall was sweeping past the ship at this moment, that no sound was heard of the usual splash, which made the sailors allege that their young favorite never touched the water at all, but was at once carried off in the gale to his final resting place!

Herman Melville reports a burial in 1843 in an account of his life aboard the USS *United States*:

"We commit this body to the deep!" At the word, Shenly's mess-mates tilted the board, and the dead sailor sank in the sea.

"Look aloft," whispered Jack Chase. "See that bird! It is the spirit of Shenly."

Gazing upward, all beheld a snow-white, solitary fowl, which —whence coming no one could tell—had been hovering over the main-mast during the service, and was now sailing far up into the depths of the sky.[18]

Sailors in those days never molested sea birds, for many mariners believed them to be the spirits of dead sailors.

In connection with funeral services, it is of interest that in the early days of the U. S. Navy the colors were half-masted only for officers

[18] Herman Melville, *White Jacket* (Boston: Page, 1892), p. 320.

of the rank of captain and above. Jones, in *Sketches of Naval Life*, written on board the frigate *Constitution* at Port Mahon, October 30, 1826, relates:

> We buried one of the officers, a surgeon's mate, and a member of our mess; application was made to have him interred in the officers' burying grounds, within the walls; but his disease, the typhus fever, alarmed them, and it was refused. I expected to see our colors half-masted; but, it seems, this is an honor due only to captains, and it was not done. The funeral was attended by nearly all of the squadron.

In the seventeenth and early eighteenth centuries it is reported that French men-of-war sometimes carried the remains of those who died at sea in the holds until the ships reached port. We are led to believe by old reports that this was a very disagreeable practice and, of course, was executed only for the purpose of burying the deceased in consecrated soil. Some tall yarns are told of the British preserving bodies of senior officers in rum until they could be buried ashore.[19]

The deep sentiment of sailors for their shipmates is proverbial. Apropos of funeral ceremonies, it is interesting after a lapse of much over a hundred years to read the epitaphs written by messmates for their lamented shipmates. The following inscription may be found in a cemetery at Port Mahon, once the base of the old United States Mediterranean Squadron.

SACRED

TO

THE MEMORY

OF

ALEXANDER GRAVES

QUARTER GUNNER ON BOARD THE

U.S. FRIGATE BRANDYWINE

WHO DEPARTED THIS LIFE JAN. 17TH

AGED 44 YEARS.

HERE LIES, BENEATH THIS CONSECRATED SOD,

A MAN WHO LOVED HIS COUNTRY AND HIS GOD:

TRUE TO THEM BOTH, I'VE HEARD HIS SHIPMATES SAY;

BUT NOW HE'S GONE; AND SLUMBERS IN THE CLAY.

A BETTER MESSMATE NEVER CROSSED THE SEAS:

I HOPE HE'S GONE TO HEAVEN. GOD BE PLEASED.

FAITHFUL IN DUTY; CONTENTED WITH HIS MIND:

AND DIED LAMENTED BY THE BRANDYWINES.

[19] Giving rise to the use of the sobriquet "Nelson's Blood" applied to rum.

Another epitaph that surely compensated in sincerity and sentiment for its deficiency in composition, runs:

SACRED

TO

THE MEMORY

OF

JAMES SMITH

CAPTAIN OF THE MAIN TOP

ON BOARD THE U.S. FRIGATE BRANDYWINE

WHO DEPARTED THIS LIFE FEB. 4TH

1826

AGED 30 YEARS

HE WHO LAYS HERE, WAS MUCH BELOVED,

BY ALL HIS SHIPMATES ROUND;

BUT HE'S NO MORE, 'TWAS ACCIDENT,

THE UNFORTUNATE MAN WAS DROWNED.

ALAS, HE'S GONE, THE DEBT IS PAID,

HE OWED FOR A SHORT TIME;

MOURN NOT FOR HIM, HE'S BETTER OFF,

HE SAILS WITH MORE DIVINE.

FIRING THREE VOLLEYS AT FUNERALS

*This the third time; I hope good luck lies in odd numbers. . . .
There is divinity in odd numbers, either in nativity, chance, or
death.*—Shakespeare

Mention has been made before of firing three volleys at funerals. By this superstitious custom it was supposed that evil spirits were driven away as they escaped from the hearts of the dead. In the Orient, firecrackers are fired to drive away evil spirits.

Before the advent of firearms, the number 3 had a mystical significance. It was used in ancient Roman funeral rites. Earth was cast three times into the sepulcher; friends and relatives called the dead three times by name, and then as they departed from the tomb they pronounced the latin word *vale*, meaning "farewell," three times.

In 1938 the Navy Department commented upon firing volleys:

> The Bureau has received advices on several occasions of the undesirable and, at times, pathetic effect of the volleys fired at military funerals upon the bereaved. It is desired that this aspect of the honors rendered at the interment be considered by commanding officers when acting upon requests for funeral escorts.

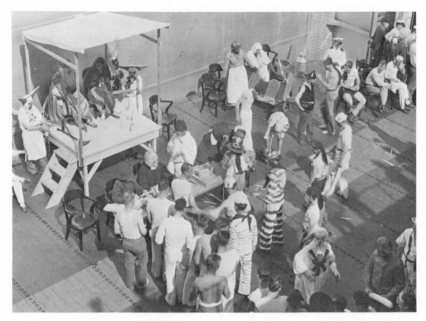

Crossing-the-line ceremony with King Neptune and party.

The following points were ordered as a guide at funerals:

(a) That the full import of the part of the firing squad be explained to the next-of-kin or those representing the next-of-kin.

(b) That those in charge of or in command of the firing squad so place the squad that it is some distance from the grave. It is not necessary that the volleys be fired directly over the grave.

(c) That the firing squad be omitted, as a matter of expedience, in the case of funerals when the omission is expressly requested by the next-of-kin or those representing the next-of-kin.

Reverence, tact and courtesy must ever govern in carrying out the ancient and solemn ceremonies of military and naval funerals.

Although not prescribed by regulations, it has become customary to hold a short religious service aboard for deceased officers and men when their remains are sent from ships on a foreign station for further transportation to the homeland. The crew is mustered aft and a religious service is held. Volleys may be omitted, but taps should be sounded as the body is lowered to the waiting boat, and the bell tolled as customary. The flag should be half-masted in accordance with regulations.

THE SOUNDING OF TATTOO AND TAPS

The word *tattoo* is derived from the Dutch word *taptoe*, time to close up all the taps and taverns in the garrisoned towns. In a quaint volume entitled *The Military Guide for Young Officers*, by Thomas Simes, Esq., reprinted in Philadelphia, 1776, there are instructions for the officer of the guard:

> The tat-too is generally best at nine o'clock at night in the summer and eight in the winter. It is performed by the Drum-Major, and all the drummers and fifers of that regiment which gave a captain of the main guard that day. The tat-too is the signal given for the soldiers to retire to their barracks or quarters, to put out their fire and candle, and go to bed. The public houses are at the same time, to shut their doors, and sell no more liquor that night.

Colonel H. L. Scott, Inspector General, U. S. Army, in the *Military Dictionary* which he published in 1861, defined "tat-too" and "taptoo" as equivalent terms meaning "drum-beat and a roll call at night."

In time, trumpets were used for tattoo. The *Century Dictionary* defines the word as a beat of drum or bugle call at night, while "taps" is defined as a signal upon a drum or trumpet at about a quarter of an hour after tattoo. The British use the term "post" for this call. Major General G. E. Voyle, Royal Bengal Artillery, defined the term in his military dictionary published in 1876: "the term Post is given to the bugling which precedes the tattoo. This is the first part; the last part, that which follows it, is the last Post." The Last Post is sounded on the trumpet or bugle at British military funerals.

Just when the American Navy adopted the custom of sounding taps at funerals seems to be unknown. The "Dead March from Saul" was all the music rendered by the musicians on board the *Constitution* at a burial at sea in 1846. Commodore Claxton was buried at Valparaiso in 1841, and at the same time mention was made of the "Dead March" and the muffled drums, but no mention of taps.

There was a melody for taps as early as the American Revolution: it was probably that of the Last Post of the British Army. Taps of the United States Armed Forces, and the Last Post of the British have a few identical notes. The St. Louis *Globe Democrat* wrote in September 1933:

> The American Army's heart-touching salute to the dead, the "song of truce to pain," the final bugle call of the night, as soldiers in field and barracks roll into their blankets, arose anew last fall. It was announced in Paris that the French Army had adopted

the bugle call for its own and that it would be used in France as it is used in America, to end the day and to mark the burial of the dead.

Vincent Norton, of Bloomfield Hills, Michigan, writes to the *New York Times* that the call was composed by General Daniel Butterfield, commander of a brigade in the Army of the Potomac, and that it was first sounded by the writer's father, Oliver W. Norton, brigade bugler, in July 1862, at Harrison's Landing on the lower James River in Virginia, where the Butterfield brigade was encamped.

The son says that he often heard his father tell how General Butterfield scribbled the notes on the back of an old envelope, summoned Bugler Norton and directed him to sound the notes. After a few trials and changes, the now world-famous call was finally arranged to suit General Butterfield who ordered it substituted that night for the regulation taps or "extinguish lights" which up to that time had been used by the United States Army.

Bugler Norton was then a young soldier assigned to brigade duty from the Eighty-third Regiment of Pennsylvania Volunteers. He later wrote a full account of the episode for his post in the publication of the *Loyal Legion of the United States* and included it in a volume of war letters privately published.

COCKBILLING YARDS—MOURNING IN DAYS OF SAIL

Yards were once "cockbilled," and rigging was slacked off to show grief. The half-masting of colors is in reality a survival of the days when a slovenly appearance characterized mourning. Even in the British Merchant Service today there are cases of trailing rope ends, "slackening off" of rigging and "scandalizing" yards to symbolize mourning. In this connection, Commander W. T. N. Beckett, RN, writes:

> I think that the last occasion that one of H.M. ships scandalized her yards as a sign of mourning, was when HMS *Exmouth* carried out the procedure in 1908 while laying off Lisbon after the murder of Don Carlos, King of Portugal. HMS *Exmouth* was commanded by Captain Arthur Henniker-Hughan and was flying the flag of Admiral the Honorable Sir Assheton George Curzon-Howe, K.C.B.

> HMS *Arrogant* was also present, and for lack of known precedent, yards were cockbilled, mainstay down to starboard, foremast down to port, lower booms were dropped. *Arrogant* copied *Ex-*

mouth and the condition prevailed from 0800 with a gun fired
every fifteen minutes until sunset.[20]

This custom was observed in the United States Navy, as shown by
an interesting item in the journal of Mr. George Jones, a schoolmaster
on board the *Constitution*:

> Thursday, 25 [September, 1826]. The Commodore sailed yester-
> day for Gibraltar and today we have been paying "honor to whom
> honor was due." Our flags have been at half mast all day; and at
> noon, twenty-one guns were fired, first by this ship, and then, by
> the *Porpoise*. This was the late Ex-President Jefferson. After an
> interval of thirty minutes, the same number were given for his
> compatriot, John Adams, by a singular coincidence so closely asso-
> ciated with him in death as well as in life. At the first gun, each
> ship cockbilled its yards. I will explain the term as far as I am able.
> On common occasions the yards are kept at right angles with the
> mast; and to a sailor's eye, nothing looks so slovenly as a different
> position; and nothing is noticed sooner, or sooner disgraces a ship.
> The slings, however, had now been loosed, and at the first gun,
> every yard was thrown into a slanting position, so as to form an
> angle of about 70° with the horizon, the lower main yards inclin-
> ing to starboard, the fore and mizen to larboard; while the upper
> yard of each mast took a direction contrary to that of the lower
> ones (*passis crinibus*.)[21] The operation[22] is an unusual one in our
> service. The French and Austrians have their ships thus in mourn-
> ing annually during the last three days of Holy Week.

But the custom has no bearing on the naive remarks a lady made
some years ago to the captain of a warship in the harbor of Ville-
franche: "Captain, I think that you have the most beautiful ship in
port, for all your rigging hangs in such beautiful festoons, and it is so
graceful to see rope ends waving in the breeze." Lesson: Smart ships
do not show "Irish pennants."

CROSSING THE LINE

*For you must know that any craft who'd fain
Cross the Great Sea Lord's Special Royal Domain,
Must pay the tribute that King Neptune wishes,*

[20] W. N. T. Beckett, *A Few Naval Customs, Expressions, Traditions, and
Superstitions.*

[21] "Like disheveled hair."

[22] The practice was carried out in 1894 by men-of-war of five nations, on
word of the death of Alexander III. The warships, including the USS *Monocacy*,
anchored at Tientsin, China, followed the movements of the Russian ship.

GREAT
ENCOURAGEMENT
FOR
SEAMEN.

ALL GENTLEMEN SEAMEN and able-bodied LANDSMEN who have a Mind to diftinguifh themfelves in the GLORIOUS CAUSE of their COUNTRY, and make their Fortunes, an. Opportunity now offers on board the Ship RANGER, of Twenty Guns, (for FRANCE) now laying in PORTSMOUTH, in the State of NEW-HAMP-SHIRE, commanded by JOHN PAUL JONES Efq; let them repair to the Ship's Rendez-vous in PORTSMOUTH, or at the Sign of Commodore MANLEY, in SALEM, where they will be kindly entertained, and receive the greateft Encouragement.---The Ship RANGER, in the Opinion of every Perfon who has feen her is looked upon to be one of the beft Cruizers in AMERICA.---She will be always able to Fight her Guns under a moft excellent Cover ; and no Veffel yet built was ever calculated for failing fafter, and making good Weather.

Any GENTLEMEN VOLUNTEERS who have a Mind to take an agreable Voyage in this pleafant Seafon of the Year, may, by entering on board the above Ship RANGER, meet with every Civility they can poffibly expect, and for a further Encouragement depend on the firft Opportunity being embraced to reward each one agreable to his Merit.

All reafonable Travelling Expences will be allowed, and the Advance-Money be paid on their Appearance on Board.

IN CONGRESS, MARCH 29, 1777.

RESOLVED,

THAT the MARINE COMMITTEE be authorifed to advance to every able Seaman, that enters into the CONTINENTAL SERVICE, any Sum not exceeding FORTY DOL-LARS, and to every ordinary Seaman or Landfman, any Sum not exceeding TWEN-TY DOLLARS, to be deducted from their future Prize-Money.

By Order of CONGRESS,

JOHN-HANCOCK, PRESIDENT.

DANVERS: Printed by E. Ruffell, at the North fide the Bell-Tavern.

Revolutionary War Recruiting Broadside. The earliest known existing American naval recruiting poster. *Courtesy The Essex Institute, Salem, Mass.*

And be received by mermaids, bears, and fishes.
We will see you on the morn,
And any who resist will wish he had not been born.[23]

The boisterous ceremonies of "crossing the line" are of such ancient vintage that their derivation is lost; such horseplay took place in the Middle Ages, and even before that when ships crossed the thirtieth parallel or passed through the Straits of Gibraltar. These early ceremonies were extremely rough and to a large degree were supposed to test the crew to determine whether or not the novices, the "boots," on their first cruise could endure the hardships of a life at sea. Then, as now, it was primarily a crew's "party." The Vikings are reported to have practiced similar ceremonies on crossing certain parallels. It is highly probable that the present-day ceremony was passed on to the Angles, Saxons, and Normans from the Vikings.

At an even earlier time there is record of ceremonies of propitiation. Neptune, the mythological god of the seas, was appeased by the seamen, and marks of respect were paid those of his under-water domain. It is plausible that a part of the present ceremony grew out of the superstitions of those days, even though Viking sailors had come to doubt the physical existence of Neptune. Nevertheless, Neptunus Rex is today the "majesty" who rules in the ceremonies.

Those who have "crossed the line" are called Sons of Neptune or "shellbacks." Bona fide Sons of Neptune always compose the cast for present-day ceremonies. It is a curious fact that men will suffer a very severe initiation in order to qualify to inflict the same on other men.

Sailors treasure their Neptune certificates, issued "in Latitude oo–oo and Longitude ————," and usually addressed to "all Mermaids, Sea Serpents, Whales, Sharks, Porpoises, Dolphins, Skates, Eels, Suckers, Lobsters, Crabs, Pollywogs, and other living things of the sea, . . ." and stating that so-and-so "has been found worthy to be numbered as one of our trusty shellbacks, has been gathered to our fold and duly initiated into the solemn mysteries of the ancient order of the deep."

The crossing-the-line ceremonies of the modern Navy are most picturesque. The discomfort of a good dousing in the tank, a slight shock of electricity from the fork of the "Devil," and the slap-happy shaving ceremony comprise the most unpleasant features of the initiation. In merchant ships the ceremony is still reasonably severe in the physical discomforts inflicted. Officers of the United States Navy could

[23] From the "Crossing the Line" ritual of the British Navy. All dialogue is in rhyme.

at one time "buy off," by giving the Neptune party a number of bottles of beer. Unless the ceremonies are very crude, however, it is a tradition that all officers, and younger officers in particular, undergo the initiation.

The oldest and most dignified senior "shell-back" member of the crew is customarily selected as Neptunus Rex; his first assistant is Davy Jones. Her Highness Amphitrite is usually a good looking young seaman who will appear well in a *deshabillé* of seaweed and rope yarns. The Court usually consists of the Royal Scribe, the Royal Doctor, the Royal Dentist, the Devil, and other names that suit the fancy of the Neptune party. The Bears have the difficult task of rounding up those to be initiated, and also standing "dousing" watches in the canvas water tank.

The night before the ship crosses the line, it is the custom that Davy Jones shall appear on board with a message to the captain from His Majesty, Neptunus Rex, stating at what time he wants the ship hove to for the reception of the Royal Party and with specific summons for certain men to appear before him. This reception of Davy Jones usually takes place after dark and may be most impressive. The ship heaves to, and amid a glare of lights and the spray of fire hoses, Davy Jones emerges from the hawse or is hoisted in over the bows to deliver his message. He is always received in a dignified manner by the captain and officer of the deck. By careful planning, supervision, and timing, the commanding officer can keep within bounds the boisterous horseplay of the oldest and most interesting ceremony of the sea. Of course, it is a "field day" for the Neptune Party and the old shellbacks, because as Harry Lydenburg writes: "What is more natural than that on later voyages the seasoned old salt should call on the green shipmates to prove that they could not only stand the terrors and strains and stresses so soon to begin, but that they also had enough of the courage and good fellow in their make-up to take in good humor the joking and the ragging and the joshing accepted as part of daily life aboard ship.[24]

---

[24] *Crossing the Line, Tales of the Ceremony during Four Centuries*: From Bulletin of New York Public Library, August 1955, quoted courtesy of writer and compiler, H. M. Lydenburg, who by years of exhaustive research located or inspected about all records that pertain to this ancient ceremony.

SAMPLE SUMMONS FOR A NEPTUNE PARTY

USS —— ON ENTERING

DOMAIN OF NEPTUNUS REX
NOTICE AND LISTEN YE LANDLUBBER

I order and command you to appear before me and my Court on the morrow to be initiated in the mysteries of my Special Royal Domain. If you fail to appear, you shall be given as food for sharks, whales, sea turtles, pollywogs, salt water frogs, and all living things of the sea, who will devour you, head, body, and soul as a warning to landlubbers entering my domain without warrant.

You are charged with the following offenses: . . . .

. . . .

THEREFORE, appear and obey or suffer the penalty.

DAVY JONES
Secretary of HIS Majesty[25]

Registered:

Decorative certificates suitable for framing, with the traditional nautical phraseology, once were furnished by the Navy Department; if they are not available they may be purchased. They should be presented within a few days after initiation; also a small card for billfold with facsimile of certificate is often issued to the new shellback. Sailors treasure such seagoing kudos and consider them particularly valuable when captains or executives of ships authenticate them with signature and title.

Over one hundred years ago, Captain Basil Hall, RN, wrote: "Its evil is transient, if any evil there be; while it certainly affords Jack a topic for a month beforehand and fortnight afterwards; and if so ordered to keep its monstrosities within the limits of strict discipline (which is easy enough) it may even be made to add to the authority of the officers instead of weakening their influence."

---

[25] Fill in specific offenses such as "too many captain's masts," "excessive liberty," "repeated seasickness," etc. Reading some of these offenses at initiation before sentence adds much to the hilarity.

SAMPLE RITUAL FOR A NEPTUNE PARTY

Davy Jones Comes Aboard

The night before crossing the line when summonses are delivered.

(Note: Shortly after dark on night before "crossing the line" Davy Jones accompanied by the Royal Navigator, possibly the Judge and the Undertaker of Royal Court of Neptune come up over the bow in boatswains chairs or come up a forward hatch amid a spray of fire hoses with the scene lit by searchlights.)

Dialogue

(Davy Jones comes aboard and hails the bridge.)

DAVY JONES *to officer of the deck:* Ship Ahoy!

OOD: Aye, aye, sir.

DAVY JONES: What ship?

OOD: USS ———

DAVY JONES: What course?

OOD: *(State course.)*

DAVY JONES: Very well. I have been awaiting your arrival. You will notify the commanding officer that I, Davy Jones, have a message to deliver from His Royal Majesty Neptunus Rex.

OOD: Aye, aye, sir.

(Permit a half-minute or so to elapse.)

OOD: Your Honor, the commanding officer awaits and will receive you now.

DAVY JONES: Very well, sir.

(Proceeding to place designated—usually forecastle. If the meeting takes place on the quarterdeck, word is passed for all hands to follow Davy Jones as he proceeds aft with a master-at-arms leading. A ceremony should be made out of the visit.)

CAPTAIN *to Davy Jones:* Greetings, Davy Jones. Welcome aboard.

DAVY JONES: My congratulations, Captain, on your fine command. Some years since we last met.

CAPTAIN: Yes, it was aboard the USS ——— about ——— years ago.

DAVY JONES: I have orders for you and some summonses for your pollywogs from Neptunus Rex.

CAPTAIN: I will be glad to receive them.

(Davy Jones then reads the general order from King Neptune.)

I, Davy Jones came out of the sea tonight to bring from His Oceanic Majesty, King Neptune, Ruler of the Seven Seas, all the summonses for the landlubbers, the pollywogs, the sea vermin, the crabs, and eels who have not been initiated into the Supreme Order of the Deep. We of the great Neptune's Court bring serious indictments against those who still have traces of heifer dust and cow dung on their feet, as well as those of the big towns who think they are real city slickers. But no matter, all will be shellbacks after the rough treatment on the morrow, at which time, those summoned will appear before the Royal Judge of His August and Imperial Majesty, Neptunus Rex, and there answer for offenses committed both aboard and ashore.

Captain, a few officers and men have already requested leniency, but be it known King Neptune has no favorites. All landlubbers since men first followed the sea have endured the strict initiation required by the King of the Sea. No! There will be no leniency—all pollywogs will receive appropriate punishment on the morrow.

And remember, sorrow and woe to those who resist or talk in a light or jesting manner of the ceremony, or of His Majesty, the Ruler of the Seven Seas, or of the Queen Amphitrite, or belittles Royal Members of his Supreme Court. So—Beware! Beware!

Good-by Captain, I will see you with the Great Neptune on the morrow.

(Leaves shouting, "Gangway for Davy Jones" as he disappears down a hatch forward or over the bow amid a fire hose spray, and with appropriate lighting effects, pyrotechnics, etc.)

Initiation in the Ancient Order of the Deep Crossing the Line

When all is in readiness for the reception of King Neptune and party, the ship's navigator reports the ship is on the "line." Davy Jones then appears forward and reports to the officer of the deck that the captain is to be informed that Neptunus Rex and the Royal Court have been sighted ahead. The personal flag of King Neptune, "the Jolly Roger" (skull and cross-bones) is broken when King Neptune and Court appear on deck. Attention is sounded on the bugle; officers and crew fall in at quarters or where designated. If convenient, at this point there can be a very brief ceremony when Neptune meets Davy Jones just before meeting the captain.

NEPTUNE *(on meeting Davy Jones)*: Well, well, what a fine ship and what a cargo of landlubbers.

(Note: About this time the officer of the deck should salute Neptune and with seriousness report that the captain awaits the Royal Party. Then all move to the place of ceremony, giving as many people as possible the opportunity to see King Neptune and the

*Royal Court before the ceremonies of initiation, such as passing
down one side of the ship as at personnel inspection.)*

CAPTAIN *(coming on deck)*: A sailor's welcome to you, King
Neptune. It is a great pleasure to have you with us.

NEPTUNE: The pleasure is mine *(then brief remarks)*. Allow me to
present Royal Navigator Shellback who will relieve you. I am so
glad to be with you, Captain, and have prepared for a busy day in
order to make all your landlubbers fit subjects of my great Raging
Main.

CAPTAIN: Your Majesty, may I invite your attention to the fact that
I have several young officers and crew members aboard who have
not been in the Navy long enough to have had the opportunity
to visit your domain and become shellbacks. I beg you to be as
lenient with them as possible.

NEPTUNE: Captain, I am very sorry, I *must* be severe, there will be
no exceptions.

*(Captain then introduces officers who have crossed the line
before, and all converse with Neptune and his Royal Court for a
minute or so.)*

CAPTAIN: Neptune, I turn over my command to you for such time
as you wish.

NEPTUNE: Very well, Captain, I thank you. *(Turns to Royal Navigator.)* Royal Navigator, proceed to the bridge and direct the ship
be put on the course assigned.[26]

*(The Royal Court is then escorted to the "throne." Solemnly,
Neptune and Court ascend and take assigned places to witness
ceremonies. On order of Neptune, initiation commences with officers first. Captain and senior officers sit back of Neptune or on
another platform.)*

The *dramatis personae* can be large or small, depending on the size
of the ship and space for ceremony. The traditional titles are: King
Neptune or Neptunus Rex and Queen Amphitrite; sometimes a daughter or Royal Princess; the Royal Baby (often the fattest man in the
crew wearing only a diaper); Davy Jones, Royal Navigator (and assistants if needed); Royal Chaplain, Royal Judge (and assistants), Neptune's Officer of the Day, Royal Chief Bear (and sufficient assistants
for the tank), Barber, Jesters, Devil, and Police. Often there is a Royal
Scribe to keep record of all initiations.

---

[26] The above dialogue was used in the ceremony aboard the USS *Augusta*,
on crossing the equator on November 23, 1936, in the Java Sea.

A NAVY CUSTOM—CROSSING THE INTERNATIONAL DATE LINE

Before World War II, when U. S. Navy transports *Henderson* and *Chaumont* made frequent cruises across the Pacific to the Far East, a ritual of initiation in some respects similar to that of "crossing the line" took place when the ships crossed the International Date Line on the voyages to the westward. The neophytes, both officers and men, were subpoenaed for appearance before the Court of the Grand Dragon, where sentence was pronounced and initiation took place. As in the preliminaries for the Neptune ceremonies, considerable amusement was derived from the mock charges and specifications, with humorous incidents stressed and slight personal idiosyncrasies exaggerated. Advance radio dispatches and bulletins supposedly received from Officers of the Court of the Grand Dragon, served "to build up the act," heightened interest, and often added to the apprehension of those about to be initiated. Those who "passed the test" were given small cards attesting to that fact. Those issued on men-of-war that crossed the one hundred eightieth meridian during the war usually stated that the ship was "on a mission of war to effect the 'Setting of the Rising Sun.'"

ARCTIC INITIATIONS

The USS *Nautilus* having first set the pace, the nuclear submarine *Skate* then made a record trip of 3,090 miles beneath the polar ice, testing new equipment and methods of breaking holes through the polar ice cap. On 17 March 1959, the *Skate* rose to the surface of the North Pole and committed the ashes of the distinguished Arctic explorer, Sir Hubert Wilkins, to the fierce Arctic winds.

Arctic initiations are already becoming the custom. Everybody who had not been to the Arctic previously had his nose painted blue and was supposed to wear paper sun glasses until midnight. But for those who had not been to the Pole before (nearly all on the *Skate*) a stiff initiation was given—beginning the day the *Skate* left the Pole. The now "old timers" were charged with various "crimes" in much the manner of "crossing the line" ceremonies, as they were brought before Borealis Rex for sentence. It was the rule that all were guilty until proved innocent, and special permission for legal counsel was only given after sentencing. Some were charged with having "nonregulation faces" and others with being "fugitives" from other submarines.

One was charged with being a "reserve officer." K.P. duty was given in most instances as sentence.[27]

Men have always liked to have proof that they were there. We have record of certificates being issued for membership in the Grand Order of Arctic Adventurers in 1956 for those of the Navy who in ships and planes helped supply the personnel stationed along the Dew Line in the Arctic.

GOLDEN SHELLBACKS

As previously mentioned, there have been ceremonies for years by Navy ships when crossing the 180th meridian (International Date Line) that entitled initiates to become certificated as members of the Grand Dragon, often called Golden Dragon. Those who cross at the intersection of the 180th meridian and the equator are certified as Golden Shellbacks by their commanding officers on wallet-sized certificates. The cards state in the left corner:

> By order of Their Majesties
> GOLDEN DRAGON
> NEPTUNUS REX

In 1965 while in the USS *Capitaine* (AGSS 336), Jimmie E. Brooks, YN 2(SS) USN, wrote to *Shipmate* that Davy Jones, speaking to all hands, said: "To pay homage to Neptunus Rex, we are not soliciting His Majesty to come up out of the sea to greet us. Rather we are going to meet him and his royal court. To say that you have crossed the 180th meridian at the equator is one thing, but to say that you have sailed *under* that point is an honor that can be bestowed only upon submariners."

DRAWING A DEAD HORSE

Often, to many a young naval officer's regret, under certain conditions one may draw an advance in pay. A colorful ceremony was once con-

[27] Fifty years after Admiral Robert E. Perry reached the North Pole, Commander James F. Calvert, USN, commanding the U.S. Nuclear Submarine *Skate*, crunched through the ice exactly at the North Pole where he and his officers planted a United States flag and stood there with their men at the top of the earth. Commander Calvert signed three certificates for all hands on the *Skate*'s first Arctic voyage: Realm of the Arctic Circle, for crossing that circle; Ancient Order of Magellan, for the round-the-world tour at the Pole; and Domain of the Royal Dragon, for crossing the 180th Meridian. "Plank Owners" certificates were given to the "charter members" of the crew.

nected with the time when the crew "stopped working for nothing."
Particularly in the Merchant Marine, seamen were permitted to draw
some money in advance; in the British Merchant Service it was approximately a month's advance when the sailor shipped. After five weeks or
so at sea, or subsequent to whatever time the debt was worked off, the
men made a horse out of canvas stuffed with old cordage and waste
material, or out of a cask with oakum tail and mane, and then permission was requested to light "the horse" and hoist it out to the end of a
boom or yard. This was done amid cheers, because it marked the time
that the crew started to accumulate wages "on the books." The advance was usually spent in riotous living at the last port; definite shore
plans could now be made for the port ahead. It was a joyous occasion.

When burning the "Dead Horse," both watches used to sing in
chorus:

> *Now, old horse your time has come,*
> *And we say so, for we know so!*
> *Altho' many a race you've won,*
> *Oh! poor old man,*
> *You're going now to say good-bye*
> *And we say so, for we know so;*
> *Poor old horse, you're going to die.*

DUELING AMONG THE OFFICERS OF THE NAVY

> *No apology can be received for a blow.*
> *For being intentionally spit on; for having wine, snuff, etc., thrown*
> *in the face, no apology is admissible, but redress must be sought*
> *by the duel, if the party aggressing rank as a gentleman.*

The above is part of the strict code in the days of dueling, and explains
why so many went to an early grave for an alleged violation of the
thirty-nine articles of *The Code of Honor.*

Between bulky tomes of historical reference in the Library of Congress is a thin, red-bound book, titled *The Code of Honor.* Written
by "A. Southron," probably a pseudonym for "A Southerner," it was
printed in Baltimore in 1847. There were originally but 175 copies,
and the one in the Library of Congress seems to be the only one extant.
The historic duels fought at Bladensburg, Maryland, such as that when
Stephen Decatur was mortally wounded, were fought under the specific rules of this little red book.

In the first half-century of our Navy there are records of numerous duels. The practice of settling by duels "affairs of honor among
gentlemen" was not confined to the senior officers, but was also a

method of redress among juniors and midshipmen. The history of the early Mediterranean Squadron of the U. S. Navy discloses a tragic record of this custom. One may read today on a tombstone near Syracuse, Sicily, the following epitaph:

> In memory of William R. Nicolson, a Midshipman in the Navy
> of the United States, who was cut off from society in the bloom of
> his youth and health, on the 18th day of September, A.D. 1804,
> aged eighteen years. His untimely death resulted from a duel
> fought with Midshipman Frederick C. DeKraft of the same ship.

Lieutenant William B. Finch, U. S. Navy, who afterwards changed his name to William Compton Bolton and who died as a commodore in command of the Mediterranean Squadron in 1849, killed Lieutenant Francis B. White of the Marine Corps in a duel fought at Boston in 1819.

Commodore Oliver Hazard Perry fought a duel with Captain John Heath of the Marine Corps with Commodore Decatur as Perry's second.

Lieutenant William Bainbridge killed the secretary of the British admiral commanding at Gibraltar in a duel fought over an alleged affair involving the "honor of the service." Stephen Decatur acted as Bainbridge's second.

There are many other cases. In fact, one historian alleges that more officers were killed in duels than in the naval actions of the period. But the most famous duel in our naval history was that between Commodore Barron and Commodore Decatur. This duel took place after a long interchange of acrimonious correspondence. The dispute centered on Barron's restoration to duty after five years' suspension of rank and pay that dated from February 8, 1808, in consequence of the *Chesapeake-Leopard* action off the Virginia capes on June 27, 1807.

The duel was fought on the morning of March 22, 1820, in a valley one-half mile from Bladensburg village, and about that distance from the present old Washington-Annapolis highway. Decatur had Commodore Bainbridge as a second; Barron had Captain Jesse D. Elliott.

The Code of Honor read: "After taking your place, you will salute your antagonist with a distant but not discourteous inclination of the head."

Just before the duel Barron expressed to Decatur the hope that "On meeting in another world they would be better friends than in this." Decatur replied, "I have never been your enemy, sir." The firing took place on the count two. Both officers fell. Decatur was shot through the abdomen, and Barron wounded in the thigh.

The brilliant, intrepid Decatur died at the age of 41, twelve hours after he was carried to his home on Lafayette Square, Washington.[28] Barron was subsequently restored to the active list and lived to become the senior commodore of the Navy, but never secured active sea service.

It is a civilized step forward that the custom of dueling is no longer part of the code of an officer and a gentleman. However, President Andrew Jackson, a duelist, believed strongly that dueling should be denied to civilians but should be permitted for the officers of the Army and Navy.

REMOVING THE RIGHT GLOVE WHEN SWORN AS A WITNESS

The custom of raising hands and eyes heavenwards when taking an oath is of great antiquity; and from early days the head was bared to the particular deity or to superior authority when taking the oath. When the Bible was published as a tome, the right hand was placed upon the Bible during the administration of the oath, and upon completion the Bible was kissed. In fact the kissing of the Bible continues in some localities, and was a general custom in this country until about seventy years ago, when the custom of raising the bared right hand, with head uncovered, became general. The Bible is still used in the Navy for the swearing of the court, judge advocate, recorder, and witnesses of courts-martial.

The practice of raising the right hand ungloved (always) came from the early days in England when all criminals were branded on the right hand. The hand was bared in order to ascertain whether or not the witness to be sworn was branded.

CUSTOM OF WEARING MEDALS ON THE LEFT BREAST

Medals and decorations are, for the most part, worn on the left breast. This custom may be traced from the practice of the Crusaders in wearing the badge of honor of their order near the heart. Also, the left side was the shield side of the Crusader, for the large shield carried on the

---

[28] Part of this house, the gift of Mrs. Truxton Beale, now houses the museum of the Naval Historical Foundation, which may be visited without charge. The handsome old mansion, presented by Mrs. Beale to the National Trust for Historic Preservation, is also open to the public at certain hours every day of the week.

left arm protected both the heart and the badge of honor. Swords were worn on the left side in order to be quickly drawn by the right hand.

"SOUNDING OFF" AT PARADE AND GUARD MOUNT

At parades and guard mounts in military and naval service, when the adjutant commands "Sound off," the band plays three chords of flourishes, which are called the "Three Cheers," before marching up and then down in front of the men under arms. When the band returns to its position, "Three Cheers" are again played.

This custom originated in Crusade days. Those soldiers designated for the Crusaders were set apart but formed in line with the other troops, and the music of the organization would march and then counter-march in front of those selected. This was a form of dedication ceremony. It is thought by authorities that the populace would give cheers throughout the ceremony, and that the three flourishes have remained symbolical of the applause accorded by the populace.

The dress parade is a survival of the days when visiting celebrities in all countries were shown the King's troops in impressive parade. The original intent was to render the display formidable and to impress the visitor with the strength of the state visited, rather than the present idea of a parade as a distinctive honor rendered the visitor.[29]

DIVINE SERVICE AT SEA

> *But our own hearts are our best prayer rooms, and the chaplains who can help us most are ourselves.*—Herman Melville

The following description of divine service at sea is taken from the *Cruise of the Frigate "Columbia,"* by William Murrell. The USS *Columbia* made a typical around-the-world cruise in 1838–41, visiting eighteen ports, spending 459 days at sea, and 313 days in port. The total mileage was 54,796.

Murrell writes:

> On Sunday mornings, immediately after quarters, should the weather permit, all hands are called to muster. The summons is instantly obeyed, by every one proceeding to the quarter-deck

---

[29] For the first time in twenty years, on February 25, 1959, the Army revived a tradition at historic Fort Myer, Virginia, by holding a horse-mounted review with the seven matched pairs of black and gray horses and white lead horse only used to draw funeral caissons at Arlington Cemetery. The salute was for retiring Chief Warrant Officer Philip A. Sellers, USA.

(the sick alone exempted) where the minister stands in readiness, arrayed in his clerical robes, and the capstan covered with the national flag to answer the purpose of a pulpit. The commodore takes his station on the weather side of the chaplain; the lieutenants, and all other commissioned and warrant officers on the weather side of the deck; the forward officers at the fife-rail, and petty officers at the fore-part of the main-mast. The blue-jackets take up their position abaft the mizzen-mast, clad in white frocks with blue collars, white trousers, and straw hats, looking the picture of cleanliness; whilst the marines are stationed and drawn up in rank, on the lee side of the deck, headed by their commanding officer, all in blue uniform. . . . After the usual routine of divine services had been performed, every monthly Sunday the articles of war are read. Punishments are always read, that is to say, death, or *worse* punishment as the sailor says. By worse punishment, he alludes to his grog being stopped, which article constitutes his principal creed.

Because of the arduous duties of naval ships, vessels have little time in port. To hold Divine Services, chaplains are often brought from larger vessels to smaller vessels and returned after services by helicopter. Without disrespect, this maneuver is known officially as "Operation Holy Joe," Holy Joe being an old sea-going name for the chaplain.

THE *CONSTITUTION* ("OLD IRONSIDES")

The U.S. Navy possesses in "Old Ironsides" the most successful and historic frigate that ever sailed the seas. She battered down enough of the stone forts of Tripoli to contribute directly to the treaty with that Barbary State. She escaped from Broke's squadron of six ships after a four-day chase. It was by the unparalleled seamanship and masterly stratagem of Captain Hull that the *Constitution* made her escape without losing a man, a gun, a boat, or an anchor. Hull's first lieutenant called it, "the advantages to be expected from perseverance under the most discouraging circumstances as long as any chance of escape may remain." She defeated the *Guerrière*, a crack British frigate, dismasting her twenty-five minutes after firing the first broadside, and she shot every spar out of the British frigate *Java*. It is a tradition that the *Constitution* did not take in her royals for this fight. She captured the British *Cyane* and *Levant* at the same time. They were smaller than "Old Ironsides," with a combined armament of 55 guns to the *Consti-*

tution's 52, but the more effective long 24s of the American frigate and Captain Stewart's excellent maneuvers carried the day.

Moses Smith, sponger of No. 1 gun on the *Constitution*, in the battle with the *Guerrière*, wrote:

> Several shots now entered our hull. One of the largest the enemy could command struck us, but the plank was so hard it fell out and sank in the waters. This was afterwards noticed and the cry arose: "Huzza! Her sides are made of iron! See where the shots fell out!" From that circumstance, the name of the *Constitution* was garnished with the familiar title, "Old Ironsides."

OFFICERS AND MEN OF THE NAVY IN THE WAR OF REVOLUTION

The list of officers of the Continental Navy comprised about 330 names. This roster includes the officers commissioned in France. There are no complete lists extant of the medical officers, pursers, midshipmen, and warrant officers. It is estimated that the number of petty officers and seamen of the Continental Navy reached a total of approximately 3,000 men.

PRIVATEERS AND LETTERS OF MARQUE

The majority of naval historians have underemphasized the work of the United States privateers. The Library of Congress has compiled a list of about 1,700 "letters of marque" which were issued to the privateers of the Continental Navy. It has been estimated that the total number of private vessels carrying arms totaled 2,000 ships, with 18,000 guns and 70,000 men.

FIRST COMMISSION FOR OFFICER AFLOAT

The first commission issued by President Washington to an officer afloat was issued to Captain Hopley Yeaton, master of a revenue cutter. The Continental Navy had been disbanded and the sole maritime defense was revenue cutters (now Coast Guard). This historic document, dated March 21, 1791, bears the signatures of both Washington and Jefferson. The Coast Guard searched for years for this first commission and secured it in 1934 from Miss Mary Yeaton, great granddaughter of Captain Yeaton.

THE ORIGIN OF "CHECKERED PAINTING" OF WOODEN SHIPS

The USS *Constitution*, "Old Ironsides," uses today the traditional out-board design of paint work: the white stripe with the black gunports. It is well established that this method of painting originated with Lord Nelson. Before Nelson attained high command, ships of the British Navy were painted buff, black, or buff and black. Black and white was used for side painting, but before Nelson's order the lines of the wales (strakes of thick outside planking) were painted white, and this gave a very narrow white band. It was ordered by Nelson that the white stripes follow the lines of the deck. Black strakes between were made wider and gun lids were painted black, all of which produced the well-known checkered broadside. After Trafalgar, and probably in memory of Nelson, this method of painting became universal in the British Navy. The same design and colors were soon adopted by other navies; from that day until sails of war left the sea, it was the general practice. The inboard vertical surface was in time painted white; red was also used for many years. Tradition tells us that the red bulkheads had practical value. They did not show blood as much as other colors.

IN MEMORY OF VASCO DA GAMA; THE PORT SIDE

The port side is designated the "honor side" in the Portuguese Navy in memory of the great navigator, da Gama, first in November 1497 to double Cape of Good Hope keeping Africa at all times on the port hand.

"*ESSEX*," FIRST AMERICAN MAN-OF-WAR TO DOUBLE CAPE OF GOOD HOPE AND CAPE HORN AND TO FIGHT IN THE PACIFIC

The *Essex*, built in 1799 by the patriotism of the people of Salem, Massachusetts, cost $154,686.77; she was the fastest sailer in the Navy for several years, and took the largest number of prizes of any vessel in the War of 1812.

In 1800 the *Essex*, under command of Captain Edward Preble, rounded the Cape of Good Hope.

Captain David Porter, in command of the *Essex*, rounded Cape Horn in 1813 and stood into Valparaiso for supplies. His object was to break up British navigation. He succeeded so well that it was only a short time until his major problem was to dispose of the merchant ship prizes and prisoners. Midshipman David G. Farragut, not quite twelve, was one of the youthful prize masters.

The final and fateful engagement came when the *Essex* was defeated by the British ships of war *Phoebe* and *Cherub*. In that fight, some of the deeds of Porter's heroic crew were truly blood stirring. Dying men who had hardly ever attracted notice among the ship's company uttered sentiments worthy of Washington. Two men, upon being told that they had lost a leg, jumped overboard rather than burden the capacity of the medical department.

RECRUITING TWO HUNDRED YEARS AGO

In 1771, one Sergeant Galbet was sent to raise recruits for the Marine Corps in Birmingham, England. His activities were announced in the following advertisement, July 22, 1771:

> *He that Works Hard is Sure to be Poor*
> *After six days hard labor come Sunday—you Rest*
> *And no sooner peeps Monday but you are quite shy of cash.*
> *Therefore to make life easy and fill your Pockets with Money*
>   Sergeant Galbet will learn any young man a Profession (without Fee or Reward) by which the Learner will be sure to earn a Guinea and a Crown the very first Hour. He will also introduce you to His Majesty's First Division of Marines, which is always quartered at Chatham, only thirty miles from London, to which Pleasure-Boats carry Passengers for Six-pence each. When you arrive at Chatham, you are immediately provided with Cloaths, free Quarters in a Public House, where you will be sure to meet with merry Fellows, a kind Land lady, and a rousing fire do nothing but on a fine day dance to the softest Music, feed on Dainties, drink the best Liquors and play at "Why won't you" with the prettiest girls, saying "Chatham for ever" and "God save the King."
>   N.B. He teaches no Militia or Apprentice
>   The Globe and Laurel

The last section of the *U. S. Naval Regulations* (1818) gives some idea of "Jack ashore" of the day and also of the system of recruiting men. The last article states:

> That seamen should be rescued, as far as practicable, from the fangs of rapacious landlords and others who frequently taking advantage of their habits of intoxication, and generally unsuspicious characters swindle them of the whole amount advanced to them by the recruiting officer, and to the prejudice of the seamen and of

the Service generally, leave them in a naked and destitute condition at the time of their appearance on board.

The section ends with advice to the recruiting officer to prevent the swindling of the men, by inducing them "to repair on board the receiving ship." The final words of the section are touched with a shade of irony, "and to take every means in his power to render [to the recruit] the Service as pleasing as possible."

NEW YEAR'S MIDWATCH LOG IN RHYME

How and when writing the New Year's Day midwatch log in rhyme began, no one knows, but custom has sanctioned it for many years. All that is prescribed in Article 1037 of *Navy Regulations* must be reported. All those facts plus the awkward names of some of the ships present, the lack of euphony in many nautical expressions, and the need to compress "the poetic form" pose challenging problems in the choice of words for the officer of the deck—the poet for a day.

USS *Newman K. Perry (DDR 883)*
The Bloomin' Newman *in a nest of four*
  At old Mike Twelve, not far from shore,
'Longside the Markab, *this year's first day,*
  Our posit Newport, Narragansett Bay.
To port is Turner *(outboard* McNair)
  To starboard Hawkins, *two mighty pair.*
SOPA *is* CO *of* DesLant, *on* Cascade,
  Other LantFleet *ships are on parade,*
But dig our Perry, *the coolest cat of all;*
  She reports all secure, watch standers on the ball.
Six crazy mooring lines, no strain and two-fold,
  Wire fore and aft, as of custom old.
On the plates, a snipe reports;
  Sparking Number One, Boiler Three snorts.
While the OOD is slowly arousing,
  On the beach, our boys are carousing.

Ens. J. C. Thompson, Jr., USN

FIRST WATCH AFTER COMMISSIONING IN RHYME

Some ships, in respect to tradition, have had all or part of the first watch of the new log book entered in rhyme, as:

First log of USS Stack
The USS Stack, *Monday the 20th, November, the year '39*
At Portsmouth, Virginia, in the Navy Yard there, this ship was
moored at the time,
To Pier Number 3 in Berth 24, with three-quarter-inch wire for
its line.
The admiral's flag was then hauled down,
The commission pennant broke in its place,
And soon of the guests and spectators,
There remained not even a trace.
But it was not the weather that caused it,
Nor was it the type of the grub
But the desire to wet their whistle,
At a party, by the ship, at the club.
Seriously—this ship commissioned,
Midst cold wind, rain, and a storm,
Though the spirit of its men and their officers
Will, *to the credit of our country, perform.*

—Lt. H. M. Heming, OOD,
Lt.Cdr. Olch, Cmdg.

THE BURNING OF THE "*PHILADELPHIA*"

The burning and boarding of the *Philadelphia*, February 16, 1804, was commented upon by Lord Nelson as the most bold and daring act of the age. The USS *Philadelphia* had been captured and was moored near the combination palace and fort of the Bashaw of Tripoli. The Tripolitans had a brig, two schooners, and a galley moored near by. A battery of 110 guns from the shore bore on the *Philadelphia*. The audacious Decatur, in a sixty-ton ketch manned by seventy-four officers and men, not only boarded the *Philadelphia* at night, but also fired and destroyed her after forcing overboard the Barbary pirate crew. Decatur made good his escape with only one man wounded. The American lieutenant was later promoted to captain at the age of twenty-four.

AN ATTEMPT AT MUTINY

For attempting to incite a mutiny, Midshipman Philip Spencer and two seamen were hanged at the yardarm of the United States brig *Somers*. The hangings took place in late November 1842 while the *Somers* was en route from Liberia to New York. Spencer, who was the son of the Honorable John C. Spencer, then Secretary of War under President Tyler, conspired with seamen Cromwell and Small to kill the officers, seize the ship, and go on a pirating expedition. Cromwell protested his innocence; Small confessed. There was overwhelming proof of Cromwell's guilt, and both seamen were hanged at the same yardarm with Spencer.

Commander Alexander Slidell Mackenzie, U. S. Navy, in command, was a stern, pious officer. He considered that his actions were warranted as, "Safety, our lives, and the honor of the flag entrusted to our charge, require the prisoners be put to death."

The national flag was hoisted at sea; drums rolled; a gun fired; and the crew walked away at the whips, hoisting the three in the air. Captain Mackenzie then talked to his crew, asked them for three cheers, and wrote:

> Three heartier cheers never went up from the deck of an American ship. In that electric moment I verily believe the purest and loftiest patriotism burst forth from the breasts of even the worst conspirators.

The captain then had the ensign half-masted, and read the service for the dead. He concluded:

> Preserve us from the dangers of the seas, and the violence of enemies; bless the United States, watch over all that are upon the deep, and protect the inhabitants of the land in peace and quiet, through Jesus Christ, our Lord.

In a rough sea and by lantern light, the bodies of Spencer, Cromwell, and Small were committed to the deep. The church pennant was hoisted above the ensign, and the crew dismissed after singing the Hundreth Psalm.

Commander Mackenzie was tried by a court-martial on the charge of murder. The general court-martial was convened at the Brooklyn Navy Yard on February 2, 1843, and lasted for six weeks. Mackenzie was honorably acquitted and the verdict was approved by President Tyler.

THE LEGEND OF SANTA BARBARA, THE PATRON SAINT OF CANNONEERS AND ORDNANCE MEN

> "Santa Barbara Virgin and Martyr" is said to have lived at the close of the third and beginning of the fourth century of the Christian Era. In the Roman, the Greek, and the Russian calendars, her feast day is celebrated on December 4, the presumed anniversary of her martyrdom.

Her rich father, Dioscorus, denounced his lovely and erudite daughter for becoming a Christian and beheaded her himself after she had been condemned by the governor. Dioscorus was struck by lightning and killed. Santa Barbara has from that time been considered the protectress against lightning, thunder, and flame and, of course, when gunpowder was used by Europeans, she became the "patron saint of cannoneers and ordnance men."

The first official recognition was by the cannoneers of Lille, France, who were commissioned in 1417 by letters patent as the "Confreres de Sainte Barbe." Other countries of Europe followed. A picture of Santa Barbara hangs in the office of the Chief of the Bureau of Ordnance.

The regimental tie (worn with civilian clothes) of the Royal Artillery, is blue with dark red zig-zags over it—symbolic of Santa Barbara's protection against flame and lightning.

INTERESTING FIRST EVENTS IN THE HISTORY OF THE NAVY

We may dispose of some questions of priority at the outset: John Manley, under a Massachusetts commission and under the Pine Tree Banner, was the first to make a British naval vessel strike her flag. John Paul Jones was the first to raise the Grand Union or American flag on a ship of war. Esek Hopkins was the first commander under a commission of Congress to carry the Grand Union flag in naval operations and to make a capture under it. John Barry was the first under a commission of the Congress and under the Grand Union flag to fight a battle with a British warship and make it strike its colors. These may be regarded as fundamental data in considering the much and often acrimoniously debated question: who was the Father of the American Navy.[30]

The Naval Academy was established at Annapolis August 10, 1845, transferred to Newport, Rhode Island, on May 5, 1861, and again established at Annapolis in September 1865. The Naval War College was established at Newport, Rhode Island, October 6, 1884. The Postgraduate School was established at Annapolis, October 1, 1909, and moved to Monterey, California, December 22, 1951.

The Bureau of Medicine and Surgery of the Navy was organized in 1842 by Dr. W. P. C. Barton. He was the first chief and the senior surgeon of the Navy at the time of his death.[31]

[30] Willis Fletcher Johnson.
[31] *Military Surgeon*, XLVI.

The first separate office to administer personnel was the Bureau of Navigation created in July 1862. At the same time were created the Bureau of Equipment and Recruiting and the Bureau of Steam Engineering.

The first Naval Militia was established by the State of Massachusetts on March 29, 1890.

The first naval officer to become an admiral was David Glasgow Farragut, so appointed on July 25, 1866.

The first naval officer to become a commodore was John Barry, senior officer in the Navy, appointed in 1794 after the Navy was reorganized.

The first naval officer to become an engineer in the U. S. Navy was Charles Haynes Haswell. He was commissioned February 19, 1836, by Secretary of the Navy Dickerson to design steam power equipment. The Bureau of Steam Engineering was created in 1862.

The first navy yard that was acquired after the establishment of the Navy Department April 30, 1798, was the Portsmouth Navy Yard, Portsmouth, New Hampshire. The property embraced 58.18 acres and had been in use as a shipbuilding yard. The price was $5,500.

The first American warship of iron using steam was the *Michigan*, built at Erie, Pennsylvania, under Act of Congress September 9, 1842. She was fabricated in Pittsburgh and transported in parts to Erie where she was completed and launched in 1844. On June 17, 1905, she was renamed the *Wolverine* and officially stricken from the naval list March 12, 1927.

The first warship with propelling machinery below the waterline was the screw warship *Princeton*, designed by John Ericsson in 1841.

The first paddle-wheeled steam warships were the USS *Mississippi* and USS *Missouri*, finished in 1841. The *Fulton the First* of 2,745 tons was built by Robert Fulton in 1814–15 for the Navy at a cost of $320,000.

The first United States warship to be docked in a government drydock was the *Delaware* at the Norfolk drydock, Portsmouth, Virginia, on the anniversary of the battle of Bunker Hill, June 17, 1833.

The first United States warship to circumnavigate the world was the USS *Vincennes*, commanded by Commander William Bolton Finch. The *Vincennes* left New York September 3, 1826, and returned via the Cape of Good Hope on June 8, 1830.

The first hospital ship definitely assigned for the purpose was the USS *Solace*, fitted out in 1898. The idea and general supervision of fitting out is credited to Admiral William Knickerbocker Van Reypen. The *Navy Register* (1864) lists *Red Rover* as "Hospital Steamer."

The first battleship and forerunner of the dreadnought was the USS *Maine*. The keel was laid October 17, 1888, and the vessel was launched in 1890. The *Maine* was destroyed by a mysterious explosion in the harbor of Havana, Cuba, February 15, 1898. This hastened the declaration of war with Spain. Of a crew of 354, only 16 escaped injury or death. The *Maine* had 12-inch side armor and two 10-inch guns in each of the two turrets.

The first electrically propelled vessel of the Navy was the *Langley* (former collier *Jupiter*). The *Langley* was commissioned April 7, 1913, and converted to an aircraft carrier April 21, 1920.

The first large floating drydock of the Navy was the *Dewey*, last at Olongapo, Philippine Islands. This dock was towed there from the Chesapeake Bay, a distance of 13,000 miles. The passage took 150 days.

The first Protestant services in California were conducted near the end of June 1846 by Commander J. B. Montgomery, U. S. Navy, at Yerba Buena Plaza, San Francisco. He requested permission to hold services after finding no Protestant church ashore. Montgomery, who commanded the USS *Portsmouth*, also hoisted the Stars and Stripes ashore at San Francisco on July 9, 1846, when official news of the war with Mexico reached him.

The first commander in chief of the Army and Navy to hold divine service for Navy personnel was President Franklin D. Roosevelt. On Easter Sunday, April 1, 1934, the President in the absence of a chaplain stood on the quarterdeck of the *Nourmahal* and read the service from the Episcopal *Book of Common Prayer*. The officers and men of the USS *Ellis* were present. The flag of the president flew from the yacht.

The first chief of the Bureau of Construction, Equipment, and Repair was a captain (line officer) of the Navy, although the law required the chief "to be a skilled naval constructor." By the Act of March 3, 1853, John Lenthall, a naval constructor, was appointed Chief of Bureau. Lenthal remained Chief of Bureau until 1871. He was not a naval officer until 1866 when Congress provided that naval constructors should have the rank and pay of officers of the Navy.

Before the passing of this Act of 1866,

> the naval constructors employed at the several navy yards and stations were not regularly commissioned naval officers, as they are at the present time, but their standing was somewhat similar to that of a foreman in a navy yard, as they were employed or laid off as the exigencies of the work in hand required.[32]

[32] From paper read before Postgraduate Department on May 22, 1913, by Rear Admiral W. G. Du Bose (C.C.), U. S. Navy.

The first surgeon and surgeon's mate were authorized by the Act of January 6, 1776. The surgeon was commissioned; the mate was a warrant officer. In 1777, an examination was provided for both surgeons and surgeon's mates. The pay of the first surgeons was increased in 1789 to $50.00 per month from $21.33 to $25.00 per month.

The first civil engineers of the staff corps were appointed in 1867. Their status had been that of civil employees before this date. In 1871, a law provided that they have such rank as the president might fix. For many years ten officers comprised this corps.

The first dental corps was established in 1912. The original act provided for a corps that could be expanded to one dentist for 1,500 of enlisted personnel.

The nurse corps (female) was authorized by an Act of Congress in 1908.

The first General Board of the Navy was established by a Navy Department order of March 13, 1900. Confidential instructions were originally issued for its guidance. The General Board had no executive functions and acted in an advisory capacity.

The first shell fired by our Navy in World War I was by J. O. Sabin, a gun-pointer on the naval collier *Jupiter*, at a sub in the Bay of Biscay, June 5, 1917. Sabin also helped sink the last German sub when he acted as gun-pointer of the crew which finished off the *U-97* in Lake Michigan at a target practice in 1921.

The first ship (a Japanese transport) sunk by a surface ship of our Navy since the Spanish American War was sunk in World War II in 1942 in the Battle of Makassar Straits by the *John D. Ford* (DD 228).

The world's first nuclear-powered submarine, the *Nautilus* (SSN-571) was commissioned September 1954. She is approximately 320 feet in overall length, has a surfaced displacement of approximately 3,000 tons, and cost an estimated $55,000,000.

The first United States ship to fly the flag of the United Nations was the USS *Putnam* at noon on July 23, 1948, when she was anchored in the harbor at Haifa, Israel. She was in the service of the United Nations, being assigned to U.N. mediator Count Folke-Bernadotte, who later met his death while trying to negotiate a truce between the Arab nations and Israel.

The USS *Higbee* is the only combatant ship which commemorates the name of a woman. Mrs. Lena Sutcliffe Higbee, who died in 1941, was the second superintendent of the Navy Nurse Corps.

The only German submarine ever boarded and captured by the U. S. Navy, the *U-505*, is at the Museum of Science and History, Chicago, Illinois. A bronze plaque tells the story: "This prize of war is dedicated to the memory of the American seamen who went down to unmarked ocean graves helping to win victory at sea."

> The *U-505* was boarded and captured on June 4, 1944, off Cape Blanco, French West Africa, by Task Force 22.3 of the U.S. Atlantic Fleet. This is the only German submarine ever boarded and captured at sea, and the first man-of-war so captured by the U.S. Navy since 1815.[33]

WAVES, the officially recognized title for "Women Accepted for Voluntary Emergency Service," was established by an Act of Congress on July 31, 1942. Recruiting ended in 1945 with a peak enrollment of 86,000. The force was greatly reduced after the war ended, and after the passage (1948) of the Women's Armed Service Integration Act, women—both commissioned and enlisted—were taken into the regular Navy. The organization was commanded until 1946 by Mildred H. McAfee, president of Wellesley College on leave and the first WAVE to be promoted to captain (in 1945).

Marine Women, the officially recognized title of the Marine Corps Women's Reserve, became a part of the Marine Corps in February 1943. By June 1944, the authorized quota of 18,000 enlisted had been met and approximately 800 officers trained and assigned. Major (later Colonel) Ruth Cheney Streeter was chosen as wartime director. As for the WAVES, after the passage of the 1948 Act, those who were retained became "Regulars." On June 30, 1965, there were approximately 1,600 enlisted women marines and 140 officers serving on active duty.

BRIEF HISTORY OF ORIGIN OF NAVY DEPARTMENT

The first agency to handle naval matters was the Marine Committee, consisting of three members, established by Congress in legislation of 1775.

In November 1776, a "Continental Navy Board" was established to consist of three competent persons and to be subordinate to the Marine Committee.

In October 1779, a Board of Admiralty succeeded the Marine Committee, and its subordinate Continental Navy Board was given direct control of all naval and marine affairs. The Board of Admiralty con-

---

[33] Captain Daniel V. Gallery, USN, commanding TG 22.3 made the capture, and as an admiral, Gallery was mainly instrumental in enlisting the interest and financial support to preserve this historic capture as a memorial and a museum. Both the Royal and Royal Canadian Navies boarded and captured a German U-boat during World War II.

sisted of five commissioners—two of the Board to be members of Congress and three to be appointed.

In February 1781, the Board of Admiralty was succeeded by a Secretary of Marine who had all powers of the preceding board.

In August 1781, an Agent of Marine was appointed, who took over all duties of agents, boards, and committees previously established.

In August 1789, a law placed the Navy under the Secretary of War and there it remained for nine years.

In April 1798, a Navy Department was established "at the Seat of Government" under the control of a "Secretary of the Navy." This marked the beginning of the present organization, the Navy Department. Government navy yards were established in 1800 and 1801. The Secretary of the Navy was directed by the president to purchase and establish navy yards at Portsmouth, New Hampshire, Boston, Massachusetts, New York, New York, Philadelphia, Pennsylvania, and Gosport, near Norfolk, Virginia. These yards are today on the original sites with the exception of the yard at Philadelphia, which was moved to League Island in 1868.

In February 1815, a "Board of Commissioners" was created to supplement the Navy Department and serve under the Secretary. The board was comprised of captains of the Navy who received appointments from the president subject to confirmation by the Senate. This board was in existence for twenty-seven years.

ORIGIN AND DEVELOPMENT OF THE BUREAUS OF THE DEPARTMENT

In August 1842, the "Board of Commissioners" was abolished and five bureaus were established under the Secretary of the Navy.

(1) A Bureau of Yards and Docks.
(2) A Bureau of Construction, Equipment, and Repair.
(3) A Bureau of Provisions and Clothing.
(4) A Bureau of Ordnance and Hydrography.
(5) A Bureau of Medicine and Surgery.[34]

In July, 1862, the Navy Department was reorganized and eight bureaus provided by law.

---

[34] Matthew F. Maury, a junior line officer of the Navy, did much to effect the bureau system by his "broadsides" on the failings of the "Navy Board"; he wrote under the *nom de plume* of "Harry Bluff."

(1) A Bureau of Yards and Docks.
(2) A Bureau of Equipment and Recruiting.
(3) A Bureau of Navigation.
(4) A Bureau of Ordnance.
(5) A Bureau of Construction and Repair.
(6) A Bureau of Steam Engineering.
(7) A Bureau of Provisions and Clothing.
(8) A Bureau of Medicine and Surgery.

Between 1885 and 1889, Secretary of the Navy Whitney effected numerous administrative reforms that made way for the expansion of the whole naval establishment in the nineties.

President Theodore Roosevelt did much in championing the cause of the Navy as to increased naval construction and new designs but was less successful in his efforts to reorganize the Navy Department.

Following World War II and after a considerable number of hearings and debate, the Army, Navy, and Air Force, for purposes of economy and coordination, were placed under a new title created by Congress—the Department of Defense. James Forrestal, able Secretary of the Navy, was the first to hold the powerful office of Secretary of Defense.

The Secretary of the Navy heads administratively the Commandant of the Marine Corps and the Chief of Naval Operations. The Chief of Naval Operations has a vice chief and various deputy chiefs for plans, policy, and operations; manpower, personnel, and training; logistics; surface warfare; air warfare; and sub-surface warfare. The Secretary of the Navy has as principal members of his staff an under secretary and assistant secretaries for manpower, reserve affairs, and logistics; financial management; and research, engineering, and systems.

The Naval Material Support Establishment (NMSE) was created on July 1, 1963, and consisted of the Chief of Naval Material, the Bureau of Naval Weapons (merger in 1960 of Bureau of Aeronautics and Ordnance), the Bureau of Ships, the Bureau of Supplies and Accounts, the Bureau of Yards and Docks, and field activities associated with the foregoing bureaus.

In a 1966 reorganization, the NMSE (reconstituted as the Navy Material Command) was placed under the Chief of Naval Operations but headed by a Chief of Naval Material under whom there are five functional commands headed by flag officers: (1) Air Systems Command, (2) Sea Systems Command, (3) Electronics Systems Command, (4) Supply Systems Command, (5) Facilities Engineering Command.

NAVAL GRADES AND SENIORITY

In concise, chronological sequence, Lieutenant Sprince, USN, presents the evolution of the naval grades of the line officer. Special attention is called to the downgrading of the boatswain, and the changes in status of the grade of midshipman.[35]

1775—Captain,[1] Lieutenant, Boatswain, and Master Mate.

1794—Captain,[1] Lieutenant,[2] Sailing Master, Boatswain, Master Mate, and Midshipman.

1806—Captain,[1] Master Commandant, Lieutenant,[2] Sailing Master, Master Mate, Boatswain, and Midshipman.

1837—Captain,[1] Commander (heretofore called Master Commandant), Lieutenant,[2] Master (heretofore called Sailing Master), Passed Midshipman, Master Mate (only if warranted as such),[3] Boatswain, and Midshipman.

1852—Captain, Commander, Lieutenant, Master, Passed Midshipman, Midshipman, and Boatswain.

1862—Rear Admiral,[4] Commodore,[5] Captain, Commander, Lieutenant Commander (heretofore senior Lieutenants called Lieutenants Commanding), Lieutenant, Master, Ensign, Passed Midshipman, and Midshipman.

1882—Admiral, Vice-Admiral, Rear Admiral, Captain, Commander, Lieutenant Commander, Lieutenant, Lieutenant J.G. (heretofore called Master), Ensign, Ensign J.G. (heretofore called Passed Midshipman), and Naval Cadets[6] (heretofore called Midshipmen).

1902—Admiral of the Navy,[7] Admiral, Vice-Admiral, Rear Admiral, Captain, Commander, Lieutenant Commander, Lieutenant, Lieutenant J.G., Ensign, and Midshipman.

1944—Fleet Admiral, Admiral, Vice-Admiral, Rear Admiral, Commodore, Captain, Commander, Lieutenant Commander, Lieutenant, Lieutenant J.G., Ensign, and Midshipman.

[1] Senior Captains of a fleet or squadron were given the courtesy title Commodore.

[2] Senior Lieutenants who had command of ships of lesser magnitude were called Lieutenants Commanding.

[3] Warrant Mates were not in line for promotion. Consequently this rate died out quickly.

[4] The titles Admiral and Vice-Admiral were established at this time; the grade of Vice-Admiral was not filled until 1864 and that of Admiral until 1866.

[5] This title was abolished by an Act of March 3, 1899.

[6] The grade of Midshipman was dropped, but it was revived in 1902.

[7] Only Admiral Dewey ever held this grade.

[35] Richard H. Sprince, "From Admiral to Midshipman," U. S. Naval Institute *Proceedings*, November 1956, pp. 1188–1193.

NOTES ON NAVAL UNIFORMS

The navies of the world have conformed in no small degree to the British in uniform regulations. The French Navy influenced the British Navy in the practice of wearing epaulets; also other navies had official uniforms before the British.

We inherit the "navy blue." British naval officers meeting at their favorite rendezvous at Will's Coffee House, Scotland Yard, decided in 1745 that they would petition the Admiralty for an official uniform in order to standardize as in other navies of the day. This was done, and the Admiralty asked certain officers to appear in what they considered a good design. Some liked grey with red facings, but Captain Philip Saumerez is reported to have worn a blue uniform with white facings.

Blue and white was subsequently chosen by the Admiralty. The story goes that since George II must make the final decision, he selected the colors from the riding habit of the First Lord's wife, the Duchess of Bedford, who was riding in the park. But it is told that the Duchess wore the colors already selected by her husband.

The cocked hat developed from the early, soft, wide-brimmed hat. The brim was first turned up on one side and then the other. Cocked hats were originally worn "athwartships" by naval officers. They were worn "fore and aft" in the British Navy by captains and below in 1795, and required as part of the uniform of all officers in 1825. Three "turn ups" were made to shape the three-cornered hats of our Colonial days. Nelson's cocked hat was triangular with the back turned up. Enlisted men wore low, plain cocked hats until about 1780.

The epaulet is a glorified, decorative amplification of the shoulder strap. The original shoulder strap had its practical use as a device to prevent the bandolier from slipping off the shoulder. In the early days of the United States Navy, lieutenants of the line wore one epaulet on the left shoulder, except "when in command"; then the decorative accouterment could be shifted to the starboard side.

Oak leaves have been used as insignia by various corps and ranks of the United States Navy since the earliest days. This decorative device was probably adopted originally as a symbol of the excellent oaken ships of the United States. In those days the government had great concern of its live oak for shipbuilding. At Boston and in other navy yards, huge oak logs were preserved under water for years.

Sailors' bell-bottomed trousers are worn large at the bottom in order to roll up easily above the knees for scrubbing decks. This feature was of great practical value when seamen went overboard in shallow water to land pulling boats.

The black silk neckerchief was originally a "sweat rag." Black hid the dirt. It was worn around the forehead and the neck. Some men used the neckerchief in "pigtail" days to protect their jackets. Black neckerchiefs were used long before Nelson's death. They were probably worn at Nelson's funeral in the manner of the ship's company of the *Berwick*, who in mourning for their captain in 1794 cut the neckerchief in two and wore half around the arm and half around the hat.

The three rows of tape on the collar of the British bluejacket's jumper were authorized in 1857. Lieutenant Commander Lowry, RN, writes:

> One of the members of the committee which drew up the 1890 uniform regulations has since said that they then suggested two rows of tape, but that the Admiralty for no stated reason decided on three, the question of commemorating Nelson's three victories never being mentioned.

It is likely that the three lines of braid were selected for decorative effect and have no special significance, tradition to the contrary notwithstanding. Also there is no basis for the story that the thirteen buttons on the old-style trousers, changed to pockets and regular fly in 1948, represented the original thirteen colonies of the United States. In 1894, the trousers had only seven buttons; the thirteen were authorized later when the "broad fall" front was put on the uniform.

After World War II, a hue and cry arose to change the sailor's uniform, with specific complaints directed against the collar, neckerchief, jumper, and bell bottom trousers. The Uniform Board had various uniforms of a landsman variety designed but submitted the idea of change to the vote of those who would wear it—the men of the service. The final score was 79 percent in favor of the current uniform, 13 percent wanted the new one, and 8 percent did not care or gave no opinion. The men wanted to keep the time-honored, characteristic, comfortable one of the tradition of the "old Navy." Naval authorities are still undecided as to the final format of enlisted uniforms.

The form-fitting, single-breasted, high-collar blouse was distinctive of the U. S. Naval officer from 1877 until 1918, when the present double breasted blouse was made regulation. It is of interest that from 1841 until 1845 gold lace was removed from officers' uniforms, and the only indication of rank was the number of buttons on a coat.

In 1886, first-class petty officers were ordered to wear regular trousers and a double-breasted coat with five gilt buttons. It must be remembered that the CPO rating did not then exist. In 1893 when the

CPO was first included in the ratings, he was authorized to wear the uniform of the first-class petty officer and the latter reverted to bell bottom trousers.

In 1899, the rank of chief warrant was established, and warrants wore the same uniform as other officers with a special distinguishing sleeve mark for chief warrants, which was the broken stripe until the change in 1954.

In 1954, the new tropical uniform for officers and CPOs was prescribed. The alternate tropical uniform is cool and practical; open neck, short sleeve shirt, with collar insignia with khaki and shoulder boards with white, long trousers, and cap cover to match. Shorts (tropical white or khaki) were permitted some time ago. A smart blue mess jacket is authorized for officers.

First mention of the enlisted men's uniform was on the arrival of Commodore Stephen Decatur with the frigates *United States* and *Macedonian* in 1813. The sailors were clothed in "glazed canvas hats with stiff brims, decked with streamers of ribbon, blue jackets buttoned loosely over waistcoats, and blue trousers with bell bottoms." The first regulations for enlisted men's uniforms were issued by Secretary of the Navy Crowninshield in September 1817. For summer, "a white duck jacket, trousers and vest" and for winter, "blue jacket and trousers, red vest, yellow buttons and black hat."

THE OLDEST UNITED STATES NAVAL VESSEL—THE *"CONSTELLATION"*

On July 22, 1955, this historic old frigate was turned over to the Star Spangled Banner Flag House Association. That organization restored the ship and maintains it as a public memorial in Baltimore Harbor. Launched in 1797, the *Constellation* participated in the naval war with France in 1799–1800 and operated at the mouth of the Chesapeake Bay until blockaded by the British Fleet in the War of 1812.

PRESIDENT TRUMAN RESTORED RANK TO AN OFFICER WHO DID "GIVE UP THE SHIP"

On August 22, 1952, the president signed a document posthumously restoring William S. Cox to the rank of third lieutenant, a rank of the Navy of sail. The reappointment dates to October 17, 1874, when Lt. Cox died.

In the *Chesapeake-Shannon* fight off Boston Harbor on June 1, 1813, James Lawrence, the commanding officer, was mortally wounded.

The only other surviving officer was Cox who had been promoted in battle from midshipman to third lieutenant. Lawrence ordered, "Don't give up the ship! Fight her till she sinks!", and then asked to be taken below for medical attention. The ship was captured and Lawrence died four days later.

A court-martial found Lt. Cox guilty of leaving his post during the brief engagement, took away his rank, and discharged him. Representative E. E. Cox of Georgia—no relation—sponsored the bill that restored Cox's rank. The president ordered the official rank of third lieutenant be placed in his naval record. Perhaps "Cox was made the whipping boy for the loss of the *Chesapeake*."

MISCELLANEOUS HISTORICAL FACTS

White Flag of Truce. Its use is so old that its origin has been lost. One writer believed it was established first by the Roman Catholic Church in the Middle Ages by an agreement reached between the church and the warring barons to suspend hostilities on certain festivals, saints' days and Sundays. Beginning in southern France, the practice of unfolding a white cloth to put an instant stop to fighting spread throughout all Europe: In 1095, Pope Urban II proclaimed it in effect throughout all Christendom. Some authorities believe that the color white was chosen as an emblem of purity and may have had some connection with the white samite which covered the Holy Grail.

Whence and Why of "Gob." "I believe," says His Excellency, Hu-Shih, "that the word 'Gob,' as meaning a sailor of the United States Navy, is most probably an abbreviation of the Chinese transcription of the Spanish word 'Captain,' pronounced 'kia-pi-tan' in Pekingese ('Mandarin'), but which the people in Canton and Hongkong pronounce 'gob-bid-dan.' The term was applied, certainly as long ago as the first decade of this century, if not earlier, to 'captains' of foreign ships and, loosely, to all foreign sailors on their ships in the ports of South China or ashore. The longer word was later shortened to the first syllable 'gob' and thus found a pretty general monosyllabic use."[36]

And the eminent scholar proceeded to state as his opinion that the continued use of the word "gob," as now applied only to sailors of the United States Navy, was essentially complimentary rather than either "unworthy" or "undignified."

Medal of Honor is frequently miscalled the Congressional Medal of Honor although it is only one of many established by Congress. It

[36] Interview with Chinese Ambassador, Washington, D.C., November 1941.

is presented by the president in the name of Congress. The Navy Medal of Honor was first authorized for enlisted men in 1861. In 1915, the same award was authorized for officers of the Navy and Marine Corps; and the Act of August 7, 1942, provided for both enlisted men and officers.[37]

Veterans Day. In 1954 Congress passed the resolution and on June 2, 1954, President Eisenhower signed a bill proclaiming November 11 to be designated as Veterans Day, to be observed in honor of all veterans—living and dead—of all the wars. The first Veterans Day found the United States paying tribute to nearly 20,000,000 living veterans, survivors of five major wars, and the thousands who made the great sacrifice for country or have since died. May the Republic never forget what they did.

Loyalty Day. On July 18, 1958, President Eisenhower signed Public Law 529, a Veterans of Foreign Wars sponsored measure that proclaimed that May 1 of each year should be observed as "Loyalty Day." For a number of years, the V.F.W. paraded and staged patriotic celebrations as a counter to the May Day activities of American Communists and their "fellow travellers."

A Historic House—A Marine Corps Tradition. The home of the Marine Corps commandant, built in 1803 on land authorized by Thomas Jefferson, is one of the oldest residential buildings in Washington and one of the oldest official buildings in Washington still in use. This house on the north side of the Marine Barracks Quadrangle, 8th and Eye Streets, in the southeast section of the District of Columbia, has been the official residence of all but two of the commandants who have headed the Marine Corps during its 191-year history.

Much interesting lore and tradition derive from the fact that this residence was not fired when the British under Admiral Cockburn and General Ross burned the Capitol, the White House, and much of the Navy Yard in retaliation for the American raid on York (now Toronto), the previous summer. One story has it that it was earmarked as headquarters for the British; another that it was spared because of General Ross's admiration for the determined resistance of Captain Samuel Miller and his marines from Washington Barracks and Captain Joshua Barney and his sailors from the gunboat flotilla, at the battle on the Bladensburg road. Both Barney and Miller were severely wounded and captured. Because of the heroic conduct of this small force, the

[37] Once called the Congressional Medal of Honor, in 1944 the Secretaries of the Army and Navy and officials of the White House agreed to use the shorter title—*Medal of Honor.*

British navy and army commanders expressed high commendation, and immediately paroled Barney, the senior officer.

Many famous commandants, a number of them of international fame, have occupied the old residence. One of the most colorful, partly by reason of his long tenure of office, was undoubtedly the fifth commandant, Archibald Henderson. When he died in 1859, General Henderson had occupied the residence for thirty-nine years, and served under eleven Presidents. It is recorded that President Buchanan and his Cabinet attended the funeral of the gallant officer.[38]

> Stories of buried treasure and of ghosts add unique interest to this house of tradition. However, a true story should be recounted which shows the narrow boundary between fact and fancy. When General Thomas Holcomb, then Commandant, told some dinner guests that he had signed that day the order establishing the Women's Reserve, he added as an interesting side-remark, that, "Old Archibald would certainly turn over in his grave if he ever found out that females could become commissioned officers in his beloved Marine Corps." And just as he finished the remark, the portrait of General Henderson, which hung in the dining room, crashed to the floor.[39]

Through the years the commandants and their ladies have added excellent period reproductions of furniture, crystal chandeliers, valuable old prints, and outside wrought iron work. One may see today the portraits of all commandants, less the fourth, and of him no likeness has been found.

There takes place in the Quadrangle, seen from the Commandant's House, the inspiring "sunset parade," and the "drill without orders." Starting with the seventh commandant and continuing until the present twenty-third, on each New Year's Day morning the Marine Band has serenaded the head of the Corps, who invites them in for a "libation" and breakfast. A tradition of "mutual surprise" has marked this ceremony through all the years. And there is, of course, the Marine Corps annual "Birthday Party" observed on November 10 wherever there are marines throughout the world.

Such enduring traditions enrich the Marine Corps and give continuity to its proud annals and unquestioned prestige. That this has

---

[38] In 1836, because of an Indian uprising, Henderson gathered all the marines he could muster and under orders of President Andrew Jackson reported to the Army. On leaving Washington, the doughty officer tacked a message on his office door that read: "Gone to Florida to fight the Indians. Will be back when the war is over."

[39] *Marine Corps Gazette*, May 1954.

been so profoundly recognized by officers of the calibre of Henderson, Barnett, Lejeune, Holcomb, Vandegrift, Cates, Shepherd, Pate, and Greene becomes itself a tradition, one that binds officers and men in loyalty to each other, and *all* to the Corps.

THE UNITED STATES COAST GUARD

Semper Paratus, Always Ready

The Coast Guard is unique in that no other nation has a comparable organization. The act establishing the Coast Guard provides that:

> The Coast Guard as established January 28, 1915, shall be a military service and a branch of the Armed Forces of the United States *at all times.*

Until 1967 the Coast Guard was administered by the Treasury Department, but by legislation enacted by the 89th Congress, it became part of the Department of Transportation. All of its functions, however, will remain the same.

Men who follow the sea should be informed of some of the historic highlights and the general duties of this active seagoing service. The Revenue Marine, as the Coast Guard was originally known, was conceived by Alexander Hamilton, first Secretary of the Treasury, as a means of putting an end to smuggling which was depriving the United States of much-needed revenue. An act of the First Congress, approved by President Washington on August 4, 1790, placed the Revenue Marine Service under the Treasury Department. The original service was really a seagoing arm of the Customs Bureau, an agency of the Treasury Department, which accounts for its being in the Treasury.

It was provided in the later act of March 2, 1799, that the cutters "shall, whenever the President of the United States shall so direct, cooperate with the Navy of the United States." The term "Revenue Cutter Service," however, did not come into use until sometime in the 1860s. The first reference to Revenue Cutter Service occurred in an article written during that period.

The Life Saving Service was amalgamated in 1915 with the Revenue Cutter Service as an organization called the Coast Guard. In the early 1870s, the Life Saving Service planned and inaugurated the beach patrol, an institution of a distinct American origin.[40]

---

[40] Centuries ago, China organized the first humane society with the mission of saving life from the perils of the sea. In 1824, the Royal National Institution for the preservation of life from shipwreck was founded, an institution which has added lasting luster to the world's life-saving annals.

These stations constituted the Life Saving Service of the United States, which long ago won its supremacy over all kindred institutions of the world. Its achievements and successes at shipwreck, many of them as brilliant as human effort can make them, have earned the praise of the civilized world. It brought to the Coast Guard in 1915 a record of 177,286 lives saved from the perils of the sea, from 1871 to 1914, inclusive.[41]

The Revenue Cutter Service, later the U. S. Coast Guard, has fought alongside the Navy in every war at sea in which the United States has been engaged. In the war without declaration with France in 1798–99, vessels of this service cruised against French privateers in the Caribbean Sea. The cutter *Pickering* made two cruises and captured ten prizes.

At the outbreak of the War of 1812, the Revenue Cutter Service, with its sixteen cutters, was prepared "to defend the coast and commerce of the country as far as the calibre of their guns and size of their vessels would admit." Those 125-ton cutters had many stubborn engagements with landing parties and boarders, but let the enemy of the time comment on the fight with the Revenue Cutter *Surveyor* at Gloster Point, Virginia, on June 10, 1813.

His Majesty's Ship *Narcissus*

Sir: Your gallant and desperate attempt to defend your vessel against more than double your number, on the night of the 12th inst., excited such admiration on the part of your opponents, as I have seldom witnessed, and induced me to return you the sword you had so nobly used, in testimony of mine. Our poor fellows have severely suffered occasioned chiefly, if not solely, by the precautions you had taken to prevent surprise; in short, I am at a loss which to admire most, the previous engagement on board the *Surveyor*, or the determined manner by which her deck was disputed, inch by inch.

You have my most sincere wishes for the immediate parole and speedy exchange of yourself and brave crew; and I cannot but regret, that I myself have no influence that way, otherwise it should be forthcoming.

I am, sir, with much respect,

Your most obedient,

John Crerie[42]

---

[41] Oliver M. Maxam, "The Life Saving Stations of the U. S. Coast Guard," U. S. Naval Institute *Proceedings*, May 1929, pp. 374–380.

[42] Captain Horatio Davis Smith, USCG, *Early History of the United States Revenue Marine Service, 1789–1849*, Bryn Mawr, Pa.: Polk Printing Co., 1932.

Of such stuff is tradition born.

Down the years, in the Mexican War, the Civil War, the Spanish-American War, the World Wars, and Vietnam, high standards of duty and a seaman's job well done have crowned the efforts of the Coast Guard—truly a formidable record of accomplishment.

The late Rear Admiral F. C. Billard, USCG, defined the community of interest with the Navy and the high professional standards of his service when he wrote:

> Having fought as a part of the Navy in all our wars, and taking an especial pride in being fully prepared to perform creditable service in the Navy whenever called upon, the officers and men of the Coast Guard are inspired not only by the high tradition and fine history of their own service, but also by the splendid traditions, history, and indoctrination of the United States Navy. They have thus two rich heritages to be proud of and two standards of the same lofty character to live up to.

The Mission of the United States Coast Guard Academy[43]

> To graduate young men and women with sound bodies, stout hearts, and alert minds, with a liking for the sea and its lore, and with that high sense of honor, loyalty and obedience which goes with trained initiative and leadership; well grounded in seamanship, the sciences and amenities, and strong in the resolve to be worthy of the traditions of the commissioned officers in the United States Coast Guard in the service of their country and humanity.

By accomplishing this mission, the Coast Guard secures the leaders that man the ships which must be ever ready to take the sea in all weather. Succor to mariners in distress when gales are strong, waves mountainous, and the seamanship hazardous, is rarely accomplished with other than "sound bodies, stout hearts, and alert minds." The Navy knows and the Navy is always proud, both in peace and war, of the brave and skilled operations of the United States Coast Guard.

[43] The Coast Guard Academy at New London, Connecticut, has lived up to its high mission, particularly in having at times of emergency sufficient "hard core" professionals to train and administer the increase incident to war. From a prewar strength of about 12,000 officers and men in the 1930s, the Coast Guard grew during World War II to a strength of about 172,000 as of June 30, 1945. More than 50,000 men and women volunteered for intermittent periods of duty as temporary members of the Coast Guard Reserve and operated their own craft without pay. And one must not forget the Women's Reserve of 10,000 women, the SPARS—the name from the old Coast Guard motto, of which they are justly so proud: "Semper Paratus."

But the men that sail the ocean
In a wormy, rotten craft,
When the sea ahead is mountains
With a hell-blown gale abaft;
When the mainmast cracks and topples,
And she's lurching in the trough,
Them's the guys that greets the cutter
With the smiles that won't come off.[44]

---

[44] Arthur Somers Roche, *The Coast Guard Cutter*.

CHAPTER 10

Nautical Words and Naval Expressions

*Out of monuments, names, wordes, proverbs, private recordes
and evidences, fragments of stories, passages of books, and the
like, we doe save and recover somewhat from the deluge of time.*
Bacon

*The sea language is not soon learned, much less understood,
being only proper to him that has served his apprenticeship:
because that, a boisterous sea and stormy weather will make a man
not bred on it so sick, that it bereaves him of legs and stomach
and courage, so much as to fight with his meat. And in such
weather, when he hears a seaman cry starboard, or port, or to bid
aloof, or flat a sheet, or haul home a cluing, he thinks he hears a
barbarous speech, which he conceives not the meaning of.*
Sir William Monson's "Naval Tracts," Seventeenth Century

It's very odd that sailor-men should talk so very queer.
Ingoldsby Legends

THOSE WHO STUDY the derivation of English nautical words and expressions—sea terms stemming from Greek, Latin, Scandinavian, Spanish, French, and Dutch words—are constantly reminded of their polyglot sources. Although many Anglo-Saxon and old English words are used at sea today, many other terms were given English shape and sound after being borrowed from foreign sources. Because British sailors and ships have from the birth of the nautical arts had a high incidence of contact with foreign people, and in particular with other races that followed the sea, it is natural that English sea language took from others about everything that could be used effectively. One of the most interesting aspects of the unique talk of sailors is the large number of nautical idioms that have been borrowed by landsmen with a metaphorical significance now understood by all.

How often do we hear and use nautical terms that have passed from sea to shore? *To take in tow; to be in the same boat with; to show one's colors; to take the wind out of the sails of some one; to tide over; at a low ebb; on the rocks; to pump ship; when one's ship comes in; left stranded; to break the ice; to be first or second rate; by and large; to pull together,* and even, *to take it easy.* All these and many more were originally part of the vigorous speech of the English-speaking sailor.

Logan Pearsall Smith wrote:

> Our oldest sea terms divide themselves into two main classes, and are derived from the two far-distant corners of Europe, where, in prehistoric times, men of European races first built themselves ships and ventured on the sea. These places were in the South among the islands and peninsulas of Greece, and in the North along the shores and shallows of the North Sea and the Baltic. From Greece the arts of navigation spread with their appropriate terms over the Mediterranean, while the sailors of the North carried their Teutonic speech along the coasts of the Atlantic. Gradually, these two vocabularies met and mingled, and the sea vocabularies of England and the other European countries are largely made up of a mixture of these North Sea and these Mediterranean terms. The most English and anciently established ones in our language are, of course, of Northern origin, and consist of those words which the Angles and Saxons brought with them to England, and which safely survived the Norman Conquest. But among these old inherited terms are a few which, though they belong also to the South, have not been borrowed from thence, but descend to us from a time, thousands of years ago, when the Northern and Southern races dwelt together, and shared in a common language. Indeed, in sorting our words, we must put a few of them aside as belonging to the Aryan speech, from which not only most of the languages of Europe, but those of the Hindoos and Persians, descend.[1]

In the glossary of the language of the sea that follows, it must be kept in mind that the great thalassocracies, sovereignties of the seas,

---

[1] L. P. Smith, *Words and Idioms. Studies in the English Language* (London: Constable & Co., 1933), p. 2.

Shipboard Activities. Top. Reefing topsails. *Center.* Lowering a lifeboat on the quarter. *Bottom.* Heaving the chip log. *Heck's Iconographic Encyclopedia*

contributed directly and indirectly to the language of the English-speaking mariner. Apart from the customary meaning of the terms for those afloat, the philologist finds in them much of interest. Usage has shaped pronunciation in many cases. The lexicographer may not agree in pronunciation with the sailor who says "starburd" for starboard; "focsul" for forecastle; "boy" for buoy; "tăckle" for tackle; and even "starn" for stern; but why should not sailors "in ships" differ in speech from those who occasionally take passage "on ships"?

ADMIRAL. The title may be traced to the Arabic *Amir-al-Bahr* or admiral (commander) of the seas. *Bahr* was dropped and the Romans called the admirals "Sarraccenorum Admirati" introducing the "d" into the Latin form. It was a title of great dignity. The term was introduced into Europe during the Crusades. There is record of its use first by the Sicilians and then by the Genoese.

The first English admiral appointed was William de Leyburn with title of "Admiral of the Sea of the King of England." This appointment was made by Edward I in 1297. The wide powers of this office gradually merged into the title of Lord High Admiral of England. In the time of Edward II, we find that the Latinized term *admiralius* had been Anglicized as *admyrall*.

There is record of the first extant Royal Commission to a British Naval Officer. It was dated 1302 when Gervase Aland was appointed "Captain and Admiral." Authorities are of the opinion that the title of "captain" delegated executive command, while that of "admiral" delegated legal powers.

On May 28, 1493, Columbus officially received the office and title of Admiral of the Ocean Sea. The latter's patent of Ferdinand and Isabella appointed D. Cristobal Colon "nuestro Almirante del Mar Oceano"; also, "Capitán General de la Armada."[2]

At the beginning of the Crusades, the Sicilians and Genoese conferred the honor of admiral on the commander of a squadron of ships.

Queen Anne acted once as Lord High Admiral of England upon the death of her consort who had held the title. It is said that the Earl of Berkeley is the only officer not of royal blood to win the flag of Lord High Admiral. At the age of twenty he had his second command, the *Litchfield*; at twenty-three he commanded the *Boyne*; at twenty-seven he was made Vice Admiral of the Blue, and the next year Vice Admiral of the Red. On March 29, 1719, at the age of thirty-eight, he

[2] Samuel Eliot Morison, *Admiral of the Ocean Sea* (Boston: Little, Brown & Co., 1942), p. 20.

hoisted his flag on the *Dorsetshire* as Lord High Admiral, with the title Vice Admiral of England and First Lord of the Admiralty.

From the seventeenth century, the colors red, white, and blue were flown to distinguish the major groups or divisions in the British Fleet, which often numbered more than 200 sail. The three seniors—usually, admiral, vice admiral, and rear admiral because of their distinctive colors (plain flags)—commanded ships that as units were known as Red, White, and Blue Squadrons. The admiral with the "Red at the fore" was in the center and senior. Or one could be Rear Admiral of the Red and take precedence over all other rear admirals if he were senior. In short, the Red seemed to denote position and seniority. In 1653 the seniority was made Red, Blue, and White. Because of the danger of confusion, Nelson ordered the whole British Fleet to hoist the White Ensign at the battle of Trafalgar. In 1864, it was ordered that all H.M. ships would in the future fly White Ensigns; that British merchant ships commanded by retired officers of the Navy or officers of the Royal Naval Reserve would fly the Blue Ensign after obtaining Admiralty permission; and that all other ships and vessels belonging to H.M. subjects would fly the Red Ensign. Yachts of members of yacht clubs that have a royal warrant may fly the Blue Ensign. Members of the Royal Yacht Squadron fly the White Ensign.

Louis IX, "Saint Louis," introduced the title of admiral to France. At that time, the rank of admiral was equivalent to a Marshal of France, but prerogatives became so great that Richelieu assumed the title and suppressed it in others. In 1669, Louis XIV revived the ancient title but he made no appointments. When the Duke of Penthièrre gave up the title in 1759, he received an annual grant equivalent to $30,000 a year until the French Revolution. In France, fifty-nine persons have held the high title. Napoleon, in 1805, made Murat a "grand admiral," but the appointment was honorary. The title of "grand admiral" was never revived in France after the 1830 Revolution.

From the beginning of our Navy, the need of higher naval commissions was urged. John Paul Jones wrote to Robert Morris, in 1776:

> I am convinced that the parity in rank between sea and land or marine officers is of more consequence to the harmony of the service than has generally been imagined.

Jones reports the British system, and then adds:

> Were that regulation to take place in our Navy, it would prevent numberless disputes and duellings that otherwise would be unavoidable.

The relative ranks with the Army were fixed on November 15, 1776. The four highest naval grades were not established, however; hence, for nearly a hundred years, *captain* was the highest grade.

Secretary Upshur wrote in his annual report for 1841:

> The rank of admiral is known in all the navies of the world except our own; it has existed through a long course of past ages; and has been fully tested in the experience of all nations. It still exists and is still approved. . . . Our naval officers are often subjected to serious difficulties and embarrassments in the interchange of civilities with those of other countries or foreign stations. . . .

Repeated attempts were made by the Secretaries of the Navy and by the press, but the opinion prevailed in Congress that the title of admiral had a monarchical connotation. Congress did not create the grade until July 16, 1862.

The Secretary of the Navy repeatedly recommended the establishment of the grades vice admiral, rear admiral, and commodore. The July 16, 1862, Act provided for nine grades of commissioned officers and carried the authority to appoint nine rear admirals.

Farragut and Porter were the only active officers who ever held the permanent grade of *admiral* (four stars)—admiral in the Navy; many have held the temporary grade. George Dewey was the only officer who ever held the title of "Admiral of the Navy," and he retired in that rank with full pay.

The titles Admiral of the Navy and General of the Armies were honorary offices which no longer exist and were specially created for Admiral Dewey and General Pershing. Both offices were abolished upon their respective deaths and have never been revived. In 1944 Congress established the ranks of Fleet Admiral and General of the Army, stipulating that there is no higher rank in the respective services.

Leahy, King, Nimitz, and Halsey were the only officers who ever held the title of Fleet Admiral with the provision made that they remain on active duty for life with full pay and allowances.

Resumé of Flag-Officer Legislation

1864—authorization to appoint a vice admiral from the rear admirals of 1862. Farragut was appointed first vice admiral.

1865—A bill made Farragut admiral and permitted one vice admiral (David Dixon Porter) and ten rear admirals.

1870—Admiral Farragut died, and Vice Admiral David Dixon Porter became admiral and Rear Admiral Rowan became vice admiral.

1875—Congress provided that grades of admiral and vice admiral should not be filled by promotion. In other words, the grades were abolished upon the death of Rowan and Porter.

August 15, 1882—The number of rear admirals on the active list was reduced to six. "Rules and Regulations for the government of the Navy of the United States" made the following provision:

> Sea officers of the Navy of the United States shall take rank in the following order: admiral, vice-admiral, rear admiral, captain, commander (hereafter called master commander), lieutenant.

March 2, 1899—The president was authorized to appoint "An Admiral of the Navy." Dewey was appointed and held the title until his death on January 16, 1917.

March 3, 1899—The Navy Personnel Act made provision for eighteen rear admirals. For purpose of pay, the grade was divided in halves. The upper nine received the same pay and allowances as major generals; the lower half, the pay and allowances of brigadier generals.

May 13, 1908—Navy Personnel Act of 1899 was changed with different pay rates for "rear admirals, first nine"—"rear admirals, second nine."

March 3, 1915—The Naval Appropriation Act authorized that the commanders in chief of the Atlantic, Pacific, and Asiatic Fleets should have the ranks of admiral while on that duty and the seconds in command, the ranks of vice admiral while on that duty.

August 20, 1916—The number of officers in the different grades was increased, and provision was made for pay and allowance of staff officers of flag rank as well as the line.

August 29, 1916—The Chief of Naval Operations was given the rank and pay of admiral and took rank after the Admiral of the Navy (Dewey).

May 22, 1917—The Act of March 3, 1915, was repeated, and the president was authorized to make a selection of six officers for the commands of the fleets (then called Atlantic, Pacific, and Asiatic), three of which, while assigned to the duty, would have the rank and pay of admiral and three, the rank and pay of vice admiral.

In 1944 legislation was enacted for creation of the title of Fleet Admiral. Leahy, King, and Nimitz were promoted to this rank in December 1944 and Halsey in December 1945. This is called "5 star rank."

ADMIRAL, VICE. This early office in the British Navy may be traced to the vice admiral of the United Kingdom which was the evolution of the ancient title lieutenant admiral or lieutenant of the Admiralty. It later became vice admiral of England in 1672; then became vice admiral of Great Britain in 1707; and finally, vice admiral of the United

Kingdom in 1801. In 1876 the office was not held and remained vacant until 1901 when King Edward VII revived it.

On December 21, 1864, the grade of vice admiral was introduced into the American Navy. David Glasgow Farragut was the first vice admiral. When Farragut was promoted to admiral in July 1866, Rear Admiral David D. Porter was then made a vice admiral. When Farragut died in August 1870, Porter was made an admiral, and Stephen C. Rowan was made a vice admiral. After the deaths of Admiral Porter and Vice Admiral Rowan, the grade of "4 star admiral" became extinct until the Act of March 3, 1915.

ADMIRAL, REAR. In order that the natural son of Charles II, Henry Duke of Grafton, could at tender years hold the title Vice Admiral of England, Admiral Arthur Herbert was made the first "Rear Admiral of England." This office was effective until 1895, but not filled until 1901, when it was revived as was that of Vice Admiral of the United Kingdom by Edward VII. Both offices are now held but carry no emoluments.

These high honorary titles brought the terms into English nautical phraseology, and for that reason are mentioned for their historical value.

The Act of July 16, 1862, to a marked degree reorganized the American Navy, authorized the commissioning of not more than nine rear admirals on the active list and nine on the reserve or retired list. The first rear admirals were selected for distinguished service. Afterwards vacancies were filled by regular promotion, now by a rigorous system of selection. The old pre–World War II board was called by some wags "The Feast of the Pass-Over."

AHOY. This was once the dreaded war cry of the Vikings—a distinct nautical hail.

AIGUILLETTE. There are various theories and traditions as to the origin of this term. The best known is that the aide-de-camp, or henchman, of a superior knight carried the rope and pegs for tethering the knight's horse, and thereby the rope became the badge of the one near the leader. Another tradition relates that it was the rope of the provost marshal used in hanging the condemned. It is a custom that aides to the president of the United States and to sovereigns, royalty, and viceroys wear aiguillettes on the right side, and that aides to all other senior officials, officers, and dignitaries wear them on the left side. Naval aiguillettes are blue and gold, while those of the Marine Corps and the Army are red and gold. Air Force aiguillettes are silver.

ANCHOR. This term is derived from a Greek word for hook or crook. Sailors say today "drop the hook," or refer to the anchor as "the old mud hook." The original Greek meaning has been lost, and the word today has only one connotation—a means of holding a ship when she is not under way.

Dr. Giles, the eminent expert on Chinese history, writes that ships carrying anchors, rudders, and oars were known as early as 2000 B.C. It is recorded that Emperor Yu invented the anchor, but emperors in those days often took credit that belonged to their subjects. Emperor Yu was said to be the first to use anchor chains. The peculiar noise of chain running out gave rise to the Chinese mariners expression "cat" or "iron cat" which in Chinese signifies "mao."

Bags of sand or stone were used as anchors by the early navigators. In time, stone anchors were used by the Greeks and Romans. In the book of Stephanus Byzantius, titled *De Urbibus*, there is the statement that the town of Ancyra in Egypt derived its name from the manufacture of anchors in its quarries.

Large lead trunks exhibited as ancient Greek anchors may be found in the archeological collections of the Museum Boreli at Marseilles, the British Museum in London, the Old Museum in Berlin, and in many smaller museums of Southern Europe.[3]

The Romans used the anchor as a symbol for wealth and commerce, while the Greeks gave to the anchor a significance of hope and steadiness, a meaning that persists in religion and heraldry today. For the early Christians the anchor symbolized steadfastness, hope, and salvation. Pictures of anchors comparable in shape to those used today may be seen in the Catacombs. The drawings sometimes have such an inscription as *spes in Christo*, "Hope in Christ." The foul anchor with a line wound around the shank may be found on the world-renowned sculptures of the Temple of Neptune at Rome.

AYE AYE. Aye is old English for "yes," probably taken from Latin verb "aio"—to affirm.

BACK. The wind backs when it changes counter-clockwise, but veers when it changes clockwise. Square sails are backed or aback when the wind blows on their forward side thrusting them against the mast. Should this occur through a shift of wind, the effect of a heavy sea, or a careless helmsman, a ship is said to be "taken aback." To back water with oars is the opposite of a regular stroke, i.e., to push instead of to

---

[3] The anchors of the aircraft carrier, USS *Forrestal*, weigh 60,000 pounds each. The 1,800 foot anchor chains weigh 246 tons and are the longest and strongest ever forged.

pull. "To back" a piece of gear means to rig or set up a preventer. "To back" an anchor means the practice of sending an extra anchor to the bottom or holding ground with its shank made fast on the chain of the first anchor in order to back it or assist it. It also means to shackle or otherwise secure the extra anchor to the chain near the lower anchor before letting go. "To back chain" is sometimes confused with "to veer chain," but in general usage it means easing out a few fathoms in deep water before letting go the anchor.

BEACH COMBER. Originally one who searched beaches and fore-shores for material washed up from wrecked or stranded ships. Beach combing in winter after a blow was quite a profitable business for the longshoremen of British ports and watering places in the old days. It has been stated that "in the happy pre-war era of gold, such a beach as that of Brighton, Hastings, or Ramsgate yielded up many a golden guinea after it had been bared by a winter gale." The expression today connotes tramps of the sea, unreliable drifters. It is also applied in some cases to impoverished and stranded landsmen in foreign sea ports.

BINNACLE. Originally spelled *bittacle*. About the size of a large corn bin or cupboard in which were placed two compasses, log board, lighted candle or lamp at night, and other navigation gear. Now only the stand used to house the compass; the binnacle list or daily sick list once hung on or near it.

BITTER END. "A bitter end is but the turn of a cable about the bits, and veare it out little and little, and the bitter's end is that part of the cable doth stay within board."—*Seaman's Grammar* (1653).
The end of anchor chain secured aboard.

BLEEDING A BUOY. To let the water out.

BLUEJACKET. The first uniform that was ever officially sanctioned for sailors in the Royal Navy was a short blue jacket open at the front. There were no definite uniform regulations for U. S. enlisted men in the War of 1812, but many wore short blue jackets.

BLUE PETER. A flag, "blue pierced with white," was used in the British Navy from 1777 as a general recall flag. In a quarter of a century the term "blue peter" was used by all to designate this flag. Civilians knew its significance, for merchant ships and convoys in the French wars would not sail until the escorting man-of-war hoisted the blue peter for passengers to come aboard.
There is on record a historic piece of doggerel, autographed "Emma," written when Nelson sailed in 1801:

Silent grief and sad forebodings
(Lest I ne'er should see him more)
Fill my heart when gallant Nelson
Hoists blue peter at the fore.

The "Blue Peter" was at the time of the War of 1812 flown at the fore preparatory to sailing.

BOARDERS. Even in 1885 one reads:

They are men detailed to attack the enemy by boarding. They are armed with pistols and cutlasses and led by the executive officer. They are summoned by verbal order and by the springing of the rattle, and assembled in the part of the ship designated, keeping under cover as much as possible—U. S. Marine Encyclopedia

On June 4, 1944, the old battle cry of the seas, "Away all boarders" or "boarding parties" was heard for the first time on loud speakers as boats from the *Guadalcanal* (CVE 60) and *Pillsbury* (DE 133) were lowered at the commencement of their capture of the German submarine, *U-505*, off North Africa.

BOATS. Derived from Anglo-Saxon *bat* that stood for boat, small ship, vessel.

BARGE. "Served for stated and ease (as for carrying the generall, admiralls, and prynce captains)." It was the admiral's boat and was rigged for ten or twelve oars.

GIG. The 1815 edition of Flaconer's *Dictionary of the Marine* calls it "A long narrow boat . . . generally rowing six to eight oars and is mostly the private property of the captain or commander."

DINGHY or DINGHEY. Small boat, an Indian word and taken from the British East India Company's service.

BOATSWAIN. The Saxon word *swein* meant a boy or servant, therefore, boatswain. The "boat" referred originally to the ship and not to her boats. "Cockswain" has a similar derivation. *Cock* is an old word for a type of small boat.

The ships were usually commanded by *batsuen* (boatswains) in the eleventh century.

He [boatswain] is to be very particular in having ready at all times a sufficient numbers of mats, plats, knippers, points, and gaskets so that no delay may be experienced when they are wanted.
—Naval Regulations (1824)

BOATSWAIN'S PIPE. Discussed in detail in chapter 9.

The parts of the pipe were called by old sailors: the "buoy," "gun," "keel," "shackle."

Technically, the parts are the bowl, the reed, the flange, and the ring. The *Bluejackets' Manual* of 1950 for the first time omits the instruction on "Boatswain's Calls" for coxswains and boatswain's mates.

The first reference to "call" on the whistle was early sixteenth century, but the use of the whistle at sea antedates Carthaginian sea power.

BOTTOMRY BOND. A lien placed on a vessel by a master in order to obtain money to get the vessel home. The funds secured are only used for repairs. This is resorted to only when the master is out of communication with the ship's owners. Such a lien takes priority for first payment over all mortgages. A lien on cargo is a *respondentia bond.*

BRIG. As a name for a sailing vessel this term did not come into use until the latter part of the eighteenth century. Mentioned by Johnson in his dictionary of 1760. It is a contraction of the older word "brigantine" or "brigandine" from robber or brigand. This was originally a general term for the fast sailing vessel used by pirates of the Mediterranean. Because Lord Nelson used a brig in battle for relieving his ships of prisoners, the sailors began to call a prison anywhere by the name "brig."

BUCCANEERS. The term was first given to early Frenchmen in Haiti, who were the original cowboys of that island. The word "boucan" was of Caribbean origin, meaning a dealer in smoked-dried meats.

In the Caribbean area, the hunters placed meat to dry on wooden lattice work, known as "boucans." "The Boucanners" eventually took to privateering and general lawlessness. After the Treaty of Ryswick, buccaneer became the common word for pirate.

BUGLE. Bugle is derived from the French, and originally meant "wild ox." Therefore, bugle horn, meaning wild ox horn, became the first expression. It was and remains in some parts of the world the true horn of the chase. Joseph Haydn, the celebrated musician, wrote the first bugle calls in about 1793, and they were introduced into navies at a much later date.

BUMBOAT. A boat selling supplies, provisions, and articles to ships. The most popular derivation is from "boomboat," signifying boats permitted to lie at booms. A British source accounts for the term as derived from "bombard," a receptacle in which beer is carried to soldiers on duty.

BUOYS. Floating beacons which by shape and color give the mariner valuable navigational information. The types in use in the United States comprise can, nun, spar, cask, bell, gong, whistle, and lighted buoys. In coming from seaward, red buoys mark the starboard, or right, side of the channel; and black buoys, the port, or left, side. A convenient way of remembering this is "red, right, returning." Red buoys are on the right when returning from sea.

BUTTONS. (On cuffs of British midshipmen). As in other matters of uniform, the origin of certain insignia and distinctions of dress is not definitely recorded, but as some old stories tell it in the case of midshipmen, buttons were placed on the cuffs for a purpose. One British commentator wrote:

> In the earlier days of the last century, small mites of boys eight or nine years old, and even younger, were sent to sea. When these small boys were first at sea, they were one and all so woefully homesick that they had continuous cases of sniffles, and for the first part of their term of service they were forever rubbing their poor little homesick and dripping eyes and noses on the cuffs of their coats. This was so detrimental to the appearance of their uniforms that it led to the sewing on of buttons.[4]

Commander W. N. T. Beckett, RN, writes:

> "Snotty" is a slang term for a [British] midshipman and is derived from the allegation that these officers used to make their sleeves do duty as handkerchiefs, and that to obviate this practice buttons were placed on the cuffs.

BY AND LARGE. Has come to mean: generally speaking or under all conditions. It is a term which was derived from the sailing terms: "by the wind" (close hauled) and "sailing large" (running free). The term "at large" stems also from that usage.

CAPTAIN. From Latin, *capitaneus*, the head or chief. The evolution of the commanding officer of ships derives from the batsuen (boatswain) or the rector in the eleventh century; about 1300, the rank of captain came in general use.[5] The master, although he sailed the ship,

---

[4] This makes a good story. British midshipmen are called "snotties" today, but as in civilian dress, the large eighteenth century cuffs went out of fashion, and the buttons were left as a dress ornament. Midshipmen may have never had the large cuffs, and buttons were added after the shift to a plain cuff.

[5] Commander R. G. Lowry, RN, writes that in A.D. 984, the Italians had a military rank *capitano* which was derived from the Latin *caput*, a head.

was of lower rank than the captain. In a British order in council in 1748, the relative rank was settled with the Army by dividing Navy captains into three grades. It was deemed at that time that any officer in command was entitled to the title of captain while in command, regardless of rank. All captains not eligible on the list for promotion to rear admiral were originally called "masters and commanders" and had "C" after their names. The rank was shortened to commander in 1794. The term "cdr." in the British Navy was used after the names of commanders in 1826.

"Post captain," a term used in the Royal Navy and once used in the American Navy, distinguished captains commanding frigates from master commanders or commanders next in rank. There never was a commission of "post captain." In 1747, the rank of captain was first clearly defined in the British Navy. Captains who commanded post ships took rank, if of three years standing, with colonels in the Army. Until the year 1824 the Royal Navy list classed such captains as post captains.

Until 1862, captain was the highest commissioned officer in the United States Navy, and according to his duty, ranked with lieutenant colonel, colonel, or brigadier general.

CARGO. Comes directly from the Latin *cargo* or *carga*, a load, freight.

CATHEAD. Projections on bows for rigging tackles for purposes of hoisting anchor aboard—"To cat and fish." The term appears in English as early as 1626. A cat was sometimes carved on wooden timber for good luck; hence the term, cathead.

CAULK, To TAKE A. To take a sleep or nap; as sailors often take them on the deck, the term is derived from the possibility of one's back becoming marked by the pitch of the seams.

CHAINS. Where shrouds (mast supports) were secured to platforms on the ship's side, "chains" were used to brace the platform. This platform was used for leadsmen to stand upon when heaving the lead; today it means that platform or position from which the lead is hove.

CHANTY. Gershom Bradford gives an excellent description of a chanty. He writes that it was

> a song formerly always and now rarely sung aboard ship to
> lighten and unify labor at the capstan, sheets, and halyards. The
> soloist is known as the chanty-man and is usually a man of leader-
> ship in the forecastle. He is something of an improviser, for those

especially successful made their verses applicable to the existing conditions in the ship, indulging in slight hits at the peculiarities of the different officers, the vociferousness of the chorus indicating the relative delight with which these squibs are received by the men. This was the only privilege allowed to pass in the old days of iron-fisted discipline. They were composed for various kinds of work such as capstan chanties, which were timed to be rhythmic with the steady tread around the capstan. They usually dwell upon the joys of being homeward-bound and farewells to the port (and ladies) when heaving up the anchor to leave. The topsail halyard chanties are the most stirring as they, at their best, are sung in a gale when the reefed topsail is being mastheaded. There are also long-pull and short-pull chanties.[6]

As Arnold Bennett once remarked about limericks, some of the best chanties are not for general publication. They were for the most part tuneful and melodious, and smacked of the romantic age of sail. Pronounce as if spelled *shanty*.[7] Probable derivation is Norman-French.

The well-known American chanties have passed from the sea. However, here is some authoritative, first-hand information about chanties (or chanteys):

> *Whiskey is the life of man*
> *O, whiskey Johnny!*
> *I'll drink whiskey while I can*
> *Oh, whiskey Johnny.*

There are, or used to be, three kinds of chanteys—single-pull, double-pull, and capstan, or marching. The first, as its name implies, was used where tremendous effort was required and single pulls, with a breathing spell in between, were all that could reasonably be asked of men—hauling aft the main-sheet is an example. "Haul on the bowline" is a single-pull chantey, and the pull comes on the last word "haul"; in some ships the pull was made immediately after the word and, in my experience, it gave the best results. "Haul on the bowline" was not nearly as popular as "Haul Away, Jo" or "Oh, Do, My Johnny Bowker," both single-pulls;

---

[6] Gershom Bradford, *A Glossary of Sea Terms* (New York: Yachting, Inc., 1927), p. 34.

[7] Captain David W. Bone, British Master Mariner, and author of books of life at sea, wrote in his authoritative book on chanties, *Capstan Bars*, that these songs of sailors fell under the general heads of Short Haul Chanties, Halyard Chanties, Debt and Credit Chanties, Capstan Chanties, Windlass and Pump Chanties, and those "Out of the Blue." Bone, the expert, believed the chanty Shenandoah, of American origin, to be the most beautiful. Always sung at weighing anchor, it is a chanty of "haunting melody" and "tender cadences."

"Paddy Doyle's Boots" was invariably used for bunting the sail on top of the yard, when furling any of the courses or lower square-sails.

The double-pulls were used for fairly long pulls, such as mastheading the topsails, or even to'gallant sails in vessels with single to'gallant yards. The chanteyman sang a line and the hands pulled twice on each bit of chorus; for instance, in "Blow, Boys, Blow," the chanteyman sang "A Yankee ship came down the river" (chorus) "BLOW, boys, BLOW." "And all her sails they shone like silver" (chorus) "BLOW, my bully boys, BLOW," the pulls coming only on what your correspondent calls upper-case.

There are dozens of double-pulls; probably the most popular was "Blow the Man Down," with "Whiskey for My Johnny" and "Reuben Ranzo" close seconds. A good chanteyman made up his lines as he went along, after the first line or two, but naturally the choruses remained the same.

Capstan chanties could be, and were, almost any song with a good rhythm and chorus: "Away for Rio" (pronounced rye-o) being perhaps the most popular; also "A-Roving"; but I've hove up the anchor many times to "Marching Through Georgia."

Incidentally, the only chanty I know of that is written in a minor key is "On the Plains of Mexico" and is of American origin.[8]

CHAPLAIN. Chaplains have been stationed aboard warships from the earliest days. Charles I appointed a chaplain to each ship of the fleet of England. Chaplains and doctors were once paid by the seamen—the chaplain receiving from each seaman four pence per month. The chaplains did not live in the wardroom until the end of the eighteenth century. The chaplain, purser, and doctor on almost all ships messed in their respective cabins, but some chaplains messed regularly with the captains. In the old days, the chaplain had the authority to give a midshipman sixpense for learning a psalm.

Tradition gives the origin of the title as follows: St. Martin divided his coat with a poor begger on a cold wintry day outside of Amiens. It is related that the coat was "miraculously preserved" and thereby became a sacred banner for the Kings of France. This cloak or cape (French *chape*) was preserved in an oratory that took the name of *chapelle*, while the gentleman charged with its keeping was called the *chapelain*.

A British Commission that in 1618 inquired into the state of the Navy set forth among other abuses that "in the narrow seas there is

[8] William Applebye-Robinson in letter to the *New York Times*, January 20, 1939.

an allowance demanded for a preacher and his man, though no such devotion be used on board. . . ."

The practice of daily prayers on British men-of-war commenced in the days of Cromwell and the Commonwealth. At this time, Admiral Blake instituted the practice of singing hymns or psalms at eight P.M., when the watch was "set."

The second article of Navy Regulations written in 1775 states that "The commanders of the ships of the United Colonies are to take care that Divine services be performed twice a day on board and a sermon be preached on board on Sundays." Many chaplains in the early days served as secretary to the captain; often they were also instructors of midshipmen, and one chaplain served as the ship's medical officer. In 1794 provision was made for a chaplain on each of the new ships being constructed. At about that time the pay was raised from $20 per month to $40.

A chaplain in the Royal Navy holds no rank. "He is considered to be of equal rank with the man he stands next to at any moment." He has a special cap badge with laurels mostly black picked out with gold. In the Royal Canadian Navy he wears officers' buttons and cap badge. Sleeve lace is never worn. The Armies and Air Forces of the British Crown do not follow this practice. Black braid for stripes was worn in the U. S. Navy until 1917, when gold lace took its place. Chaplains never wear side arms.

CHARLIE NOBLE. Sailor's nautical term for the galley smokepipe. Derived from the British merchant service Captain Charlie Noble, who required a high polish on the galley funnel. The funnel of his galley was of copper and its brightness became known in all ports visited.

CHART. From Latin *charta*, Greek *charte*, a kind of papyrus. In middle English, the chart or maps were known as "scacards" or sea-cards. There are many references in the early day to "the cards" for the charts.

CHIT. (Hindu word *chitti*.) Letter, note, bill, voucher, or receipt. It came from the old East India Company. The word has wide use in the Far East and is used throughout the British Army and Navy. The U. S. Navy on the Asiatic Station adopted it many years ago from the "pidgin" (business) English.

CLERKS. The institution of "captain's clerk," as the United States Navy knew it, came from the British Navy. There was no commission or warrant for the duties; although the captain appointed the clerk and dismissed him if necessary, he was complimentarily considered an officer of the Navy.

The acme of position of official clerical work became in time the "commodore's secretary" or "commodore's clerk." This billet led to the flag secretary of today. Both the "commodore's secretary" and "captain's clerk" wore a uniform much like that of the midshipmen of their day. They lived with the midshipmen in the "after cockpit." In fact, a few became midshipmen.

In the early days should no civilian be employed by the captain, a midshipman was appointed to the office. In 1779, Commodore John Paul Jones appointed Midshipman Nathaniel Fanning "commodore's secretary."

In 1835, one finds secretaries to "commander of squadron commanding in chief" and to "commander of squadron." There were also the titles "clerk to commander of squadron" and "clerk to commander of ship," as well as "clerk to paymaster," at a later time. A derivative of the old "purser's steward" was the clerk to paymaster or paymaster's clerk. The top secretaries were ranked later with lieutenants in the matter of certain privileges, such as messing in the wardroom.

Eventually the work of the "clerk to commander of ship" was done by a midshipman, while later the chief yeoman ordered to perform the clerical duties of the captain became styled the "captain's writer." The "ship's writer" was the old title given to the chief yeoman who assisted the executive officer. The executive officer is now assisted in clerical work by an officer classified as a personnel specialist. Because of the increase of reports and paperwork, the supply officer in time had pay clerks and yeomen as assistants.

CLIPPER. Properly taken from old English *clip* meaning to run, fly swiftly. "The knife-edged clipper with her ruffled spars." The fast, trim clipper ships mark the golden age of the United States in merchant ships. World-famous, record-breaking passages to San Francisco, China, and Australia placed American shipbuilding at the top. The *Flying Cloud* of builder McKay was, on long voyages, the fastest sailing vessel that ever flew the American flag. This beautiful craft logged 374 miles for a day on her trials. "How they succeeded is endured in records unbroken while time lasts." It was a vital and glorious maritime period in American history.

COMMANDER. As explained under "captain," the lower grades of captains were originally styled "master and commander" and commanded small ships of war. The title was introduced in England by

William III and was originally "commandeur." The British in 1827 first appointed commanders as second in command on large ships.

The title was introduced in the United States Navy in 1838 when the law read that "master commandants" should be known as "commanders."

The pay bill approved March 3, 1835, recognized the new title. A commander was originally supposed

> to command vessels of the third and fourth classes; may be employed as chief of staff to a commodore, or duty under a bureau; or as aide to a flag officer of either grade on shore stations.[9]

COMMISSION PENNANT. The distinctive mark of a ship of the Navy in commission, other than the national ensign, is a flag or pennant at a masthead.

In the days of chivalry, knights rated a small pointed flag or pennon. The mark of a squire was a long pennant very similar to the "coachwhip pennant" of modern men-of-war. Bannerets ranked the knight and took precedence below a baron. They carried a knight's pennon with a slit in the end. It was customary to create barons on the battlefield by the king or general cutting off part of the fly of the pennon. This square flag was then a symbol of increased rank. Edward, the Black Prince, tore the tail off the pennon of Lord John Chandos after battle saying, "Sir John, behold, here is your banner; God send you much joy and honor with it." One may trace directly from these customs the commission pennant, "coachwhip," broad command pennant, and broad flags worn by commanding officers of ships, and by commodores, as well as the square flags of the admirals of our own and other navies.

> When Maarten Harpertszoon Tromp, the Dutch admiral, hoisted a broom at his masthead to indicate his intention to sweep the English from the sea, the English admiral hoisted a *horsewhip*, indicating his intention to chastise the insolent Dutchman. Ever since that time, the narrow, or coachwhip, pennant symbolizing the original horsewhip, has been the distinctive mark of a vessel of war, adopted by all nations.[10] [Commander Kemp, an authority, believes both Tromp's broom and Blake's whip apocryphal. A broom at the masthead once indicated that a ship was for sale.]

[9] *Marine Encyclopedia* (1881).
[10] George Henry Preble, *History of the Flag of the United States of America* (Boston: A. Williams & Co., 1880), p. 659.

However, Commander R. D. Merriman, Royal Indian Navy (Ret.) wrote in 1943: "I do not think that Blake's whip 'at the fore' is the real origin of the Commissioning Pennant. It is much more likely to be an attenuated survival of the 'Pennon' used by every noble family in the Middle Ages, and on which were emblazoned the Arms of the bearer. These 'pennons' or 'streamers,' sometimes of great size and length, were flown on board ships in which the owners were embarked. The Commissioning Pennant of today is, of course, standardized, but it represents, none the less, the PERSONAL insignia of the officer appointed to command the ship."

COMMODORE. This title came from Holland. In the Dutch Wars of 1652, there were not sufficient admirals and the Dutch desired to create others without calling them admirals. The title was brought to England by William III. The broad command pennant or burgee was used by the Dutch at the same time. The rank was officially recognized by the British in 1806. The American Navy used the rank as an honorary title in the Revolution—"Commodore" John Paul Jones; "Commodore" Esek Hopkins, appointed as "commander in chief."

Until 1861 all captains in the United States Navy, commanding or having commanded squadrons, were recognized as commodores, though never commissioned as such. They wore a broad pennant distinctive of that rank. In 1862 it was established as a fixed rank, as in July of that year eighteen were commissioned on the active list and seventeen on the retired list. The grade was abolished in 1899. During World War II, the temporary grade of commodore was given to some officers both of the line and the staff corps. President Franklin D. Roosevelt made the original suggestion that the old title be revived.

A captain in the United States Navy who commands a flotilla or squadron of destroyers is called a "commodore" by courtesy. The British Admiralty continues to make appointments of a small number of commodores. The broad stripe of rank is worn by those appointed and the "burgee" of a commodore is flown.[11]

COMPASS. Some writers hold that the Chinese made use of the compass long before European navigators. This rather interesting statement has never been verified by conclusive proof. The early Chinese records disclose that the Chinese knew of the extraordinary properties of the magnet from the third century A.D., but in all the documents relating to voyages at that earliest date no mention is made of the magnet as an

---

[11] On January 1, 1959, there were sixty-six commodores on the retired list, none on the active list, and none being commissioned.

aid to direction and navigation, until the Chinese water compass of the twelfth century.

The Arabians, who learned most probably of the water compass from the Chinese, were acquainted with the magnet ashore as well as were the Greeks who used it for purposes of instruction in their academies. Plato wrote of the magnet in a humorous vein when he spoke of its use by jealous husbands to detect wifely virtue, but there is no record of its use at sea until much later.

The following interesting description of what may have been a compass was recently found in a Latin volume dealing with the art of ship handling.

> Take a number of small iron bars [needles] and paint them with a mixture of cinabro and oprimento well powdered and mixed with the blood of the crest of a rooster. Heat them well and, after the Astrologer has carried them next to his skin for a period of a full lunation, lay them on straws floating on the water and they will point south.[12]

The water compass, first seen in Europe about 1190, was probably brought back by the Crusaders after seeing those of the Arabs.

In 1248, Brunetto Latini, a Florentine, made reference in his poem "Tresor" to the instrument used on the Norman ships:

> In a tub of water placed in the center of the ship there floats the Mariniere, which is a round piece of cork with a thin hollow shaft filled with lodestone inserted through its center so that it lies parallel to the plane of the water, and the quill of a goose sealed at both ends, also inserted through the cork at right angles to the one filled with lodestone; over this there lays a bird's skin with the *fleur-de-lis* upon it, and even as our august King is our constant guide on the land, so does the *fleur-de-lis* upon the Mariniere guide the mariner by constantly pointing to Boreas (north) no matter how the ship may go.

The *fleur-de-lis* has remained to this day on the north point of practically all compass cards.

About 1295, Messere Flavio Gioja, of Amalfi, gave to the world the first practical compass. He used a large copper bowl instead of the wooden tub of the Mariniere in order that, when the ship's head swung in azimuth, the current of the electro-magnet induction was such as

---

[12] Captain John M. L. Gorett, M.S.R., C.A.A., in his comprehensive compass research brought to light the Latin book, title and author unknown, with the title page missing. He places its writing in the third century A.D.

to dampen the oscillations of the compass and thereby bring the needle to rest sooner than the old method in the wooden tub. He balanced the compass card on a vertical shaft in the bowl and placed on the card all the cardinal points of the compass. The *fleur-de-lis* was left for the north point, and although Gioja was not the first to use the symbol, it was indeed a graceful compliment to Charles d'Anjou, whose armorial device it was, and who at the time was the reigning King of Sicily.

Prince Henry, the Navigator, did much to perfect the compass by his establishment of a school for navigation in Portugal. When Vasco da Gama sailed on July 8, 1497, it may be correctly said that his compass cards were the result of Norman invention, Italian adaptation, and Portuguese improvement.

CON, CONN. A very old word and the exact derivation is not known. It was used first about 1520 in the present sense of directing the steering or giving orders to the helmsman, by the captain but more often by the officer-of-the-deck. One writer says that it "doubtedly had an affinity to cunning."

COOK. Michael Scott in *Tom Cringle's Log* writes:

> The cook of a man-of-war is no small beer; he is his Majesty's warrant-officer, a much bigger wig than a poor little mid, with whom it is condescension on his part to jest.
> It seems to be a sort of rule, that no old sailor who has not lost a limb or an eye, at least, shall be eligible to the office, but as the kind of maiming is so far circumscribed that all cooks must have two arms, a laughable proportion of them have but one leg. Besides the honour, the perquisites are good; . . .

In the seventeenth century the cook was, in most cases, an unscrupulous individual. For many years, it was the custom that the cook received his meat from the steward, and was by order to cook it and give it to "such persons as are chosen by every mess (mess cooks) for the fetching of it away from him." We learn in many cases that cooks were bribed to furnish double rations to a mess. In the time of Charles II, men who had been maimed in the Dutch Wars were given appointments as cooks in the Royal Navy. We have record of John Gamble who, although minus both arms "in fight the 11th of August, 1673," was recommended for cook of the navy ship *Sweepstakes* while James Davis, "who lost all the lower part of his face in the engagement May 28, 1692," was made cook of the *Revenge*. The record reads, "that forasmuch as he is not able to eat sea biscuits or meat that he would be permitted to perform cook's duty by deputy."

At seven bells, "The ships cook brings a sample of the crew's dinner aft for inspection and is directed 'to serve out.'" At this point Lieut. P. W. Hourigan, USN, in his *Manual of Seamanship for the Officer of the Deck, Ship Under Sail Alone* (1903), inserted a footnote: "Under the new commissary system or 'general mess,' this custom may die out as the commissary is responsible for the proper preparation of food. The old call of 'roast beef,' to serve out provisions is extinct, and 'serve out tea water' is no longer heard."

CORVETTE. The word derived from Latin *corbita* or a basket which was lashed to the mastheads of Egyptian grain ships to show their trade. These ships known as the *naves onerariae*—vessels of burden.

In the Middle Ages, the corvette was a light and fast Italian galley with one mast and propelled by either sails or oars. In the year 1687, the corvette was first seen in the French Navy as a fast light ship used for lookout duty. In time the class ranked just after frigates. Various navies have used this title in modern times for small, fast ships.

COXSWAIN or COCKSWAIN. From *cock*, a small boat, and *swain*, a servant. It originally meant one who had charge of a boat and a crew in the absence of an officer.

It was once the custom that in single-banked boats the coxswain pulled the stroke oar; the boat was generally steered by an officer; in double-banked boats the coxswains usually steered.

CRUISER. Derived from *crusal* or fast, light vessel used by pirates in the Mediterranean. They were not essentially fighting vessels, but were used for raiding and pillaging.

CUT OF HIS JIB. In the days of sailing ships, nationality and rigs could often be distinguished by their jibs. A Spanish ship, for example, had a small jib or none at all; the large French ships often had two jibs; English ships seldom but one.

> From ships, the phrase was extended to apply to men; approximately enough, for the nose, like the jib, is the first part of its wearer to arrive. Figuratively, it implies the first impression one makes on another.

CUTTING A DIDO. A rather recent expression and one used considerably in some sections, by shorefolk. HMS *Dido*, a very smart and clean ship in commission about fifty years ago in the British fleet, often cruised around the fleet before anchoring, some said as a "show off" hence "to cut a dido."

DAGO. From James, the Spanish patron saint, called Iago, Santiago, San Diego, Diego. Yankee sailors first called Spanish sailors "Diego men" or "Dagos." Extended to the Latin race, then restricted by usage to Italians.

DEAD MARINE. An empty bottle, "a marine," "a dead marine." In the old days of hard drinking at sea, this expression was generally accepted as synonymous with an empty bottle. The story is told that William IV, when Duke of Clarence and Lord High Admiral, pointed at some empty bottles at an official dinner and said, "Take away those marines." A dignified and elderly major of marines rose from the table and said, "May I respectfully ask why your Royal Highness applies the name of the corps to which I have the honor to belong to an empty bottle?" The Duke, with that tact and characteristic grace that was his, retorted promptly, "I call them marines because they are good fellows who have done their duty and are ready to do it again."

In Grose's *Dictionary of the Vulgar Tongue*, one finds under the word "marine officer" the libelous explanation, "an empty bottle."

DEAD RECKONING. A reckoning kept so as to give the theoretical position of a ship without the aid of objects on land, of sights, etc. It consists of plotting on a chart the distance believed to have been covered along each course which has been steered.

In the seventeenth and early eighteenth centuries, this was always referred to as "deduced reckoning" or "deduced position." The old log books had a column for entering the "deduced position" but because of lack of space at the top of the column, it became a general custom to write "ded reckoning." Mariners referred to this position by its shorter and abbreviated top-of-column term, which by another strange change in spelling but with the same pronunciation became "dead reckoning."

DERRICK. From the name of Thomas Derrick, a well-known hangman of the time of Queen Elizabeth, an ingenious fellow, who devised a spar with a topping lift and purchase for his gruesome work, instead of using the old-fashioned rope method. Derrick was the executioner of the Earl of Essex in 1601.

DAVIT. Not used until 1811; tackle on main and foremost shrouds were used for hoisting heavy boats and weights out and in. In more modern times applied to the swinging metal or wood fixture to which tackle is rigged. Called first *davitt*, and by Captain John Smith, "*the Davids end*" in 1626. Derived from *Daviet*, a diminutive for David, it being customary to give proper names to implements, as *billy*, *jack*, etc.

DEVIL TO PAY. "The devil to pay and only half a bucket of pitch" was the original expression. This is understood when it is known that the "devil" was the longest and most difficult seam to pay (fill with oakum and tar) and was found near the garboard strake; hence, "between the devil and the deep blue sea." "Pay" is from the French word *poix*, meaning pitch, "to pay the seams" or "to pitch the seams." "Devil to pay" still means "trouble."

DITTY BOX. The small box formerly carried by sailors in which were kept letters, small souvenirs, toilet articles, and needles and thread. These articles were, before the use of the box, kept in a bag of "Dittis" or "Manchester stuff"; hence a "ditty box." Possibly derived from the Saxon word *dite*, meaning tidy.

DOCTRINE OF THE LAST FAIR CHANCE. A doctrine which provides and asserts that a person in authority (senior officer) shall, when a collision is imminent, do all that is possible to avert or lessen the damage of the disaster.

DOG WATCH. Several possible origins are given. It may have come from *docked* or short watch. Admiral Cradock, in his *Whispers from the Fleet*, called it a watch "curtailed."
One of the watches of two hours duration from 4 to 8 P.M. The first dog watch is from 4 to 6 P.M., and second dog watch, from 6 to 8 P.M.

DUTCH COURAGE. This term, used by the English-speaking world, is of nautical origin and may be traced to the Dutch. It is related that when Cornelius Van Tromp and de Ruyter were in command, Dutch sailors were given, before going into battle, suitable libations of the well-known "square-faced gin." The English, who were their enemies at the time, called this practice "Dutch courage."

DUTCHMAN'S BREECHES. Mariners look for that small patch of blue sky that denotes the breaking up of a gale. No matter how small the patch, it has been said to be "enough to make a pair of breeches for a Dutchman."

ENGINEER CORPS. The first appointment of an engineer in the United States Navy was in 1836; the first in the British Navy in 1837. The corps was not incorporated in the United States Navy *Register* nor regularly organized until 1843.

ENSIGN (FLAG). Direct from old Norman *enseigne.* Anglo-Saxon *segne* meant flag. *Signum* in Latin meant sign. Signal comes from the same root word.

The British Navy borrowed the word from land service in the sixteenth century when the large flag was hoisted on the poop of sea vessels. One may read in *The Theorike and Practike of Moderne Warres*, in 1598, that

> we Englishmen do call them [ensigns] of late "colours" by reason
> of the variety of colours they may be made of, whereby they
> may be better noted and known to the companie.

Ensign bearer, shortened to ensign, was the rank, at an early date, of a young officer in the French Army and was afterward introduced into the French Navy as a naval rank. After the British in 1861 adopted the rank of sub-lieutenant to supplant the rank of mate, the American Navy in 1862 adopted the rank of ensign. The rank existed in the American Revolutionary Army and today is used in the British army for the color bearers. It is also used by some of the old, honorary state and city military organizations in the United States.

EPAULETTES. They were common in the French service long before they were introduced in the British Army. The British Navy first used them as an optional part of the dress, although no uniforms were standardized. In time, British officers in France were not recognized as commissioned officers without them. Nelson met Captains Ball and Shephard in France and wrote in regard to these officers, "They wore fine epaulettes, for which I think them coxcombs. They have not visited me, and I shall not count their acquaintance." Epaulettes were originally dubbed "swabs" and are so known today. This ornament of uniform consisted originally of bunches of ribbon.

In the War of 1812, American naval officers wore epaulettes. Commodores then had a uniform the same as captains except a silver star was worn on each epaulette. Naval surgeons wore the same uniform without epaulettes. Master commandants and lieutenants wore the same as the captain except that only one epaulette was worn on the right shoulder, no button on the collar, nor lace around the pocket flaps. Neither chapeaus nor epaulettes have been authorized in the U. S. Navy since just before the U. S. entered World War II, and probably such accouterments will never be authorized again.

EXECUTIVE OFFICER. The second in command of ships of the United States Navy. Captain W. T. Truxtun, writing in 1881, said:

The title of executive officer is of quite recent date and has been the cause of much discussion, bad temper, and bitter opposition. It has grown from the ashes of the old first lieutenant and finds its parallel in the Army adjutant, and in all corporations or factories employing large bodies of men, in the name of superintendent or manager. The executive officer holds by far the most onerous, most difficult, and most thankless office on board ship. . . . He is held responsible for the cleanliness of the ship, her good order, neat and man-of-war-like appearance, and above all, he is to do as he is told by his captain, to promulgate and execute his orders; and, last of all his duties, never to go ashore except on the sheet anchor.[13]

EYES OF THE SHIP. Most of the early ships had heads of mythological monsters or patrons carved in the bow; hence, the terms "figurehead," "forecastle head," "the heads," and the term "eyes of the ship" followed from the eyes of the figures placed there. Large "eyes" are still painted on bows of Chinese junks.

FATHOM. From Anglo-Saxon *faehom*; Dutch *vadem*; Latin *patene*, act of stretching two arms wide as rough measurement of six feet.

FIGUREHEADS. Research does not disclose when the custom of placing figures and images over the prow, cutwater, and between the "eyes of the ship" began. We do know that the ancient Phoenicians, Egyptians, Greeks, Carthaginians, and Romans, as well as the Norsemen, placed images of animals, renowned leaders, and the deities over the prows of their war vessels. It was originally a superstitious custom intended to propitiate the gods of storms. The early Greeks named their vessels of war after goddesses and had an image of the goddess aboard. Spanish galleons in the sixteenth century carried images of patron saints of ships. On the sterns of ships of the Middle Ages scrolls were often carved with *Dieu Conduit* (God leads).

The *Constitution*, "Old Ironsides," originally had a figurehead of Hercules. Later Andrew Jackson's figure in wood was placed there, but the head was sawed off clandestinely by a navy yard clique of

---

[13] In the British navies the executive branch corresponds to the line branch of the U. S. Navy, and its members are referred to as executive officers irrespective of rank or appointment. The Royal Canadian Navy has adopted the American usage of "Executive Officer" instead of Commander or First Lieutenant. However, traditional names were retained in unofficial sea language: "Jimmy" (lower deck), and "Number one" (wardroom). Acknowledgment to Lieut. Chaplin, RCN(R).

opposite politics. The *Constitution* later carried a carved scroll. One of the most famous figureheads in America is that of the one-time Chief of the Delaware Indians, Tamanend. This stern Indian chief once adorned that proud old ship of the line, the USS *Delaware*. In order to preserve this historic relic of sail and reminder of cherished tradition, the Naval Academy Class of 1891 donated the amount necessary to cast a duplicate in bronze; and with suitable ceremony preserved the "patron saint" of "wooden" midshipmen, "the god of 2.5" (lowest passing mark). The old figurehead of Tamanend is called Tecumseh—a name and a memory that no Naval Academy man will ever forget.

Figureheads, in some cases, and shields on the majority of ships, were worn as late as 1909. They were both removed prior to the new instructions for painting ships, effective late in 1908. White hulls were then changed to the slate or man-of-war color we know today. Figureheads went out with the clippers. The figureheads balanced the harmony of design of these "aristocrats of the sea."

FLAG OFFICER. A "flag officer" is an officer of the Navy above the grade of captain. It comprises in the United States Navy rear admiral, vice admiral, admiral, and fleet admiral. The President of the United States appoints vice admirals and admirals by letter.

The United States Navy had "flag officers" before the square flag was flown and before the grade of admiral was created by Congress. On January 16, 1857, an Act of Congress directed that "captains in command of squadrons" should be denominated *flag officers*. The square flag was not prescribed at the time.

The following order is of interest in that it is a fore-runner of the rank of admiral and prescribed the flag (See "Admiral"):

> Navy Department, May 18, 1858.
> It is hereby ordered that in lieu of the broad pennant now worn by "flag officers" in command of squadrons, they shall wear a plain blue flag of dimensions proportionate to the different classes of vessels prescribed for the jack in the table of allowances approved July 20, 1854.
>
> Flag officers whose date of commission as captain is over twenty years shall wear it at the fore; all others at the mizzen.
>
> Isaac Toucey, Secretary of the Navy

Admiral George H. Preble wrote: "This order introduced the flags of vice and rear admirals into our Navy, although the title was considered too aristocratic for republican ears at the time."

FLEET. From Anglo-Saxon *floet*, *floetan*; old Spanish *flota*; hence, *flotilla*.

FLOGGING. A flogging entry from the log of the USS *Constitution* reads:

> May 10 (1834). At 6:30 P.M. punished at the gangway with one dozen of "the cats," Thomas Frazier and Thomas Webb, also Peter Hudson six, with "the cats."

The Quarterly Report of Punishments of the USS *Columbus* reports twenty-nine men flogged from May 28th to June 27th in 1846. Entries such as: James Johnson . . . Ordinary Seaman . . . Knocking down master at arms . . . twelve lashes with cats, and, Thomas Childs . . . Landsman . . . Fighting . . . twelve lashes with boy's cats. Note the variation from the "king size" to "boy's cats."

In 1850, Senator John P. Hale (New Hampshire) a liberal and champion of the "under dog," added an antiflogging clause to the Naval Appropriation Bill. Commodore Uriah P. Levy was instrumental in interesting Senator Hale in the measure.

In 1851–53, Commodore R. F. Stockton, Senator from California, further restricted flogging by legislation and on July 17, 1862, Congress abolished flogging.

The Navy Department reported that "it would be utterly impracticable to have an efficient Navy without this form of punishment." The Department reported that the "colt" (a single whip) was in most instances used instead of the "cat-o'-nine-tails." Senator Hale showed where a seaman had been sentenced by court-martial "to receive 500 lashes, and actually received 400." This was given in twelve-lash installments.

Many sailors as well as writers had long advocated reform in punishment. But paradoxical as it may seem, groups of sailors presented memorials to Congress requesting no change in the system, stating that without drastic punishment the good men would have to do the work of the shirkers. After the act was passed, Secretary of the Navy Gideon Welles reported on December 4, 1862, that it was impossible to re-enlist the better class of seamen. The sober, hard-working men considered that they had been performing duties of the shirkers and the indolent. This led to a change in the enlistment system and the training of the Navy.[14]

---

[14] Man's brutality for his fellow man at sea reached shocking heights in execution of the practices of flogging and, in particular, "flogging around the fleet." A British officer in the early nineteenth century who had charge of the launch gives a long, detailed account of a "five hundred lash" sentence around the fleet: "Two hundred lashes had now been inflicted with a cat-o'-nine-tails, or eighteen hundred strokes with a cord of the thickness of a quill. The flesh from the nape

FORECASTLE. In the twelfth century, castles to fight from, similar to those towers of wood used ashore, were placed forward and aft on the Norman ships. The word "forecastle" survived.

FOUL ANCHOR. An anchor that is foul of the cable or chain. The symbol is found in various Admiralty and Navy crests. This device is also on the cap badge of the American naval officer, the collar of the midshipman, and the buttons and cap badges of the British officer. It is regarded by many true sailors as an emblem of careless and poor sea-manship, although artistic to the landsmen, and is sometimes called the "sailor's disgrace." It was the badge of Lord Howard of Effingham in 1601, when he was Lord High Admiral, and was used first in this con-nection as a naval seal. As a badge, it was used previous to this time.

FRIGATE. *Frigata* originally designated a class of Mediterranean ves-sels which used both oars and sails. The French were the first to use frigates on the ocean for war or commerce.

Theodore Roosevelt wrote in *The Naval War of 1812*: "Towards end of the eighteenth century the terms frigate and line-of-battle ship had crystallized. Frigate then meant a so-called single-decked ship; it in reality possessed two decks, the main, or gun-deck, and the upper one, which had no name at all until our sailors christened it spar-deck. The gun-deck presented a complete battery, and the spar-deck an in-terrupted one, mounting guns on the forecastle and quarterdeck." In the two victories of the *Constitution*, her broadside was fifteen long 24s on the main deck, and one long 24 on the spar deck. Also ten or eleven 32-pound carronades. The broadside was 704 or 736 pounds. A few days before her action with the *Guerriere*, the *Constitution* had a muster roll of 464 names (including 51 marines). Roosevelt wrote: "Our three 44-gun ships [*Constitution, President,* and *United States*] were the finest frigates then afloat."

FURL. Probably from the old English *furdle*, corruption of *fardle*, meaning to make up a bundle.

---

of the neck to below the shoulder blades was one deep purple mass from which the blood oozed slowly. At every stroke a low groan escaped, and the flesh quiv-ered with a sort of convulsive twitch; the eyes were closed, and the poor man began to faint. Water was administered, and pungent salts applied to his nostrils, which presently revived him in slight degree." Five weeks after this the man was lashed again, "then every blow brought away morsels of skin and flesh." Then there was a two years' prison, "where he fell into consumption and ended his days." Clark, *Battles of England.* The last official flogging in the British Navy was in 1882, but the order in council removing authority to award corporal pun-ishment was not made until 1949.

FUTTOCK SHROUDS. Futtock is a contracted term for "foot hooks," for the toes have to be hooked or bent around the ratlines to go over them.

GALE. From old Norse *galem*, Danish *gal*, mad or furious. In the seventeenth century, Butler wrote:

> When the wind blows not too hard, so that the ship may bear out
> her topsail a-trip (that is, fully hoisted, no reefs) it is called a
> loon gale; when it blows much wind it is called a swift and strong
> gale, or at least a fresh gale.

He describes the conditions when no sail could be carried, and this was considered a degree higher than a storm. The force of wind in nautical miles per hour, with equivalent designations such as "calm," "light airs," "fresh breeze," "gale," and "full gale" are employed today for logging weather. They were originally devised by Admiral Beaufort, RN, and are known as the Beaufort Scale or Table.

GALLEY YARN. A "scuttle-butt rumor," a rumor. In the early days the cook was often the originator of much startling news passed on to the crew.

GANGWAY. From Anglo-Saxon *gang*, to go; make a passage in, or cut out, or through.

GIG. The captain's boat. It is usually a light boat of whaler build with a gilded arrow on each bow. Much pride is taken in the gig: the general appearance of the crew and the cleanliness and neatness of the boat are usually excellent indications of the condition of the ship. In a gig under oars, it is customary for the captain to steer the boat and make the landing, after which the coxswain who is stroke oarsman takes charge.

GIG STROKE. A stroke used by the single-banked crew of gigs, requiring a distinct pause after each stroke of the oars. This stroke has fallen into disuse in the United States Navy and is now only a memory.

GIG AND GALLEY. The clinker-built "gig," as a substitute for the pinnace as the captain's boat, came in with the nineteenth century. The 1815 edition of Falconer calls it "A long, narrow boat used for expedition, generally rowed with six or eight oars, and is mostly the *private property* of the captain or commander." The one-horse, two-wheeled vehicle called by the same name was introduced only a few years earlier, and the two land and sea terms may have the same etymology. Elisha Coles (1692) and Bailey (1724–90) in their dictionaries give, as the *only* meaning of word "gig," a "wanton woman" but "gig-manity" in a man-of-war has always been as much a guarantee of "respectability" afloat as Carlyle assures us it was ashore. The term "galley," now so universal for the long six-oared "gig" of the captain of a man-of-war, is not older on board ship than the middle of the nineteenth century, and at the date of the Crimean War was exclusively applied to the boat of the captain of a line-of-battle ship; but it has never been officially recognized by the Admiralty. In Crimean days it was an unpardonable offense for an officer of the watch, when the captain of a line-of-battle ship ordered his boat, to call away the "1st gig" instead of the "galley."[15]

GIVE QUARTER. Came from a practice that originated in the wars between the Dutch and the Spaniards, when a captured officer was given life and liberty for a ransom fee estimated at one-quarter of his yearly pay.

GLASS. Employed nautically to refer to such articles of the mariner's craft as barometers, telescopes, and time glasses. "How's the glass?" means, "What is the barometer doing?" "To flog" or "to sweat the glass" was a sharp practice of olden days, whereby the "glass" was agitated; the sand flowed faster, and the watch was more quickly terminated. "Clear glass" was used in reference to the heaving of the chip log and signified to clear all sand out of one end of the glass before heaving the log. "To cook a glass" meant to heat either a time glass or a telescope in order to remove moisture.

"GONE WEST." An expression dating back to the Norsemen. When a Viking chief died, his body was placed in a special bier aboard a Viking war boat, the steering oar was lashed, and the sails set with the intent that the body would sail on toward the setting sun. Chiefs were occasionally buried in their boats.

GRAPE. Small iron balls an inch or so in diameter bound together in clusters. This type of ammunition played an effective part in our early frigate actions.

GROG. A sailor's expression for watered rum. Admiral Vernon, RN, in 1740 ordered that the rum be watered.[16] It was Vernon's custom to

---

[15] Rear Admiral Sir R. Massie Blomfield, RN, "Man-of-War Boats, II," *Mariner's Mirror* (January, 1912).

[16] "Whereas it manifestly appears by the return made to my general order of 4th August, to be the unanimous opinion of both Captains and Surgeons that

wear a boat cloak of a coarse material, called "grogram" (like stiff Irish frieze—rain proof). His nickname was "Old Grog"; hence the name applied to the beverage. Sailors of long ago sang:

For grog is our starboard, our larboard,
Our mainmast, our mizen, our log—
At sea, or ashore, or when harbour'd,
The mariner's compass is grog.[17]

Very early we pursued the policy, "*Buy American.*" The Secretary of the Navy in 1806 wrote:

Being persuaded that whiskey is a more wholesome drink as well as a much more economical one, I am anxious to introduce the use of it into our Navy generally; but this cannot be immediately effected. I have therefore made experiment to introduce it, and the result has satisfied me that in time the Sailors will become perfectly reconciled to it, and probably prefer it to Spirit [rum]. Our annual consumption of Spirit is about 45,000 gallons.

The legislation that led to the abolishment of grog in the Navy is of some historic interest. The spirit ration when abolished consisted of "two dips" a day and in lieu thereof a commutation of five cents per day.

Gustavus V. Fox, Assistant Secretary of the Navy, in 1862 wrote to Senator J. W. Grimes, "I beg of you for the enduring good of the service . . . to add a proviso abolishing the spirit ration. . . ." Senator

---

the pernicious custom of the seamen drinking their allowance of rum in drams, and often at once, is attended with many fatal effects on their morals as well as their health, which are visibly impaired thereby, and many of their lives shortened by it, besides the ill consequences arising from stupefying their rational qualities which makes them heedless slaves to every brutish passion, and which cannot be better remedied than by the ordering their half pint of rum to be daily mixed with a quart of water: which they that are good husbandmen may from the savings of their salt provisions and bread, purchase sugar and limes to make more palatable to them. . . ." *August 1740*. By Edward Vernon, Esq., Vice Admiral of the Blue and Commander in Chief of His Majesty's ships and vessels in the West Indies.

[17] Compare "A Sailors Will": "To my old friend and messmate, Capstan, I leave all my gin tubs, rum kegs, beer jugs, glasses, and all them other public-house rigging and tackle. To Tom Hallyard, my best blue jacket and trousers, provided they ar'n't worn out before I die. . . . And as to what money may happen to be aboard the bank when I slips my cable, why, they may be spent in grog after all my funeral expenses are paid. My funeral to be attended by such of my messmates as can get leave to attend (provided they don't get too much grog aboard before the service begins); and as for an epitaph at the top of my grave, why, just write—'Here lies Jack Helm, Stormy Jack, becalmed at last.' "

Grimes championed the bill that abolished a spirit of rum ration aboard United States men-of-war.[18]

On May 23, 1872, Congress made provision for a liberal issue of coffee and prescribed its use—"an additional ration of coffee and sugar to be served at his [the seaman's] first turning out. . . ."

"General Order 99," of June 1, 1914, signed by Secretary of the Navy Josephus Daniels, prohibited "the use or introduction for drinking purposes of alcoholic liquors on board any naval vessel, or within any navy yard or station. . . ."

"General Order 244," of March 21, 1934, signed by Secretary of the Navy Claude A. Swanson, permitted intoxicating liquors on naval shore establishments and confined such use to "officers' quarters, officers' messes, and officers' clubs. . . ."

General Order No. 15, of November 4, 1948, extends this privilege to all chief petty officer messes (open) and staff noncommissioned clubs, and to clubs and recreation centers of enlisted personnel beyond the continental limits of the United States.

GUARD AND BAND FOR COLORS. Although originally a ceremony at sunrise, Lord Saint Vincent established a new regulation after the 1797 mutinies in order to make it a most impressive ceremony. In 1844 the British Navy, for the sake of uniformity, set a fixed time for this ceremony.

GUESS OR GUEST WARP ROPES. A rope carried to a distant object in order to warp a vessel towards it, or to make fast a boat. "Haul out" also meant to haul out in its original sense. A ship's boat would come alongside, the crew would be ordered aboard, and the boat would be made fast while alongside to a guess warp and "hauled out."[19]

GUN, SON OF A. In the early days, sailors were permitted to keep their "wives" on board. Lord Exmouth, after the bombardment of Algiers in July 1816, reported that "even British women served at the same guns as their husbands, and during a contest of many hours, never shrank from danger but animated all around them."

The British Admiralty issued an order in 1830 prohibiting officer's wives to be carried in men-of-war; however, in many cases the order

---

[18] "On September 1, 1862, the spirit ration shall forever cease and thereafter no distilled spirituous liquor shall be admitted on board vessels of war, except as medicine and upon the order and under the control of the medical officer of such vessel and to be used only for medical purposes." U. S. *Stat.*, XII, 565.

[19] W. H. Smyth, *The Sailor's Word Book: An Alphabetical Digest of Nautical Terms* (London: Blackie & Sons, 1867), p. 354.

was evaded. The term was actually used to refer to children born alongside the guns of the broadsides. In fact, the expression questioned the legitimacy of anyone. The old definition of a man-o'-war's man was:

> Begotten in the galley and born under a gun. Every hair a rope yarn, every tooth a marline spike; every finger a fish hook and in his blood right good Stockholm tar.

A British officer commanding a brig off the Spanish coast in 1835 wrote in his diary:

> This day the surgeon informed me that a woman on board had been laboring in child for twelve hours, and if I could see my way to permit the firing of a broadside to leeward, nature would be assisted by the shock. I complied with the request and she was delivered of a fine male child.
>
> The Gunnery Department made a perfect score!

GUNNEL (GUNWALE). Wale comes from Anglo-Saxon *wala*, a weal, a strip, a ridge. First in English in 1330. Derived from the custom of firing the top row of guns over planking which had been reinforced by "wales"; hence "gunwales." In small boats never permit anyone to sit on the "gunnels."

GUNNERY. Although China had powder long before its invention in Europe, 1330 is given as the date of the invention of gunpowder. Powder-burning guns, breech-loading and discharging a stone projectile, were reported in England in 1338. The Spaniards were armed with cannon in a sea fight against the English and the people of Poitou, off La Rochelle in 1392. This is the first naval battle wherein mention is made of artillery. In 1824, Blunt, in his *Theory and Practice of Seamanship*, writes in regard to gunnery:

> The machines, which owe their rise to the invention of gunpowder, have now totally supplanted the others; so that there is scarcely any but the sword remaining of all the weapons used by the ancients. Our naval battles are therefore almost always decided by fire arms, of which there are several kinds, known by the general name of artillery. In a ship of war, fire arms are distinguished in the cannon mounted upon carriages, swivel cannon, grenades, and musketry. Besides these machines, there are several others used in merchant ships and privateers, as cohorns, carabines, fire arrows, organs, stink-pots, etc.

In the British *Naval Regulations* (1790) the following may be found under "The Gunner":

Also every gunner ought to know that it is a wholesome thing for him to eat and drink a little meat before he doth discharge any piece of artillery, because the fume of saltpetre and brimstone will otherwise be hurtful to his brain, so it is very unwholesome to him to shoot in any piece of ordnance while his stomach is full.

Melville, writing of the quarter gunners and gunners' mates, refers to them as,

a class full of unaccountable whimsies. They were continually grumbling and growling about the batteries; running in and out among the guns; driving the sailors away from them, and cursing and swearing as if all their consciences had been powder singed and made callous by their calling.

HAMMOCKS. In 1498 in the Bahamas, Christopher Columbus found that the natives used woven cotton nets as beds, called "hammacs." The Spanish changed the word to *hamaco*. The Spanish spelling was used when the word entered the English nautical vocabulary in the Elizabethan reign.[20]

In 1596, they are officially mentioned as hanging "cabbons" or "beddes." After an action, as many sails as possible were expended to provide new hammocks and white trousers for the crew. "Up hammocks" and "down hammocks" are expressions derived from the days when hammocks were stowed in topside, upper-deck nettings; hence comes the meaning "up all hammocks."

HAND, LEND A, or BEAR A. Long usage has decreed that "lend a hand" is a request for assistance, while "bear a hand" implies an order, and especially, an order to hurry.

HANDSOMELY. An order to do something slowly and carefully.

HARTER ACT. By this act and law, a ship owner is protected against claims for damage incurred through the acts of the ship's officers or crew, provided the ship was seaworthy and was fully equipped and manned on leaving port.

HARVEST MOON. The phenomenon in high latitudes of several moonlight nights at the full moon nearest the autumnal equinox in which that body rises nearly at the same time. The moon ordinarily rises later each night by an average of 51 minutes, but at this time it is coming northward very rapidly in declination, causing an earlier rising

---

[20] Hammocks were first issued in 1629 to British ships on foreign stations. Each hammock was shared by two men; one man was always on watch.

which almost overcomes the natural retardation due to its eastward movement of revolution.[21]

HAUL. It means literally to pull or to drag. The wind "hauls" when it changes in direction with the sun. When a ship's course is so changed that her head lies nearer the wind, she is "hauled up." "To haul off" is to remove to a greater distance.

HAWSE PIPES. Hawse is an old name for throat; and since the head was forward as well as the "eyes," the term throat pipe or hawse pipe came into being.

HAWSER. From French *hausser*—to hoist. In the early eighteenth century and before, cables made of hemp, bass, or Indian grass were used for the anchors. The change from hemp to chain cables came in 1812. Hemp cables for a 1,000-ton ship were 8″ in diameter and usually 120 fathoms long. The friction of the cable through the hawse was enormous; tar on the surface of the hemp often took fire and men stood by with buckets of water. It was a common saying of those enlisted men who became officers that "they came through the hawse," meaning, of course, that they once worked forward or on the forecastle.

HOLYSTONES. So named because fragments of broken monuments from Saint Nicholas church, Great Yarmouth, England, were used at one time to scrub the decks of ships of the British Navy. In the British service, holystones were also called "ecclesiastical bricks." The name is now used for bricks, sand stones, or medium-soft sand rock used for the scrubbing of wooden decks. They were moved fore and aft on the wet decks by means of a wooden handle placed in a depression of the stone. Holystones were of sufficient importance to become the subject of a general order issued by the Secretary of the Navy.

General Order 215 of March 5, 1931, states:

> 1. The use of holystones for cleaning the wooden decks of naval vessels wears down the decks so rapidly that their repair or replacement has become an item of expense to the Navy Department which cannot be met under limited appropriations.
>
> 2. . . . .
>
> 3. It is therefore directed that the use of holystones or similar material for cleaning wooden decks be restricted to the removal of stains.

[21] Bradford, *A Glossary*, p. 85.

Small holystones were called "prayer books"; larger ones were called "Bibles."

HORSE LATITUDES. A belt of light and variable winds between the "Westerlies" and the "Trade Winds" in the northern and southern hemispheres where sailing vessels were often becalmed for some time. The name had its origins in the mid-nineteenth century, when numerous horses were transported from Europe to the Americas. The belt in the North Atlantic was often studded with the carcasses of horses that died during such times.

IDLERS. Falconer's *Marine Dictionary* (Revised 1815) defines "idlers" as all those on board a ship of war, who from being liable to constant day duty are not subjected to keep night watch, but nevertheless must go up on deck if all hands are called during the night. The term today includes sick bay attendants, cooks, yeomen, etc.

JAMAICA DISCIPLINE. A name for the "Articles for the Government of Pirate Ships," in the eighteenth century. The articles stipulated that the captain took two shares of all stolen booty, the officers one and one-half and one and one-quarter depending upon rank, while all the crew shared alike. In order to prevent quarrels and brawls aboard ship, gambling and the bringing of women aboard ship was prohibited. Indulgence in strong drink could only take place on deck after 8:00 P.M.

JAVA or "JAMOKE." Used by bluejackets of the United States Navy to designate coffee. Some sailors call coffee, "joe," which some say is a derivative of Foster's song "Old Black Joe." Others call coffee, "java," "jamoke," "murk," a "shot" or "shot-in-the-arm." For twenty years before grog was legislated out of the Navy, the rum ration had been diminished, while tea and coffee were "experimentally supplied as a substitute." In the Congressional Bill of May 23, 1872, further provision was made for "an additional ration of coffee and sugar to be served at his [the bluejacket's] first turning out." The United States Navy uses more coffee per man than any other military or naval organization in the world. In March 1954, the Bureau of Supplies and Accounts estimated the Navy used 50,668 pounds of coffee a day.

KEELHAULING. A call down or reprimand; "getting on the carpet" is its general meaning as used by older seamen. In the early days this term signified one of the most drastic and cruel forms of punishment. The victim was hoisted by a whip or light tackle to a fore yardarm and thence dropped into the sea. A weight was attached to the unfortunate to ensure that he would sink deep enough for a whip to drag him under the keel and up again to the opposite yardarm on the other side.

There is record that this was originally a punishment in vogue among the pirates of the Mediterranean in the sixteenth century, and that it was afterwards introduced into the English and the Dutch Navies.

Boteler describes this punishment in a book called *Dialogical Discourse on Marine Affairs*, written probably about 1630, but published in 1685, and dedicated to Samuel Pepys, as follows:

> The duckinge at the marine yarde arme is when a malefactor by haveing a rope fastened under his arms and about his middle and under his breech is thus hoysted up to the end of the yarde from whence he is againe violently let fall into the sea, sometimes twice, sometimes three, severall tymes, one after the other, and if the offense be very fowle, he is also drawn under the very keele of the shippe, the which is called, keele-rakinge, and whilst he is thus under water a great gunne is given fyre unto, right over his head, ye which is done as well to astonish him the more with thunder thereof, which much troubles him, as to give warninge unto all others to looke out and beware of his harms.

Keelhauling, flogging, tongue-scraping and gagging were common practices as early as the sixteenth century. It was in 1645 that ship court-martial was instituted and written records of all punishments kept in the Royal Navy. An historical entry from a ship's log of 1675 reads: "A scolding woman was well washt today." It could have been by keelhauling.

KNOTS. Captain Gershom Bradford describes in detail the old method of computing speed:

> Chip log is a device now restricted to a few sailing vessels. It consists of a wooden quadrant about 5 inches in radius, with lead placed in the circular edge, which causes it to float upright. It is made fast to a log line by a three-part bridle. The part fitted to the upper corner has a socket and a pin which pulls out when a strain is placed upon it with the desire to haul it aboard. The chip is cast over (streamed) with the pin in position. The first 15 or 30 fathoms of line is called the stray line which is marked by a piece of red bunting. The line from this point is divided into parts of 47 feet 3 inches, each called a knot. They are marked by pieces of cord tucked through the strands with knots in their ends corresponding to the number of knots out. Each knot is subdivided into fifths and marked with a white rag. The log line is allowed to run

out while a 28-second glass is emptying itself. The result is the
rate of speed of the vessel. The length of the knot was derived
from the proportion that one hour (3,600 sec.) is to 28 seconds as
one mile (6,080 ft.) is to the length of a knot (47 ft. 3 in.). The
clipper ship *Flying Cloud* off Cape Horn once ran out 18 knots
and there was still a little sand in the glass."

LANGRIDGE. Knife blades, old nails, copper slugs, iron bolts, and
scraps of metal in cans. Used in cannon at the time of the War of
American Independence and War of 1812. Bayonet blades bound with
rope yarn were shot from cannon for the purpose of cutting rigging
in order to effect the fall of masts. There were shells of that time
known as starshots, chain shots, "sausages," double headers, "porcu-
pines," and "hedge hogs."

LARBOARD. The "load board" was the left side of the ship, in distinction to the right side of a ship where the steering gear was carried,
known as "steer board." Larboard was confused with starboard and
hence the term "port" or loading entrance was adopted.

The expression "steer bord" may be traced to the Vikings. Viking
ships have been found in a remarkable state of preservation, wherein
the remains of chieftains were buried. From these ships the arrangement for steering on the right or starboard quarter may be observed
in detail. The Gokstadt ship discovered in 1880 was built of oak, was
72 feet long and 15 feet 6 inches beam, and had a displacement of about
30 tons. The quarter rudder was used by the Vikings in the ninth century, but about the twelfth century a second rudder was placed on the
larboard side. Eventually the stern rudder replaced the two quarter
rudders.

LASHING BROOM TO FORE TOPMAST. Maarten Harpertszoon Tromp,
a Dutch admiral, ordered that brooms be lashed to the masts when the
great sailor sailed to meet the fleet of Cromwell. This gesture signified
that he would sweep the English Channel of the English Navy.

The American Navy has for many years hoisted brooms at the
mastheads of the ships that won the battle efficiency pennants. Even
before the present form of competition, brooms were hoisted by ships
standing one in gunnery, also in engineering competition. Christmas
trees are hoisted at both the foremast and mainmast trucks of United
States ships during the Yuletide; the tips of yards are also decorated
with evergreens.

LAUNCH CANNONADE. This short piece of ordnance was in reality
the forerunner of the antiaircraft gun. It was the most effective gun of

its time for shooting at sharpshooters in the tops. It is recorded that by a launch cannonade the mizzentop of the *Chesapeake* was cleaned of sharpshooters before the daring Broke boarded her from the British *Shannon*.

LIEUTENANT. A word derived from the French, meaning "holding in lieu of" or "one who replaces."

The introduction of this rank into the British Navy in 1580 was for the purpose of providing the captain with an assistant and qualified relief if necessary. The first lieutenant was for years, both in the British and American services, the executive officer of the ship. In smaller British ships, the title First Lieutenant still obtains, and he is referred to unofficially as No. 1.

In the latter part of the Elizabethan reign, the following rule is on record:

> The lieutenant must have a care that he carry not himself proudly or presumptuously, nor that his captain give him power or authority to intermeddle with the master's office; for where there is heart burning between the lieutenant and master, it will make it burst out into open discontent and then will follow mischief and and factions among the company.

LIEUTENANT COMMANDER. This title was introduced in the United States Navy in 1862 with the reorganization of the service. Previous to this time, all lieutenants in command of smaller men-of-war were called "lieutenant commanding." For example, in the roster of the North Atlantic Blockading Squadron in 1862 one reads:

> (USS) *Valley City*, Lieut. Commanding S. C. Chaplin, bearing the flag of Flag Officer Goldsborough; also (USS) *Commander Perry*, Lieutenant Commanding C. W. Flusser.

The title lieutenant commander was derived from the term "lieut. commanding."

"LIMEY." A friendly name that through the years has been used by American bluejackets in referring to British bluejackets and merchant sailors in particular, and when pluralized, to the British in general. It was derived from the old practice in the British Navy of giving lime juice to prevent scurvy. Lime or lemon juice was issued from the time of the early French wars until this century.[22] Until 1860, this

---

[22] "The lime juice lives on too; it was still issued in 1941 when I was in West Africa but supplies ran out soon afterwards. I remember the WRENS were given it when the main brace was spliced (drinking time) at the RNVR centenary in London, 1953—they felt gypped." Lieut. Chaplin, RCN (R).

antiscorbute was obtained from Malta and Sicily; in fact, it was the juice of the lemon, then called a lime. Medical authorities then considered the acid quality of citron fruit an excellent means of combating scurvy. Due to the expense and difficulty of getting lime juice from the Mediterranean area, the British authorities commenced after 1860 to secure lime juice from St. Kitts in the West Indies. Scurvy cropped up again in the British Navy during World War I, and a committee of experts was delegated to study the question. It was found that certain vitamins played a most important part. Investigation disclosed that lime juice contains a negligible percentage of those vitamins, while lemon juice had a large percentage. The acid quality had little or nothing to do with the prevention of scurvy. Scurvy, that dread disease of sailors, has been practically eliminated by short voyages and modern refrigeration, but the old word "limey" lives on.

"Lemon juice," wrote Surgeon A. Farenholt, USN, in the U. S. Naval Institute *Proceedings*, "as an antiscorbutic was first carried to sea by Captain Lancaster, in an expedition sailing from England for the East Indies in January 1600. Three ounces were given daily to each man. When Cape Town was reached, Captain Lancaster's ship, the *Dragon*, alone was free of scurvy, and his ship's crew hoisted out the boats of the entire squadron and landed the sick, 105 of whom died there."

LOGGERHEAD. The word was derived from *logger-heat*, a piece of iron on a long handle used for melting pitch. The iron after heating was placed in the cold pitch. It was a deadly weapon when men came to "loggerheads."

LONG SHIP. An expression once used in our service and still used in the British service to signify a ship in which it was a long time between drinks or a long way from the fount of hospitality.

Some British ships hoist a green pennant in port at noon to signify that the time for the cup that cheers has arrived and friends are welcomed aboard. This is known in the Royal Navy as the "gin pendant" (always pronounced "pennant").

LUCKY BAG. Now a small compartment or large locker where masters-at-arms stow articles of clothing, bedding, etc., picked up on the decks. Originally, these articles were placed in a bag called the "lucky bag" which was in the custody of the master-at-arms. In a narrative of a cruise in the USS *Columbia* in 1838, the writer relates that the bag was brought to the mainmast once a month, and the owners of the articles "if their names are on them, get them again, with a few lashes for their carelessness in leaving them about the deck." The term "lucky" in this case is sailor's humor for "unfortunate."

In 1839, Matthew Fontaine Maury wrote a series of articles entitled "Scraps from the Lucky Bag, by Harry Bluff" and published in the *Southern Literary Messenger*.

MARINES (see United States Marine Corps, chapter 8).
Admiral Luce wrote:

> The United States Marine Corps has well sustained the high reputation for steadfast courage and loyalty which has been handed down to it from the days of Themistocles.

At least five centuries before the Christian Era, the Phoenicians and the Greeks used marines. The marines were the fighting men, while the seamen were the rowers. There is mention of marines in the time of Darius, King of Persia, about 497 B.C. In the battle of Lade between the Greeks and the Persians, one hundred Greek ships had forty armed citizens on board, and those were picked men. The Greeks called these sea soldiers *epibatoe*. The Scandinavians called them *bat-karler* or sea soldiers. They have been called *suprasalientes*, a word still retained in the Spanish *sobresaliente*, and as a military term meaning "over-leapers." In 1740, three regiments of marines were raised in the American Colonies and were assembled at New York.

The United States Marine Corps antedates the organization of the regular Navy, and even the Declaration of Independence. On November 10, 1775, the Continental Congress, to promote a "publick defense"

> *Resolved*, that two battalions of Marines be raised consisting of one colonel, two lieutenant colonels, two majors. . . . That particular care be taken that no person be appointed to offices, or enlisted into said battalions, but such as are good seamen or so acquainted with maritime affairs as to be able to serve to advantage by sea when required; that they be enlisted and commissioned to serve for and during the present war between Great Britain and the Colonies. . . . That they be distinguished by the names of the First and Second Battalions of American Marines.

It would require a long essay to trace the history of the Marine Corps from the British Navy in 1664 to our present organization. The first corps was known as the Lord Admiral's Maritime Regiment and was commanded by the Duke of York (later James II). Its history is long and interesting. In 1802, they were styled Royal Marines by order of the King as a mark of the King's pleasure for their conduct during the War of the French Revolution and their action during the great mutiny.[23]

In 1827, new colors were presented to the Chatham Division of the Royal Marines, and at the presentation, a device or badge was given them. The Duke of Clarence said:

> From the difficulty of selecting any particular places to inscribe on these standards, your Sovereign has been pleased to adopt "The Great Globe itself," as the most proper and distinct badge . . . the anchor which is your distinctive bearing was also adopted.

The cap device of the American marine was formerly a bugle, but in 1869 a metal hemisphere on an anchor and surmounted by an eagle was adopted.

MARTINET. A stickler for discipline, "a sundowner." The name comes from a French army officer, the Marquis de Martinet. A "cat-of-nine-tails" is still called in French nautical slang a "martinet."

MASTER. Six things required of a master in the Elizabethan age were "the cards (charts), the compass, the tides, the time, the wind, and the ship's way." The detailed duties of a master in the United States Navy are outlined elsewhere.

MASTER-AT-ARMS. Master-at-arms evolved from the sea corporal and was introduced into the Royal Navy during the reign of Charles I. His department included all the muskets, carbines, pistols, swords; and he exercised the ship's company, seeing that their bandoliers before going into action were filled with good powder. In the days of the USS *Constitution* and other early ships, there is record of drill under arms for the seamen by direction of the master-at-arms. He not only had police duties and was "chief of police," but was supposed to be qualified in close-order fighting under arms. Records of more than a hundred years ago indicate that these drills were received by the crew with no more enthusiastic welcome than landing force exercises today.

MATE. An old rank in the Navy. The mate, although an officer, was not in the line of promotion and held his position by appointment. He usually messed in the steerage or with the warrant officers and was ordered to duty in charge of boats, mate of the deck, or any special

[23] The Lord Admiral's Maritime Regiment is not to be confused with the Royal Maritime Regiment of the Royal Artillery, which served at sea in merchant ships in World War II, to make up for the shortage of naval gunnery ratings.

duty prescribed by the commanding officer. This term must not be confused with the boatswain's mate, gunner's mate, etc. Originally, he was known as Master's Mate, but later was down graded.

MESS. Middle English—*mes*, meaning a dish; hence, a mess of pottage. The word in English originally denoted four, and at large dinners the diners were seated in fours.[24] Shakespeare wrote of Henry's four sons as his "mess of sons" (*King Henry VI*, Part II, Act. I). The word mess, meaning confusion, is from the German *mischen*, meaning to mix.

MESSMATES. Those eating together, comrades. "Messmate before shipmate, shipmate before stranger, stranger before a dog."[25]

MIDSHIPMAN. Men or boys originally stationed amidships to carry messages, to bring up ammunition, and to relay messages from aft to the gundecks. It was a ship's rating in the British Navy until the end of the Napoleonic wars. A midshipman could be disrated at any time by the captain. In 1740, admirals and captains were permitted a certain number of followers; in some cases a flag officer was permitted fifty. They were rated midshipmen, tailors, barbers, fiddlers, footmen, and stewards. It was in 1815 that midshipmen became a naval rank in the British service. The midshipman's time on the books counted towards promotion as a lieutenant, for two years of the six years' service required at sea had to be served as a midshipman or mate. Often midshipmen were entered on the books a year or so before actual service. It was a British personnel problem in 1755 how to bring up officers and gentlemen who should be able seamen, skilled to manage a ship and maintain a sea fight judiciously, be of discretion and courage, and able to speak to the seamen in their own language.

"Middy" is a term disliked by midshipmen and used most frequently by elderly ladies, some land-going writers of sea stories, and a few Annapolitans.

Until the advent of steam, the life of the midshipman was often most disagreeable. The food was bad; the quarters cramped and located below the waterline; and the duties were onerous and manifold. Without the full status of an officer and still not a member of the crew, his position aboard ship was quite indefinite until regulations became more specific. The *United States Naval Regulations* (1818) state: "The commanding officers will consider the midshipmen as a class of officers, meriting in an especial degree their fostering care." From all accounts this "fostering care" was capable of wide interpretation.

---

[24] The mess of four is still in use at the Inns of Court in London.
[25] Smyth, *The Sailor's Word-Book*, p. 478.

The midshipman's berth. *Courtesy Naval Records and Library, Navy Department.*

This apprenticeship for a commission is set forth in a realistic manner by Rear Admiral Baron Jeffrey de Raigersfeld in *The Life of a Sea Officer*. As to midshipmen, it is recorded:

> In the latter part of the eighteenth century it was not uncommon for midshipmen to be flogged, mastheaded, and disrated, if not turned before the mast.

Admiral de Raigersfeld writes of his midshipman days under Captain, afterwards Admiral, Lord Collingwood:

> On board the *Mediator* all these punishments were inflicted at various times; and one morning after breakfast, while at anchor in St. John's Road, Antigua, all the midshipmen were sent for into the captain's cabin, and four of us were tied up one after the other to the breech of one of the guns, and flogged upon our bare bottoms with a cat-o'-nine-tails, by the boatswain of the ship; some received six lashes, some seven, and myself three. No doubt we all deserved it, and were thankful that we were punished in the cabin instead of upon deck, which was not uncommon in other ships of the fleet.[26]

Although a midshipman is an officer in a very qualified sense, it will forever stand as a record that Samuel Barron was appointed and given a midshipman's warrant on April 11, 1812, when he was three years and four months old. He was "on duty" at half pay (midshipman's pay $19 per month) and a few cents in place of his grog ration. At the age of eight, in 1816, he reported for active duty at the Norfolk Navy Yard, and went to sea in the USS *Columbus* in 1820. Farragut was a midshipman at nine and one half, and Louis M. Goldsborough, who became a distinguished Civil War officer, received his warrant at the age of seven years and ten months. In the British Navy there is record of babies being entered on the rolls at age one. In most cases the captain collected all pay and allowances and the original five pounds of "bounty money."[27]

[26] Being bent over the breech of a gun for caning or flogging is still known in British wardrooms as "kissing the gunner's daughter," but as a British officer wrote, "no modern gun is well adapted for this purpose."

[27] The Barrons left a most distinguished record as a "sea-going" naval family. "The family tree shows one commodore and six other officers in the Virginia Navy during the Revolution, two commodores and a captain and many other officers in the U. S. Navy, and one commodore and other officers in the Confederate Navy. Of the twenty-seven male members of the family, twenty-one followed the sea. Nine of them were lost at sea. Through seven successive generations, Barrons served as officers in the armed forces holding continuous high command for 125 years." *All Hands*, January, 1952.

As to the many duties of the "young gentlemen" (midshipmen were so referred to even before Nelson's time), the late Vice Admiral J. K. Taussig, U. S. Navy, told the writer that he was ordered with another midshipman to heave the lead from the chains of the *Newark* upon her departure from New York City in 1899, notwithstanding the fact that both of the young gentlemen were in dress uniform. Vice Admiral Taussig also relates that because of a mix-up in a salute from a British captain to an American rear admiral, his senior officer ordered him as a midshipman "to go aboard that British ship and make the British captain feel sorry for his mistake." It took courage, quick wits, and above all the spirit of youth to perform creditably the duties of a midshipman at sea. The most amusing and thrilling events in a sea officer's career take place in his midshipman and junior officer days.

To classify a midshipman as an officer has always been subject to qualification. The present *United States Navy Regulations* state that, "Midshipmen are, by law, officers in a qualified sense and are classed as being in the line." In other days, their relative rank, as established in the reorganization of the Navy by the Act of 1815, was as follows.[28]

> The order in which officers shall take precedence and command
> in the ship to which they belong is as follows:
>   Captain or commander
>   Lieutenants, agreeably to date or number of their commissions
>   Master
>   Master's mate
>   Boatswain
>   Gunner
>   Carpenter
>   Midshipman

In days of sail midshipmen were frequently called "reefers."

The old title "passed midshipman" in the United States Navy meant originally a midshipman who had passed his examination, entitling him to promotion to a lieutenant. When the title of ensign was introduced into the United States Navy, those awaiting promotion were called midshipmen while undergraduates were called cadet midshipmen. In 1819 a board, of which Commander Bainbridge was senior member, met in New York to give the first examinations that had ever been given midshipmen in our Navy for promotion. This, incidentally,

---

[28] Midshipmen are known as Subordinate Officers in the British Navies, and since World War II the term has been adopted by the British Armies and Air Forces for analogous officers. The term includes cadets.

was the first examination of any kind instituted for officers in the American Navy.

MOOR. From Dutch word *marren*, to tie, to fasten.

NOT ROOM TO SWING A CAT. A very old naval expression, meaning not room to swing a cat-of-nine-tails—low overhead.

OAR. Used by mankind at the dawn of history but our word comes from the *ayr* of the Middle Ages.

OFFICER—OFFICIALS. The following interesting history was taken from a foreign service examination pamphlet issued by the Department of State:

> Historically, the employment of the word "officer" to denote a person holding a military or naval command as representative of the State, and not as deriving his authority from his own powers or privileges, marks an entire change in the character of the armed forces of civilized nations. Originally signifying an official, one who performs an assigned duty (Latin, *officium*), an agent, and in the fifteenth century actually meaning the subordinate of such an official (even today a constable is so called), the word seems to have acquired a military significance late in the sixteenth century.
>
> It was at this time that armies, though not yet "standing," came to be constituted almost exclusively of professional soldiers in the king's pay. Mercenaries, and great numbers of mercenaries, had always existed, and their captains were not feudal magnates. But the bond between mercenaries and their captains was entirely personal, and the bond between the captain and the sovereign was of the nature of a contract. The non-mercenary portion of the older armies was feudal in character. It was the lord and not a king's officer who commanded it, and he commanded in virtue of his rights, not of a warrant or commission.[29]

OPEN MUSTER. The general muster in the American Navy was derived from the British open muster. The British "mustering by the open list" was forced upon the British service to counteract the sharp practices of pursers in underpaying men. The original idea was that each member of the crew would report who he was and for what he was paid. General muster was abolished in the American Navy in 1914. Division quarters each morning was introduced by Admiral Kempenfeldt, RN, in 1780.

[29] At sea the relatively clear partition of actual duties amongst the authorities of a ship brought the adoption of the term "officer" somewhat earlier.

PASSING TO WINDWARD. Vessels were supposed to pass to leeward of their superiors. This was strictly observed if the inferior happened to be a merchantman. For it was then written:

> If the opposite procedure took place, it is as accounted as unmannerly a trick as if the constable of a parish should jostle for the wall with a justice of the peace dwelling in the same country.

Whether in men-of-war or merchantmen, the weather side was the traditional side at sea for the admiral and captain, the starboard side is the "sacred ground" when the ship is at anchor. In the days of sail, it is explained as the side where,

> he [the captain] can feel the wind and weather upon his cheek, can sniff the land, or sight the coming squall. It was once always customary for all weather gangways to be used by superiors.

PAYING YOUR FOOTING. The following anecdote gives the meaning of this old expression. Captain's Clerk Mr. E. G. Wines, U. S. Navy, who served on the USS *Constellation* 1829–31, wrote:

> On the twenty-first of August [1829] I went for the first time to the main top-gallant masthead—to me a dizzy height. . . . The old tars laughed heartily at my timidity. I asked them if they were never afraid. "Afraid!" they replied, "what good would it do to be afraid? Mr. Wines, have you never been in a top before?" "No." "Then you must pay for your footing" was the next thing. Paying for your footing is treating all hands to a glass of grog on your first visit to a top. This they never fail to demand, always promising in return, to teach you all they know themselves about the rigging of the ship. At first I offered them money. "Oh," said they, "give us the grog, what good will money do us here?" I then told them I would pay my footing in their own way, if they would get permission from the first lieutenant. I thought this would stagger them, but was mistaken. "Poh! Poh!" they replied, "never mind the first lieutenant, send it up by a boy and call it water." More than two years afterwards, I asked the captain of the top if I didn't owe him a glass of grog. "Yes, Sir, I believe you do, Sir. Why, Sir, I believe it's to pay your footing in the main top, Sir."

PAYMASTER (PURSER). Records of the fourteenth century show "clerks" or "bursers" in English ships. In the early days their pay came from profit in the sale of supplies, which sometimes led to the purchase of assignment to lucrative positions. In 1842, the British Navy created the title paymaster and purser.

Melville, writing of life on the USS *United States* in 1843, says:

Of all the non-combatants of a man-of-war, the purser perhaps stands foremost in importance; though he is but a member of the gunroom mess, yet usage seems to assign him a conventional station somewhat above that of the equals in Navy rank—the chaplain, surgeon and professor.

The purser's steward in those days acted as postmaster.

The title purser was derived from bursar. This was the old name for keeper of the cash, and hence the word disburser or one who pays out money. The term "burse magister" may be found in the English Merchant Marine in the time of Henry VI. The title "purser" was used in the United States Navy from its birth until 1860. The pursers were civilian appointments made only for a vessel's cruise. Their compensation was based upon a commission on expenditures. By a general order, legalized by Act of Congress in 1854, pursers of more than twelve years' service were to rank with commanders and those of less than twelve years with lieutenants, and to take rank with surgeons according to date of commission. In 1860, it was enacted that pursers in the Navy of the United States should thereafter be styled "paymasters." They were designated supply officers in 1917 and were authorized to be addressed by the military titles, ensign, lieutenant, lieutenant commander, commander, captain, and rear admiral. This order gave military titles to all officers of the Staff Corps.

PEA-COAT. Probably from the Dutch word *pij*, a coarse, woolen cloth. For two hundred years it has been the name for the heavier top coat worn by seafaring men in cold weather. The coat was originally made of a material called pilot cloth.

PORT. Larboard signified the left side on board ship in the United States Navy until about 1846. It is recorded that in that year the following word was passed on board an American man-of-war cruising off the coast of Africa:

Do you hear there fore and aft? The word "larboard" is to be forever dropped in the United States Navy, and the word "port" is substituted. Any man using the word "larboard" will be punished.

The British Navy made the change some years before. Admiral Penrose Fitzgerald states in his memoirs that the word "port" was adopted in the British Navy from the orders of the Portuguese Tagus River pilots (See "Larboard").

PORTHOLE. James Baker, a shipbuilder, when ordered by King Henry VI who desired heavier guns on his ships, pierced the sides of

The Great Harry. Baker resorted to the French method of a watertight door to close the opening when the battery was not in use. This door was called a port; hence the term porthole which was originally a hole for a gun. Technically, a port is closed with a port lid. Old port lids had scuttles or bulls eyes in them. We call the old scuttles portholes.

PROFESSORS OF MATHEMATICS. The first appointments were made in 1831 for the purpose of instructing midshipmen aboard ship. Eventually, this practice was found impracticable, but after the establishment of the Naval Academy, the professors then on the list were detailed to duty at the Academy. Professors of mathematics were at an early date detailed to the Naval Observatory. The title of Professor of Mathematics no longer exists.

QUARTERDECK. From the *Marine Encyclopedia* (1881) prepared by officers of the Navy:

> The upper deck abaft the mainmast. Naval etiquette requires all persons to salute coming on the quarter-deck, and to conduct themselves in decorous manner while thereon.
>
> The starboard side in port and the weather side at sea are reserved for the use of the commanding and executive officers, and officer of the deck.

Originally the term referred to a deck which covered a quarter of the ship, a raised platform from which the ship was "conned" or controlled. Additionally, it served as a repository of the ancient shrines, etc. Therefore, there is a traditional precedent for its role as an area of both temporal and religious superiority. For more on this subject, see chapter 9.

Irrespective of design or type of ship, there will always be a part of the deck set aside for ceremonies and honors.

QUARTERMASTER. A quartermaster originally had nothing to do with the bridge or steering a ship, but was assigned to the specific duty of looking after troop quarters. In later years these men were retained aboard after troops debarked and were assigned to other duties. The army uses the word in its original connotation.

ROGUE'S MARCH. An old tune played when drumming bad characters out of a ship or a regiment.

ROGUE'S YARN. The yarn in rope which is twisted either the opposite way from the other yarns, or is colored. This is a means to detect the theft of government cordage.

ROPE. Most ropes are called lines by sailors. Old sailors assert there are only seven ropes on a ship, although some are called lanyards—the man rope, head rope, hand rope, foot rope, bell rope, buoy rope, and dip rope.

Master mariner of sail and distinguished writer of the sea, the late Captain Felix Riesenberg, in his review of the first edition of this book, wrote:

> I can think of a few more, such as wheel rope or tiller rope, back-ropes (the head stays, from the martingale up, aft, to the cat heads), mast rope (used in sending up and down masts), yard rope (same for yards), boltrope (on sails), and ridgerope (on ship's awnings).

Admiral Hugh Rodman, USN, who had thirty-two years' sea service with all early days under sail, adds: anchor rope (small boats), boltrope, yokerope, wheel or tiller rope, yardrope, mastrope, backrope, and bullrope.

ROUND ROBIN. "This morning we all signed a round robin, setting forth our 'willingness to return to duty on the liberation of the three men.' Our names are written in radiating lines, like the spokes of a wheel, so that there are no leading names on the list." On this point William M. Davis queries, "Is it from this custom of signing dangerous papers that the term 'ring leader' was derived?"

ROUND TURN. To take a turn around a bitt or bollard, to check a strain or weight.

"To bring up with a round turn" is nautical phraseology for a "call-down" or reprimand.

RUDDER. Originally placed on "steer board" or starboard (right) side of Viking ships. Derived from the old Anglo-Saxon *rother*, that which guides. The sternpost rudder came into use in the twelfth century. In 1262, there is record of ships paying certain dues if they had "helm-rothers," and smaller dues for "hand-rothers." This is considered as a distinction between the quarter rudder and the sternpost rudder.

RUNNING. Originally to impose upon the credulity of "greenhorns" at sea, whether it be the crew or midshipmen. In a description of a cruise in the *Constellation* over a hundred years ago: "The men were fond as the 'reefers' of 'running' each other, and imposing upon the credulity of landsmen." Confined now generally to midshipman slang, it connotes mild hazing.

SAILING MASTER. This was the title for a warrant (warranted) officer as early as 1798. In the *Regulations of the United States Navy*, issued by command of the president, January 25, 1802, certain duties required of the sailing master were:

> To inspect the provisions and stores. . . . To take care of the ballast. . . . To give directions for stowing the hold and spirit-room. Trimming the ship, and preservation of the provisions; to take special care of the rigging; to navigate the ship and see that the log and log book are duly kept.

These duties are now assigned to officers of other titles. In 1813, there were 162 sailing masters on the list of the Navy. George Farragut, father of the admiral, was on this list. The title was changed to master in 1839. In 1846, the term "masters in the line of promotion" was used to signify certain of the grade of passed midshipmen to fill the vacancies by death of the old-time masters. In 1861, there were thirty-six of the grade on the active list. In 1862, on reorganization of the Navy, they were all merged into the grades. Then master became a commissioned grade between lieutenant and ensign, with the duties of a watch officer. In 1881, there were four old-time warranted masters on the retired list.

SAILOR. From Middle English *saylor*, root unknown.

On shipboard, one who has made a long sea voyage other than his first, and who is qualified to go aloft and tend the sails. A sailor is not necessarily a seaman.

Mariner is usually restricted to legal documents. Technically speaking, sailor means one before the mast; nevertheless, that Farragut and Nimitz were great sailors will not be denied. Officer-seamen are proud to be called sailors.

SALLY SHIP. An all hands evolution used to "rock" a ship off mud, sand, and other obstructions. On orders, men rushed *en masse* from one side of a ship to the other in the attempt to get a roll on her. Ice breakers use the same principle to break out of ice by quickly pumping large amounts of water from tanks on one side to the other.

SALT JUNK AND HARD-TACK. Salted meat and sea biscuits, at one time the principal diet of seafaring men. This expression is seldom heard today. One who has eaten the old hard-tack fully agrees with Charles XII when he said, "It is not good but it can be eaten." In old sea narratives mention is made of "lobscouse," a delicacy in its day, although easy to prepare—potatoes and salt beef hashed together.

Junk was originally a vegetable fiber from which rope was made. In time the word junk was used in referring to old rope. The meat, in sailing ship days, was carried in the "harness cask." Probably as a result of its resemblance to old rope, both in texture and stringiness, it was called salt horse or salt junk.

> Here the individual who was acting 'cook of the mess,' had set our supper out on a 'mess cloth' on deck. It consisted of a sea-bread, raw salt pork, cold boiled potatoes, and vinegar. We gathered around the cloth, each one bringing his tea and a seat, although some squatted right down on deck. When all was arranged an old salt said, "Well boys here's every one for himself, and the devil for us all—Jack pass the pork."[30]

SCHOONER. The schooner is an American rig, and the type was originally built in Gloucester, Massachusetts, in 1713. Andrew Robinson, shipbuilder, had not decided on a name for the new rig, and tradition relates that as she left the ways a bystander sang out, "See how she scoons." Robinson heard this remark and said, "A schooner she shall be."

SCRIMSHAW. Called the "folk art of the American whaleman." Some work of this description was done by the naval men of the day, in particular those who were unlucky enough to be captured in the wars and placed in shore jails, where some made ship models and small articles from the bones of animals. A hundred years ago, the majority of New England households either displayed or had knowledge of the interesting art of *scrimshaw*: engravings, etchings, and carvings on sperm whale's teeth, cribbage boards of walrus tusks, and scenes done on the jaw-bones of sperm whales—handiwork often functional but usually decorative.

SCUTTLE. This meant "hold" in Anglo-Saxon. In reality, to scuttle a ship means literally to hole her deliberately.

SCUTTLE BUTT. The sailors' source of fresh drinking water. Here men have ever gathered for exchange of gossip; hence, "scuttlebutt": rumors, unconfirmed information.

Melville, in *White Jacket*, describes the scuttle butt in the USS *United States*, 1843.

[30] Charles Nordhoff, *Man-of-War Life* (New York: Dodd, Mead, 1855), p. 30.

The scuttle butt is a goodly, round, painted cask, standing on end, and with its upper head removed showing a narrow circular shelf within where rest a number of tin cups for the accommodation of drinkers. Central within the scuttle butt itself stands an iron pump, which, connecting with the immense water tanks in the hold, furnished an unfailing supply of the much admired Pale Ale. . . .

A long way from the refrigerated drinking fountains aboard ship today.

SEA. The sea was called *saivs* from a root *si* or *siv*, the Greek *seiō*, to shake; it meant the tossed-about water as opposed to stagnant or running water.

SEA TIME. There is record in the earliest days of navigation of a division of the sea day into watches.

Pigafetta, in his detailed account of Magellan's ill-fated voyage, refers to the captain-general when he

> ordered that three watches should be set at night. The first was at the beginning of the night, the second at midnight, and the third towards break of day, which is commonly called *la diane*, otherwise the star of the break of day.

Sir Henry Mainwaring explains the early watches in his *Seaman's Dictionary*:

> at sea the ship's company is divided into two parts, the one called the starboard watch, the other the larboard watch. The master is the chief of the starboard and his right-hand mate, of the larboard. These are in their turns to watch, trim sails, pump, and do all duties for four hours; and then the other watch is to relieve them. Four hours they call a whole watch.

It is believed that "dog watches" came at a later date than the time of the *Seaman's Dictionary*.

Sandglasses were used ashore before clocks were invented. Because of the rolling and pitching of a ship, sandglasses remained for many years as ships' timepieces after the pendulum clock was invented.

It appears that before ship's bells the sandglass was turned each half hour for the "trick at the wheel." This original watch probably lasted only one-half hour, due to its strenuous nature. Lyde writes in his *Friends Adventure* that one sailor sat down on a low stool by the helm, to look after the sandglass and to call to pump, which they had to do every half hour because the ship leaked so much.

Ships' bells came in later. The first clue that can be found is from an unknown author of a book of travel and adventure. He wrote in the middle of the seventeenth century and describes a Dutch ship which he boarded in Leghorn, Italy. Among other things this unknown writer said:

> Every half hour the steersman . . . at the ringing of a bell is changed. The bell is rung also every time they change the watch and for prayers, breakfast, and dinner.

"There is an old story," writes Commander R. G. Lowry, RN, "that one bell has been struck at 6:30 P.M., instead of five bells, since the Mutinies of 1797. In one port the signal to mutiny was to be the striking of five bells in the dog watch; the officers got wind of this, and, instead of striking five bells, ordered one to be struck, and the mutiny was averted. How true this may be is not known, but it is quite a common yarn."

The eight strokes on the bell is derived from the number of turns of the hour glass during the watch. The hour glass became obsolete, but the ship's bell remains.

An old custom, once strictly observed, was that of having the oldest man in the ship, be he admiral or jack-of-the-dust, strike eight bells at midnight, on December thirty-first. This was immediately followed by eight bells for the New Year and always struck by the youngest boy on board. It was, of course, the only time of the year when sixteen bells were struck.

SEVEN SEAS. Antiquity: Mediterranean, Red, Persian Gulf, Indian Ocean, China, West African, and East African. Today: North Atlantic, South Atlantic, North Pacific, South Pacific, Indian, Arctic, and Antarctic.

SHAKEDOWN CRUISE. A cruise made in a new vessel for the purpose of testing machinery, adjusting instruments, and getting officers and men familiar with administration and drill aboard.

SHIPMATE. "A term once dearer than brother, but the habit of short cruises is weakening it."[31]

---

[31] W. H. Smyth, *The Sailor's Word-Book*, p. 618.

SHIPPING OVER. Reenlisting. Since men first followed the sea, imagination has pictured the end of the cruise, the getting "paid off," the decommissioning, the shore leave, and shore work. Often the sailor exclaims, "Never again!" and that he will quit the sea, but the idle boasts usually come to naught, and the old-timer is back aboard, after a little hectic life ashore. In 1843, the following conversation took place after a long cruise on an American man-of-war. It is heard in substance today, but without the nautical verbiage of deep-water men of other days:

> "Sink the sea!" cried a forecastle man. "Once more ashore, and
> you'll never catch old Boom bolt afloat. I mean to settle down in a
> sail loft. Shipmates, take me by the arms and swab up the lee
> scuppers with me, but I mean to steer a clam cart before I go again
> to a ship's wheel. Let the Navy go by the board, to sea agin,
> I won't."
> "Start my soul-bolts, maties, if any more blue peters and sailing
> signals fly at my fore!" cried the captain of the head. "My wages
> will buy a wheelbarrow if nothing more."
> "I have taken my last dose of salts," cried the captain of the
> waist. . . . "Blast the sea shipmates! says I."

Needless to say, after spending their accumulated wages, nine out of ten shipped over.

In commentary, Melville wrote in *White Jacket*:

> But do men ever hate the thing they love? Do men forswear the
> hearth and the homestead? What then must the Navy be?

Thus it was and ever shall be, as long as men follow the sea.

SHOW A LEG. An expression used generally by boatswain's mates and masters-at-arms to rouse and turn out sleeping men. "Rouse and shine" has been corrupted to "rise and shine" in the American Navy.

The call "show a leg" is derived from the days when women were carried at sea, "the wives of seamen"; these women, who put out a leg for identification, were not required to turn out at first call.

The old original call, says Commander Beckett, RN, was,

> Out or down there, out or down there, all hands, rouse out, rouse
> out, rouse out. Lash and carry, lash and carry, show a leg or else
> a purser's stocking. Rouse and shine, rouse and shine. Lash up and
> stow, lash up and stow, lash up and stow, it's tomorrow morning
> and the sun's a-scorching your (bloody) eyes out.

SHROUDS. When cordage was of inferior grade, so many stays of rope were used to support a mast athwartships that the mast was practically obscured in the manner that a shroud covers a corpse. Ratlines were placed fore and aft on shrouds to provide footing on going aloft.

SICK BAY. Originally called "sick berth." The term probably was introduced by Lord St. Vincent in 1798. After round bows were introduced about 1811, the contour of the bulkhead effected the change of name to "sick bay."

SILENCE IN A MAN-OF-WAR. The American Navy has always insisted, as the British Navy did at an earlier date, that silence be observed at all drills and evolutions. When Napoleon, as prisoner, was aboard the *Bellerophon* in July 1815, he remarked as the ship was getting under way:

> Your method of performing this evolution is quite different to the
> French. What I admire most in your ship is the extreme silence
> and orderly conduct of your men. On board a French ship every-
> one calls and gives orders and they gabble like so many geese.

SKIN OF A SHIP. The outer planking or plating of a ship is called the "skin." It is believed that there is a direct connection with our ancestral sailors of many centuries ago, who first sailed the seas in wicker-work coracles covered with the skins of animals. The skins were sewed together at "seams." Both "skin" and "seam" have lived in the language of seamen.

SKIPPER. Derived from the Scandinavian word *schiffe*, meaning ship; or the Dutch word *schipper*, which means captain.

SKY PILOT. The chaplain aboard ship is called the *padre* or "sky pilot" by sailors. The older sailors had a religious vein that was mingled with superstition. The bluejackets of sail seldom showed any fear of a hereafter. Their philosophy as expressed by an old "sky pilot" was that since they lived hard, worked hard, and died hard, they thought it would be hard indeed to have to go to hell.

SLOPS. A general term for ready-made clothes and outfits furnished seamen. The name was first used in this sense by Maydman, in 1691. The word is an old one, for in Chaucer's time *sloppe* designated a kind of breeches.

In an original manuscript account of Queen Elizabeth, one finds an order to John Fortescue to deliver some Naples fustian for "sloppe for Jack Green, our Foole."

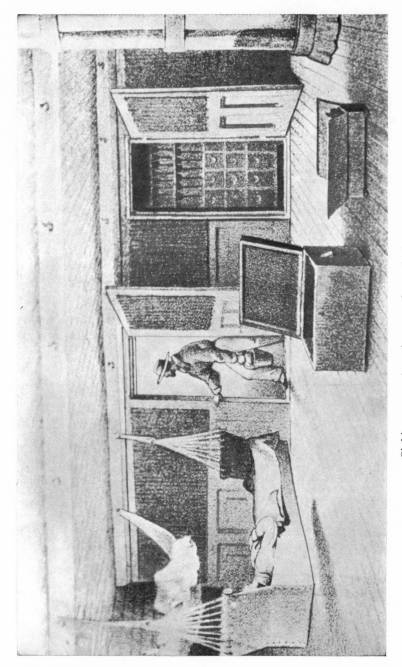

Sickbay on an American naval vessel, about 1845.

SNOW. A two-master, square-rigged vessel with a boom mainsail set on a trysail mast, and often with a spritsail rigged beneath the bowsprit. The rig was most common at sea in the War of American Independence. It is said to be pronounced as rhyming with "cow." A model may be seen in the Smithsonian Institution, Washington, D.C.

SPEAKING TRUMPET or MEGAPHONE. History records that Alexander the Great used one in 335 B.C. It is used by the officer of the watch for hailings, and is of particular use in wind and fresh breezes.[32]

SPLICING THE MAIN BRACE.[33] Tradition relates that, in the days of sail, those who performed this rather important and difficult task of marlinespike seamanship received upon completion of the job an extra ration of rum.

A copy of the following historic message may be seen today in the United States Navy Department. The dispatch was sent, or "signal made" as the British say, by Admiral Sir David Beatty, RN, to the Allied Fleet at Rosyth on November 11, 1918, at the end of World War I.

> The Armistice commenced at 11:00 today, Monday, and the customary method in the H. M. Service of celebrating an occasion is to be carried out by the ships' companies splicing the main brace at 19:00 today. Hands are to make and mend clothes.

It is interesting to observe that in the dispatch one may read, "Negative 6 B.S." The Sixth Battle Squadron was composed of American ships under the command of Rear Admiral Hugh Rodman, USN, but operating under the orders of Beatty. Spirits were forbidden in the United States Navy, but there are still pleasant recollections by some American officers and men who visited the ships of their British allies on that memorable day.

SPRIT. From old Saxon with very ancient meaning "to sprout." We have the bowsprit which sprouts out from the bow. The spritsail in older ships was set under the bowsprit.

STARBOARD. (See "Larboard.")

STEERAGE. A term supplanted by junior officers' mess. In the *Marine Encyclopedia* (1881), a steerage officer was

---

[32] Lieut. P. W. Hourigan, U. S. Navy, in *Manual of Seamanship*, said: "Bawling through a trumpet in a 'reef-topsail' voice is to be avoided; the boatswain's mate is usually on hand and can use the necessary vehemence."

[33] Today in the British Navy, Sir Geoffery Callender defines it: "To serve out an allowance of drink to all hands to celebrate a special occasion."

an officer living or messing in the steerage. Steerage officers in the
U. S. Navy are clerks, midshipmen, cadet midshipmen, mates,
cadet engineers, ensigns when not in charge of a watch or division,
and all officers ranking with ensign.

SUNDOWNER. Derived from the strict captains who once required
that all officers and men be aboard by sunset; now used for a martinet
or strict disciplinarian.

SUN OVER THE YARDARM OR FORE YARD. In other days the well-
known expression meant about time for the first drink, "a nooner."
Some ships never waited; they had "universal joints" on the yardarm.

SUPERCARGO. Much of the early success of the British and American
China and India trade was due to these business diplomats who handled
the sale and collection of cargo. E. Keble Chatterton writes:

> He has to combine the ability of a banker and merchant, the tact
> of an ambassador and the loyalty and incorruptibility of an honest
> man. . . . His job was to sell the vessel's cargo, buy a new one, and
> establish relations with the highest Indian natives or with the
> loftiest Chinese officials.

In 1690, French priests were given free passage out to the Orient in
English ships, in order that their knowledge of languages and conditions might be used in the capacity of supercargoes. An idea of the
tremendous amount of business with the huge profits of those days
may be seen in the investment of £430,000 by England's East India
Company in 1674, whose ships brought home £860,000 worth of com-
modities. In New England's early maritime development and China
trade, the supercargoes were often the scions of families of shipowners,
and their trade reports were some of the earliest submitted to our government.

SUPERSTITIONS, SAILORS'.[34] Literature abounds in superstitions and
explanations that the early mariners gave to phenomena actually observed at sea. Some of the great superstitions of the sea arose from the
love of travelers to exaggerate in relating great adventures after long
voyages to distant, strange lands.

Smollett says that in his day Davy Jones was "the fiend who pre-
sides over all the evil spirits of the deep and is seen in various shapes.

[34] Lieutenant Commander A. W. Meyerson of the former Imperial Russian
Navy reports old Russian Navy superstitions: Bad luck to whistle aboard ship; to
kill sea gulls or albatross; to have priest and women aboard ship together; to come
on deck without a hat. Never write the port of destination in a log book until
reached. Always scratch a mast to get a wind.

He sometimes appeared, a giant breathing flames from his wide nostrils, and having big eyes and three rows of teeth."

A naval officer wrote in the last century: "Sailors always personify ships and boats. A venerable commodore in our own Navy, still living [in 1881] was one to talk to the mizzenmast of his ship. This is a common idea among old sailors, who often believe as the old captain said, 'She can do anything but talk, and sometimes she can even do that. A ship which is about to sink makes her lamentations just like any other human being.' "[35]

Much has been written of the superstitions of men of the sea, from the journey of the Argonauts and the legend of floating rocks on through *Flying Dutchman* "appearances" to the pig tattooed on a modern sailor's foot as a charm against drowning.

The phenomena of the sea—waterspouts, phosphorescence, St. Elmo's light, winds and storms, enchanted islands and rocks, mermaids, and sea monsters—all have generated among the seagoing races numerous legends, superstitions, and customs of propitiation with charms against dangerous effects.

Phantom ships and apparitions were often reported by mariners. Many people believe in omens and prognostics; for example, the "Friday superstition" still obtains among some landsmen as well as among some seamen. Do we not have the old proverb, "Friday's noon, come when it will, comes too soon?"

The "Fore-Topman" of *Old Ironsides* (1839–41) wrote:

Many clever writers have affirmed that sailors are generally the most superstitious beings in existence, and I believe with some reason, for since my sojourn on the boundless ocean, I have never seen an accident occur on shipboard but what someone would step up with prophetic countenance, and engross the attention of every bystander with a relation of some little circumstance that he had taken notice of prior to the occurrence, which he considered as a forewarning. . . . Sailors put great faith in the predictions of fortune tellers or persons supposed to be skilled in magic charms.[36]

[35] Columbus in his *Journal* chronicles the appearance of three mermaids. Henry Hudson reported one of his men on a voyage saw a white mermaid, and "long hair hanging down behind, of color black. Seeing her go down, they saw her tail which was like that of a porpoise, speckled like a mackeral." F. S. Bassett in *Legends and Superstitions of the Sea and of Sailors*.

[36] "Sea shells, fish amulets, the caul, coral, amber, bunches of garlic, bits of seaweed, turf from the church yard—the belief of the sailor in these many omens, lucky signs, auguries, etc., is a survival of ancient superstitions—reminiscent of the many impositions, practiced by Chaldean magicians, and astrologers, Greek and Roman augurs, medieval sorcerers and cunning charlatans of all ages."—Lieut. Fletcher S. Bassett, USN (1881).

SURGEONS (MEDICAL CORPS).[37] The title surgeon cannot be found in any record of the British Navy before 1557. However, there is little doubt that some went to sea before that date. Doctors of medicine commanded regiments of cavalry and infantry in the civil wars of Charles I's time.

The title is a contraction of the French word *chirurgien*, or is from the Latin *chirurgus* and from the Greek originally, and means "operating with the hand." Gallant old Sir William Monson says:

> The surgeon is to be placed in the hold where he should be in no danger of shot; for there cannot be a greater disheartening of the company than in his miscarrying, whereby, they will be deprived of all help for hurt and wounded men.

In the British Navy in the eighteenth century, the pay of surgeons and chaplains came from the seamen aboard. Each sailor was required to pay to each two-pence a month. In 1776 when pay for officers and men was established by Congress for the "'new commissions under the free and independent states of America," surgeons on ships of twenty guns received $20 per month and their mates $15. By 1825 the monthly pay for surgeons had increased to $50.

TAKING A SIGHT. This term is well known by all who follow the sea as the act of taking with sextant or octant the altitude of the sun, moon, or stars; but it has another meaning. Captain Marryat refers to it as the act of spreading the fingers out and placing the right thumb to the nose. Rabelais gives it the same meaning in his *Pantagruel* (Book II).

TAR. General name for a sailor and derived from the old custom of a sailor tarring his trousers, as well as other wearing apparel, in order to make them waterproof.

TARPAULIN MUSTER. In practice, the term is applied to a collection of money by a group of sailors. In the old days, a "tarpaulin" or black tarred hat was passed. At times sailors used to collect money for the family of a deceased shipmate. The name comes from the hat passing of a hundred years ago.

---

[37] Oak leaf insignia. In 1880, the gold oak leaf with silver acorn imposed thereon became the official insignia of the Medical Corps. The oak leaf and the caduceus (staff) according to tradition became symbols of the medical profession because of their connection with the Druids, physician-priests of ancient England. Oak groves were their temples and their robes are said to have been embroidered with designs of oak leaves and acorns.

The Old Navy. Left to right. David Ireland, aged 55; Gilbert H. Purdy, aged 60; John T. Griffith, aged 62; and John King, aged 54. *Photograph by Asst. Surg. H.W. Whitaker, USN, 1888.*

TATTOOING. The *Century Dictionary* defines tattoo:

To mark, as the surface of the body, with indelible patterns produced by pricking the skin and inserting different pigments in the punctures. *Sailors and others mark the skin with legends, love emblems, etc.; and some uncivilized peoples, especially the New Zealanders and the Dyaks of Borneo, cover large surfaces of the body with ornamental patterns in this way. . . .*

"They [the Tahitians] have a custom . . . which they call *Tattowing*. They prick the skin so as just not to cause blood."[38]

Although savage races have from early times decorated the body with designs which were supposed to give beauty to the individual, one must examine other reasons for the origin with military and seagoing men. It is thought that seafaring men imitated at an early date the custom as practiced by the military.

[38] James Cook, *First Voyage.*

Tattooing was the original identification tag of the soldier. Various researches that have been made arrived at the conclusion that the art of tattooing with Europeans originated as a mark of identification for the dead and wounded on the field of battle. It was by such an identification that Edith of the Swan Neck found the body of Harold on the field of Hastings. Tattooing was also once used to mark permanently a thief or a deserter. Charles Kingsley wrote in *Hereward the Wake*:

> May not our soldiers' and sailors' fashion of tattooing the arms and chests with strange devices be a remnant of the very fashion kept up, if not originated, by the desire that the corpse be recognized after death?

In this connection, because of the custom of refusing burial to Protestants in wholly Catholic communities and islands, as in the islands of Madeira when at one period a Protestant stranger was not permitted to be buried upon the island, the sailors, irrespective of creed, found a way to ensure a shore burial. The Reverend Fitch W. Taylor, a chaplain of the United States Navy, wrote in 1838:

> And so prevalent was this refusal of the rites of burial to Protestants, by Catholic communities, that there is even a custom among sailors to have a cross tattooed upon their arms, that if by chance chance they should die in a Roman Catholic country, their bodies might be respected, and be allowed a quiet interment on the shore.

From a means of identification, tattooing in time became the fashion of sailors of all nations. It was as much a part of the sailor as was nautical phraseology; it marked him as a mariner. Even now elaborate tattooing is considered by many sailors to give an added degree of "saltiness" to the one tattooed.

The practice of tattooing in the United States Navy is on the wane. Commenting on the new type of man, an old chief boatswain's mate remarked:

> Yes, sir, we had bracelets tattooed on our arms, but the "rookies" now wear wrist watches, and what hurts me is where we tattooed our girl's name and the ports we made is today just a place where these landsmen wear garters. No, sir! She ain't what she used to be.

Since the practice is dying out, it may be well to comment briefly on some of the conventional designs of tattooing that will soon be no more as the old school passes on. The design varied from a small crest, anchor, star, or shield to a large design of Christ on the Cross, flanked by the two thieves. The latter design, pricked on the sailor's back, was the *chef d'oeuvre* of the tattoo "professor"; but due to its size and the time required for execution, it was one of the most painful pieces of work. Nudes were once quite popular, but it was required on reenlistment that the girls be dressed. This was done by tattooing a dress of color over the nude. "Miss Liberty" in red and blue was one of the favorite costumes.

In order to express sentiment for the girls ashore, initials of the fair ones would be tattooed on the arms or legs. Sometimes the sailor's initials as well as those of the girl would be intertwined in a heart. One of the most competent and artistic of the "professors" of tattooing told the writer that sometimes the girl would have the identical design tattooed on her body after the sailor had submitted to the pricking. It was a token of true love. A sailor told the writer forty years ago that "the initials help you to remember their names." Some of the more robust fellows would have a dagger that appeared to pierce the skin with a motto, "Death before dishonor." The cross is sometimes used alone as a design, but more frequently it takes the form of a tombstone placed under a willow tree. A sailor stands by the stone, and underneath or on the cross is placed "In memoriam" to "father" or "mother" or both. The word "hold" was sometimes tattooed on the fingers of one hand, and "fast" on the fingers of the other. It was considered by the more superstitious that a pig tattooed on the foot was an effective means of preventing death by drowning. As designs go out of style, some of the younger men have a log of the ports, and the years in which they were visited, tattooed on the forearm. This is a convenient means of refreshing the memory; also battles are added.[39]

Tattoo work may be partially removed by means of acid; it is most painful, and a blur always remains under the skin.

To Break a Flag. Normally a flag or pennant is attached to a halyard and to a downhaul and hoisted to its proper place. If it is desired to have a flag or pennant at its proper place ready for instant showing, as in the case of a man overboard; or for smartness, as at a change of command ceremony; or to avoid rigging obstructions when hoisting,

---

[39] "And many sailors not Catholics," writes Melville, "were anxious to have the crucifix painted on them, owing to a curious superstition of theirs. They affirm—some of them—that if you have that mark tattooed on all four limbs, you might fall overboard among seven hundred and seventy-five thousand white sharks, all dinnerless, and not one of them would so much as smell at your little finger. We had one foretop-man on board, who, during the entire cruise, was having an endless cable pricked round and round his waist. . . ."

a different method is used. The flag or pennant is attached to a halyard at its top and to a downhaul at its bottom. It is then folded, and the folds secured by two or more stops made of light string. When so made up, it can be hoisted to its proper place and left aloft until needed. At the proper time a sharp jerk on the downhaul will break the stops allowing the flag or pennant to fly free instantly. This procedure is known as breaking a flag.

In reference to battle flags, Admiral Dewey at Manila Bay wrote: "We broke our flags from the mastheads with the conviction that we were to see the end of the story. . . ."

"Upon the completion of the reading of his orders, he will direct the commanding officer to break his flag."[40]

TO BOX THE COMPASS. It is derived from the Spanish *boxar*, to sail around.

TO SAW AWAY THE BULWARKS. The first record of this practice in the American Navy is found in the chase of the American cruisers *Lexington*, *Dolphin*, and *Reprisal* by an English ship of the line. The *Dolphin* and *Lexington* by separating escaped with little difficulty but it is recorded by Cooper in his *Naval History* that the

> *Reprisal*, commanded by Lambert Wickes, was so hard pressed as to be obliged to saw her bulwarks, and even to cut away some of her timbers; expedients that were then much in favor among the seamen of the day, although of questionable utility.

This questionable practice was supposed to limber a ship and make her sail faster.

The *Reprisal* took Dr. Franklin to France. The sheltering of American men-of-war and French prizes was so vigorously protested by the English that France ordered the *Reprisal* and *Lexington* seized until ordered to leave France. The *Lexington*, the first vessel of the American Navy to have borne the American flag (not the later official one) in a victory on the seas, shortly after sailing from France was captured by the British *Alert* in a prolonged gun duel, and thus ended her brief but successful career. The *Reprisal* met a tragic fate. On her voyage to the American shores, the ship foundered and all the officers and crew were lost with the exception of the cook. Thus ended the career of Captain Lambert Wickes, one of our most outstanding and brilliant officers, to whom little recognition has been given. These two cruisers captured many prizes in European waters and also were the first two of our national cruisers to dispute British commerce in those seas.

To SKYLARK. An expression that is distinctly nautical. Lark, meaning a spree, is a corruption of the old Anglo-Saxon word *lac*, to play or have fun. The word skylark was derived from the practice of young sailors laying aloft to royal yards and sliding down the backstays. A skyraker or skyscraper is any sail above the fore, main, or mizzen royal. Skylarking is used in the Navy and at the Naval Academy, meaning "to play,"—"to cut-up" when at drills or in ranks. The earliest record of the use of this term was in the early nineteenth century.

To WHISTLE FOR A WIND. A very old expression of sailing-ship days. It is derived from the expression "you can whistle for it if you want it," and came from the custom of supplying a certain number of drinkers in English taverns and ale houses with whistles in order to summon the drawer for refills of tankards.

TOM SAWYER'S TRAVERSE. An old term that at the present time is not used in the Navy. It meant the course and movements of a "soldiering" (no reflection on the Army) sailor to kill time, such as frequent trips to and long stays at the scuttle butt and in the head. The art of work dodging. An American variant of Tom Cox's Traverse (British) "up one hatch and down another."

TRANSOM. In sailing ships a transom was a horizontal timber that was a part of the stern frame and sternpost. This beam or timber was used as a seat; hence, any seat that is built in officers' country and is a permanent fixture is by usage called a transom.

TYPHOON. A corruption of the Chinese *t'ai-fun*, or great wind.

WARDROOM. In the early part of the eighteenth century, there was a compartment aboard British ships below the "great cabin," called the "wardrobe." It was used for storage of valuable articles taken from prizes. The officers' staterooms were near. When the wardrobe was empty, particularly when outward bound, the lieutenants met there for lounging and for meals. In time the compartment was used entirely as an officers' messroom, and the name was changed to wardroom. Such was the designation of the lieutenants' messroom when the United States Navy came into being.

WARRANT OFFICER. For many years the officers of the Navy have been listed as "commissioned," "warrant" and "petty" officers. These designations derived from the manner of appointment. Commissioned officers are commissioned by the president, by and with the advice and consent of the Senate. Warrant officers are warranted by the Navy Department or the president. Petty officers are rated or designated as such by the Chief of Naval Personnel. In November 1956, the Court of Claims ruled that warrant officers are not "commissioned officers." The court made this distinction in deciding that retired warrant officers may work for the federal government as civilians earning more than $3,000 a year and still get their retirement pay. Although a warrant officer is sometimes called a "commissioned warrant officer," the court said it is clear that commissioned officers have the rank of ensign, lieutenant, etc.

WATCHES. Herman Melville, in *White Jacket*, describes life on the USS *United States* in 1843. Speaking of watches and details, he writes:

> Now the fore, main, and mizen topmen of each watch, starboard and larboard, are at sea, respectively, subdivided into quarter watches. . . . Besides these topmen who are always made up of active sailors, there are sheet-anchor men, old veterans, all whose place is on the fore-castle; the fore yards and anchors, and all the sails on the bowsprit being under their care. . . . These are the fellows, that it does your soul good to look at; hearty members of the old guard; grim sea grenadiers. . . . Then there is the after guard stationed on the quarter-deck, who under the quarter-master and the quarter gunners attend to the mainsail and spanker, and help haul the main brace, and other ropes. . . . They acquire the name of "sea dandies" and silk socks gentry. . . . Then there the waisters, always stationed on the gundeck. These haul aft the fore and main sheets, besides being subject to ignoble duties, attending to the draining and sewerage below hatches. . . . They are the tag-rag and bobtail of the crew and he who is good for nothing else is good enough for a waister.

WEIGH. Anglo-Saxon *woeg*. To lift the anchor from the ground. This term must not be confused with "way" as is often the case.

WHERRY. Said to be another form of the word *ferry*, because wherries in early days were often ferry boats on rivers.

WINDFALL. The word "windfall" came about as the result of the old custom that some of the British nobility held lands on condition that no timber would be cut except for the Royal Navy; however, those trees blown down by wind were exempt. It was therefore considered a godsend and good luck when gales effected windfalls.

WOMEN AT SEA. Women were carried on many British men-of-war until after the beginning of the nineteenth century. There is record of

Mary Ann Talbot, who received a pension of £20 a year "for wounds received in action when she was before the mast in the Navy." Rebecca Anne Johnson served on a Whitby collier for seven years when in 1808 her sex was discovered. It is related that her mother served at sea and fell at the battle of Copenhagen as a member of a gun's crew.

The marriage of two sailors as reported in a London journal is of interest.

> At St. Dunstane's in the East, in May 1802, David Jones was mar-
> ried to Anne Robinson. They had been old shipmates on board
> *Le Seine*, frigate on the West Indian Station, during most part of
> the war, where the lady bore a most conspicuous part in the differ-
> ent actions in which the frigate was engaged. She was always an
> attendant in the surgeon's department and waited upon Jones in his
> wounded state. An attachment took place which ended in their
> union.

WRECK. From old English *wrack* or seaweed; cast ashore; drifted or driven ashore.

SOME PROVERBS AND PHRASES OF THE SEA

> *The genius, wit, and spirit of a nation are discovered in its
> proverbs.*

DAVY JONES'S LOCKER.

A familiar name among sailors for Death, formerly for the evil spirit who was supposed to preside over the demons of the sea. He was thought to be in all storms, and was sometimes seen of gigantic height, showing three rows of sharp teeth in his enormous mouth, opening great frightful eyes, and nostrils which emitted blue flames. The ocean is still termed by sailors Davy Jones's locker.
—William A. Wheeler

> *As ships go to Old Davy, Lord knows how, Sirs,*
> *While heaven is blue enough for Dutchman's trowsers.*
> —Thomas Hood, "Love and Lunacy"

> *He dies, by not a single sigh deplor'd.*
> *To Davy Jones' locker, let him go.*
> *And with old Neptune booze below.*
> John Welcott, "Ode to the K———

HE THAT WOULD BRING HOME THE WEALTH OF THE INDIES MUST CARRY THE WEALTH OF THE INDIES WITH HIM.

As the Spanish proverb says, "He who would bring home the wealth of the Indies must carry the wealth of the Indies with him." So it is in traveling; a man must carry knowledge with him, if he would bring home knowledge. Boswell. "The proverb, I suppose, sir, means, he must carry a large stock with him to trade with." Johnson. "Yes, sir."—James Boswell, *The Life of Samuel Johnson.*

It Is an Ill Wind That Blows No Man Good. This very old expression came directly from the sea and is derived from the fact that every wind is a fair wind for some ship under sail.

Like a Fish Out of Water.

Ne that a monk, whan he is rekkeles,
Is like to a fish that is waterles.
                              —Chaucer, Prologue to *Canterbury Tales*

Shipshape and Bristol Fashion. Neat, clean, all rigging coiled and flemished down.

The Fish That Is Bred in the Sea Swims Best.

"My lord mayor," he said, "there is a proverb in my country which says, 'Fish swim best that's bred in the sea,' which means, I take it, that men do best what they are trained for."—Sir E. Bulwer-Lytton, *The Last of the Barons.*

To Be Above Board. To have nothing concealed, nothing below deck, frank, honest, open minded.

"Now, for my part, d'ye see, I'm for carrying things above board, I'm not for keeping anything under hatches, so that if you b'ent as willing as I, say so a'God's name, there's no harm done." —William Congreve, *Love for Love.*

To Be at Sea. To be doubtful; to "mull" around; to be hesitant.

To say the old man was at sea would be too feeble an expression.—G. W. Cable.

To Be Three Sheets in (to) the Wind. A phrase which refers to the lines used to control the sails of sailing vessels. When these sheets are cast to the wind (let go), it would cause the old sailing ships to shudder and stagger and the resulting track would be the same as that of a drunken sailor, out of control, and "three sheets to the wind." The phrase has been taken into general usage for one who is *very* drunk.

To Catch a Crab. To fail to keep in stroke in rowing and ofttimes thereby to jam and foul other oars. The Venetians called a green hand or novice at rowing a "crab."

> It was a scene of much confusion—the half-drunken boat's
> crew catching crabs, and falling forward upon the others.
> —F. Marryat, *Peter Simple.*

To Know One by the Cut of His Jib. To size up; to make a personal estimate of; to judge character and capabilities by appearance.

> A vessel is known by the cut of her jibsail; hence the popular
> phrase, to know a man by the cut of his jib.—Hotten.
> We shall be very good friends, sir, I'll answer for it, if I may
> judge from the cut of his jib.—F. Marryat, *Jacob Faithful.*

To Rejoice the Cockles of One's Heart. To gladden and to cheer. Derived probably from the old English term "cockling seas," or short and quick ones; hence, applicable to that which brings short, quick heart beats. The cockles of the heart are of course unknown to doctors and surgeons.

To Shoot Charlie Noble. To clean the galley smokepipe of soot and dirt by firing a pistol therein.

Between Wind and Water. That part just below the waterline when sailing in smooth water that becomes exposed when the ship rolls. It refers to the vulnerable part of anything.

> *And just e'en as he meant, sir,*
> *To loggerheads they went, sir,*
> *And then he let fly at her*
> *A shot 'twixt wind and water,*
> *That won this fair maid's heart.*
> —William Congreve, *Love for Love.*

To Write in Water.

> *Men's evil manners live in brass; their virtues*
> *We write in water.*
> —Shakespeare, *Henry VIII.*

On John Keats's tombstone in Rome, one may read:

> This grave contains all that was mortal of a young English poet,
> who on his deathbed, in the bitterness of his heart at the malicious
> power of his enemies, desired these words to be engraved on his
> tombstone: "Here lies one whose name was writ in water."

WET YOUR WHISTLE. To take a drink of liquor.

As any jay she light was and jolyf,
So was hir joly whistle wel ywet...

—Chaucer, *Reeve's Tale.*

SLIPPED HIS CABLE. Means he died.

The sailor's analogy of a ship being free from all attachments to land and able to sail as intended, is very close to the soul's being free from earthly ties.

The ship is clear at last, she leaps!
She swiftly courses from the shore ...

Whitman, "Joy, Shipmate, Joy!"

WHY IS A SHIP CALLED "SHE"? Fleet Admiral Chester Nimitz said in a talk to the Society of Sponsors of the United States Navy; "A ship is always referred to as 'she' because it costs so much to keep one in paint and powder."

> A boat is called a she because there's always a great deal of bustle around her . . . because there's usually a gang of men around . . . because she has a waist and stays . . . because she takes a lot of paint to keep her looking good . . . because it's not the initial expense that breaks you, it's the upkeep . . . because she is all decked out . . . because it takes a good man to handle her right . . . because she shows her topsides, hides her bottom and, when coming into port, always heads for the buoys.—George L. Moses in Falmouth, Mass., *Enterprise.*

IRON MEN IN WOODEN SHIPS[41]

SEA CAPTAIN. Upon his first popping up, the lieutenants sheer off to the other side, as if he was a ghost indeed; for 'tis impudence for any to approach him within the length of a boat hook.

A SEA LIEUTENANT is a gentleman, he'll tell you, by his commission, and hence it is he always carries it about with him to give you demon-

[41] The above excerpts are taken from a scurrilous but entertaining work, called *The Wooden World*, first published in 1707 by Edward Ward, one-time British seaman. "Plain Ned" Ward, as he was known, ran an inn after retiring from the sea. He had a decided talent for writing and with engaging frankness and wit, wrote various compositions, coarse, racy, but always descriptive. Some of the bawdier extracts of the old sailor's philosophy and observations would not be appropriate in a work of this kind. Grateful acknowledgment to Sir Geoffrey Callender for the extracts from a new edition of *The Wooden World.*

stration proof, in case you call it in question: He lays it out as often as he does his watch, and believes both together convincing proofs of his gentility.

A Sea Chaplain is one that in his junior days was brought up in the fear of the Lord; but the university reasoned him out of it at last, and he has oftimes thanked his good stars for it.

The Master of a Ship of War. His language is all heathen Greek to a cobbler; and he cannot have so much as a tooth drawn ashore without carrying his interpreter. It is the aftmost grinders aloft, on the starboard quarter, will he cry to the all-wondering operator.

The Purser is a kind of Pythagorean philosopher, not because of his pocket holes, for his breeches are commonly well lined, but for his many transmigrations, having lived in various regions, and rubbed through many callings, before he came to be a purser in the Navy.

The Surgeon. He adjusts his prescriptions, as a country shoemaker does his lasts; he makes one and the same recipe serve to a hundred various tempers and circumstances. For there's no standing upon niceties, he cries, with fellows that have the constitution of a horse.

The Gunner. As heavy as his guns are, they are certainly more active than he is, and do the King fifty times more service, for his grand amusement is eating and drinking; his sleeps are moderate enough, just to suffice nature, and make him ready for a fresh attack: Were it not for these, he would be a list man, for his mates do all his other business for him.

The Carpenter. Tho' he is generally but a rough-hewn fellow, yet he values himself upon a well-built hull; and as for his intellects, they are much about the same model with the master's, for he has little more of the mathematicks than the boatswain.

The Boatswain. It is not so much his fine silver-coil, as the illustrious chain that it hangs by, that is the distinguishing badge of his post, and which he's as proud of as my Lord Mayor is of his and prouder.

He has a thousand pretty phrases and expressions pickt up at Billingsgate and elsewhere, which he never sends abroad without bedecking them with all the embroider'd oaths and curses that can be had for love or money.

He has wit in his liquor, that's certain, for though he's often tipsy, it's at other men's cost.

A SEA COOK. The captain's cook and he are opposites as well in their practice as in their habitations, and seldom or never make incursions into each other's provinces. . . . He cooks by the hour glass as the parsons preach sermons. . . .

A MIDSHIP-MAN. He's elevated as high as Flamsteed, in his own conceit, and is often times shewing you a sample of his ingenuity. He can prove the purser a rogue by Gunter's scale, and compose a bowl of punch by the rules of trigonometry. . . . He's one that sometimes passes under the discipline of the cane or fist; that is when he is guilty of that great sin of omission of not giving timely notice of the captain's going from or coming into the ship.

THE CAPTAIN'S STEWARD. But he's too staunch a knave to trust to vain hopes and fair promises; so he takes care to make hay while the sun shines; and shuffles and cuts with everyone that has to do with him.

A SAILOR. He's one that is the greatest prisoner, and the greatest rambler in Christendom; there is not a corner of the world but he visits . . . but when he does get ashore he pays it off with a vengeance; for knowing his time to be but short, he crowds much in a little room and lives as fast as possible.

APPENDIX A

Some Makers of Tradition

Every drop of blood of me holds a heritage of patriotism.
Elias Lieberman

Men who when the tempest gathers
Grasp the standards of their fathers
In the thickest fight.
Edward Henry Bickersteth

I drew my sword [for the American Colonies] in support of
the violated dignity and rights of human nature.
John Paul Jones to the King of France

God give us men! a time like this demands
Men whom the spoils of office cannot buy
Men who have honor; men who will not lie . . .
Josiah Gilbert Holland

He was not named '31-Knot Burke' for nothing. He had made it
his way of life and his way of meeting the enemy. To go into
action at the best speed possible, to concentrate on the job to be
done, to take no half measures when an all-out effort would win.
These are qualities we need in our public life and in our armed
forces establishment.[1]

---

[1] The *New York Times* in a May 27, 1955, editorial concerning Admiral Arleigh Burke's selection as CNO.

FROM TIME TO TIME, there is considerable discussion by the press, also the services, and the Congress, as to whether or not military-naval careers may be made sufficiently attractive to secure a high percentage of superior individuals in the way of professional commissioned and noncommissioned officers. Because of this question and at a time when the country requires as never before the most intelligent and compe-

Perry's Victory on Lake Erie. Perry's battle flag and a facsimile of his dispatch to General William H. Harrison.

tent young men for the defense of the country, it is interesting to examine the records of some of the outstanding officers of our Navy from Captain John Paul Jones to the late fleet admirals of WW II, to the more contemporary officers of our times.

Who are the outstanding officers in the history of the Navy? That is an extremely difficult question to answer without the application of empirical criteria and without consideration of their times and their problems. The concern of this appendix is to point out those desirable qualities that the officer of this generation should endeavor to develop and emulate—in a word, to emphasize characteristics of military leadership that are immutable. Such a study is worthwhile if we quicken only our awareness of the importance of high personal *esprit* in that never ending job of striving to be a competent leader. Trying to live up to the best traditions of the naval service will show us what we might become if we are given the opportunity.

"Each man has his special gift,'" said Mahan, "and to succeed must act in accordance with it." The names of some who did may now be seen carved high in the marble amphitheater at Arlington Cemetery: John Paul Jones, Thomas Truxtun, Edward Preble, Isaac Hull, Stephen Decatur, Oliver Hazard Perry, Thomas Macdonough, Charles Stewart, David Glasgow Farragut, David Dixon Porter, Andrew Hull Foote, John Lorimer Worden, George Dewey, and William Thomas Sampson.

A committee of admirals, captains, and college presidents selected these names three decades ago as the most distinguished officers of the old Navy. Many naval historians would disagree with the board as to some of the selections. For example, where are Barry and Barney? Yet no one can deny that the names chosen represent a Roll of Honor of eminent sea officers who made the best of their opportunities and were tested and not found wanting in times of critical decision.

Some on that list, as well as others not on it, will be discussed in ensuing pages with particular emphasis on their careers as makers of tradition. Thereby we trace the Navy from its humble beginnings to its position as the world's greatest sea power. It is interesting to observe the marked continuity of naval tradition in the several generations since 1776. Let us take Jones first, often referred to as "the father of the Navy."

JOHN PAUL JONES

I have not yet begun to fight.—John Paul Jones

Jones took part in several gallant actions in the early stages of the Revolutionary War off the North American coast. He was ordered to his first command, the *Providence*, on May 10, 1777. Later he commanded a squadron with his flag in the *Alfred*. On June 14, 1777, Congress appointed Jones to command the *Ranger*, and he sailed her for France late the same year. It was on this voyage that the first recognition of the American flag by a foreign government occurred, when Vice Admiral La Motte Picquet, Commander of the French Fleet, returned the *Ranger's* salute of thirteen guns with nine.

Bust of John Paul Jones. Executed from life by Jean Antoine Houdon, it stands in a niche in Jones's crypt at the U.S. Naval Academy. It was commissioned by the Lodge of the Nine Sisters in Paris, and was bequeathed to the Naval Academy Museum by Marshall Field of Chicago in 1958. *Courtesy U.S. Naval Academy Museum.*

In an effort to divert the British naval forces and relieve the pressure on General Washington's sea supply lines, Jones planned raids on the coasts of England proper. The *Ranger* sailed from Brest on April 11, 1778, and boldly headed for the Irish Sea, taking prizes en route. On April 22, Jones landed at Whitehaven, spiked the guns at the fort and set fire to the shipping in the harbor. The following day he made another surprise landing at St. Mary's Isle and planned to seize the Earl of Selkirk as hostage for American seamen imprisoned in England—but the Earl was absent.

One day later, the *Ranger* encountered the British warship *Drake*, and in a bloody one-hour fight, defeated and captured her. The *Drake* was the first man-of-war to surrender to a Continental Navy ship flying the Stars and Stripes. The *Ranger* returned to Brest with her prizes and Jones became a hero to the French as well as the Americans.

Jones next outfitted a small squadron and put to sea with his flag in the *Bon Homme Richard* to intercept a fleet of British merchantmen. By the time he had sailed around the British Isles, circling Ireland to the west and around Scotland to the north, all but two of his ships had deserted him. He was to rendezvous with these two ships off Flamborough Head, a promontory on the east coast of England near the Scottish border. He arrived there on September 23, 1779, and there before him was a fleet of some forty-odd British merchantmen, escorted by the superior British frigate *Serapis*. Jones headed straight for the frigate and engaged her.

The battle, which began at sunset and lasted for four hours, was not only the most brilliant sea fight of the war, but one of the most remarkable single ship actions in history.

The superior guns of the *Serapis* began taking their toll almost immediately and it was all Jones could do to bring the battered *Bon Homme Richard* alongside the frigate, where a rather one-sided slugging match began. Finally, with the *Richard*'s hold filled with four to five feet of water and in a sinking condition, with all her guns out of action except three nine-pounders, with half her crew killed or wounded, with rudder and rigging shot away and fires fast approaching the magazines, Captain Pearson of the *Serapis* hailed Jones, asking him if he surrendered. Jones and his men suddenly boarded the *Serapis* and he shouted his challenging answer: "I have not yet begun to fight!" Jones captured and took command of the *Serapis*. He had to, for despite the use of pumps and every effort to save her, the *Bon Homme Richard* sank the following day from the severe damage to her hull.

Jones was given a vote of thanks by the Congress and authorized to receive the first medal ever awarded to an American naval officer by Congress—the only officer of the Continental Navy to be so honored.

John Paul Jones's victory was a historical naval milestone because, incredibly, a fine new frigate of the then "Invincible Royal Navy" had been defeated and captured by an American captain. This action gave hope to the American cause; it inspired our infant Navy with the possibility of rendering substantial aid to our struggling colonies.

We gained from Jones another tradition to which historians seldom refer, namely, that of magnanimity to foe when our arms are victorious. After the *Bon Homme Richard-Serapis* action when the gallant Pearson presented his sword to Jones, tradition relates that this captain of the Royal Navy said: "I cannot, sir, but feel much mortification at the idea of surrendering my sword to a man who fought me with a rope around his neck." The reference was to the English allegation that Jones was a pirate.

Jones received his sword but returned it at once saying: "You have fought gallantly, sir, and I hope your king will give you a better ship."

An American naval tradition was born. For example, in the War of 1812, after the battle of Lake Erie, Perry returned the swords of the British captains as a mark of recognition of their stubborn resistance.

This tradition was continued when Captain "Fighting Bob" Evans took the surrender of Captain Eulaté, Spanish commander of the *Viscaya*:

> . . . the captain [Eulaté] covered with blood from three wounds,
> with a bloodstained handkerchief about his bare head. Around
> him sat or lay a dozen or more wounded men. . . . The captain
> [Spanish] was tenderly placed in a chair and then hoisted to the
> deck, where he was received with the honors due his rank. As the
> chair was placed on the quarter-deck he slowly raised himself to
> his feet, unbuckled his sword belt, kissed the hilt of his sword, and
> bowing low, gracefully presented it to me as a token of surrender.
> I never felt so sorry for a man in all my life. Of course I declined
> to receive the sword, or rather I hastily handed it back to Captain
> Eulaté, but accepted the surrender of his officers and men in the
> name of Admiral Sampson, our commander in chief. My men were
> all crowded aft about the deck and superstructure, and when I
> declined the sword the brave hearts under the blue shirts appreciated my feelings and they cheered until I felt ashamed of myself.[2]

---

[2] Robley D. Evans, *A Sailor's Log* (New York: D. Appleton & Co., 1908), p. 451.

THE QUASI-WAR WITH FRANCE AND THE
TRIPOLITAN WAR

The small Navy of the War of the Revolution was finally disbanded with nothing left behind it except "the recollection of its service and sufferings," but traditions lived on. Some splendid naval leaders and seamen had been developed in a rugged school that fully qualified them to take command of the new American-built ships—all constructed under the act of March 27, 1794, and superior to any of their class in Europe.

When the famous frigates, the *Constitution*, the *President*, the *United States*, the *Chesapeake*, the *Constellation*, and the *Congress* were completed, heroes of the Revolution—Barry, Nicholson, Barney, Dale, and Truxtun—were chosen to command. Truxtun gave a glorious account of himself in the *Constellation* when he captured the *Insurgente* and crippled the *Vengeance* in the short maritime war with France.

Our naval activities then turned to another part of the world. Preble attacked the forts of Tripoli. Captain Somers, Wadsworth, and Israel went to their deaths in the daring explosive-boat attack. Before Preble's atttack on Tripoli, the *Philadelphia*, commanded by Bainbridge, was lost to the Tripolitan pirates. The ship went aground in shoal water before the surrender. The resistance, to say the least, was faint-hearted. Frost writes:

Stephen Decatur at Tripoli. Oil painting by William A.K. Martin. *Courtesy of the U.S. Naval Academy Museum*

It is true that then we had no naval tradition—but Germans also had none when they entered the World War. Yet they knew how to die! True, for Bainbridge there are many good excuses. But how we wish that he had stood forth there and spoken to his comrades, in the words of Beowulf:

Each of us must his end abide
in the ways of the world; so win who may
glory ere death! When his days are told,
that is the warrior's worthiest doom.

Stephen Decatur afterwards attacked and burned the captured *Philadelphia* that his father had once commanded. Nelson, the master seaman, in his cabin in the *Victory* off Toulon said the feat was "the most bold and daring act of the age." Truly, it established an inspiring tradition of naval enterprise that will never die. With but few exceptions, the war with Tripoli was a brilliant naval campaign and resulted in eliminating forever the tribute that had been paid to the Barbary Coast "racketeers." And it also added to the prestige of the Republic.

THE WAR OF 1812

Next came the "second war for independence," the War of 1812. Hull's victory in the *Constitution* against the *Guerrière* astonished both sides of the Atlantic. Congress thanked Hull in the name of the nation and gave the officers and crew $50,000 in prize money. This victory strengthened morale in that it gave our new Navy confidence, and dispelled the prevailing idea that the British Navy was omnipotent.

In fact, with a measure of alarm, Great Britain's attention was directed to the daring exploits of the "Yankee sailors" and their frigates. The London *Times* wrote:

It is more than merely that an English frigate has been taken, after what, we are free to confess, may be called a brave resistance, but that it has been taken by a new enemy, an enemy unaccustomed to such triumphs, and likely to be rendered insolent and confident by them. . . . Never before in the history of the world did an English frigate strike to an American; and though we cannot say that Captain Dacres, under all circumstances, is punishable for this act, yet we do say that there are commanders in the English Navy who would a thousand times rather have gone down with their colors flying than have set their brother officers so fatal an example.

The London *Times* was correct as to the confidence engendered, because the American Navy had achieved the first of the long list of impressive victories that astounded our own people. Decatur in the *United States* captured the *Macedonian*; the *Constitution* shot every spar out of the frigate *Java*, and shortly afterwards captured both the *Cyane* and *Levant* in the same action.

It was an era when fighting slogans were coined, such as Lawrence's dying words in the *Chesapeake*, "Fight her till she sinks and don't give up the ship." Perry carried the watchword on to Lake Erie, thus demonstrating the continuity of tradition, when he hoisted at the main royal masthead of the *Lawrence*, a flag upon which were sewn Lawrence's last words, "Don't give up the ship."[3] Then after the battle came Perry's dispatch which has been so often quoted, *We have met the enemy and they are ours, two ships, two brigs, one schooner, and one sloop.* American shipbuilders and seamen "delivered the goods" in practically all of these actions.

In the 1812–1815 naval war, the Yankee sailors also demonstrated a coolness that was inherent in their native English stock, and a daring that derived from their pioneer spirit. Because of the constant gun drills, American marksmanship was unexcelled. Dashing American seamen dealt some powerful blows in this second war of independence.

DAVID GLASGOW FARRAGUT

The continuity of this splendid sea tradition is illustrated by the career of Farragut. Trained by David Porter, Farragut was appointed prize master of the *Barclay* at the age of twelve. Half a century later, Farragut won the battle of New Orleans.

The masterful ship and fleet handler, the loyal and audacious David Glasgow Farragut, who was to be the first admiral of the United States Navy, was born near Knoxville, Tennessee, and spent his earliest years on the rugged East Tennessee frontier. As a child, on a flatboat trip down the Mississippi, he remembered the river pirates on the way, and at New Orleans, first saw men-of-war on which he was destined to win imperishable fame. At the age of eight, Farragut was adopted by Commodore David Porter; at the age of nine years and five months, he received a midshipmen's warrant; and at ten went to sea under Porter in the *Essex*. At the age of twelve, he was given his first command —the captured *Barclay*.

---

[3] This flag now hangs in Bancroft Hall at Annapolis.

Thereafter, however, his career for many years was unspectacular, and when the Civil War came, he was hard put to prove his value to the Navy because of his Southern birth and connections, even though he had remained loyal to the Union cause and had moved from Virginia to New York. The chance to prove himself finally came in 1862 when Farragut, now over sixty, was given command of the West Gulf Blockading Squadron. His heroic role as a maker of tradition evolved from this assignment that led to critical and decisive victories at New Orleans and Mobile Bay. It was in the latter campaign that he made

David Glasgow Farragut. The first officer in the U.S. Navy to hold the rank of admiral. Photograph by Mathew B. Brady. *Courtesy U.S. Naval Academy Museum.*

his famous decision in stirring words that have become an American byword for courage and determination.

It was at Mobile Bay in 1864. Farragut, lashed in the rigging of the *Hartford*, after noting that one ship had stopped after reports of "torpedoes ahead," that another had been sunk, and that the line of battle seemed hopelessly tangled up directly under the guns of Fort Morgan, made an immediate and inspiring decision: "Damn the torpedoes! Four bells! Captain Drayton, go ahead—Jouett, full speed." This order led to the capture of Mobile Bay, hastened the end of the Civil War, and gave the American Navy a new tradition for ships propelled by steam. Farragut became the epitome of the all-out offensive attack, most evident in his order for the attack on New Orleans when he asserted that "the best protection against the enemy's fire is a well-directed fire from our own guns." Farragut had written to his wife before the battle: "As to being prepared for defeat, I certainly am not. Any man who is prepared for defeat would be half-defeated before he commenced. I hope for success; shall do all in my power to secure it and trust to God for the rest."

DAVID DIXON PORTER

Porter's family was one of unsurpassed American naval tradition. His grandfather and granduncle commanded ships in the American Revolution. His father, Commodore David Porter, who adopted Farragut, served in the French and Tripolitan wars, and then the War of 1812. The exploits of the Commodore in the *Essex* make thrilling sea lore. David Dixon Porter, who had more continuous fighting time from 1861 to 1864 than any "officer of distinction," rose from lieutenant to rear admiral in the Civil War period and became the second American officer to attain the grade of full admiral; his adopted brother, Farragut, was the first.

At the age of ten, Porter made his first cruise. As a midshipman in the Mexican Navy at the age of fifteen, he fought the Spaniards. In this baptism of fire, his cousin, the commanding officer, was killed; Midshipman Porter was taken prisoner; and over one-third of the crew were killed or wounded. He became a midshipman in the United States Navy at the age of sixteen. After some daring exploits in the Mexican War, Porter had his great opportunity. While on monotonous blockade duty off the Southwest Pass of the Mississippi in 1861, Porter evolved a plan for the capture of New Orleans. He made a trip to Washington and received the general approval of two senators and the Secretary of the Navy. The Secretary took him to see President

Lincoln who commented: "This should have been done sooner. The Mississippi is the key to the whole situation." The plan was adopted, and it is of distinct interest that Porter recommended his brother, Farragut, to command the operation.

After Farragut's fleet was assembled in the lower reaches of the Mississippi, Porter, with small vessels often under heavy fire, made a survey of the channel; this hydrographic reconnaissance made safe navigation possible. He was then ordered to command gunboats on the upper Mississippi, after completing a short command of a mortar flotilla on the James River in Virginia. The Mississippi command, which included all forces from St. Louis to Vicksburg, was of invalu-

Rear Admiral David Dixon Porter

able assistance to General U. S. Grant in the capture of Vicksburg. Porter distinguished himself as a brilliant commander of gunboats.

Porter's Civil War career was climaxed with the bombardment, siege, and capture of Fort Fisher and Wilmington, North Carolina. At this time he commanded sixty vessels, of which five were ironclad, the largest force that had ever been brought together under the American flag. Throughout, he impressed President Lincoln by his original ideas, his quick grasp of situations, and his superb leadership.

A vice admiral at fifty-three, Porter was ordered to the Naval Academy as superintendent. From 1865 to 1869, he made enormous strides in rebuilding the Academy. Because he introduced baseball, rowing, and boxing there, some have called him "the father of Navy athletics." He certainly knew from experience what the Navy required in stamina and endurance, and few senior naval officers ever surpassed him in these qualities.

GEORGE DEWEY–ADMIRAL OF THE NAVY

George Dewey, to whom President Theodore Roosevelt wrote on May Day, 1908, the tenth anniversary of the battle of Manila Bay: "Surely no man in any country could hope for a higher reward than is yours, for no other man living stands to his countrymen in quite the same position that you do," was an officer supremely conscious of our naval tradition in the War with Spain. The hero of the battle of Manila Bay, our first four-star admiral, with the title "Admiral of the Navy," recognized as much as any officer of his time the tremendous but imponderable effect of lofty tradition:

> I have often asked myself, "What would Farragut do?" In the course of preparations for Manila Bay I often asked myself this question, and I confess that I was thinking of him the night that we entered the Bay, and with the conviction that I was doing precisely what he would have done.

Thus, he looked back thirty-six years to the time when he was a lieutenant with Farragut when he commanded the Union fleet and ran the gauntlet of the forts below Mobile.

After Dewey's fleet steamed at night past the island defenses of Manila Bay, he waited for first light to attack, at which time he gave the classic order, the casualness of which caught the American imagination: "You may fire when ready, Gridley." Dewey also gave another order "which also contributed to his subsequent reputation for laconic imperturbability, that is, the order to 'draw off for breakfast.' " Dewey afterwards said that this was done to check remaining ammunition, and also because smoke was so heavy that it was impossible to fire accurately.

Although the news was seven days late arriving in the United States, never had a United States naval victory so caught the admiration of the American people. It inspired speeches, editorials, a congressional memorial, a "Hymn to Dewey," dozens of songs, and the manufacture of souvenirs of all descriptions.

Amid all the unprecedented national adulation there were perhaps not many Americans who at the time sensed the long-range historic

Dewey at Manila Bay

significance of the battle of Manila Bay, since at the time there still remained a military campaign to quell the insurrection and make victory complete.[4] Many historians believe that this defeat of the Spanish Navy at Manila, together with the defeat of the Spanish fleet by Rear Admiral William T. Sampson at Santiago de Cuba, marks the emergence of the United States as a world power. In reality, it was "one of those feats," wrote Theodore Roosevelt, "which mark the beginning of new epochs." The sailor, author, and inventor, Admiral Bradley A. Fiske, believed:

> The battle of Manila Bay was one of the most important ever fought. It decided that the United States should start in a direction in which it had never traveled before. It placed the United States in the family of great nations, and it put Spain into outer darkness. Before the battle, British Navy officers treated the United States Navy officers with condescension. In fact Europeans as a body treated all Americans so. They have never done so since.[5]

It is of interest that Dewey's life (1837–1917) spanned the period from sailing frigates and wooden ships of the line, through the days of the steam frigates and armored vessels, to the battleship and the birth of the aircraft carrier. Four battleships that were at Pearl Harbor on that fateful day in 1941 were launched while Dewey was alive. Dewey, who knew Farragut and Porter, veterans of the War of 1812, also knew King, Halsey, and Nimitz of World War II.

In his Message to Congress the day after Dewey's death, Woodrow Wilson summed up some of the most outstanding characteristics of the only Admiral of the Navy in American history:

> It is pleasant to recall what qualities gave him his well-deserved fame; his practical directness; his courage without self-consciousness; his efficient capacity in matters of administration; the readiness to fight without asking any questions or hesitancy about any details. It was by such qualities that he continued and added lustre to the best traditions of our Navy. He had the stuff in him which all true men admire, and upon which all statesmen must depend in hour of peril.[6]

---

[4] *The Military Order of the Carabao*, with membership consisting of officers of all services who have served in the Philippine Islands, keeps alive today the tradition and songs of those distant "empire days."

[5] Written by Admiral Fiske to Henry Cabot Lodge in reference to Lodge's book, *History of the Spanish War*. Quoted by Mark Sullivan in *Our Times*.

[6] Woodrow Wilson, *Message to Congress*, January 17, 1917.

STEPHEN B. LUCE

Admiral Luce is best known for his effort in establishing the Naval War College. During the Civil War, he came to the attention of the Navy Department for his superior work in training midshipmen in seamanship at the Naval Academy. His text book on this subject was used throughout the Navy for years. Luce was a superb seaman, but he was an equally good strategist. For years he fought the civilian bureaucracy in an effort to establish a Naval War College at Newport, Rhode Island, where naval strategy would be taught to naval officers.

Rear Admiral Stephen B. Luce

After the Naval War College was at last firmly established, Admiral Luce continued to lecture there until he was eighty years of age, and it was he who brought Commander (later Admiral) Mahan to the War College as one of its first department heads. Luce insisted that naval officers should master international law, history, the latest naval technology, and naval strategy in a formal intellectual atmosphere. This tradition is continued today.

ALFRED THAYER MAHAN

Admiral Mahan entered the Naval Academy in 1856 as a third class midshipman, the only person ever permitted to skip the fourth class year. Subsequent to his graduation, he rose through the ranks, carrying out the usual assignments of the period, until 1885, when he was assigned to the Naval War College as a lecturer and as department head of Naval Tactics and History. This began a long association with the War College during which Mahan served as president, lecturer, and writer even after his retirement. In 1890 Mahan wrote *Influence of Sea Power on History, 1660–1783*, the first of twenty books and many essays on this subject. He held many prestigious appointments on commissions and in organizations during the latter part of his career. Mahan's major contribution to naval tradition was his codification of the elements of sea power in such a fashion that they could be grasped by naval students of our own Navy and of the world.

WILLIAM SOWDEN SIMS

There is one officer in World War I who, by virtue of his attention to important detail and his organization of the convoy system, will live in naval history as a symbol of our Atlantic operations in that war: Admiral William Sowden Sims, Commander Naval Forces Europe.[7]

To Sims, a stormy petrel of the Navy in his younger days, history accords major credit for the doctrine and organization of the convoy system. His idea of the planned escort of merchant ships by naval vessels, with relentless war against submarines by all conceivable weap-

---

[7] At that time Admiral William S. Benson was Chief of Naval Operations and Admiral Henry T. Mayo, Commander of the Atlantic Fleet. Conspicuously and commendably assisted by Admiral Hugh Rodman of the Fifth Battle Squadron, British Grand Fleet; Admiral H. B. Wilson, Commander U. S. Naval Forces France; Admiral Albert T. Gleaves, Commander Transport Service; and Admiral Joseph Strauss with Captain R. R. Belknap of the American Mining Squadron, Sims coordinated and had general direction of the naval activities that to a great degree contributed to the winning of the war at sea.

William Sowden Sims. Commander, U.S. naval forces operating in European waters in World War I.

ons and devices, permitted the United States to place 2,086,000 soldiers in Europe; one-half the number were carried in British ships. This is remarkable in light of the fact that German submarines destroyed 6,618,623 tons of ships in 1917, while the shipbuilding of the whole world (less Germany and Austria) in that corresponding time was but 2,703,345 tons. The efficiency of Sims's plan speaks for itself in view of the fact that these troops were delivered with scarcely any loss of life en route or any ships sunk.

However, the situation was critical when the United States entered the war in April 1917. Just prior to our entry, Admiral Sims was sent to confer with the British Admiralty and make a special report on general conditions in the war area, with special attention to methods used by the British to counter the submarine menace. He found it was so serious that unless a more successful system for merchant ships were devised, it was indeed probable that Great Britain would have to sue for peace.

Although there was a great shortage of escort vessels, Admiral Sims strongly advocated the convoy system from the start. The British Admiralty admitted the failure of the existing antisubmarine measures, and with the support of Prime Minister Lloyd George and some progressive British naval officers, the British Cabinet ordered a trial of the escort-convoy system in May 1917.

These figures tell the story: From February 1, 1917, to August 1, 1917, the Germans destroyed an average 640,000 tons of Allied shipping per month; from August 1, 1917, to February 1, 1918, 300,000 tons a month; and from February 1, 1918, to the Armistice 200,000 tons a month.

A British naval officer once said that the outstanding characteristic of an American naval officer is "his open-mindedness," whereas "we [British] cling too much at times to the practices of Lord Nelson." Sims's professional life epitomized the quality of "open-mindedness." In his specialty—gunnery—he was one of the most progressive and best-informed officers of his time. Despite considerable Navy Department resistance, Sims, with the backing of Theodore Roosevelt, revolutionized gunnery practices and greatly improved the efficiency of the fleet in target practice. Always an indefatigable worker and a profound student of war, he nevertheless took great interest in his men. His tireless quest for new ideas inspired his subordinates, and qualifies him as a maker of tradition.

Sims set high standards for conduct of personnel and battle readiness. In particular, the admiral took great pride in the condition of readiness of our ships of the Sixth Battle Squadron under Admiral Hugh Rodman at Scapa Flow, Scotland.[8]

Sims inspired more than the respect of the enlisted men who served with him. A young officer serving in the *New York* wrote: "Each time when the sailors learned that Sims was to come, they were overjoyed and seemed to take particular interest in having the ships in the very pink of condition. Perhaps this is because a number of our chief petty officers at one time or another during their careers had served directly

---

[8] Sixth Battle Squadron comprised U. S. ships *New York*, *Texas*, *Wyoming*, *Florida*, and *Delaware*. When accompanying George V, the sailor king, on an inspection of the *New York*, Sims must have been proud to hear His Majesty remark: "In the American Navy, the precept of cleanliness being next to godliness has been effectively adopted."

It would have been poor taste to have said, though it is true, that cleanliness of ship and crew has always been a proud naval tradition. May our ships on missions of goodwill ever remain "show ships," as well as effective fighting units. Good impressions of us by foreigners can never be underestimated.

under Sims. The verdict of such men is perhaps, after all, the greatest test of a good commander. *They loved him.*"[9]

SECRETARY OF THE NAVY JOSEPHUS DANIELS

Most Secretaries of the Navy serve briefly and do not change the nature of the service much. Secretary of the Navy (1913–1921) Josephus Daniels was an exception. He served for eight years, including all of World War I. He is best known for his action in banning alcoholic beverages from Navy ships, but this is a social injustice, for he is really

[9] Francis T. Hunter, *Beatty, Jellicoe, Sims and Rodman* (Garden City, N.Y.: Doubleday, Page & Co., 1919), p. 51.

Secretary of the Navy Josephus Daniels. Shown here with the Prince of Wales, who later became King Edward VIII.

the Father of the American Navy as far as enlisted men are concerned. Daniels established the recruiting system which remains virtually unchanged to this day. By various General Orders he set up the service school system, the recruit training center system, the Navy rate training courses, and he made it possible for enlisted men to enter the Naval Academy via the Preparatory School. He also superintended the entrance of women into the Navy in World War I. He originated the unsatisfactory discharge to rid the Navy of those who were damaging its ability and efficiency and converted the Naval Prison System from a holding institution to a rehabilitation organization. All of these changes were made over the objection of the uniformed leaders of the Navy, and the wisdom of Daniels's actions has been proven by their lasting nature.

WORLD WAR II

Naval, military, and state archives will be combed for years to come for all the facts of the small- and the large-scale operations of World War II. In 1962 Rear Admiral Samuel Eliot Morison completed his superb fifteen-volume series *United States Naval Operations in World War II*, that proves Machin's dictum: "The decisive battles of the world decide the destinies of nations." Because there were such decisive battles as Midway, and because certain senior officers of the Navy had the responsibility of planning, approving, or executing these voluminous coordinated joint plans, their names will ever live in naval and national history as the makers of naval tradition in World War II.

This section is primarily concerned with naval traditions and that which bears on the genesis and perpetuation of tradition. The last major citations received by our Fleet Admirals, terse résumés of service to country with their implications of fearless acceptance of awesome responsibility, prove best that these officers were makers of tradition—exemplars to devotion to country and duty.

FLEET ADMIRAL WILLIAM D. LEAHY, USN

Admiral Leahy graduated from the Naval Academy in 1897 and served through all ranks to admiral, retiring in 1939. He was then appointed as governor of Puerto Rico. After approximately a year he was appointed ambassador to France, and in July, 1942, was recalled to active duty as Chief of Staff to the Commander in Chief of the Army and Navy. In 1944 he was made a Fleet Admiral and appointed as the president's representative on the newly created National Intelligence

Fleet Admiral William D. Leahy

Authority. He retired again in 1949. Admiral Leahy fulfilled to the highest degree the tradition that U. S. naval officers can serve in high governmental positions.

FLEET ADMIRAL ERNEST J. KING, USN

> *It is the particular business of the Navy to gain and keep control of the seas for the support and execution of our national policies. To accomplish this duty, we of the Navy must be prepared to defeat the enemy wherever he may be found on the seas or on the coasts bordering them.*—Admiral E. J. King, in *Air Power*

Admiral King was graduated from the Naval Academy in 1901 and served in a variety of surface ships and submarine units before taking flight training in 1927. After Pearl Harbor he was appointed Commander in Chief U.S. Fleet. In March 1942 the office of Chief of Naval

Operations was reestablished and assumed by Admiral King. In 1944 he was made a Fleet Admiral.

For distinguished service concurrently as Commander in Chief of the U. S. Fleet, and Chief of Naval Operations, during the World War II period Fleet Admiral King was awarded a Gold Star in lieu of the third Distinguished Service Medal with citation, in part, as follows:

> In his dual capacity (he) exercised complete military control of the Naval Forces of the United States Navy, Marine Corps, and Coast Guard and directed all activities of these forces in conjunction with the U. S. Army and our Allies to bring victory to the

Fleet Admiral Ernest J. King

United States. As the United States Naval Member of the Joint Chief of Staff and the Combined Chiefs of Staff, he coordinated the naval strength of this country with all agencies of the United States and of the Allied Nations, and with exceptional vision, driving energy, and uncompromising devotion to duty, he fulfilled his tremendous responsibility of command and direction of the greatest naval force the world has ever seen and the simultaneous expansion of all naval facilities in the prosecution of the war. . . .

On news of the death of Fleet Admiral Ernest J. King on June 25, 1956, President Eisenhower said: "The Nation has lost a great American and an outstanding naval officer . . . Admiral King carried heavy responsibility with courage, brilliance and continued devotion to duty."

At the impressive religious ceremony at the National Cathedral, Washington, D.C., before burial at the Naval Academy Cemetery, the Very Reverend Francis B. Sayre, Jr., Dean of the Cathedral, in a special prayer, said:

> Oh Almighty God, who by silent stars does guide those who go down to the sea in ships, we praise Thee for the steadfast course of Thy servant's life. . . . By a staunch mariner, Thou has blest our people and brought us safely to this day.

FLEET ADMIRAL CHESTER W. NIMITZ, USN

The Lord gave us two ends to use: one to think with and one to sit with. The war depends on which we choose—heads we win, tails we lose.[10]

Under the leadership of Admiral Nimitz, we had a combination that could—and did—go anywhere in the Pacific.[11]

Admiral Nimitz was graduated from the Naval Academy in 1905 and served in surface ships until entering the submarine service in 1908. Shortly after the attack on Pearl Harbor he was appointed Commander in Chief Pacific Fleet and retained that command throughout World War II. Later he served as Chief of Naval Operations and was appointed a Fleet Admiral. He was best known for his ability to exercise effective command over a large variety of forces and areas, thus contributing to the Navy tradition of command ability.

---

[10] Sent as a motto by Admiral Nimitz to Admiral Halsey.

[11] Admiral Raymond A. Spruance, USN (Ret.), in his introduction to *Beans, Bullets, and Black Oil* by Worrall Reed Carter (Washington, D.C., 1953), p. ix.

Fleet Admiral Chester W. Nimitz

On September 1, 1945 (U.S. time), Fleet Admiral Nimitz was one of the signers for the United States when Japan formally accepted the surrender terms aboard the battleship *Missouri* in Tokyo Bay.

On October 5, 1945, which had been officially designated as "Nimitz Day" in Washington, D.C., Fleet Admiral Nimitz was presented a Gold Star in lieu of the third Distinguished Service Medal by the president of the United States personally, who cited him:

> For exceptionally meritorious service . . . from June 1944 to August 1945. Initiating the final phase in the battle for victory in the Pacific, (he) attacked the Marianas, invading Saipan, inflicting a decisive defeat in the Japanese Fleet in the First Battle of the Philippines and capturing Guam and Tinian. In vital continuing operations, his Fleet Forces isolated the enemy-held bastions of the Central and Eastern Carolines and secured in quick succession Peleliu, Angaur and Ulithi. With reconnaissance of the main beaches on Leyte effected, approach channels cleared and opposition neutralized in joint operations to reoccupy the Philippines, the challenge by powerful task forces of the Japanese Fleet resulted in a historic victory in the three-phased Battle for Leyte Gulf, October 24 to 26, 1944. Accelerating the intensity of aerial offensive

by pressure exerted at every hostile strong point, Fleet Admiral Nimitz culminated long-range strategy by successful amphibious assault on Iwo Jima and Okinawa . . . (and) finally placed representative forces of the United States Navy in the harbor of Tokyo for the formal capitulation of the Japanese Empire. . . . He demonstrated the highest qualities of a naval officer and rendered services of the greatest distinction to his country.

Nimitz, last of the Fleet Admirals, died 20 February 1966. President Johnson in tribute said: "Admiral Nimitz loved the country and the sea. His devotion to one inspired his mastery of the other, earning for his quiet courage and resolute leadership the undying gratitude of his countrymen and an enduring chapter in the annals of naval history."

FLEET ADMIRAL WILLIAM F. HALSEY, JR., USN

Admiral Halsey graduated from the Naval Academy in 1904 and spent the majority of his early years at sea in destroyers. In 1935 he completed flight training and was designated a naval aviator at the age of 52. When World War II began he was Commander Carrier Division II

Fleet Admiral William F. Halsey, Jr. Shown here with President Harry S. Truman.

with his flag in the *Enterprise*. After some early raids on Japanese-held islands, Admiral Halsey commanded the ships which took part in the Doolittle raid on Tokyo. He was then placed in command of the South Pacific Force in an effort to restore its morale and effectiveness. He did so, beginning his reputation for attacking whenever possible. He is best known for his forceful tactical command and continued this tradition later when in command of the Third Fleet at the time of carrier raids on the Philippines and Japan. He was not a very good strategic commander, as he proved in the Battle of Leyte Gulf, but his pugnacious aggressiveness earned him a place in history and promotion to the rank of Fleet Admiral.

ADMIRAL RAYMOND A. SPRUANCE

Admiral Spruance was graduated from the Naval Academy in 1907 and served in surface ships throughout his career. Unlike Admiral Halsey, he did not qualify as a naval aviator. He was a quiet, studious officer and through his studies at the Naval War College was firmly grounded in naval strategy. At the outbreak of World War II he was a rear admiral in command of a cruiser division. Shortly before the Battle of Midway Admiral Halsey became ill and recommended that Admiral Spruance be placed in command of the U. S. Task Force that was being assembled to confront the Japanese at Midway. Spruance's knowledge of tactical aviation was limited, but his strategic knowledge

Admiral Raymond A. Spruance

carried the day at Midway. Later, in command of the Fifth Fleet, he demonstrated superior strategic judgment numerous times in the best traditions of the U. S. Navy.

ADMIRAL ARLEIGH A. BURKE

Admiral Burke was graduated from the Naval Academy in 1923. He served in surface ships, but at the beginning of World War II found himself on shore duty. His repeated attempts to go to sea were rewarded with orders to command two destroyer divisions and two destroyer squadrons. His service was in the South Pacific at the height of the operations in that area. Destroyer Squadron 23, known as the "Little Beaver" squadron, participated in twenty-two different engagements. Admiral Burke went on to higher commands in World War II and eventually became Chief of Naval Operations for an unprece-

Admiral Arleigh A. Burke

dented six years. He was best known as "31-Knot Burke" and he forged a new tradition for the destroyer, that of a versatile, fast, aggressive, hard-hitting ship always at the forefront of the toughest fighting.

ADMIRAL HYMAN G. RICKOVER

Admiral Rickover was graduated from the Naval Academy in 1922. He served in surface ships and submarines until 1937 and was then designated for engineering duty. In 1947 he began duty in the Bureau of Ships and with the Atomic Energy Commission. Admiral Rickover is generally credited with being the driving force behind the development of nuclear power for submarines and surface ships. The first such ship, the *Nautilus*, was launched in 1953, and twenty-five years later

Admiral Hyman G. Rickover continues a new tradition, established by him, of welding the sponsor's initials to the keel of a ship by welding his initials to a steel beam of Rickover Hall, the Naval Academy science and engineering building.

there were 125 nuclear-powered vessels. Admiral Rickover set up a system of extreme thoroughness in the selection and training of personnel and in construction methods. As a result, there were no accidents in the nuclear program, and a new Navy tradition of safety, reliability, and performance was established.

VICE ADMIRAL WILLIAM F. RABORN, JR.

Admiral Raborn was graduated from the Naval Academy in 1928. He was designated as a naval aviator and saw combat in World War II. After the war he entered the field of guided missiles. When the Navy decided to construct guided-missile-bearing submarines, the program was given the name POLARIS and Admiral Raborn was designated head of the Special Projects Office which was to produce it. He was responsible for the entire system less the nuclear propulsion system of the submarine and was given top priority in personnel, money, and

Vice Admiral William F. Raborn, Jr.

material. Within ten years and without delay or accident, he brought into being the most important weapon system ever produced by the Navy or the country. The POLARIS system was followed by the improved POSEIDON and TRIDENT systems. Together they provided our country with an invulnerable, reliable, and powerful deterrent system which prevented the Soviet Union from attacking. Admiral Raborn was awarded the Collier Trophy and the Distinguished Service Medal, but never received adequate credit from press or public. History will record his accomplishment as being in the finest tradition of our Navy.

VICE ADMIRAL JAMES B. STOCKDALE

Admiral Stockdale was graduated from the Naval Academy in 1946. He served as a naval aviator in the war against Vietnam before being shot down over that country. He was a prisoner of war for approximately seven years. As the senior prisoner of war in his camp, he exercised strong control over his fellow prisoners in spite of torture, isolation, and brutal treatment. His personal conduct was an example to all. After release he resumed his naval career, rising to the rank of vice admiral. Together with other senior prisoners of war, he established a new tradition of outstanding conduct while a prisoner of war.

Vice Admiral James B. Stockdale

APPENDIX B

Army and West Point Regulations, Customs, and Courtesies

A little experience of Army life will convince anyone that the Service is among the remaining strongholds of good manners. . . . And where in contemporary civil life will you find a profession in which a man can be fired from his job "for conduct unbecoming a gentleman?"

Hoffman Nickerson, *Officer and Gentleman*

Here die I, Richard Grenville, with a joyful and quiet mind, for that I have ended my life as a true soldier ought to do that hath fought for his country, queen, religion, and honor. Whereby my soul most joyfully departeth out of this body, and shall always leave behind it an everlasting fame of a valiant and true soldier, that has done his duty as he was bound to do.

Last words of Sir Richard Grenville, 1591.

Major, tell my father I died with my face to the enemy.[1]

I. E. Avery

We proudly trace the traditions of our service directly back to the Order of Knighthood, which for centuries furnished the brain and spirit and sinew to European armies, and indelibly stamped its impress upon our profession.

Brigadier General Lincoln C. Andrews, USA

[1] A blood-stained note addressed to Major Samuel Tate, found clasped in the hand of Colonel Isaac Erwin Avery of 6th Regiment, North Carolina Confederate Troops. The paper is now on exhibition at State Museum, Raleigh, North Carolina. Avery, who commanded Hoke's Brigade, was killed on the evening of the second day at Gettysburg. The Colonel wrote his last message with his left hand because his right arm was paralyzed by the fatal wound.

THE UNITED STATES ARMY officer has with justifiable pride maintained the honor, the integrity, and the gentility that is ever implied by "soldier and gentleman." As with all military and naval services that are worthy of the name, the traditions of yesterday influence the services of today. The devotion to cause of Washington, the inspirational leadership of Andrew Jackson, the gentility of Lee, and dogged perseverance of Grant, the religious cast and military genius of Stonewall Jackson, the knowledge and scholarship of MacArthur, the dignity and the strategic and administrative "know how" of Marshall, and the genius to effect team-work in foreign armies as characterized by Eisenhower, comprise superior military traits that have been seldom equaled in the military history of any state.

Great generals, in nearly all cases, have been great gentlemen. For some the development commenced in childhood; for others it was developed through a conscientious observance of regulations, customs, and courtesies of the Army service tempered by sound character with a sense of the value of tradition and example to *ésprit de corps*. Greatness is reflected in defeat as well as in victory; at death as well as on the heights of success. The inner man was reflected when the wounded Sydney passed his cup of water to the dying soldier on the battlefield; when Grant, in recognition of a gallant and brave foe, displayed a magnanimous spirit towards Lee at Appomattox.

Wherever subject matter in this work touches upon manners, social usages, and courtesies it is generally true, whether the courtesies be military, naval, or civil, that they may be epitomized by the expression of thoughtfulness and respect for others. In fact, thought of others in all strata of humanity reflects one of mankind's most precious attributes; but when that consideration is expressed by the vehicle of best usage, it reflects the gentleman in an exalted sense of the word.

West Point has been concerned in laying the foundation stones of good usage by a definite course for all cadets. The West Point course requires the embryo Army officers to learn what is meant by good usage, and standardizes the outstanding courtesies expected of the Army officer. Extracts of *Army Regulations* pertinent to the course are also included. West Point considers that a course of this description, properly imparted to cadets, will help to mold the representative young men and women into "soldiers and gentlemen."

In substance, the social usage of the Army and Air Force is identical with that of the Navy. There are, of course, departures that result from the differences in the organization and life of the respective services.

The West Pointer was taught:

The relationship between an officer and his men must be given careful thought and study. Our *Army Regulations* and customs of the service forbid undue familiarity between the two. This is not due to any difference in birth or social status but is countenanced solely to maintain discipline. There is an old saying which is especially applicable to the military service and that is "familiarity breeds contempt." Any officer who ignores the distinction which prevails in the Army between himself and his men will be a failure as a commander. Soldiers understand the necessity for the relation which exists between an officer and his men and have only contempt for one who oversteps the bounds.

Remember in all of your dealing with subordinates to avoid language or remarks which lessen self-respect. Employ a tone of voice and a manner such as you would ordinarily employ in a conversation with another.

Set a high standard as a gentleman and a soldier and your men will recognize in you a leader whom they will gladly follow.[2]

EXTRACTS FROM OFFICIAL AND SOCIAL COURTESY, USMA

Military Courtesy

1. *General.* a. Courtesy is the expression of consideration for others. It pays the largest returns for the least effort of anything one can do. In military life, where individuals are required to live and work together more intimately than in civilian life and where cooperative effort is all-important, courtesy is of vital importance in promoting coordination and developing a proper *ésprit de corps.*

b. Courtesy is shown to all, to juniors as well as to seniors. The courtesy shown a senior is a recognition of the responsibility and authority of his position. That shown a junior acknowledges the essential part he plays as a member of the military team.

c. The methods of expressing military courtesy are distinctive and precise. Slovenly, grudging, or perfunctory display of these methods is discourteous.

d. The courtesy which marks military ceremonies has a profound meaning. A salute to the flag is a declaration of loyalty to the United States and the principles of liberty and justice on which the Nation was founded. When a military man presents arms at retreat or salutes a senior, it is a recognition of the organized authority of the Nation, as represented by the Army which is charged with its protection.

[2] Quoted by permission of the superintendent of the U.S. Military Academy.

2. *Salutes.* The salute is an important military courtesy because it is the most obvious and the most used. The manner of executing the salute is an indication of the individual's attitude toward his duties as a military man and the state of training and morale in the unit of which he is a member. Executed willingly and smartly, it indicates pride in himself and his unit and confidence in his ability to perform his military duties well. A sloppy, grudging salute indicates neglect or ignorance of his duties, lack of confidence in his ability to perform them, lack of pride in the military team of which he is a member, a stubborn, defiant spirit unsuited to cooperate with others in a common effort, or some similar deficiency which marks him as a poor soldier and his unit as a poor unit from which the best results cannot be expected.

5. *Saluting in vehicles.* a. Drivers of motor vehicles salute only when the vehicle is at a halt and the engine is not running.

b. The exchange of salutes is not required between persons mounted in different moving vehicles, persons mounted in moving vehicles and persons mounted in halted vehicles and dismounted persons, except (1) when a vehicle is clearly marked by methods prescribed in regulations to indicate the presence of a general officer, and (2) when required as part of a ceremony. In case a detail is riding in a vehicle, the individual in charge renders the hand salute for the entire detail.

c. Salutes are rendered between persons in a halted vehicle and dismounted persons.

d. Salutes are not rendered in public conveyances.

9. *Honors to the National Anthem or "To the Colors" (Standard).* a. *Outdoors.* Whenever and wherever the national anthem or "To the Colors" is played (not in formation)—(1) At the first note, all dismounted personnel present will face the music, stand at attention, and render the prescribed salute, except that at the "Escort of the Colors" or at "Retreat" they will face toward the colors or flag. The position of salute will be retained until the last note of the music is sounded.

(2) Vehicles in motion will be brought to a halt. Persons riding in a passenger car or on a motorcycle will dismount and salute as directed in (1) above. Occupants of other types of military vehicles remain at attention in the vehicle, the individual in charge of each vehicle dismounting and rendering the hand salute. Tank or armored car commanders salute from the vehicle.

(3) The above marks of respect are shown the national anthem of any friendly country when played upon official occasions.

b. *Indoors.*—When the national anthem is played indoors at a formal gathering individuals will stand at attention and face the music or the flag if one is present. They will not salute unless under arms.

10. *Other honors.* a. *To colors.* Military personnel passing uncased colors (standard) salute at six paces distance and hold the salute until they have passed six paces beyond it. Similarly, when uncased colors (standard) pass by, they salute when it is six paces away and hold the salute until it has passed six paces beyond them. Small flags carried by individuals are not saluted.

b. *Personal honors.* When personal honors are rendered, military personnel present, not in formation, salute at the first note of the music and hold the salute until the completion of the ruffles, flourish, and march. When a cannon salute is rendered, military personnel being saluted and other persons in the ceremonial party will render the hand salute during the firing of the gun salute. Other persons in the vicinity of the ceremonial party will stand at attention. Acknowledgment by persons in civilian dress may be made by standing at attention. A cannon salute to the nation requires no individual action.

c. *Military funerals.* Military personnel will salute during the passing of a caisson or hearse bearing the remains in a funeral procession. Those attending a military funeral in their individual capacity or as honorary pallbearers will stand at attention, uncovered (except in cold or inclement weather), and hold the head dress over the left breast at any time when the casket is being moved by the pallbearers and during the service at the grave, including the firing of volleys and the sounding of "Taps." During the prayers they will also bow their heads. In cold or inclement weather they will remain covered and will execute the hand salute at any time when the casket is being moved by the pallbearers and during the firing of volleys and the sounding of "Taps."

11. *Uncovering.* Individuals *under arms* uncover only when—
a. Seated as a member of or in attendance on a court or board. Sentinels guarding prisoners do not uncover.

b. Entering places of divine worship.

c. Indoors when not on duty.

d. In attendance at an official reception.

Customs of the Service

Customs of the service comprise the unwritten law for the social and official conduct of the Army of the United States.

Calls of courtesy. "The interchange of visits of courtesy between officers is of great importance and the well-established customs of the Army in this respect will be scrupulously adhered to. Failure to pay the civilities customary in official and polite society is to the prejudice of the best interests of the Service." (A.R. 605-I25.)

It is highly desirable that officers of the Army, wherever they might be stationed, take advantage of every opportunity to meet and to maintain social contact with the better element of the civilian community. In the case of officers on duty with the National Guard, Organized Reserves or R.O.T.C., this becomes a definite obligation.

As calling varies somewhat on different posts, it is wise always to ascertain local practices from the adjutant as soon as practicable after arrival. (NOTE: *This check on local rules for calling is important in all services.*)

Formal calls. Formal calls are those made in the discharge of a social obligation.

A formal call should not exceed fifteen minutes duration. A gentleman should always be exceedingly punctilious about his formal calls. Calls should be returned within two weeks, if possible.

An officer arriving at a post at which he expects to remain longer than twenty-four hours should check with the post adjutant for rules on calling. He is normally expected to call on the post commander. If assigned to duty there, he should normally call on all of his intermediate commanders. These calls should be immediately after the call of the post commander and should be at the office of those concerned. If unable to wear uniform, an explanation should be made for appearing in civilian clothes.

If in keeping with local rules as verified by the adjutant, the official visit to the post and intermediate commanders should be repeated at their residences within seventy-two hours after arrival. If the commander is married and his wife is present on the post, it is the custom of the officer making the visit to be accompanied by his wife. These calls should be formal and should ordinarily last no longer than fifteen minutes.

It is not necessary for the new arrival to make other calls until the officers of the battalion, regiment or garrison have called on him, except that junior officers should make the first call on field officers in the chain of command of their unit.

It is customary for all officers of a unit or garrison to call upon the commanding officer on New Year's Day. (Again, the commanding officer's desires in this matter should be ascertained by contacting his aide or adjutant.)

It is customary for officers to call on a new arrival as soon as he is situated so that callers can be received comfortably and without embarrassment. If the newcomer is married and his family is present, ladies call with their husbands.

In case of a death in the family of a friend or acquaintance, leave cards at the home.

Days at home. Hostesses might occasionally have a "day at home." Information as to the day at home of any particular hostess, if it be the same day of the week, or month, throughout the season, is common knowledge among her friends and may be ascertained. When a hostess is known to have a day at home, calls, except dinner calls and similar immediate obligations, should be made on that day, and on no other.

Farewell calls. Upon departing permanently from a station or community, an officer calls on the commanding officer and other friends. In such cases his cards should be marked p.p.c. (pour prendre congé) in the lower left corner in small letters. When obliged to leave hurriedly, he should mail these cards to his friends —also place one on the club bulletin board.

Calling hours. On a post, determine from the post adjutant.

In civil life, as local custom directs.

Social functions. It is customary for officers of all grades to make a point of speaking to the senior officers present and to dance or chat with their wives.

Officers should not discuss official subjects at social functions.

Miscellaneous rules. When the commanding officer says, "I desire," or "I wish" rather than, "I direct you to do so-and-so," this wish or desire has all the authority of a direct order.

Never keep anyone waiting.

Custom demands that officers be meticulous about their personal appearance. When the average civilian thinks of a soldier he remembers only those he has seen on parade. In his mind, a soldier, to be a soldier, must be on parade. Our uniform singles us out from the populace. Officers and cadets are constantly on parade before civilian population. Every day we represent the United States Army and everyone who sees us forms an opinion of the officer personnel by our behavior and appearance.

Never explain unless an explanation is called for.

Be courteous. Courtesy to subordinates is more important than courtesy to superiors. A sure test of an individual is his employment of his authority. Commendation when commendation is due, and admonition when admonition is necessary, are vital in developing morale.

Avoid the impolite practice of approaching an individual whom you know or remember well but haven't seen for some time, expecting him to remember your name and where he has known you before. When you speak to such an individual, introduce yourself by name and refresh his memory regarding where he has known you.

Social Customs

Gentlemanly conduct arises in the first instance from ingrained qualities and in the second from a knowledge of social customs.

Social customs are the forms, fashions and manners observed in the society of educated and cultivated people. They constitute a code of behavior the purpose of which is to foster ease and grace in living while eliminating the coarse and offensive. At the same time, social customs are intensely practical. They aim to facilitate life, to get things done quickly, to smooth the course of friendly gatherings, and to eliminate friction in our daily contacts with one another.

A knowledge of social customs comes inevitably with experience. To depend entirely on experience is, however, a slow and costly procedure.

On arrival in a strange community always inquire what the customs are, but great care should be exercised in selecting an authoritative source for this information. One should never adopt a standard which his good taste tells him is low.

Attitude toward ladies. Nothing so quickly discloses the presence or absence of manners in a man as his attitude toward ladies.

Special consideration should be accorded older women. At social gatherings men of all ages should pay their respects to the elderly women present.

Social Affairs

Entering a reception room. On entering a reception room one should immediately seek out the hostess and pay his respects to her. His movements to her from the door should be direct. Having greeted the hostess, he proceeds to greet each of the other ladies present. He then exchanges greetings with the host and with the other men present and joins in the conversation.

Leaving a reception room. When one wishes to take one's departure from a reception room, as for example at the termination of a call or after a dinner party, the first thing to do is to rise. This at once indicates to the hostess what is intended and no explanations or excuses are necessary unless the departure is premature. It is not necessary to wait for a lull in the conversation; on the contrary, such a course, particularly in the case of a short formal call, would probably result in an over-extended visit. Having risen, the guests should at once go to the hostess, make their adieus briefly and depart at once. Under no circumstance should they continue the conversation after having risen to go. After a dinner party it is the usual custom for other guests to remain, as a matter of courtesy, until the guests of honor have departed.

Teas, receptions, etc. All guests should present themselves to the hostess and those receiving immediately upon arrival. In going down the receiving line a lady precedes her escort. Guests should, on presenting themselves to the hostess, pronounce their names clearly and distinctly.

Acknowledging courtesies. A gentleman renders appropriate acknowledgment for every courtesy extended to him, and for every kindly, generous or helpful act of which he is the beneficiary. It is rude to accept the hospitality of one's friends without expressing appreciation, and it is both rude and selfish not to attempt to reciprocate. In the majority of cases there can be no value relationship between the courtesy received and that offered in return. People in moderate circumstances are not expected to return on a money basis the entertainment extended to them by wealthy friends and acquaintances. Nevertheless, within the limit of their resources, they must discharge the obligations they have accepted. Just what form the acknowledgment should take depends on all related circumstances. As a general rule, obligations of the sort contemplated may be satisfied by personal thanks, by calling or mailing cards, by sending an inexpensive gift, or by offering in return the same or similar courtesy or one which, even though of an entirely different nature, is equally enjoyable.

At the beginning of the succinct and excellent pamphlet from which the above extracts were taken, Colonel John K. Waters, Commandant of Cadets said in a foreword: "The phrase 'a fine officer' is inclusive of the phrase 'a gentleman.' An officer must be well mannered, poised, courteous, and considerate in every respect if he is to succeed either as a gentleman or a leader of men." And he ended the preface with emphasis on the basic rule of all good manners, "Be thoughtful and considerate of the rights and feelings of others."

Wardroom Etiquette
and Toasts in
H.M. Navy[1]

THE FOLLOWING RULES of protocol and custom obtain in the Royal
Canadian Navy but are essentially the same as those of the Royal Navy
and the navies of the Commonwealth that maintain consistently the
highest formal officer mess standards of the maritime countries.

It is customary to assemble in the anterooms of British ships about
one-half hour before dinner.

At 2000, the Senior Steward reports to the Mess President
"Dinner is served, Sir" and the President leads the way into the
wardroom. Drinks and smokes are deposited and members follow
the President to the table. The Vice-President is normally last—
rounding up strays and stragglers on his way. On taking their
places at the table, members wait until the President is seated before seating themselves. (If guests are present, they also wait on the
President.) When all are seated, the Senior Steward reports to the
President—"Gentlemen or table—seated, Sir" and the President raps
for silence. Grace is then said—by a Chaplain, normally, if one is
present—or by the President—or by any member requested by
the President. The usual Naval Grace is either "God Save the
Queen; Bless this food, and make us thankful" or "For this food we
are about to receive, thank God." "Amen" is usually chorused by
all members and while highly improper if classed as "singing," it is
not unusual for a long harmonized "Amen" to be given.

[1] Commanding Officer Naval Divisions, RCN (R) *Officers Divisional Course*,
January 1955.

From Grace until after the Loyal Toast, dining rules are rigidly observed.

The President's gavel, the Vice-President's gavel (or rap), or a member's standing, demand immediate silence.

During dinner, one may not—without the President's permission—

(i) Come in and sit down at the table
(ii) Leave the table—or return to it after being permitted to leave
(iii) Read or write
(iv) Commence a course before the President
(v) Smoke
(vi) Use foul language or tell smutty stories
(vii) Discuss or place bets or wagers
(viii) Mention specific sums of money
(ix) Discuss political or controversial issues
(x) Talk shop. ("Shop" in this instance refers to matters within the Command—it does not include matters of general interest to the service.)
(xi) Mention a woman's name (unless she is a celebrity)
(xii) Speak a foreign language
(xiii) Propose a toast. ("Cheerio" forms a toast, for this ruling.)

During dinner, the President is always served first and no dish is removed after a course until the last diner has finished eating that course.

When the last course has been eaten, the table is cleared of everything but the table decorations. Members should not retain unfinished drinks when the table is cleared. (It is permissible, though not usual, to obtain the President's permission to do so, however.)

When the table is cleared the senior steward reports to the President, "Table cleared, Sir."

The President raps the gavel on table for silence and Grace is said as before, the customary one being, "For what we have received, thank God."

DRINKING TOASTS IN THE BRITISH NAVIES

Rules for drinking toasts are contained in QRCN 61.03, which reads as follows:

(1) The health of Her Majesty the Queen shall be honoured while seated in all naval messes, whether on shore or afloat, on all occasions except those where:

    (a) the National Anthem is played, when the toast shall be drunk standing; or

(b) toasts to heads of states of other than Commonwealth countries are included, when they and that to Her Majesty shall be drunk standing, whether national anthems are played or not.

(2) Whenever officers or officials of India are entertained officially on board ships or in naval establishments on occasions when it is customary for toasts to be exchanged, the first toast shall be to Her Majesty the Queen followed by a toast to the President of India.

(3) Whenever officers or officials of other than Commonwealth countries are entertained officially on board ships or in fleet establishments on occasions when it is customary for toasts to be exchanged:

(a) the Canadian officer acting as host proposes as the first toast the health of the head of the state (sovereign or president) of the country to which the visitors belong; and

(b) after this toast has been honoured, the Senior Officer of the guests of the other nation proposes the health of Her Majesty the Queen.

(4) (a) When more than one nation is represented among the guests, the host proposes a collective toast to the heads of the several states represented, naming them in the order of the rank and seniority of their respective representative officers present.

(b) In a port of another nation, however, when officers of the state visited are present, the head of that state shall invariably be named first in the collective toast, the remainder being named in the order prescribed in (a) of this paragraph.[2]

(c) If the head of the State visited is present in person at an official function, the host proposes an individual toast to him, and immediately after this has been honoured, the collective toast to the heads of the remaining States represented is proposed.

(d) The senior and highest in rank of the visiting officers or officials responds to the collective toast on behalf of all the foreign guests by proposing the health of Her Majesty the Queen.

---

[2] At a luncheon to honor a South American Minister of Marine given by a British admiral aboard his flagship in a South American port and at which an admiral of the U.S. Navy was a guest, the following procedure for toasts was requested by the British admiral and so executed: The British admiral toasted the head of the South American country, the South American admiral, the president of the United States; and the U.S. admiral toasted, "the King."

(5) The procedures prescribed in (2), (3) and (4) of this article should be arranged beforehand between the Canadian officer who is the host and his guests.

(6) The first toast shall always be proposed in English, but if practicable, shall also be repeated in French or the language of the visitors.

(7) Subsequent toasts may follow as the occasion demands.

(8) When a national anthem of another nation is played in accompaniment to a toast, an abbreviated version shall not be used unless it has been ascertained that this is in accordance with the custom of the country concerned.

After the Loyal Toasts, mess rules are relaxed and cigarettes and cigars are passed. Cigarettes or cigars must not be lit, however, until after the President has lit his own or given permission for smoking to be carried on. Pipes must not be smoked without the President's permission.

Anyone who wishes may leave the table after smoking has commenced except officers in charge of sets of decanters—unless these officers charge the member on their left with the responsibility of "decanter custody." Officers leaving decanters without relieving themselves of their responsibility, may be fined the contents of the decanters which are passed around the table at the offender's expense.

When ladies are present at the table, it is usual for the President to announce—when smoking commences—"The ladies may leave the table." This is interpreted by many—both male and female—as equivalent to "Ladies, leave!"

The President may order the decanters removed at any time after the toasts are drunk, but it is usual to pass them at least once more. After the second passing, decanters are left unstoppered until removed.

It is not permissible to pick up a decanter at any time to refill a glass—one must wait until the decanters are passed in their normal rounds.

Members who do not take wine when the decanters are passed for the Loyal Toast are not permitted to take any at any subsequent passing.[3]

There are a few officers who apparently think that dining in the mess is the most appropriate occasion for horse-play and concentrated infringement of rules. Whether or not this line of

---

[3] Note that this is the basis for the ceremony of the passing of the port. See following section.

thought is in order is dependent on whether it may be accepted as conduct becoming mature gentlemen when dining. Your lead!

The Loyal Toast is given on every occasion of dining in Naval messes—whether nightly or infrequently. When dining is a nightly routine, it is not unusual for one of the traditional daily toasts to follow the Loyal Toast. These traditional dailies are:

Monday—"Our Ships"
Tuesday—"Our Men"
Wednesday—"Ourselves" (and may no one be like us!)
Thursday—"A bloody war, or a sickly season"
Friday—"A willing foe and sea room"
Saturday—"Sweethearts and wives"[4]
Sunday—"Absent Friends"

The popular custom is for the President to call on a junior member of the mess for the toast to .... day, with a stiff fine to the one who doesn't jump to his feet and respond correctly and without delay.

There are other points which could be mentioned with respect to rights, wrongs and customs when dining in the mess, but the foregoing cover the fundamentals. After all—we should leave a couple of loopholes for zealous Presidents and knowledgeable members!

Good Dining!

THE OLD CEREMONY OF PASSING THE PORT

The port is placed on the table after the table is cleared. In a small mess it is placed before the president, in larger ones the vice-president and, possibly, other officers have decanters placed in front of them as well.

When the decanters are all placed on the table, the senior steward reports to the president, "The wine is ready to pass, sir." The president then unstoppers the decanters in front of him, and other officers with decanters before them follow suit.

The president passes the decanters one at a time to his *left*, the other officers doing the same. Remember, the president and other officers in charge of decanters do *not* help themselves before passing the decanters.

---

[4] The custom of drinking to "sweethearts and wives" was the practice as early as 1650. In that time there is record that the captain's table had such delicacies as "ribbs" of beef, plum pudding, "roosted hens," "raysings," almonds, "minct" pies, woodcock pies, English pippins, and "punch galore."

The decanters should be at least one place apart during their trip around the table. They should never be allowed to "pile up" beside a member. They should be "slid" from place to place, not lifted from the table.

If, due to shortage of members, there is a gap at the end of the table, the stewards in that area should move the decanters across it.

When a set of decanters arrives in front of an officer who has charge of a set, he helps himself to what he wants and keeps the new set in front of him. The stewards move the stoppers on from one officer to the other, so that they remain with their own decanters.

Remember that a decanter may never be passed to the right. If an officer thoughtlessly does not help himself when he desires wine, he is out of luck. Although not very good form, it is permissible for him to pass his glass down to the officer who has the decanter at the moment and ask him to fill it.

No one may touch his wine until the Loyal Toast has been proposed.

It is not necessary to take wine if you do not want it, but if you do not take it on the first round of decanters, you may not take it subsequently.

In civilian circles if you do not take wine, your glass will be filled with water, but in the Navy we never drink a toast in water, as superstition says that the subject of our solicitude will die by drowning.

When the wine has been passed and all decanters have reached their destination, the senior steward reports to the president, "The wine has been passed, sir." The president then stoppers the decanters in front of him and the other officers follow suit.

The president taps the table for silence and says, "Mr. Vice, the Queen." If there is a band in attendance, it then plays the national anthem, after which the vice-president responds, "Gentlemen, the Queen." All members raise their glasses and repeat, "The Queen," and those with wine drink the toast.

APPENDIX D

"The Laws of the Navy"

Now these are laws of the Navy,
    Unwritten and varied they be;
And he that is wise will observe them,
    Going down in his ship to the sea;
As naught may outrun the destroyer,
    Even so with the law and its grip,
For the strength of the ship is the Service,
    And the strength of the Service, the ship.

Take heed what ye say of your seniors,
    Be your words spoken softly or plain,
Lest a bird of the air tell the matter,
    And so ye shall hear it again.

If ye labour from morn until even'
    And meet with reproof for your toil,
It is well—that the guns be humbled,
    The compressor must check the recoil.

On the strength of one link in the cable,
    Dependeth the might of the chain.
Who knows when thou mayest be tested?
    So live that thou bearest the strain!

When the ship that is tired returneth,
    With the signs of the sea showing plain,

Men place her in dock for a season,
    And her speed she reneweth again.
So shall thou, lest perchance thou grow weary
    In the uttermost parts of the sea,
Pray for leave, for the good of the Service,
    As much and as oft as may be.

Count not upon certain promotion,
    But rather to gain it aspire;
Though the sight-line end on the target,
    There cometh, perchance, a miss-fire.

If ye win through an Arctic ice floe,
    Unmentioned at home in the Press,
Heed it not, no man seeth the piston,
    But it driveth the ship none the less.

Can'st follow the track of the dolphin
    Or tell where the sea swallows roam;
Where leviathan taketh his pastime;
    What ocean he calleth his home?
Even so with the words of thy seniors,
    And the orders those words shall convey.
Every law is as naught beside this one—
    "Thou shalt not criticise, but obey!"
Saith the wise, "How may I know their purpose?"
    Then acts without wherefore or why.
Stays the fool but one moment to question,
    And the chance of his life passeth by.

Do they growl? It is well: be thou silent,
    So that work goeth forward amain;
    Lo, the gun throws her shot to a hair's breadth
    And shouteth, yet none shall complain.
Do they growl and the work be retarded?
    It is ill, speak, whatever their rank;
The half-loaded gun also shouteth,
    But can she pierce armor with blank?

Doth the funnels make war with the paintwork?
    Do the decks to the cannon complain?
Nay, they know that some soap or a scraper
    Unites them as brothers again.
So ye, being Heads of Departments,
    Do your growl with a smile on your lip,

Lest ye strive and in anger be parted,
  And lessen the might of your ship.

Dost think, in a moment of anger,
  'Tis well with thy seniors to fight?
They prosper, who burn in the morning,
  The letters they wrote over-night;
For some there be, shelved and forgotten,
  With nothing to thank for their fate,
Save that (on a half-sheet of foolscap),
  Which a fool "Had the honor to state—."

Dost deem that thy vessel needs gilding,
  And the dockyard forbear to supply;
Place thy hand in thy pocket and gild her,
  There be those who have risen thereby.

If the fairway be crowded with shipping,
  Beating homeward the harbour to win,
It is meet that, lest any should suffer,
  The steamers pass cautiously in;
So thou, when thou nearest promotion,
  And the peak that is gilded is nigh,
Give heed to thy words and thine actions,
  Lest others be wearied thereby.
It is ill for the winners to worry,
  Take thy fate as it comes with a smile,
And when thou art safe in the harbour
  They will envy, but may not revile.

Uncharted the rocks that surround thee,
  Take heed that the channels thou learn,
Lest thy name serve to buoy for another
  That shoal, the Courts-Martial Return.
Though Armour, the belt that protects her,
  The ship bears the scar on her side;
It is well if the court acquit thee;
  It were best hadst thou never been tried.

Now these are laws of the Navy,
  Unwritten and varied they be;
And he that is wise will observe them,
  Going down in his ship to the sea.
As the wave rises clear to the hawse pipe,
  Washes aft, and is lost in the wake,

So shall ye drop astern, all unheeded,
  Such time as the law ye forsake.

Now these are the Laws of the Navy
  And many and mighty are they.
But the hull and the deck and the keel
  And the truck of the law is—OBEY

Captain Ronald Hopwood, RN

APPENDIX E

"The Navy Hymn"

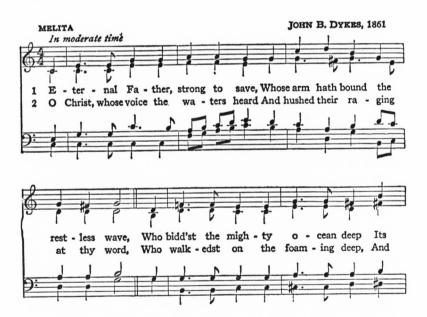

MELITA   JOHN B. DYKES, 1861

In moderate time

1 E - ter - nal Fa - ther, strong to save, Whose arm hath bound the
2 O Christ, whose voice the wa - ters heard And hushed their ra - ging

rest - less wave, Who bidd'st the migh - ty o - cean deep Its
at thy word, Who walk - edst on the foam - ing deep, And

    [1] In 1860, the Reverend William Whiting, a clergyman of the Church of England, after passing safely through a violent gale in the Mediterranean, composed what is popularly called "The Navy Hymn." John Bacchus Dykes of England wrote the music. This beautiful hymn, "Eternal Father Strong to Save," was initiated in the United States in 1870 and in 1879 a young officer, Charles J. Train, in charge of the midshipman choir initiated the singing of the hymn in the Chapel of the Naval Academy. The first stanza is always sung at the close of each Chapel service.

349

own ap - point - ed lim - its keep: O hear us when we
calm a - mid its rage didst sleep: O hear us when we

cry to thee For those in per - il on the sea.
cry to thee For those in per - il on the sea. A-men.

3 Most Holy Spirit, who didst brood
  Upon the chaos dark and rude,
  And bid its angry tumult cease,
  And give, for wild confusion, peace;
      O hear us when we cry to thee
      For those in peril on the sea.

4 O Trinity of love and power,
  Our brethren shield in danger's hour;
  From rock and tempest, fire and foe,
  Protect them wheresoe'er they go;
      Thus evermore shall rise to thee
      Glad hymns of praise from land and sea.   Amen.

William Whiting, 1860, *alt.*

"Anchor's Aweigh"

Many Americans, including practically all Navy officers and men, have been stirred by the strains of "Anchor's Aweigh."

The music for this remarkable composition was written by Lieutenant Charles Adam Zimmerman, member of the Naval Academy band, which he had joined when he was 21 years of age. The band was then a civilian contract organization. Zimmerman was still with the band when its status was changed to Regular Navy on 21 April 1910, at which time he was appointed band leader and given the pay and allowances of a second lieutenant in the Marine Corps.

Lieutenant Zimmerman composed the music of "Anchor's Aweigh" in 1906, with dedication to the Class of '07. It was first played publicly at the Army-Navy football game in the autumn of 1906 and, of course, ever thereafter.

Zimmerman became a highly valued institution in his capacity as leader of the Naval Academy band for more than thirty years. In 1916, a memorial monument was erected on his grave in the Naval Academy Cemetery by "his midshipmen friends."

"The Navy Hymn" is played only at religious services. "Anchor's Aweigh" is a football song and is played at athletic events, parades, and at other similar events. It is not customary for naval personnel or Naval Academy graduates to stand when it is played. Naval Academy graduates stand when their Alma Mater, "Navy Blue and Gold," is played.

APPENDIX F

"The Marine's Hymn"

proud to claim the ti - - tle Of U - nit - ed States Ma - rine. . .

2 Our flag's unfurl'd to ev'ry breeze,
        From dawn to setting sun,
    We have fought in ev'ry clime and place
        Where we could take a gun;
    In the snow of far off northern lands,
        And in sunny tropic scenes,
    You will find us always on the job—
        The United States Marines.

3 Here's health to you and to our corps,
        Which we are proud to serve.
    In many a strife we've fought for life,
        And never lost our nerve.
    If the Army and the Navy
        Ever look on Heaven's scenes,
    They will find the streets are guarded
        By United States Marines.

The "Marine Hymn" is not a religious song but is played at parades and athletic events. Marines and their families customarily stand when it is played.

APPENDIX G

A Note on the Much-Quoted Letter of John Paul Jones

THE LETTER so frequently quoted and ascribed to John Paul Jones is given below. Recent research has disclosed that this letter as commonly printed was not written by Jones, but was a composite letter of collected phrases and clauses of Jones, published for the first time by Augustus C. Buell in his work, *Paul Jones, Founder of the American Navy*.

Without entering into details of the literary argument, the facts of which have been adequately and conclusively covered by the late Professor L. H. Bolander, for many years Librarian at the Naval Academy, it will suffice to set forth the first paragraph of Jones's letter and Mr. Buell's version of it.

The following quotation is from a letter, a copy of which was made by Jones's secretary, and may be found in the Library of Congress. It is part of an open letter to the Marine Committee, dated January 21, 1777.

> None other than a Gentleman, as well as a Seaman, both in theory and practice is qualified to support the character of a Commissioned Officer in the Navy, nor is any man fit to command a Ship of War who is not also capable of communicating his Ideas on Paper in Language that becomes his Rank.

Please note the first two paragraphs of the letter as interpreted by Mr. Buell. There is no proof that John Paul Jones ever wrote the letter;

but as Mr. Bolander states, "That he truly was the author of such phrases is beyond doubt."[1]

In short, Mr. Buell drafted a letter that covered many of Jones's suggestions and opinions; and, although this literary sharpness is not condoned, the Buell letter of Jones is quoted as the essence of that brave, dashing officer's code; that because of the variety of influences that have shaped our naval tradition, none have had a greater impact than the deeds and writings of the "Founder of the American Navy." He deserves that title better than does any other.

QUALIFICATIONS OF THE NAVAL OFFICER

A Collection from Jones's Reports and Letters in Modern Version as Arranged by A. C. Buell

It is by no means enough that an officer of the navy should be a capable mariner. He must be that, of course, but also a great deal more. He should be as well a gentleman of liberal education, refined manners, punctilious courtesy, and the nicest sense of personal honour.

He should not only be able to express himself clearly and with force in his own language both with tongue and pen, but he should also be versed in French and Spanish—for an American officer particularly the former—for our relations with France must necessarily soon become exceedingly close in view of the mutual hostility of the two countries towards Great Britain.

The naval officer should be familiar with the principles of International Law, and the general practice of Admiralty Jurisprudence, because such knowledge may often, when cruising at a distance from home, be necessary to protect his flag from insult or his crew from imposition or injury in foreign ports.

He should also be conversant with the usages of diplomacy, and capable of maintaining, if called upon, a dignified and judicious diplomatic correspondence; because it often happens that sudden emergencies in foreign waters make him the diplomatic as well as the military representative of his country, and in such cases he may have to act without opportunity of consulting his civic or ministerial superiors at home, and such action may easily involve the portentous issue of peace or war between great powers. These are general qualifications, and the nearer the officer approaches the

[1] L. H. Bolander, "Two Notes on John Paul Jones," Naval Institute *Proceedings,* July 1928, pp. 548–550.

full possession of them the more likely he will be to serve his country well and win fame and honours for himself.

Coming now to view the naval officer aboard ship and in relation to those under his command, he should be the soul of tact, patience, justice, firmness, and charity. No meritorious act of a subordinate should escape his attention or be left to pass without its reward, even if the reward be only one word of approval. Conversely, he should not be blind to a single fault in any subordinate, though, at the same time, he should be quick and unfailing to distinguish error from malice, thoughtlessness from incompetency, and well-meant shortcoming from heedless or stupid blunder. As he should be universal and impartial in his rewards and approval of merit, so should he be judicial and unbending in his punishment or reproof of misconduct.

In his intercourse with subordinates he should ever maintain the attitude of the Commander, but that need by no means prevent him from the amenities of cordiality or the cultivation of good cheer within proper limits. Every Commanding Officer should hold with his subordinates such relations as will make them constantly anxious to receive invitations to sit at his mess-table, and his bearing towards them should be such as to encourage them to express their feelings to him with freedom and to ask his views without reserve.

It is always for the best interests of the Service that a cordial interchange of sentiments and civilities should subsist between superior and subordinate officers aboard ship. Therefore, it is the worst of policy in superiors to behave towards their subordinates with indiscriminate hauteur, as if the latter were of a lower species. Men of liberal minds, themselves accustomed to command, can ill brook being thus set at naught by others who, from temporary authority, may claim a monopoly of time and sense for the time being. If such men experience rude, ungentle treatment from their superiors, it will create such heartburnings and resentments as are nowise consonant with that cheerful ardour and ambitious spirit that ought ever to be characteristic of officers of all grades. In one word, every Commander should keep constantly before him the great truth, that to be well obeyed he must be perfectly esteemed.

But it is not alone with subordinate officers that a Commander has to deal. Behind them, and the foundation of all, is the crew. To his men, the Commanding Officer should be Prophet, Priest, and King. His authority when off shore being necessarily absolute, the crew should be as one man impressed that the Captain, like the Sovereign, "can do no wrong."

This is the most delicate of all the Commanding Officer's obligations. No rule can be set for meeting it. It must ever be a question of tact and perception of human nature on the spot and to suit the occasion. If an officer fails in this, he cannot make up for such failure by severity, austerity, or cruelty. Use force and apply restraint or punishment as he may, he will always have a sullen crew and an unhappy ship. But force must be used sometimes for the ends of discipline. On such occasions the quality of the Commander will be most sorely tried. . . .

When a Commander has, by tact, patience, justice, and firmness, each exercised in its proper turn, produced such an impression upon those under his orders in a ship of war, he has only to await the appearance of his enemy's top-sails upon the horizon. He can never tell when that moment may come. But when it does come, he may be sure of victory over an equal or somewhat superior force, or honourable defeat by one greatly superior. Or, in rare cases, sometimes justifiable, he may challenge the devotion of his followers to sink with him alongside the more powerful foe, and all go down together with the unstricken flag of their country still waving defiantly over them in their ocean sepulchre.

No such achievements are possible to an unhappy ship with a sullen crew.

All these considerations pertain to the naval officer afloat. But part, and often an important part, of his career must be in port or on duty ashore. Here he must be of affable temper and a master of civilities. He must meet and mix with his inferiors of rank in society ashore, and on such occasions he must have tact to be easy and gracious with them, particularly when ladies are present; at the same time without the least air of patronage or affected condescension, though constantly preserving the distinction of rank. . . .

APPENDIX H

Homeward Bound Pennant[1]

1. The Chief of Naval Operations has received many inquiries requesting information concerning the "homeward bound" pennant. The following codifies all known authentic information.

2. The use of the "homeward bound" pennant is traditional. The specifications of the design and rules for display apparently have never been adequately set forth; however, the following usage is believed to conform with tradition:

(a) A vessel which has been on duty in foreign waters outside the continental limits of the United States continuously for a period of nine months (270 days) or more flies the "homeward bound" pennant upon getting under way to proceed to a port of the United States.

(b) The "homeward bound" pennant is divided vertically into two parts: that portion next to the hoist is blue and the fly is divided horizontally into halves, the upper red and the lower white. In the blue portion is placed one white star for the first nine months that the ship has been continuously on duty in foreign waters outside the continental limits of the United States, plus one additional white star for each additional six months. The over-all length of the pennant was normally one foot for each officer and man on the ship who has been on duty outside the United States for nine months or more. Where this produces a pennant excessively long, its length is restricted to the length of the ship.

[1] Navy Department Bulletin of August 31, 1947.

(c) The relative proportions of the pennant shall be as follows:

Length of pennant 1
Width
    at hoist .... .005
    at fly .... .0015
Distance between centers of stars and from centers
    of end stars to ends of blue portion .... .004
(Hence, the length of the blue portion is derived
    by multiplying the number of stars, plus one,
    by .004.)
Diameter of stars .... .003

(d) Upon arrival in a port of the United States, the blue portion containing the star or stars is presented to the commanding officer. The remainder of the pennant is divided equally among the officers and men of the ship's company.

APPENDIX I

The History of
Navy Day and
Armed Forces Day

ARMED FORCES DAY is observed annually on a day declared as such by the president. All services hold open house at all posts, ships, and stations. Appropriate civilian organizations respond by holding dances, banquets, and otherwise honoring the Defense Department or the service of their choice. Armed Forces Day was established in 1949 as a substitute for individual service days.

Navy Day was established in 1922 with the day first set as October 27th, Theodore Roosevelt's birthday. Subsequently, and perhaps to avoid any political complications, the Navy League of the United States in its widespread national sponsorship retained the date but by fortuitous coincidence of history could also designate it as the anniversary of the day on which President Washington proposed the first bill to authorize the construction of a naval force. The establishment of Navy Day was approved by President Harding. In October 1923, President Calvin Coolidge wrote officially: "It has been pleasing to learn of the plans to continue this year the observance of October 27, birthday of the late President Roosevelt, as Navy Day." Reference to Theodore Roosevelt, naval historian and champion of sea power, has been customary in a great number of speeches and articles of Navy Day observances through the years. As the Navy League states, Navy Day has become: ". . . a spontaneous act of recognition and tribute by the people of the United States to their Navy and to the men and women who make it great."

The "story behind the story" of the establishment of Navy Day is interesting. A club known as the Navy Club for enlisted men of the

Navy and Marine Corps was established in New York City in World War I and operated by a group of ladies under the leadership of Mrs. William H. Hamilton. When reorganized in 1921, Franklin D. Roosevelt became the president of the Manhattan Navy Club. In fact, Roosevelt wrote the motto that was framed over the registration desk: "Here you will neither be robbed, instructed, nor uplifted." Mrs. Hamilton and ladies continued their support but decided that there should be a nationwide celebration of Navy Day, not only for emphasizing the importance of the Navy to the country but also to direct an appeal to the significance of Navy Clubs on a national scale. With these ideas in mind, Mrs. Hamilton visited Washington and received support from the then assistant secretary of the Navy, Theodore Roosevelt, Jr. After formal approval by the secretary of the Navy and the president, plans were made to hold the first Navy Day on October 27, 1922, the birthday of Theodore Roosevelt.

Some time afterwards, Assistant Secretary Roosevelt gave Mrs. Hamilton a letter to the effect that she was the founder of Navy Day. "Mrs. Hamilton's service as founder of Navy Day," writes J. Russell Carney, "has been too little remembered by the Navy."

Under the vigorous sponsorship of the Navy League, Navy Day became a national event, particularly on the seacoasts. After the establishment of Armed Forces Day, however, the Navy League, a civil organization, decided that an observance of the former Navy Day, voluntary in nature and entirely under civilian sponsorship, be continued. If practicable, naval personnel are given permission to participate in the celebration, but no public funds are expended in the observance.

The Honorable Carl Vinson, distinguished chairman of the House Committee on Armed Forces, on October 27, 1950 said: "We should return to a celebration of service days—Army Day, Navy Day, Air Force Day, Marine Corps Day—to keep foremost in the minds of the Americans that each service has its role to play in the defense program, and that each service is a highly specialized instrument that will be impaired if it is put into a pot and scrambled up with other services' administrative and tactical and strategic doctrines and practices."

APPENDIX J

Notes on Social Usage Abroad

THE FOLLOWING COMMENT and suggestions, as condensed and adapted from the Navy's official handbook, *Social Usage and Protocol*,[1] should be of interest to all officers and particularly those serving abroad, both afloat and ashore.

GENERAL PRINICIPLES OF OFFICIAL ENTERTAINING

Naval and marine officer hosts, when entertaining abroad, should conform as closely as possible to the best accepted usage of their own country.

Before issuing invitations for a representational function abroad, an officer should check with and obtain clearance from the counselor of embassy, in order that there be no conflict in the times of official functions. Also, chiefs of foreign diplomatic missions and other high officials should not be invited without clearance from the respective ambassador, minister, or counselor.

---

[1] This excellent official publication, used by admirals' staffs, naval and marine attachés, Department of State officials and others, was compiled by Miss Ruth Nelson Tarrant, Lieutenant Commander USNR, and a member of a prominent naval family. The information, with sample forms on best usage in the way of invitations, calling cards, formal and informal replies, and forms of American address, is authoritative and valuable. Official seating is comprehensively covered. In 1957, official permission to use this information was granted by Rear Admiral L. H. Frost, USN, Director of Naval Intelligence.

In foreign countries to which our officers are accredited, governmental, ecclesiastical, and diplomatic precedence is a matter of official record. But, should any doubtful or disputed point arise, one should consult either the Protocol Section of the American Embassy, or the Foreign Liaison Section of the Office of Naval Intelligence.

At all official luncheons and dinners, check and double check as to the correct seating of the guest of honor and the second ranking guest. A consideration of prominence, linguistic qualifications, and mutual interest should determine the seating of nonranking guests between those of official rank who are seated in order of precedence. If toasts are to be given, plan the routine, and so inform those expected to respond.

Infrequently, it is necessary to invite a high-ranking guest other than the guest of honor. If ambassadors or very senior military or civil officials are invited to such a function, it is customary to adhere to strict seating precedence, even though the guest of honor sits a few places down the table. However, relations and conditions sometimes make it agreeable for a ranking guest to waive his precedence for a guest of honor; if a stag party, the ranking guest may provide the solution by acting as co-host. A senior guest of honor should be offered the option as to the date, his staff or aide should be consulted as to the guest list and other details, and his invitation should carry in place of R.S.V.P., the notation, "To Remind."

DINNER NOTES

A table diagram and small folded cards designating dinner partners are generally used for formal dinners. Cards in small envelopes are also used to inform the men of the names of their dinner partners. A host should make sure that all male guests know or have been presented to their partners.

The host leads the way to the dining room with the ranking lady, and seats her to his right. The hostess comes last with the ranking man. There are, of course, exceptions—such as that of the president of the United States, another chief of state, members of royal families, or for a governor, if at a dinner in his own state. In these exceptions, the hostess enters first with the guest of honor, followed by the host and senior lady.

At formal dinners, one should never smoke until the host or hostess sets an example, or invites guests to smoke. Cigarettes are usually passed after toasts have been made, and often just before the last course.

"Turning the table" is a conventional term used in reference to the time when a hostess shifts her conversation from the guest at the left to the one at the right. When adhered to, this polite old custom occurs about half way through the dinner, and should be a cue for other guests to conform in general with the hostess.

It is a long-established custom, at American and British formal dinners, that after dessert the hostess leads the women from the table to the drawing room for coffee and liqueurs; the men remain at the table or adjourn to the library or other room, and later join the ladies. It is a general European custom for the men and women at a formal dinner to have coffee and liqueurs together in the drawing room.

Irrespective of any man present who outranks her, the ranking lady should make the move to go home. Custom dictates about ten o'clock for a very formal dinner, and about ten thirty or eleven for less formal ones. Other guests may then follow in any order desired.

Formal dinner calls are made by few people today. But in place of this old custom, punctilious guests write notes of appreciation or send flowers. Sometimes, in official Washington, calling cards with p.r. (*pour remercier*) written in the lower left-hand corner are sent as an expression of appreciation. The note is more gracious and thoughtful.[2]

SEATING ARRANGEMENTS—MIXED DINNERS

Except when women have official positions, they are seated in accordance with the rank of their respective husbands.

The simple rule to remember—seat the ranking lady to the right of the host, and the ranking man to the right of the hostess; then the second ranking man to the left of the hostess, and the second ranking lady at the left of the host.

An unmarried host, or one entertaining in the absence of his wife, often requests one of the senior women guests to act as hostess.

If there is an equal number of men and women, then at tables of eight, twelve, or any multiple of four, the host and hostess cannot sit opposite to each other without two men or two women together. This can be corrected and the table balanced if the hostess moves one seat to the left, thereby putting her right hand guest opposite the host. This is often done.

---

[2] *Service Etiquette*, published by the Naval Institute Press in 1977, gives in a social sense "the rules of the nautical road." This comprehensive book contains much social usage that should be of interest to all. It contains information on the art of conversation and table manners, how much to tip, both at home and abroad, and includes some very important chapters on military social life.

At a horseshoe table, the host, hostess, and ranking guests sit on the outside of the center of the curve of the horseshoe, with other guests down the sides.

In order to balance the table at official stag dinners, a co-host may be designated, usually the senior U.S. guest; on occasions, the senior foreign guest is seated opposite the host.

There are times when the toastmasters or speakers are of relatively low rank; however, they should be seated as near the center of the table as possible without upsetting the seating precedence too much. Great care must always be given to the seating of prominent guests who are not active officials of government. The *Navy Department Handbook* gives an example of the exercise of good judgment in this respect: To the right of the host in the center—ex-president of the United States, civic leader, U.S. representative to United Nations, and an Air Force general on the end. To the left of host—foreign ambassador, senior Red Cross official, congressman, and Protestant bishop.

RECEPTIONS

U.S. service attachés invited to official functions by their chief of mission are expected to wear uniform with aiguillettes and act as aides. At some American embassies, the attachés meet guests at the door, escort them to the receiving line, and introduce them to the ambassador. At other posts, service attachés and their wives are only expected to assist by circulating among the guests. They should arrive early and stay until the end.

At afternoon receptions women wear afternoon dresses or suits; men, dark suits or uniform. Women guests wear gloves, but not the women in the receiving line. For evening receptions, the type of dress to be worn will be indicated on the invitation.

The host should be first in the receiving line, then the guest of honor and his wife, then the host's wife and another man. Take care not to leave a lady at the end of the line. An aide, or butler, should announce or present the guests at the beginning of the line. At the White House and at many embassies abroad, it is customary for the officer to precede his wife on the receiving line.

It is no longer customary to leave cards at formal receptions.

MAKING SOCIAL CALLS ABROAD

Social Usage and Protocol gives general guidance for the new attaché as to calls. It advises that an officer who is ordered to report to a legation or embassy should call promptly with his wife at the residence of the chief of mission; and as soon as possible, he and his wife, after this first and senior call, should call upon the wife of the counselor of embassy, or in her absence the next ranking wife, in order to learn the more important social customs of the post. It is suggested that this call be arranged by telephone.

The protocol officer of the embassy or legation should be consulted as to the foreign civil and military officers to call upon. It is, of course, presumed that the officer being relieved, if present, will be most helpful and give his relief a thorough briefing.

In the large capitals, senior officers rarely return the calls of relatively junior officers; however, an invitation to some form of reception or entertainment is usually sent after the junior leaves cards. Keep in mind that some foreign officials do not care to be called upon at home; therefore, it is advisable to consult the protocol officer regarding calls on the wives of foreign officials. In England, one "signs the book" in the front halls of naval and military officials, without being received. Check at all times for local customs.

Official calls are made abroad in much the same manner as those made at home. Cards are handed to the servant who opens the door. If a member of the family should open the door and the caller is received, then cards should be left inconspicuously in the hall or living room. If the family is not receiving, the caller should say to a member of the family, "May I leave these?"—then place the cards on the hall table himself. When one wishes to leave cards without being received, or finds the hostess not at home, he should leave cards with the request, "Please give these to Mrs. Otis." Remember that leaving cards is considered a personal call, whether one is received or not.

NOTES FOR NAVAL ATTACHES

1. Remember that you are a representative of the United States, and the Navy of which you are a part.

2. Be scrupulous in obeying all the laws and regulations of the country wherein you are stationed.

3. Be punctilious in the exercise of social amenities.

4. Be discriminating in the making of friends.

5. Give complete, wholehearted cooperation to your colleagues of the Army, Air Force, and Foreign Service.

6. Advise and assist visiting naval officers as much as possible.

7. Keep well informed on precedence and protocol, but when in

doubt check with the protocol officer, or the secretary of the chief of mission, who is often the "unofficial social arbiter."

8. Attachés have found that small unofficial luncheons and dinners are more conducive to making friends and cultivating good relations than formal and larger affairs. However, it is a fact, whether liked or not, that the cocktail party is almost the only means of discharging numerous obligations. Never invite more people than one can comfortably entertain.[3]

---

[3] Apart from the important *do's* and *don'ts* set forth above, it is a point of personal observation that the most effective attachés and the ones most highly respected by foreigners gave considerable attention to a study of the language of the country, gained fair knowledge of its history and culture, and never failed to reflect the good manners expected of an officer and gentleman.

APPENDIX K

Swallowing the Anchor

(A Note on Retirement)

. . . thereafter go thy way, taking with thee a shapen oar, till thou shalt come to such men as know not the sea, neither eat meat covered with salt; yea, nor have they knowledge of ships of purple cheek, nor shapen oars which serve for wings to ships. And I will give thee a most manifest token, which cannot escape thee. In a day when another wayfarer shall meet thee and say that thou hast a winnowing fan on thy stout shoulder, even then make fast thy shapen oar in the earth and do goodly sacrifice to the lord Poseidon, even with a ram and a bull and a boar, the mate of swine, and depart for home and offer holy hecatombs to the deathless gods that keep the wide heaven, to each in order due. And from the sea shall thine own death come, the gentlest death that may be, which shall end thee foredone with smooth old age, and the folk shall dwell happily around thee. This that I say is sooth.

The Odyssey, Book XI

Bibliography

Many things contained in this book are no other than collections of other authors, and my labor is no more therein than theirs who gather a variety of flowers out of several gardens to compose one sightly garland.

Sir Wm. Monson (1703)

SOCIOLOGICAL AND PSYCHOLOGICAL CONSIDERATION OF CUSTOMS, TRADITIONS, AND USAGE

Ellis, Havelock. *The Dance of Life.* Boston and New York: Houghton Mifflin Co., 1924.
Ludovici, Anthony M. *A Defence of Aristocracy.* London: Constable and Co., Ltd., 1933.
Rapport, Dr. Angelo S. *Superstitions of Sailors.* London: Stanley Paul Co., Ltd., 1928.
Spencer, Herbert. *Principles of Sociology.* 3 vols. Part 4, "Ceremonial Institutions," New York: 1880.
Veblen, Thorstein. *The Theory of the Leisure Class.* New York: 1899.

SEA LORE, CUSTOMS, TRADITIONS, USAGE, MEMOIRS, AND NAVAL HISTORY

Alden, Carroll Storrs, and Earle, Ralph, Captain, USN. *Makers of Naval Tradition.* Boston: Ginn and Co., 1925.
Allen, G. W. *Our Naval War with France.* Boston: Houghton Mifflin Co., 1909.

Ammen, Daniel, Rear Admiral, USN. *Old Navy and the New*. Philadelphia: J. W. Lippincott Co., 1891.

Arnold-Forster, D., Rear Admiral, RN. *The Ways of the Navy*. London and Melbourne: Ward, Loch and Co., 1932.

Barney, Mary. *A Biographical Memoir of the Late Commodore Barney*. Boston: 1832.

Beckett, W. N. T., Commander, RN. *A Few Naval Customs, Expressions, Traditions, and Superstitions*. 2d ed. Portsmouth, England: Gieves, Ltd., 1932.

Clark, George R., Rear Admiral, USN (Ret.); Stevens, W. O.; Alden, Carroll S.; Krafft, Herman F. *A Short History of the United States Navy*. Rev. ed. Philadelphia and London: J. B. Lippincott and Co., 1927.

Chatterton, E. Keble. *Sailing the Seas*. London: Chapman and Hall, 1931.

Coggeshall, George. *History of American Privateers and Letters of Marque*. New York.

Conrad, Joseph. *The Mirror of the Sea: Memories and Impressions*. Garden City, New York: Doubleday Page & Co., 1921.

Cooper, J. Fenimore. *The History of the Navy of the United States*. 2 vols. Philadelphia: Lea and Blanchard, 1839.

Duncan, Robert B. *Brave Deeds of American Sailors*. Philadelphia: George W. Jacobs & Co., 1912.

Field, C., Colonel, RMLI. *Old Times Afloat: A Naval Anthology*. London: Andrew Melrose, Ltd., 1932.

Gleaves, Albert, Lieutenant Commander, USN. *James Lawrence, Captain, United States Navy, Commander of the "Chesapeake."* New York: G. P. Putnam's Sons, 1904.

Green, Fitzhugh, Lieutenant Commander, USN. *Our Naval Heritage*. New York and London: The Century Co., 1925.

Hall, Basil, Captain, RN. *Fragments of Voyages and Travels*. London: Edward Mixon, 1846.

Jones, George. *Sketches of Naval Life: A Series of Letters From the "Brandywine" and "Constitution" Frigates*. New Haven: 1829.

Kimball, H. *The Naval Temple: Complete History of the Battles Fought by the Navy of the United States*. Boston: 1816.

DeKoven, Mrs. Reginald. *Life and Letters of John Paul Jones*. 2 vols. New York: Charles Scribner's Sons, 1913.

Lowry, R. G., Lieutenant Commander, RN. *The Origin of Some Naval Terms and Customs*. London: Sampson Low, Marston & Co., Ltd., 1930.

Mackenzie, A. S. *Life of Stephen Decatur*. Boston: Chas. C. Little and Jas. Brown, 1846.

Mahan, A. T., Captain, USN. *Types of Naval Officers: Drawn from History of the British Navy*. Boston: Little, Brown and Co., 1918.

Masefield, John. *Sea Life in Nelson's Time*. New York: Macmillan Co., 1925.

Monson, Sir William. *Naval Tracts*. 6 books written in 1703.

Montgomery, James Eglington, of the Admiral's Staff. *Our Admiral's Flag*

Abroad: The Cruise of Admiral D. G. Farragut. New York: G. P. Putnam's Sons, 1869.

Morris, Charles, Commodore, USN. *The Autobiography of Commodore Morris.* U. S. Naval Institute *Proceedings*, vol. VI, 1880.

Porter, D. D. *Memoirs of Commodore David Porter.*

Puckle, Bertram S. *Funeral Customs: Their Origin and Development.* New York: Frederick A. Stokes, 1926.

Robinson, Charles N., Commander, RN. *The British Tar in Fact and Fiction.* New York: Harper and Bros., 1909.

Robinson, William Morrison. *The Confederate Privateers.* New Haven: Yale University Press, 1928.

Rogers, Stanley. *Sea Lore.* New York: Thomas Y. Crowell Co., 1929.

Russel, Phillip. *John Paul Jones, Man of Action.*

Sayer, Edmund S. *Ships of Other Days.* Limited ed. Nice, France: Imprimerie Gastaud, 1930.

Sherburne, J. H. *Life and Character of the Chevalier John Paul Jones.* Washington, D.C., 1825.

Snow, Elliot, Rear Admiral (C.C.), USN (Ret.) *Life in a Man-of-War: or Scenes in "Old Ironsides" during Her Cruise in the Pacific.* Boston and New York: Houghton Mifflin Co.; Cambridge: Riverside Press, 1929.

Snow, Elliot, Rear Admiral (C.C.), USN (Ret.), and Gosnell, A. H., Lieutenant Commander, USNR. *"On the Decks of 'Old Ironsides.'"* New York: Macmillan Co., 1932.

Stewart, C. W., ed. *John Paul Jones Commemoration at Annapolis . . . 1906.* Washington: Government Printing Office, 1907.

Swan, Oliver G., ed. *Deep Water Days* (A collection). Philadelphia: McCrae, Smith Co., 1929.

Ward, Edward W. *The Wooden World.* (First published London, 1707). Edwin Chappell, 1929.

Wells, Gerard, Rear Admiral, RN. *Naval Customs and Traditions.* London: Philip Alan, 1930.

Yexley, Lionel. *Our Fighting Sea Men.* London: Stanley Paul & Co., 1911.

MARINE ENCYCLOPEDIAS; NAUTICAL DICTIONARIES OF WORDS, PHRASES, AND EXPRESSIONS; ROUTINE BOOKS, ORDER BOOKS, AND NAVAL REGULATIONS

A Naval Encyclopedia, A Dictionary of Nautical Words and Phrases, Biographical Notices, and Records of Naval Officers. Prepared by officers of the Navy. Philadelphia: L. R. Hammersly and Co., 1881.

Ansted, A. *A Dictionary of Sea Terms.* Brown, Son and Ferguson, Ltd., 1933.

Belknap, Reginald R., Captain, USN. *Routine Book.* Annapolis: U. S. Naval Institute, 1918.

Blunt, Edmund H. *Theory and Practice of Seamanship* . . . . With Rules, Regulations, and Instructions for the Naval Service. New York: 1824.

Bradford, Gershom. *A Glossary of Sea Terms*. New York: Yachting, Inc., 1927.

Cowan, Frank. *A Dictionary of the Proverbs and Proverbial Phrases of the English Language Relating to the Sea*. Greensburgh, Pennsylvania: Olivier Publishing House, 1894.

Falconer's Marine Dictionary. Rev. by Dr. Wm. Burney. London: 1815.

Heinl, R. D., Jr. *Dictionary of Military and Naval Quotations*. Annapolis: Naval Institute Press, 1966.

Neeser, Robert Wilden. *Statistical and Chronological History of the United States Navy*. 2 vols. New York: Macmillan Co., 1909.

Noel, John V., Jr., and Beach, Edward L. *Naval Terms Dictionary*. Annapolis: Naval Institute Press, 1978.

Plunkett, Honorable R., Commander, RN. *Modern Officer of the Watch*. 5th ed. London: John Hogg, 1913.

Smith, Logan Pearsall. *Words and Idioms. Studies in the English Language*. 4th ed. London: Constable and Co., 1933.

Smyth, W. H., Vice-Admiral, RN. *Sailor's Word Book: An Alphabetical Digest of Nautical Terms*. London: Blackie and Sons, 1867.

REGULATIONS OF THE COLONIAL AND UNITED STATES NAVY

(1) *Rules for the Regulation of the Navy of the United Colonies; Pay Tables; Articles of Enlistment and Distribution of Prize Money*. Philadelphia: 23 November, 1775. Text appears in Way & Gideon editions of journals of American Congress, vol. 1, pp. 185–391 (Congressional library book No. Z2:7:1), and in Journals of Continental Congress, edited from original records.

(2) *Naval Regulations* (1802), reprint 1809; these are entitled *Naval Regulations Issued by Command of the President of the United States of America*, and are signed "by command, Rt. Smith, secretary" and dated 25 January, 1802.

(3) *Naval Regulations* (1814).

(4) "American State Papers," *Naval Affairs*. Vol. 1, 1794–1825, p. 512 *Rules, Regulations, and Instructions for the Naval Service*. President Monroe to the House of Representatives, 20 April 1818. Prepared by Board of Navy Commissioners in obedience to act of Congress 7 February 1815 entitled "an act to alter and amend the several acts for establishing a Navy Department, by adding thereto a board of commissioners."

(5) *Report on the Rules for the Naval Service*. 29 December 1819, Sec't. Smith Thompson, *Senate document No. 15*, 16th Cong., 1st Session, vol. 1, "showing wherein the rules, regulations, and instructions adopted by the naval service are at variance with the existing laws, and suggesting amendment of the laws so as to make them conform."

(6) *Rules and Regulations of the Naval Service.* Sec't. Smith Thompson, 11 January 1821, *Senate Document No. 65*, 16th Cong., 2d Session, vol. 2, "the rules and regulations for the naval service prepared and reported under the authority of an act of Congress of 7 February 1815, with a schedule of alterations and additionsh as have been deemed necessary."

(7) *The Rules of the Navy Department Regulating the Civil Administration of the Navy*, city of Washington, printed at the Globe office, by F. P. Blair. This was called the "Red Book" and was published in 1832; the *Rules, Regulations*, etc., of 1818 was called the "Blue Book" and was effective in 1832 for the military administration as distinguished from the civil.

(8) *Rules and Regulations Prepared by the Board of Revision for the Government of the Navy, 23 December 1833.* House of Representatives *Executive Document No. 20 and 375*, 23d Cong., 1st Session, serial No. 254 and 258.

(9) *Book of Regulations for Use of Commanders, Pursers, and Recruiting Officers* (1838).

(10) *Financial Regulations for Naval Officers* (1838).

(11) *General Regulations for Navy and Marine Corps*, published in Washington, by J. and G. S. Gideon, 1841. These were prepared in obedience to joint resolution of Congress of 24 May 1842, 72 Cong., 3d Session, *House Document 148*, serial No. 421. Poore's reference on this is "Jan. 13, 1843, copy of proposed new regulations," Sec't. A. P. Upshur, in response to House of Representatives resolution.

(12) *Regulations, Circulars, Orders and Decisions for Guide of Officers of Navy* (1851). In 1853 the *Orders and Instructions* for the Navy were declared not legal by the Attorney General and were withdrawn. Poore refers to 1851 amendments necessary due to abolishing of flogging in the Navy.

(13) *Regulations of Navy* (1863).

(14) *Regulations for Government of Navy* (1865).

(15) *Regulations for Government of Navy* (1869). Various amendments and additions were issued.

(16) *Regulations for Government of Navy* (1870). Various amendments and additions were issued.

(17) *Regulations for Government of Navy* (1876). Various amendments and additions were issued.

(18) *Regulations for Government of Navy* (1893). Various amendments and additions were issued.

(19) *Regulations for Government of Navy* (1896). Various amendments and additions were issued.

(20) *Regulations for Government of Navy* (1900). Various amendments and additions were issued.

(21) *Regulations for Government of Navy* (1909). Various amendments and additions were issued.

The above references are listed in *Check list of U. S. Public Documents, 1789–1909* and *Poore's Index to U. S. Publications*, as well as appearing in original and state papers indicated.

(22) *U. S. Navy Regulations* (1913). Various amendments and additions.
(23) *U. S. Navy Regulations* (1973) with amendments, which is effective at this writing.

WAR OF 1812

Abbot, Willis J. *Blue Jackets of 1812: A History of the Naval Battles of the Second War with Great Britain.* New York: Dodd, Mead and Co., 1887.

James, Wm. *Naval Occurrences of the Late War between Great Britain and the United States of America.* London: 1817.

Roosevelt, Theodore. *Naval War of 1812.* New York: G. P. Putnam's Sons, 1882.

FLAGS, HERALDRY, AND ARMS

Boutell. *Manual of Heraldry.* London and New York: Frederick Warne and Co., Ltd., 1931.

Preble, George Henry, Rear Admiral, USN. *History of the Flag of the United States of America: Symbols, Standards, Banners, and Flags of Ancient and Modern Nations.* Boston: H. Williams and Co., 1880.

Origin and History of American Flag. 2 vols. Philadelphia: Nicholas L. Brown, 1907.

Johnson, Willis F. *The National Flag: a History.* Cambridge, Mass.: Houghton Mifflin Co., 1930.

Smith, Colonel Nicholas. *Our Nation's Flag: In History and Incident.* Milwaukee: The Young Churchman Co., 1908.

Spanish Franciscan. *Book of Knowledge of All Kingdoms, Lands, and Lordships That Are in the World, and the Arms and Devices of Each Land.* London: Old ed., printed for the Hakluyt Society, 1912.

The Flag Code adopted at the National Flag Conference, June 14–15, 1923, as revised and endorsed at the Second National Flag Conference, May 15, 1924.

SOCIAL CUSTOMS, CONVENTIONS, PRECEDENCE, ETIQUETTE, AND SOCIAL CORRESPONDENCE

Ageton, Arthur A., Rear Admiral, USN (Ret.), and Mack, William P., Vice Admiral, USN (Ret.). *The Naval Officer's Guide.* Annapolis: Naval Institute Press, 1970.

Armiger. *Titles, A Guide to the Right Use of British Titles and Honours.* London: A. and C. Black, Ltd.

Burke's *Peerage, Baronetage, and Knightage.*

Castiglione, Count Baldesar. *The Book of the Courtier.* (Latest of more than 140 editions). New York: Charles Scribner's Sons, 1903.

Ebbert, Jean. *Welcome Aboard.* Annapolis: Naval Institute Press, 1974.

Jacobsen, K. C., Commander, USN. *The Watch Officer's Guide*. Annapolis: Naval Institute Press, 1979.

Meyers, Elizabeth. *The Social Letter*. New York: Brentano's, 1918.

Post, Emily. *Etiquette*. New York: Funk & Wagnalls Co., 1959.

Regulations of the Navy, Army, and Foreign Service.

Satow, Sir Ernest Mason. *A Guide to Diplomatic Practices*. New York: Longmans, Green and Co., 1917.

Swartz, Oretha D. *Service Etiquette*. 3rd rev. ed. Annapolis: Naval Institute Press, 1977.

West Point Monograph. *Military Discipline, Courtesies, and Customs of the Service*. West Point: 1930.

Whitaker's *Peerage, Baronetage, Knightage, and Companionage*, 1933.

Wedertz, Bill, and Bearden, Bill. *Bluejacket's Manual*. 20th rev. ed. Annapolis: Naval Institute Press, 1978.

SHIPS AND NAVAL PRINTS, SEA PAINTINGS, ETC.

Chatterton, E. Keble. *Old Sea Paintings*. New York: Dodd Mead and Co., 1928.

Chatterton, E. Keble. *Old Ship Prints*. New York: Dodd Mead and Co., 1927.

Colasanti, J. M. *Our Navy and Defenders*. Portsmouth, Virginia: 1905–1906.

Culver, Henry B., text; drawings by Gordon Grant. *The Book of Old Ships*. Garden City, New York: Doubleday, Page and Co., 1924.

Laughton, L. G. Carr. *Old Ship Figure-Heads and Sterns*. New York: Minton Balch and Co., 1925. Printed in Great Britain.

Walton, William, and others. *The Army and Navy of the United States 1776–1890*. Philadelphia: George Barrie, 1890.

Zogbaum, Rufus Fairchild. *All Hands*. New York and London: Harper and Bros., 1897.

MISCELLANEOUS

Bone, Captain David W. *Capstan Bars*. Edinburgh: Porpoise Press, 1931.

Freuchen, Peter. *Book of the Seven Seas*. New York: Julian Messner, Inc., 1957.

Paullin, C. O. *Paullin's History of Naval Administration*. Annapolis: Naval Institute Press, 1968.

Richmond, Sir Herbert, Vice Admiral, RN. *Command and Discipline*. London: John Murray, 1927.

Shuon, K. *U.S. Marine Corps Biographical Dictionary*. New York: Franklin Watts, Inc., 1963.

Shuon, K. *U.S. Navy Biographical Dictionary*. New York: Franklin Watts, Inc., 1964.

Van Denburgh, Elizabeth Douglas. *My Voyage in the United States Frigate "Congress."* New York: Desmond Fitzgerald, Inc., 1913.

Index